PRINCES ÒF THE CHRISTIAN PULPIT AND PASTORATE

SECOND SERIES

PRINCES *of the* CHRISTIAN PULPIT *and* PASTORATE

SECOND SERIES

By HARRY C. HOWARD

PROFESSOR OF HOMILETICS AND PASTORAL THEOLOGY, EMORY UNIVERSITY
AUTHOR OF "PRINCES OF THE CHRISTIAN PULPIT AND
PASTORATE" (FIRST SERIES)

———

"We preach not ourselves, but Christ Jesus as Lord"

———

NASHVILLE, TENN.
COKESBURY PRESS
1928

To
LUTHER LANE SMITH
AND
LESLIE POWELL HOWARD
EACH OF WHOM WAS CUT DOWN BY DEATH
WHEN HE HAD BUT WELL BEGUN
A BRIGHT AND PROMISING
MINISTRY

PREFACE

EVERY name chosen to be embraced within the composition of this volume meant the rejection of another. As some had to be taken, others had to be left. Even this seems a part of the incompleteness of the world.

Who would not like to write on themes such as these until all the great preachers of Christendom had been included? Why should Chrysostom have been omitted? or Augustine? or Dominic? or Hugh Latimer? or innumerable others, both in earlier and later times, in England, in the United States, in France, in Germany, and in lands still beyond?

In many cases good biographies and other necessary literature could not be had. This is particularly true of the author's own Church and of other Churches of the South. Something has been done; but much more remains to be done. A great literature awaits the creation of some competent hand in this field. But it will require a hand not already full of important work.

The names which have been introduced met two conditions at least: They possessed a permanent interest to catholic Christianity, and an especial interest to the author's own mind. There is not one of them who has not been a blessing to his own life and ministry. His sincere desire is that he may be able to cast the mantle of that benediction about the shoulders of his brethren in the ministry, while he is not entirely without hope that at least the shadow of it may fall upon some of the laity.

In writing thus I have had also in mind a former volume, "Princes of the Christian Pulpit and Pastorate" (First Series).   H. C. HOWARD.

EMORY UNIVERSITY, GA.,
    March 20, 1928.

(7)

CONTENTS

(9)

I

BERNARD OF CLAIRVAUX

(1091–1153)

A Long Lasting Splendor

BERNARD OF CLAIRVAUX was French; he was medieval, a mystic, a monk; he was a Roman Catholic, and a Churchman in the strictest sense which that term implies. But the impulses of the man break through all these terms of outward distance and difference, and he admonishes the world still to better paths. Across all these gulfs of difference which are so often made to be dividers of men the splendor of his character and fame illuminates our later time. The able and brilliant Hildebrand and the earnest Pope Urban had made their contribution toward a better world by their zeal for a cleaner and more effective Church within that world. But the extreme depression and darkness of a former time still held the world in the thrall of their ascendancy over the mind of man when Bernard came. And here he so lived as now to have lived in the long centuries since in the affections and admiration of men. When Dante saw him in Paradise he was not in contemplation more devout than he had been here:

> "I thought I should see Beatrice, and saw
> An old man, habited like the glorious people;
> O'erflowing was he in his eyes and cheeks
> With joy benign, in attitude of pity,
> As to a tender father is becoming.
>   .   .   .   .
> As he who peradventure from Croatia
> Cometh to gaze at our Veronica—
> Even such was I while gazing at the living
> Charity of the man, who in this world
> By contemplation tasted of that peace."

CRADLED IN A CASTLE

Bernard was nobly born in an ignoble age. Fontaines, near Dijon, was the place, and the year 1091 was the date of his birth. He died in 1153, August 20 being the exact date, so that the period of his life was nearly coincident with the central portion of the Middle Ages. Tescelin, his father, though a vassal to the Duke of Burgundy, was himself a knight and in all the outward relations of his life pledged to fighting and feudal warfare. His very rank in life in that turbulent age made him a fighting man. The more rare was it, therefore, that he was also a man of gentle manners and kindly spirit, a lover of the poor, a succorer of their need, a man very ardent too in his inward piety, and very zealous in his advocacy and practice of justice among men. On one notable occasion when he had been drawn into a personal quarrel he had the courage to appear a coward and to seek a reconciliation with his foe without resort to the code of the times. In no case would he take up arms except in defense of his own land or in duty to his lord of Burgundy. The castle, therefore, in which Bernard was cradled was as nearly as might be an instance of Christianity in a medieval castle.

Moreover, he had from his mother more than he had from his father. More devout was she even than her husband, and more devoted to the duties of piety. Likewise toward the poor also she was quite as kindly as he. She bore the beautiful name of Alith, or Aleth, or Aletta, or to go still farther back to the French, Alêthe; and she gave additional luster even to such a name. Indeed, she visibly increased the moral luster of the dark age in which she lived. Her sons—and there were six of them, and one daughter—she offered to God as soon as they were born. The charism of this infant consecration was upon Bernard, in particular, down to the very day of his death. He owed to her scarcely less than Augustine owed to his mother Monica. "If ever a mother's wish and prayer, and Christian counsel," says Dr. Storrs, "determined the character and career of a son, those of the mother of Bernard determined his." She died while he was still a youth, but her influence never ceased to be exerted powerfully upon him. All compact of moral passion as he was, he owed it more to her than to any other human source. He preserved through his youth and throughout his life a chastity of body which was but the lower form of his chastity of soul, and in it all there was the image of the chastity of his mother. When she died the abbot of a monastery at Dijon came to Fontaines and begged for her remains, and having obtained his request he "caused six images to be made and placed upon her tomb, in memory of her six sons, where they may be seen to this day."

At a very early age Bernard had been entered as a pupil in a cathedral school at Chattillon. He accomplished his tasks with great proficiency, and his notable grace and genius distinguished him among his fellows. At a still earlier age the land had been shaken with the tread of the crusaders going on their first fateful journey to the East. He was probably too young for any of the seeds of some of his later exploits to have been sown at this time in his mind.

CHOICE OF A CAREER

The death of his mother removed the first outward constraint Bernard had toward a career. His older brothers, Guido and Gerard, had already entered the pursuit of arms. Should he follow them? This would be the natural, and, ordinarily, the almost inevitable thing for him to do. His father and his brothers would hardly wish it otherwise.

Or he might have graced any court of the time by his presence and service had this been his preference. The accomplishments of his person, the grace of his manners, the readiness of his command of himself and of the occasion all commended him to such a career. Or he might have turned to literature and letters with gifts amply able to command success. Abelard, with whom he was afterwards to be so unhappily connected, was already drawing thousands across seas and through distant lands, who in the thirst for learning which characterized the time came to enroll as his students and hear his famed lectures in philosophy. Or if he were going into the Church he might enter by other paths than those of a monastery. Some of his family seem to have hoped that the effect of his attendance upon the school at Chattillon might be to shape his career toward preferment rather than self-abnegation should the Church be his choice. But his determination to be a monk in so far as that had been formed remained unshaken. "Between the clash of arms and the din of wars comes a silvery peal of convent bells. In the deep, hushed winter's night, the chorus song of matins is heard in measured cadence, and the last chant of compline goes forth as the summer sun approaches the horizon. There, in the thick woods, sleeps the monastery, from whence these voices and bell tones are heard."

His brothers and friends, however, opposed his purpose. So strongly did they present their dissuasion to a monastic life that they were near to prevailing over him. They seem especially to have desired him to be a disputer in the schools rather than a monk. And what career, indeed, could be more attractive to a young man of fine gifts and noble birth?

The effect of their plea was lessened by the fact of his physical frailty. He was not able to take up a career at

arms. He brought a frail body into the world, and bore it
in a fashion frailer still to the grave. But much more effective as a persuasive toward the monastery was the
memory of his mother and the power of her early and
insistent dedication of his life to God. Setting out one
day on horseback toward the camp of the Duke of
Burgundy to join his brothers engaged there in besieg-
ing a castle, he could only have been in a very doubtful
and perturbed state of mind. Neither his heart nor
his conscience could have gone with him. The thought
and image of his mother, as had often before been the
case, took insistent possession of him. Swift self-rebuke
entered into his soul. He retired to a roadside church to
pray. There with streaming eyes he lifted up his face and
stretched out his hands to God, imploring his mercy.
That hour of wayside pleading profoundly affected his
course and fixed in him an inflexible purpose to devote
himself to a religious life. All other prospects completely
faded out, and definite and intense Christian purpose directed all his after career. Henceforth there was no admixture of doubt or hesitation in his determination to be
a monk.

In his new access of zeal for God and the devoted life
he went forth to gather others within the sweep of his own
consuming purpose. His uncle, the rich Lord of Touillon,
was won without great difficulty, though one would think
a lord would hardly wish to be a monk. His brother
Gerard, deeply absorbed in the business of soldiering and
attaining in it already a conspicuous success, was a richer
prize, though not so easily won. His brother Guido, though
happily married and the father of children, was with much
difficulty drawn into the enthusiastic venture, his wife
having reluctantly agreed to enter a convent. Soon there
were as many as thirty under bonds to make the great

resolve. Entering a church with the companions thus associated in purpose with him, while they practiced certain exercises in preparation for the fuller sacrifice of the monastic life, Bernard heard read the text: "Faithful is God, because he who hath begun a good work in you himself will perfect it, unto the day of Jesus Christ." He took it as a word directly from the Spirit of God, and submitted himself and his company with still deeper resolves to the divine purpose and guidance. He had literally preached up a company for a convent.

Monastic Experience and Expansion

At the early age of twenty-two, heading his band of spiritual crusaders, Bernard appeared at the gates of the monastery of Citeaux and asked admission. The strength of his resolution appears in the very character of the convent to which he came. Hard by stood the famous abbey of Clugni, rich and prosperous, ever in the eye of Rome and offering every opportunity for preferment which ecclesiastical ambition could ask. Instead he turned to the poor and depleted Citeaux, founded only fifteen years before, and now sustaining a very doubtful prospect for the future. It was under the strict rules of the Benedictines, and kept them very strictly. Its poverty and strictness had failed to attract novices and the number of its monks decreased until after the devastation wrought among them by an epidemic illness hardly any were left. The coming of Bernard and his company was like a visit of angels, only the coming of the right sort of men just then might be more serviceable than angels.

The austerities practiced at Citeaux could hardly be supposed to have left anything undone. The rule as to the substance of it consisted of much doctrine and more discipline, with little comfort for the outward man. A report is circulated of Horace Walpole that when he was asked why he did not become a Roman Catholic he replied that "it would give him too much to swallow, and too little to eat." The monks of Citeaux might have copied his complaint. Dr. Storrs thus summarizes the regimen to which they were subjected: "One meal a day, usually at noon, without meat, fish, or eggs, commonly without milk, with a slight supper of fruit or herbs; an utter poverty of dress, such as had been common in imperial days for the Italian serf working on farms, from which indeed it had been copied; nothing except assiduous labor to interrupt the succession of song, meditation, reading, writing, prayer, which began with matins at earliest morning, and ended with compline, at eight or after on the following evening—this was the rule of life at Citeaux."

This was all too lavish for Bernard and he went beyond the rule in the austerity of his own practice. He need not have done it. He ought not to have done it. How easy it is for those who have done less, and still less, to say that. Still we say he ought not to have done it. He essayed to count sleep as wasted time. He could go a good way in wakefulness, but could not get through the entire night. Nature vetoed his new statute. It was clearly unconstitutional. He denied himself food until he lost all relish for it, and almost lost the power to assimilate it. He fixed an infirmity upon himself which he could never put off. He was more than half an invalid all his public life.

There were two or three reasons why he entered the monastic life. In the first place it was congenial to his temperament and his desire. He loved seclusion. Cities oppressed him. He loved the solitudes more than the multitudes so far as his tastes in the matter were concerned. When he was repeatedly called out of Clairvaux to settle French, Italian, and other European disputes he

2

still longed for the quiet of the monastery. Above all he loved nature and all the mystery with which she broods over a susceptible soul. Nature he said taught him far more even about the Bible than books. Such knowledge as he had of the Scriptures "he had acquired chiefly in the woods and fields; and beeches and oaks had ever been his best teachers in the Word of God."

In the next place the monastic discipline appealed powerfully to his moral and spiritual intensities. It was given him not so much to possess these as to be possessed by them. Instead of his excessive austerities it were truer to speak of his overmastering intensities. Neither he nor his age was able either to appreciate or to appropriate that great saying of Jesus that he would not have his Church taken out of the world, but he would have it kept from the evil. But Bernard found Jesus in spite of any blundering he may have done. To say that he went into a monastery because at bottom he had legalistic conceptions of religion is to miss the point both as to the man and as to certain deeper meanings of monasticism itself. He appropriated the best and largely escaped the worst of all that there was in the monastic system. Whatever its vices, the system had its virtues, and one of the most important of these is seen in the contribution the cloisters made to Christian preaching. A striking instance of this is Bernard himself. Furthermore, this was the age when monasticism attained to much of the best there ever was in it. Here, too, Bernard had his place. Who more than he contributed toward the best there was in the long-tried system?

At the end of a year at Citeaux, Bernard made his final profession as a monk in a celebration of all the usual ceremonial of the occasion. At the end of still another year, at the age of twenty-four, he went out, with twelve other monks accompanying him, to found a new monastery.

His going out was a sign of the prosperity of Citeaux.
His accession to Citeaux with his remarkable ability and the
unusual character of those who went in with him had
opened there a new era, and the springing up of new
monastic establishments was one of the chief consequences
of it. The abbot of Citeaux at the time, Stephen Harding,
an Englishman, possessed unusual ability for his position,
and was especially gifted in his discriminating insight into
character. It is a gift without which leadership is sure to
blunder, without which authority in its very strength becomes
weakness. It was an unusual, but, as the event proved in
the case of Bernard, a very wise thing to send out a young
man of only twenty-four to found a monastery.

The new settlement was made in the valley of Clairvaux—*Clara Vallis*—in a wild and hilly country about one
hundred miles to the north of Citeaux. They had gone
unequipped into a wilderness. The earliest apostles had
gone unequipped into a peopled world. These had gone
unequipped into aboriginal forests. They had lands,
though these were not cleared. Houses they had none.
The privations they suffered while securing a lodgment
amid such surroundings were very severe. Winter was
near and would not wait on the labor of their hands. Their
food in summer had consisted of barley bread and millet,
"partially cooked, with a relish of beech leaves steeped in
water, and bits of vetch. Beechnuts and roots of herbs
must furnish food for the winter." Their supply of salt
failed them entirely, and Bernard sent a monk without
money to go on the market-day and buy at the most ac-
cessible village. He thought if he went without money
he should return without salt. "Where is the money?"
he asked. "Believe me," said Bernard, "I know not the
time when I had gold or silver. . . . Fear not, my son,
go in peace." Proceeding upon an ass, "the solitary animal

in the possession of the community," he came near to his destination and met a priest, who asked him: "Whence comest thou, brother, and whither art thou bound?" On hearing of the object of his expedition and the sad state of his monastery, the priest carried the monk to his own house, ministered to him of its comforts, gave him a half bushel of salt and money besides. Hastening back to Clairvaux, he told the prosperity of his journey, and Bernard said to him: "I tell thee, my son, that no one thing is so necessary to a Christian as faith."

Clairvaux prospered and occupied the chief place among all the branches of Citeaux. Bernard was in due time formally ordained as its abbot and under his government and direction the establishment obtained a remarkable development, as many as one hundred and sixteen colonies having gone out from it in the lifetime of its founder. The remains of the settlement of one of these may be seen to-day as far away as Yorkshire in England. In the end there are said to have been as many as eight hundred abbeys thus affiliated with the original Clairvaux, all of them following the austere morality and rigid rules of Citeaux.

THE EUROPEAN EXTENSION OF HIS FAME

Clairvaux through the personal influence and action of Bernard became the uncanonical center of European Christendom. It was as if the papacy had left the Vatican Hill and settled in the convent of Clairvaux, as if Rome itself had forsaken the Tiber and preferred the streams that purled through the valleys of northern France. The center of the world's gravity is in men, not in places. The center of the world's influence is in personal will and worth, and not in statutory standards nor official functions. Bernard had taken the valley of Clairvaux in its virginity and erected upon its silent slopes a throne of European in-

fluence and action. He had made his monastery a mother
of institutions, and a dispenser of grace and good will to
the nations. He had gone into the woods and like his
Master kept nothing for himself, and was "clean forspent,
forspent." But he kindled a light that burned on all the
heights of European prestige and power.

He did not so much seek as he was sought. His fame
went forth as a harbinger of his action, and men called
him out into the world's conflict. "No man is free until
he can dispose of himself, until he is sought after instead
of seeking." Bernard was an eminent example of this
kind of freedom. Was there trouble in Aquitane? There
was; and only he was found to compose it. Duke William,
whose territory extended over the fine country in the south-
west of France, and whose rule embraced a still wider collateral sovereignty, a man who in all his wide domain was
without any restraint of legal authority, had expelled certain bishops from their sees out of mere caprice or arbitrary
personal displeasure; and he could not be prevailed upon
to reinstate them. He was a giant in strength and stature,
violent and intractable in temper, and his fierce and sensual
animal nature was sunk in sensual-mindedness and sensual practice. Bernard had met him four years previously,
but had left him practically unimpressed. Coming to him
again in the time of the contested election to the papacy
between Innocent II and Anacletus, he had readily prevailed upon him to recognize Innocent as pope. But he
stubbornly refused to restore the deposed bishops. They
had offended him past all forgiveness, and he had taken
an oath to abide his decision. To persuade him seemed
impossible. "Bernard," says Storrs, "broke off the useless
discussion, and proceeded to the church to celebrate mass.
The count was compelled to remain at the door, as one
beneath the censure of the Church. When the host had

been consecrated, Bernard, with lifted arms and flashing face, and with eyes that burned with indignant menace, advanced directly to him with the paten in his hands, and said in tones of terrible authority: 'We have besought you, and you have spurned us. . . . Behold, here comes to you the Virgin's Son, the Head and Lord of the Church which you persecute. Your Judge is here. . . . Will you spurn him, also? Will you despise him, as you have despised his servants?' . . . The furious and implacable count, pierced in spirit, fell to the ground with loosened and unsupporting limbs, and lay there prone, speechless, insensible. Lifted by his knights, he could not stand or speak or see, and fell again, foaming at the mouth. Bernard bade him rise, and listen standing to the judgment of God. He presented the Bishop of Poictiers, who had been violently expelled from his see, and commanded the count to give him then and there the kiss of peace, and restore him to his throne." This man of will so obstinate had also an army at his back. But both army and obstinate will were swept into one swift act of obedience, and the count with a kiss led the bishop to his place.

In a way that was nothing short of peremptory in its boldness he dealt with the powerful Count of Champagne within whose jurisdiction lay the convent of Clairvaux. The count had treated very unjustly one of his vassals, and Bernard had been moved to intervene in the matter, saying to him in a written admonition after a verbal request had failed, "If I had asked of you gold, or silver, or anything of that sort, I trust you so far as to believe that without doubt I should have received them. But why do I say 'if I had asked'? since, not asking at all, I have received many gifts from your generosity. But this one thing which I *have* asked, not for my sake, but for God's sake, not for myself so much as for you, from yourself—what reason exists why I am not worthy to receive it?" The count promised to right the injustice; but when he had failed to do this, apparently through the opposition of some who had profited by the wrong action, and wished to retain the fruit of it, Bernard wrote again: "Falsely, not truly does he esteem you, fraudulent and not faithful is his counsel, who tries to obscure your noble fame for truth in the interest of his own avarice; who, through what malice I know not, to accomplish his purpose on the suffering poor, would empty of meaning the word which your own lips have spoken, a word well-pleasing to God, worthy of yourself, religiously just, and righteously religious. . . . Let the inheritance of Humbert be restored to his wife and his children." Such a friend to the poor in such an age was about the only guarantee they had that they should have the right to their own, though it were never so little. Instances of this kind—his boldness toward the two dukes and his intercession for the poor and others who were defenseless—could on authentic grounds be multiplied almost to the point of wearying the attention required to follow them.

Bernard's intervention in European affairs by correspondence was more extensive and scarcely less important than by his actual attendance upon the scene. His *Letters* as preserved and published aggregate a considerable number, and are marked by a sanity, sincerity, and courage such as his personal presence was wont to lend to the occasion.

His repute for miracles also had much to do with the European extension of his fame. Most circumstantial evidence is offered of miracle after miracle; and it is not the sincerity of the witnesses which must be questioned, but their credulity which must be charged with excess. So credulous was the age that belief in the supernatural itself was in some ways turned into materialistic profit and advantage. But of every highly credulous age this is true.

By the time of the second Crusade Bernard had acquired such an undisputed European influence that he was appointed to preach it up; and at one of the popular assemblies held to promote it he was even elected to its military leadership. From this extremity of folly he was only saved by his own good sense, and the protests of his convent.

This "infirm man ruled Europe, from the arbor and the cell." On his passage upon his journeys multitudes thronged the public ways and did him the honor which no mere official position, civil or ecclesiastical, can ever command. "The rustic shepherds of the Alps . . . forsook their flocks and rushed in crowds to seek his blessings." All Europe was astir to greet him.

An Uncrowned Pontificate

Bernard would accept no ecclesiastical office. Perhaps the greater its immunities and emoluments the less he desired it. He might have had without a word except that of acceptance any of the more attractive bishoprics where there was a vacancy—Langres, Chalons-sur-Marne, Genoa, Pisa. The archbishopric of Milan, seat of the illustrious Ambrose, the spiritual father of Augustine, was all but thrust upon him. The whole population turned out to greet him in their streets, and to press upon him their desire that he should become their archbishop. He only escaped their importunity, not wishing to do it rudely, by a specious device. "To-morrow," he said, "I will mount my horse, and leave it to Providence to direct him." If the horse left the city, he himself should be free. If the horse remained within the city, he himself would stay, and accept the charge and be their pastor. This looks like

taking the advantage both of Providence and the people.
It looks like putting the horse in the place of Providence.
But he thought he knew what the will of God was and
merely used the horse to help him in following that will.
For he knew, and the people ought to have known, that
the horse would go home. He cared no more about an
archbishop's trough than Bernard cared about his throne.
So on the morrow, following the lead of his faithful horse,
he galloped away from the walls of Milan.

Such self-renunciation could but react powerfully in his
favor in the public mind and conscience. The people, unless
utterly blinded and corrupted, have a way of finding and
crowning their own kings. With their instinct for justice and
insight to true worth they elect their rulers in the affection
of their hearts and crown them with their confidence.
Rulers thus chosen may not wear the titular crown, but
they are the real rulers. The cardinals may elect those who
wear the tiara and sit in the official seat. This may be very
well done; and if so, very well. But if not so the popular
verdict might go to another. The Bernards are the real
popes. And so our Bernard was the uncrowned pontiff of
his time. All the wisdom and the grace and the power of
a true pontificate were gathered together in him.

It is not the crown that makes the king, but the king
who makes the crown. It is not the staff that makes the
shepherd, but the shepherd who makes the staff. Cowards,
and rascals, and thieves, and the despicable hireling, who
combines all bad offices in one, may, alas! get the shep-
herding of Christ's flock. But it is not according to the
will of Christ, nor by the consent of wise and good people.
It was the eminent distinction of Bernard that he could
exercise the franchise and function of the high offices of
the Church without outward suffrage or prestige. Such
pontificate as he held was by the suffrage of his own man-

hood and by the warrant of his own lofty character. There was a religious aspect, always serious and sometimes severe, in all that he did. But his special interest was religion, and the Church was his chosen sphere of action.

There was the matter of a divided papacy. Some of the cardinals had elected and enthroned Innocent II, rather precipitately, perhaps. Others of them, more in fact than had voted for Innocent, had stood for Anacletus. There were thus two popes, each claiming to be the true and lawful incumbent of the office. Bernard advocated the claims of Innocent. Anacletus was enthroned in Rome, and was supported by Roger, Duke of Sicily, whose motive was political rather than religious. He might be the inferior man, but he was the better pope, as Roger saw it. Anyway he judged it convenient to have a pope of his own. It was a long and weary contest, won by Bernard, but not completely till Anacletus disappeared by death from the scene. But he had, mainly by the exertion of his sheer personal influence and force, won over through their rulers the French, the English, and the Germans, and, though not with complete success, had invaded Italy itself.

Meantime, in matters of whatever general worth or importance, he was a man of influence far surpassing that of either titular pope. Though but the unofficial adviser of both bishops and popes, there was secured through his action a much wiser and more prosperous administration of the affairs of the Church in general than had been possible through any other means. He was not without fault, nor without weakness, some of the errors and limitations of medievalism infected both his habit and his character, there were some crudities in his early writings, he was not as charitable toward heretics as higher standards might require, the notable case of Abelard being an especial witness; but after all he was much bigger than all his faults and much stronger

than all his weaknesses. The sun itself renders the very
spots which are upon it conspicuous.

But the mere counseling of official opinion did not always
suffice. As occasion required, Bernard was an accuser of
both the episcopal and the pontifical conscience. If they
did not have the ability to see the issue clearly, he had.
If they did not have the courage to proceed upon the issue,
he had. To Pope Innocent II, whose cause he had coura-
geously espoused, he boldly wrote when things were not
going as they ought: "There is but one voice among our
faithful bishops, which declares that justice is vanishing
from the Church; that the power of the keys is gone; that
episcopal authority is dwindling away; that a bishop can
no longer redress wrongs, nor chastise iniquity, however
great, even in his own diocese; and the blame of all this
they lay on you and the Roman Court. What they or-
dain aright, you annul; what they justly abolish, that
you reëstablish. All the worthless contentious fellows,
whether from the people or the clergy, or even monks expelled from their monasteries, run off to you, and return
boasting that they have found protection, when they ought
to have found retribution. Your friends are confounded,
the faithful are insulted, the bishops are brought into contempt and disgrace; and while their righteous judgments
are despised, your authority also is not a little injured."

To Henry, Archbishop of Sens, he wrote with equal
warmth, and in the same accusing tone: "I wish to retain
your friends for you. This you disdain. I should be glad
to reconcile to you your enemies. You will not suffer it.
You are determined not to have peace; you seek, you
summon, your confusion, your destruction, yea, your
deposition. You multiply your accusers; you diminish
your defenders. You excite against yourself old dissensions
that have been allayed. You provoke your adversaries;

you offend your friends. Your own self-will is your law.
All you do is for your ambition, never from the fear of God.
Which of your enemies does not laugh? Which of your
friends does not weep?" These were days, to be sure,
when the papacy was less securely established in absolut-
ism, much less than in the time of Savonarola, for instance.
Nevertheless these excursions into disjointed papal and
episcopal affairs are examples of refreshing candor and
boldness.

In his excellent tract *De Consideratione* Bernard addresses
Pope Eugenius III, who had been one of his own monastic
pupils, on the moral image of a true pope: "Remember,
first of all, that the holy Roman Church, over which thou
art chief, is the mother of churches, not their sovereign
mistress; that thou thyself art not the Lord of bishops, but
one among them, a brother of those delighting in God, and
a partaker with those that fear him. For the rest, regard
thyself as under obligation to be the figure of justice, the
mirror of holiness, the exemplar of piety, the restorer of its
freedom to truth, the defender of the faith, the teacher of
nations, the guide of Christians, the friend of the Bridegroom, the bridesman of the Bride, the regulator of the
clergy, the pastor of the people, the master of the foolish,
the refuge of the oppressed, the advocate of the poor, the
hope of the suffering, the protector of orphans, the judge
of widows, eyes to the blind, a tongue to the dumb, the
staff of the aged, an avenger of crimes, a terror to evil-
doers, and a glory to the good, a rod for the powerful, a
hammer of tyrants, the father of kings, the director of
laws, the superintendent of canons, the salt of the earth,
the light of the world, the priest of the Most High, the
vicar of Christ, the anointed of the Lord. Remember what
I say, and the Lord give thee understanding." At the
same time he could say to the same man: "The whole

Church is full of ambitious men, and has no more ground to be horrified at their schemes and plots than has a den of thieves at the spoils of wayfarers."

To see that justice was done in all Europe, and that the honor of the Church was preserved in all the earth, was indeed a large undertaking. But Bernard was so much absorbed in it as not to be able to realize how large it was. A man who held the scales of justice for the doings of a continent, and stood sponsor for the honor of the Church universal, did not have time to take the measure of his task.

The Power of a Monastic Pulpit

Bernard's early preaching was done in the convent at Clairvaux. Cloistral preaching it was called, because it was done in the cloister and by the monks. If the incumbent of the cloistral pulpit, though, indeed, the meager arrangements made for the service could hardly be called a pulpit, displayed unusual gifts, he would attract hearers from the outside, and would be advanced to the convent church, and at length to some outside church. It was the cloistral preaching which for the most part saved the character of preaching in the Middle Ages. It was better sustained by both the ability and character of the preacher than any other. The monks surpassed the priests. The parochial preaching, or that done by the priests in their parishes, if it were attended to at all, was hardly an apology for preaching; and it was ill sustained by the character of the preachers. The missionary preaching was good, but it had the most of its springs in the monasteries. Savonarola began to preach in the cloister. And Luther's first reluctant preaching was done there.

Bernard's preaching and personal character attracted great crowds to Clairvaux. His was another voice crying in the wilderness. But he cried, not without ears to be entered as in tones of thunder, and not without consciences to be penetrated as in strokes of the swift lightning. Where the preacher is, there is the pulpit, whether in the silences of the desert, or where the multitudes press upon the centers of traffic amid the great city's concourse. There were many conversions at Clairvaux; and the manner of it all was almost as stern as at the Jordan. Henry, son of the king of France, came one day to see Bernard on some secular business. He saw the monks assembled and asked for their prayers. "I trust in the Lord," said Bernard, "that you will not die in the state in which you now are, but rather that you will soon test by your own experience what these prayers which you have just asked for can effect for you." In a little while afterwards, on the same day, he announced his intention to become a monk. His action astounded the monks, but much more those of his own party. One of them in particular was outraged and disgusted, and expressed himself in language which was not in the vocabulary of the monks. "Leave him alone," said Bernard; "his soul is bitter now: but be not troubled overmuch about him, for he is certainly yours." The young man overheard the remark and went away the next day more enraged than ever and imprecating curses on the monastery in which he had lost his master. But he was ill at ease in his own bed on the very next night, and arising before the dawn he sped back to Clairvaux and asked that he himself be admitted as a monk. His conversion was likened to that of Saul of Tarsus.

At an earlier time Bernard had gone on a journey to Paris. Being invited to preach in the schools, he had done so, but there were no conversions. Such preaching was so entirely unlike that to which the young clerks were accustomed that they could not at once comprehend it.

Bernard returned to the home of the archdeacon, where he
had entertainment, in a state of profound dissatisfaction.
In the vehemence of his prayers he poured out his tears in
torrents and uttered such groans and sobs as to be heard
on the outside. His host asked what could be the cause of
such grief. A monk replied: "That wonderful man . . .
cares for nothing in this world save only to recall the wandering to ways of truth, and to gain their souls to Christ;
and because he has just sown the word of life in the schools,
and has gathered no fruit in the conversion of the clerks,
he thinks God is angry with him. Hence this storm of
groans and outpouring of tears; wherefore I firmly antici-
pate that a full harvest to-morrow will compensate for
to-day's sterility." And so it was, when he preached again
the next morning. Several of his hearers immediately expressed their desire to become monks. This was their
means of signifying their conversion.

Setting out for Clairvaux with this precious fruit of his
labor, Bernard passed the night a day's journey out of
Paris. The next morning he announced: "We must return to Paris, as there are some there who belong to us."
Reëntering the city, they saw three young men at a distance approaching them. As they came nearer Bernard
said: "God has helped us. Behold there are the clerks
for whom we returned." On recognizing him, the young
men greatly rejoiced, and exclaimed: "O most blessed
father, you have come to us who desired you so much."
They then said that they had set out to follow him, but
had hardly hoped to overtake him; and certainly not in
this remarkable manner.

1. In the convent Bernard preached a series of sermons on
The Canticles. It seems now a strange source of so many
sermons. But to his mystical mind it offered many at-
tractions. There he found Christ. And his finding was

to him very real, whatever other interpretations others might make of the book. And there his homiletical ingenuity found, too, the expository substance of many a practical application. "Love is everywhere the speaker," he says. But he does not lose the ethical sense. "Learning without love inflates one," while "love without learning is liable to error."

He has left eighty-six sermons upon the book and had only entered the third chapter. He has seven sermons on the verse: "Let him kiss me with the kisses of his mouth." He was engaged eighteen years upon the series, the object of which, as Garvie states it, is "to lead the monks of his own order into the intimate relation of the individual soul to Christ as the Bridegroom."

His long engagement upon this particular task reveals one of the permanent needs of preaching as exemplified in him. This sort of thing in itself was a fine apprenticeship to preaching. The man who thus devotes himself to his task of preaching can but secure some of the highest ends to be sought both in the preparation and the delivery of sermons. The study, the prayer, the meditation to which he is drawn during a long season of attention to a single book will bring to any serious preacher uncalculated resources of highest homiletical value. The man who will thus absorb himself and his time and his purpose in devotion to the demands of his pulpit will carry his meditation into camp and court and highway and will never cease his brooding upon the evangel. He will never lose the unction of his commitment to such a manner of ministry as this. It is meditation the preacher needs, and prayer, and tears, and the sweating of blood. Men want too easy a way to pulpit perfection and power. But there is no easy way to the heights. We must be forever climbing. "We do not say the same things to ourselves with sufficient frequency," says Mark Rutherford; "in these days of big reading fifty fine thoughts come into our heads in a day and the next morning are forgotten. Not one of them becomes a religion." "Meditation is not easy," says Cardinal Newman; "we have stony hearts, hearts as hard as the highways, and the history of grace makes no impression on them." *The history of grace*, indeed. Who has meditated sufficiently on Christ's sufferings, and on the grace of which they are but the expression, to give to grace a real history in his thinking and experience?

Bernard meditated his sermons. His whole system of homiletics might be said to be comprehended in two things: preparation of his sermons through intense and protracted meditation; and extemporaneous delivery. On Christ's sufferings he meditated, and found the reality of grace culminating in them. In the fields, under the oaks, in his cell, in the arbor where in prayer he sought his sermons, these were the chief theme of his thought. In the intensity and absorption of his contemplation he would seem almost to pass the boundaries of the rational. But when he preached it was testified that he had found the only rational.

His preaching before great assemblies was but an extension of his convent preaching. The Cistercians were a preaching order, but he excelled them all. He was devoted to his monks and had a passion for preaching, and when the occasion fused the devotion and the passion the conditions of very high achievement were secured. The frequency of his monastic preaching is indicated in his own suggestion to his convent audience that he addresses them "more frequently than is customary in our order." The circumstances of the convent preaching are described by Morison: "The hour of the sermon varied, from early morning to approaching sunset. When Bernard was at

3

home and well enough to preach, the assembly of grown, silent men would noiselessly gather in the auditorium, whether from the night's vigils and psalmody, or the day's labor in the hot fields. A strange company it must have been: the old, stooping monk, whose mortifications were nearly over; the young beginner, destined perhaps to pass half a century in painful self-denial; the lord of wide lands, and the peasant who had worked on them—one after another came in with soft glide and took their places, waiting for the man whose thoughts and conversation they verily believed came from another world."

2. With the mystical Bernard combined a very practical bent of mind. The mystic in him constituted a large part of his fitness for the ministry. His conception both of theology and the Church was mystical. There was some exaggeration in his conception at both its main points of contact. Nevertheless, in his hands it was turned to singularly beneficent results. He exalted the Church as the one divine institution on earth, all others, whether feudal, royal, or imperial, being secular only, and existing only for secular ends. And, as in the case of his theology, this view fitted in well with the temper of his action.

He had the soul of a mystic. But he was practical too. There was in him a rare combination of the practical with the meditative. The practical saves the meditative and the mystical from excess and from unreality. The meditative and the mystical save the practical from hard and mechanical routine, which at the last is more ineffective than anything else can be. Had Bernard been mystical only, and not also practical, he might have kept closer to his convent as a certain tendency in him constrained him always to do. But no convent could confine him, constituted as he was. His practical sagacity gave his mysticism a wider currency, and made him serviceable to Europe.

Even in lesser matters the practical in him asserted itself. Pigs are practical, if anything is. Some pigs intrusted to his care by a neighbor abbot who had gone to Rome had been stolen by vassals of the Count of Champagne. Said Bernard in writing to the Count: "I would greatly have preferred that they should have stolen my own pigs; and I require them at your hand."

3. Speaking in the English language, the Hebrew Psalmist says: *Thy gentleness hath made me great.* Speaking in the native language of Bernard he says: *Ta debonnairrété m'a fait devenir fort grand.* This divine gentleness is the crowning attribute of all the hierarchy of the humble.

The great must be humble. Above all it consists in seeing God. And the man who sees God is humble. In the soul of every great man there is a secret sanctuary where he hides himself from himself, and feels that he ought to hide himself from God. Bernard had an unaffected sense of his unfitness for the great offices he fulfilled. When acclaimed by great popular assemblies as the most commanding figure of the time and with the most astonishing success crowning his almost every attempt, he still seemed to himself not to be the man who had done these things, and certainly not the man to whom these plaudits were due. Being praised by a bishop, he said: "If the good seed, sown upon good ground, is seen to bring forth fruit, His is the glory who gave the seed to the sower, the fruitfulness to the ground, the increase to the seed. What can I take to myself in these things? Certainly the law of the Lord converteth souls, and not I; the testimony of the Lord maketh wise the simple, and not I."

Truly it was his lowliness among his monks that raised him to the great heights they saw him attain in the great outside world. Not better than the very least of these did he count himself; and from none of the lowliest of their tasks did he absolve himself. He acquired such an influence over them that in his frequent and protracted absences the affairs of the convent went on as if he had been there. An instance of his unaffected self-forgetfulness is afforded in a visit he made to the monks of the Carthusian Order at La Grande Chartreuse. They were greatly rejoiced to see him, but noticed that the saddle upon which he had ridden was much too magnificent for the equipage of a Benedictine monk. They whispered their surprise about until the matter reached the ears of Bernard himself. True, he had sat upon those fine trappings all the way from Clairvaux, but had not in the least noticed them before. Both the horse and the saddle had been loaned to him by an uncle who was a Cluniac monk, and his only concern about them had been that they had brought him on his journey.

4. Out of the lowliness of his mind the singular loftiness of his courage was born. Unexpressed, or expressed, his prayer had been:

> "O, make me strong like some great tree,
>   Root-grappled through the sod—
> My strength in that humility
>   Which clasps the feet of God."

The wonder of the Christian humility is that it is the root of what seems to be its opposite. Meekness, humility, when Christ came was not at all esteemed to be a virtue, but rather a vice. Yet of this lowly virtue the high virtue of courage springs. Bernard had an intensity of conviction which was the child of his gentleness. He had a moral earnestness which was the child of his convictions. He had a spiritual purpose which was as lofty as his own mind was lowly. His very life and character were a constant rebuke to all monkly softness and self-indulgence, and to all papal and episcopal arrogance and cowardly compliance. He had a courage which shattered pretense to atoms, and called a coward world to bolder action, a courage which gave him the mastery of kings and their occasions, and made him the greatest moral force and the greatest preacher of his century.

He had sought to enlist the support of Conrad, Emperor of the Germans, in the second Crusade. He had seen him twice without definite results. At last Conrad said he would consider the matter, consult his advisers, and give his answer on the following day. "On that day Bernard officiated at the mass, the Emperor being present. Suddenly, without invitation, moved as he felt by the Divine Spirit, he began to preach. At the end of the discourse, turning to Conrad in the crowded cathedral, and feeling himself as much alone with him as if the earth had swung out of sight and only they two remained to remember it, he addressed him not as an Emperor but as a man." He brought the authority of Christ as he should appear at the tribunal of the Last Judgment to bear upon the whole occasion. It was perhaps as much like a scene out of the drama of that searching day as it has been given this world to see. All were overwhelmed, and Conrad was completely subdued. Bursting into tears as Bernard was still speaking, he exclaimed: "I acknowledge the gifts of the Divine favor; nor will I prove ungrateful for them. He assisting me, I am ready to serve Him, seeing that on his part I am so admonished."

5. Bernard's whole career was characterized by an utter self-renunciation. His attitude toward official place and power was astonishing at the time, and it is inexplicable to the worldly-minded still. "As the Lord liveth, before whom I stand, I will receive none." The Gehazis cannot understand the Elishas. They run after the honors which

cannot be thrust upon their worthier masters. The bishoprics Bernard refused profited him more than any he could
have accepted. His traditionary portrait shows him with
miters lying unregarded upon the book which itself lies
just at his hand, and lying unnoticed at his feet. The portrait is less than true to the facts of history. The gleam of
a miter could not turn him by so much as the glance of an
eye from the clear path of duty; his feet would sooner
tread upon miters than swerve from their destined way.
He was for an entire generation "the most commanding
man in Europe"; but his hands went empty of any rewards
Europe had to give. Great acts of renunciation passed
into fixed habits of his life. By disregarding the world he
brought the world to his feet. He was bound up with
nothing which could make duty a calculable thing to him.
He had renounced, and could call others to renounce. At
Vezelai, rendezvous of Richard the Lion-Hearted at the
outset of the third Crusade, he preached for the second
Crusade. The king, though accompanied by his beautiful
queen, and grand prelates in the flashing robes of their
office were all forgotten, and all eyes turned to Bernard
and every ear was attentive to him. The cry of "Crosses!
Crosses!" rolled like a storm upon the wave through the
mighty assembly; and these insignia of sacrifice and service were grasped as if they had been scepters, and the great
crusade, the disastrous consequences of which reflected
so seriously upon Bernard's confident advocacy of it, was
well under way.

6. A heart of living and poignant sympathy subdued
the tone of his preaching, or lifted its courageous accents
to the level of the requirements of every occasion. It was
that deep and chastened quality of sympathy which so
surely kindles the imagination, and awakens one tender
heart to its truest converse with another. One of the most

remarkable of all the funeral sermons which have been
preserved from the past is that of Bernard for his brother
Gerard whom he so tenderly loved. There is hardly one
of the finer qualities of such a sermon which it does not
admirably exemplify. Going on for a while as if he would
avoid coming to the real poignancy of the occasion, he
deals with what is only general and distant. But it is impossible for him so to continue. If ever there was a time
when his heart must speak, it is now. "But I must desist," he says; "my grief and the calamity I have suffered
command it. How long shall I dissemble? How long
shall I conceal the fire which is within me, scorching my
sorrowful breast and consuming my vitals? The more I
repress its flames, the more fiercely it burns and rages.
. . . While others wept, I, as ye may have observed,
followed his body to the grave with unmoistened eyes; I
stood by his tomb, and dropped no tear till the burial of
the dead was over. Clad in my priestly robes, I pronounced with my lips the usual prayers; with my own hands
in the wonted manner, I cast the earthly mold on the
body of my beloved, soon itself to be dissolved to earth.
Those who watched me wept, and wondered why I wept
not also, for their pity was less for him than for me—for
me who had lost him. Would not even a heart of steel be
moved, to see me the survivor of Gerard? . . . Who
would not have had pity on the sweet bond of our mutual
love but death, the enemy of all sweetness? . . . I look,
as I have been wont to do in every emergency, to Gerard,
and he is not there. Then do I groan as one that hath no
help. . . . Alas, my cares and anxieties entered more
deeply into Gerard's breast than into my own, ravaged it
more freely, wrung it more acutely. . . . It was fitting
that I should depend for everything on him who was everything to me. He left me but little besides the name and

honor of superintendent, for he did the work. I was called abbot, but he monopolized the abbot's cares. Justly did my spirit repose on him, through whom I could delight in the Lord, preach more freely, pray more confidently. . . . I was slain when he was cut off. For who could call him killed whom the Lord has planted in life? But the portals of life to him were death to me; and I would say that I died with that death, not he who fell asleep in the Lord."

7. The very figure and presence of the man preached. "Bernard is an eloquent preacher much more by nature than by art," said Erasmus; "he is full of charm and vivacity and knows how to reach and move the affections." There was in him a peculiar attractiveness of character, of person, and of utterance. "His very character seemed an evangel." "Remember," said he to a young abbot, "to give your words the voice of a noble virtue." "What went ye out into the wilderness to see? a reed shaken with the wind? . . . a man clothed in soft raiment?" Surely not: "they that wear soft raiment are in kings' houses."

Bernard's austerities increased and fixed his native frailties upon him. But his very frailty preached. He so impaired his taste that he could not distinguish flavors, drinking wine or oil indifferently. He so wasted his body that it became, as Victor Hugo says of an early character in his "Les Miserables," a mere "pretext for a soul to remain on earth." But all this only assisted his moral power, and gave to his utterance an almost supernatural attractiveness and effect. "Reduced almost to the tenuity of the spiritual body," says a contemporary, "he persuaded the eye before the ear heard him." He acquired through his very severities that peculiar attractiveness and power which the Baptist had by the desert aspect of his habit and life, preaching repentance by the very girdle of his loins, and proclaiming a fast by the very scantiness of his own food. There is a principle laid very deep even in the philosophy of preaching, to say nothing of the plenitude of its spiritual implications, which requires that he who would be a prophet of the Most High must separate himself from the world.

8. The age was plastic to the preacher's action, and not without response to the grace of God to which he summoned it. And he did preach the grace of God and salvation by faith. His preaching itself he regarded as a potent instrument of God's grace, a means of planting and nurturing in the lives of men the knowledge of God and love toward him. In one of his noble hymns he said:

> "Jesus, the very thought of thee
>   With sweetness fills the breast;
> But sweeter far thy face to see,
>   And in thy presence rest.
>
> O hope of every contrite heart!
>   O joy of all the meek!
> To those who fall, how kind thou art!
>   How good to those who seek!"

Of another of his hymns, that beginning, "O Sacred Head once wounded," Dr. Philip Schaff has said: "This classical hymn has shown in three tongues, Latin, German, and English, and in three Confessions, Roman, Lutheran, and Reformed, with equal effect, the dying love of our Saviour and our boundless indebtedness to Him."

Bernard was neither bigot nor fanatic, but held that "faith is to be produced by persuasion, not imposed by force." No otherwise could he have displayed such warmth and zeal in his preaching; as, for instance, witness his effect upon the Germans, who, though they "could not understand a word he said, were carried away with his preaching equally with his more excitable countrymen." His sermons even among his own countrymen seem to have been delivered in Latin, and not in French.

Plastic as he himself was to the action of God's grace, he found the age plastic to his personal genius. Dreary centuries had dragged out their dismal and ineffectual length. Pope John XII had in his time "turned the pontifical palace into a vast school of prostitution." Courtesans had bestowed the papacy at their will on their lovers or bastard sons, and such elevation had not served to break the bonds of licentious love. Men in their weariness had looked through the gloom for the world's end. There had been some reviving of hope, and then this man came. He came and by his genius made the valley of Clairvaux the center of European Christendom. He lifted in his bosom and in his own slender arms the tides of the world's better destiny, and quickened humanity's sense of God.

Luther counted him "the best of all the doctors," the one from whom he drank most deeply as of the river of the water of life. It has been thought that only Augustine could contend with him for the place of foremost preacher in the whole history of Latin Christianity. In that long age between the Apostles and the Reformation it is perhaps only Chrysostom and Augustine who can dispute with him the premiership of preaching. He is indeed "a link in the evangelical succession of Paul, Augustine, Luther, Wesley."

Long, long after he had gone from the scene ennobled by his presence and his action here there was found by explorers in his tomb, among the bones and a little dust, and among other of his most intimate effects, a faded piece of yellow cloth, folded and crumpled, on which he had inscribed the words: "A bundle of myrrh is my well-beloved unto me." From this home of the heart's finest fragrance he had drawn the unfading fragrance of his own devoted life.

II

MARTIN LUTHER

(1483–1546)

A Monumental Man

THERE are men whose actions attain to the dignity and importance of events of history. Their deeds are achievements of the cosmos. They are the monumental men. In action they are prophetic. In influence they are colossal.

To Martin Luther more than to most men it was given to be such a man and the author of such actions, and to build himself into the structure of the world. There are those who will dispute his claim to such eminence. But there are also those who just as confidently will decline to stay for the dispute. Whether he be a boor or a sinner, or no, they do not care to argue. One thing they do know, that whereas the world was blind and enslaved to hard tradition, it now lives in the light of a clearer seeing, and man's soul "walks abroad in her own majesty." Luther's composition and publication of the ninety-five theses, the public burning of the papal bull and the whole of the protracted dispute with the papacy, his appearance at the Diet of Worms, his translation of the Bible into German, his masterful and majestic preaching—these at any rate must be admitted to the category of world events. This monumental estimate of the man has not been allowed to go unchallenged. He did not stand as the chief figure in the midst of events toward which men could easily assume a neutral attitude. And the strong projection of his character into history has not invited any neutrality of attitude. Men cannot take him indifferently. They either decidedly favor or strongly dislike him. Either the one attitude or the other is a tribute to the unusual character of the man. The elements were so mixed in him that he would be either tremendously right or tremendously wrong. To the Roman Catholic, still pleased to be bound as Luther found all men bound, he is the arch-heretic of a divided Christendom. To the earnest Protestant waxing in unregulated enthusiasm he is the sole founder of the modern world. And all men who will may know him well enough to have some opinion about him. "I do not know that in all history," says Tulloch, "there is any one to whose true being, alike in its strength and weaknesses, we get nearer than we get to that of Luther." He has outlived his own contemporaries, and made himself a contemporary to other ages. "Four potentates ruled the mind of Europe in the Reformation," says Dr. Krauth; "the Emperor, Erasmus, the Pope, and Luther. The Pope wanes, Erasmus is little, the Emperor is nothing, but Luther abides as a power for all time. His image casts itself upon the current of ages, as the mountain mirrors itself in the river that winds at its foot—the mighty fixing itself immutably upon the changing."

EARLY EDUCATION

Luther was heir to a long line of poverty. As far back as his ancestral search could go he discovered only peasants. "I am a peasant's son," he said. "My father, grandfather, and ancestors were all peasants." Some of the writers say that his mother was also a peasant. But Lindsay, who should be the better authority, says that Hans Luther married above his rank, and that Margarethe Zeigler came of the burgher class.

A distinguished Christian scholar, traveling in Germany, tells us that, standing one day in a common room in an old inn in the market-town of Eisleben, four hundred years after the event, where, amidst the confusion of a market day and the bustle of a public house, Luther's mother was taken with sudden surprise and gave him birth, he reflected on the meanness of the circumstances about him until he realized for the first time the poverty of the birth of One who was first laid in a manger because there was no room for his mother in the inn.

The date of his birth, which is now itself noted as one of the events of history, was November 10, 1483. His father was a slate-cutter by trade whose home was on the western slope of the Thuringian forest, his sojourn at Eisleben at the time of Martin's birth being only temporary. The home was a religious one after such fashion as prevailed, to some extent at least, among the German peasants of the time. The position of the peasant was extremely bad. He was "the pariah of medieval society," cut off from noble, burgher, and ecclesiastic, and preyed upon by all of them. He was "so dependent on his overlord that the character of the proprietor counted for much in the condition of the people." Luther was born on the eve of St. Martin, and was carried to church the next morning and baptized after the name of the patron saint of the day.

The children of the house were subjected to a very rigid discipline. Luther remembered being whipped for a trivial offense until the blood came; and he afterwards said that his mother's strictness and the rigorous life she compelled him to lead drove him into the monastery and made him a monk. Still he learned from her the simple elements of religion. The peasant life out of which he came had in it the elements of his sure corruption unless "the wise severity of his parents" saved him from it; so he had in their hard treatment of him much more to thank them for than had it been a weak indulgence. They taught him that "pardon comes from the free grace of God," and that alone was a sure seed of the Reformation just so soon as it found a lodgment in his experience.

His school days began at a very early age. The teaching was hardly worthy of the name, and the administration of discipline extremely harsh. No less than fifteen times in a single morning was the blundering and inconceivable peda-gogue to whom he was sent known to beat him while he was yet a mere child, and that for not knowing some sub-ject which had not been taught him. At the age of four-teen he had a better school at Magdeburg, where he spent a year. Being thrown on his own resources through his father's lack of ability at this time to support him in school, he sang for alms at the houses of the more prosperous citizens, a custom which the mendicant friars had estab-lished and rendered respectable. He was, however, never a wandering student after a certain miscellaneous fashion of the times, an employment which was wanting in re-spectability.

The next year he was sent to Eisenach, where he would be among his mother's people. Here his open countenance and sweet voice so strongly attracted Madam Ursula Cotta that she invited him to her house, and eventually gave him a home for the rest of his stay of four years.

He came next to the University of Erfurt, which stood at the head of the German universities of the time. He was entered as "Martin Luther from Mansfeld," to which the family home had by this time been changed. His father had grown more prosperous in his financial affairs, and now provided for his schooling, but with a view to his becoming a lawyer. He had begun to discern in him un-usual ability, and wished to have him enter a profession rather than follow a trade. Nevertheless, his future course

was as yet wholly undetermined. No human hands could
lay the lines of the great career to which he was destined.
He could not be forced by the paternal choice into the law.
He was not intended to be a jurist after the law of a carnal
commandment. At Erfurt, so Melanchthon says, he displayed such conspicuous ability as to become the wonder
of the whole university. He obtained his bachelor's degree in 1502 and his master's in 1505. He had just passed
his twenty-first birthday when he was graduated with the
higher degree.

Upon the whole the religious influences exerted upon
him were good and served to quicken and to deepen the
instruction of his earlier life. He began to be given to the
habit of prayer which so strongly marked the later periods
of his life; and in the library of the university he found a
copy of the Latin Bible and had for the first time the entire volume in his hands. He was surprised to find that
there was more of the Gospels and the Epistles than in the
lectionaries, and actually seems not previously to have
known what constituted the whole of even the New Testament. It is recorded that in his reading his eyes first
lighted on the idyllic passage which delineates the early
life of Samuel and exhibits the godly devotion of his mother.
This made him think of himself and his own mother.

Convent and Conversion

The circumstances which precipitated Luther's sudden
entrance upon the monastic life have been variously related. What he well knew would be his father's objections
to such a course must have borne with considerable weight
upon his mind. Other circumstances were more personal.
It was said that the sudden death of a friend, with a narrow escape of his own from death by lightning shortly
afterwards, combined to draw from him an impulsive vow

that he would become a monk. This action, though ill-considered, if indeed it can be said to have had any mature consideration at all, was really in the direction which his life was destined to take. Two weeks later he invited a company of his more intimate friends to an evening of song and mirth at his house, and the next morning they accompanied him on his way to the Augustinian convent at Erfurt and bade him farewell at its gates.

The discipline of the monastic life was strict and severe. He himself was not less strict and severe in his obedience to it. He swept, he scoured, he scrubbed. He was sent out to beg from door to door. He was carefully instructed how to stand, to sit, to walk, to kneel, how to conduct himself in the presence of priests and other superiors, and so on, and so on, and so forth, and so forth. Think of the man of Wittenberg and of Worms as the subject of these trivialities. And yet it was no doubt from this very extremity of triviality that his spirit revolted at last to the deeper truth and experience of the gospel.

Such time as he could filch from triviality to study he gave to the Scriptures. He went through the Psalter and the Epistles to the Romans and to the Hebrews with such care and attention that it was said that each sentence was weighed word by word. He finished his probation within the prescribed time and order and was allotted a cell of his own, which would be provided with a table, a chair, a couch, and a lamp. He was now introduced to the study of the scholastic theology, but continued his devotion to the monastic regulations with a strictness which surpassed all others. "If ever a monk could win heaven by monkery, I must have reached it," he said long afterwards. And yet he felt no nearer God, and still was without any sense of pardon or peace. In this rigorous life he spent more than two years, and this was the religious fruit of it.

The question would inevitably arise: "If monastic observances were to advance his salvation, how could he
ever be satisfied that they were performed with sufficient
perfection?" He tortured himself—and torture is the
word—with fasts, vigils, and prayers, having gone at one
time three whole days without either food or drink, but
his heart could never come to the assurance that God was
pleased with what he had done. The mind and the habit
may be ceremonial and ritualistic, but the heart is at last
evangelical and craves the good tidings of grace. Luther
could not be sure that he had the Holy Spirit. And only
so could he have peace. The heart's lack of peace raises
the whole issue between the evangelical and the legal
means of salvation. So it is the heart in another way than
we have been wont to think that makes the theologian.

In all his stress of soul Staupitz, Vicar-General of the
Augustinian order, was his surest and most valued human
guide and comforter. Luther spoke of being afraid of
Christ. "That is not Christ," said Staupitz, "for Christ
does not terrify; he only consoles." Proceeding still
further he admonished him that he could not trust to his
own powers, and taught him man's inability to do anything, except by the grace of God. An aged monk came
to him in the time of an illness brought on by the excess of
his mortifications, a condition which gave abundant occasion to his old terrors to renew their assault upon him, and
recited to him the Creed. Coming to the clause, "I believe in the forgiveness of sin," he paused and pressed
Luther to answer whether he believed that. "Then put
the word 'my' in," he continued; "say, 'I believe in the
forgiveness of *my* sins." That was a truly evangelical way
in which to proceed, but it brought to Luther only momentary comfort.

He began the study of the Epistle to the Romans over

4

again. He had begun to see that "the righteousness of
God for every one who trusts in Christ is *on the sinner's
side*, and not against him." He gives his own account of
his wrestling with the *Romans* and his way to peace: "I
sought day and night to make out the meaning of Paul; and
at last I came to apprehend it thus: Through the gospel
is revealed the righteousness which availeth with God—
a righteousness by which God, in his mercy and compassion,
justifieth us; as it is written, 'The just shall live by faith.'
Straightway I felt as if I were born anew. It was as if I
had found the door of Paradise thrown wide open. Now I
saw the Scriptures altogether in a new light—I ran through
their whole contents as far as my memory would serve, and
compared them, and found that this righteousness was
really that by which God makes us righteous, because
everything else in Scripture agreed thereunto so well. The
expression, 'the righteousness of God,' which I so much
hated before, now became dear and precious—my darling
and comforting word. That passage of Paul was to me the
true door of Paradise."

Luther was ordained to the priesthood in 1507. He
found his first celebration of the Mass a great trial. The
special attendance of his father, with a group of his friends,
who was faithful to the expectation of his attendance on
the occasion, though he had not yet become reconciled to
the course his son had pursued, was a source of no slight
embarrassment to the conscientious young celebrant of
his initial mass. But a further and far more potent cause
of the sensible agitation of his spirit was a deep sense of
his own unworthiness.

MATURING CONVICTIONS

The next year after his ordination Luther was called by
Staupitz, who had been made dean of the newly founded

University of Wittenberg, to the chair of philosophy in
that institution. Wittenberg has been described as "a
truly denominational college of the sixteenth century."
Though Luther was appointed to teach philosophy, a
subject which at the time embraced a much broader curriculum than now, he much preferred theology. Very
soon he became a Bachelor of Theology, with authority to
lecture upon the text of the Holy Scriptures. Melanchthon
reports that no less distinguished a man than Dr. Pollich,
who had been instrumental in the founding of Wittenberg,
declared after hearing several of Luther's lectures that he
was destined to change the entire method of instruction
then prevailing in the universities.

His service at Wittenberg was interrupted while he went
on a mission to Rome in a matter related to the adjustment
of some of the affairs of his order. From his early monastic
days his administrative ability had attracted the attention
of his superiors. His conduct of the mission to Rome won
for him the esteem of all who were interested in its outcome, though its immediate object seems not to have been
accomplished. Upon Luther himself the impressions of the
visit were most profound. Rome awed him and drew from
him emotions of deepest reverence. Coming first within
sight of its walls, he raised his hands in sheer delight, and
exclaimed, "I greet thee, thou Holy Rome." He swallowed
wholesale "all the legends his guides repeated to him."
It was only in the new light of after years that he remembered how much he had seen in Rome that his conscience
could not approve.

On returning to Wittenberg he assumed the chair of
theology in the university. He said no sad farewell to the
scholastic philosophy, on which he had had to enter as a
preparation for the law to which his father had destined
him. The theology itself was scholastic, but anyway it

was theology. And he was to prove that scholasticism could not curb him.

On October 19, 1512, he became a Doctor of Theology and rose rapidly to a commanding position in the university. He had long resisted the wish of Staupitz that he should prepare himself for this degree and for the work for which it equipped him. He had "yielded not to persuasion but to commands." And now he was speedily to make his university famous. His work consisted of lectures in the form of expositions of the Scriptures. He began with the book of Psalms, which to him was "the Bible within the Bible," and which was his prayer book in all the great crises of his life. It lay so close to his experience and affections as to draw most effectively upon his powers of exposition. He taught it as if he himself had fought in all these ancient battles and prayed beside all these far-away altars. He conquered the Psalms as Joshua had conquered Canaan: "Every place that the sole of your foot shall tread upon, to you have I given it." After the Psalms he made the Epistle to the Romans the basis of his exposition, and then the Epistle to the Galatians. Wittenberg students were awakened to a new sense of the Bible, the fame of the lectures spread into the town, and sedate burghers came and enrolled in his classes. Gradually there appeared at "the small, poor, and remote University of Wittenberg students from all parts of Germany, and then from all parts of Europe." But it was to no merely easeful spontaneity in the exercise of his native powers to which he trusted for the accomplishment of these results. All these early years of his work as a professor he was a very hard student.

Furthermore, his new degree embraced a more definite and additional obligation to preach. This he was at first very reluctant to do. He was even more unwilling to preach than he had been to teach. It was as if he had to be drawn to it with a cart rope. It was only at the command of his superior and under stress of his vow of obedience that he had first preached in the refectory of the cloister at Erfurt. And now ere he will so much as preach in the little chapel of the cloister at Wittenberg he has to be impressed by the authority set over him. Ten years afterwards he pointed out to some of his friends a pear tree under which he had pleaded with Staupitz to release him from the proposed promotion and its attendant preaching responsibilities. But once he began to preach the taste of it grew upon him and soon he was preaching by request in the town church of Wittenberg.

CRISES IN THE CONTEST WITH THE PAPACY

The contest with the papacy constitutes the next stage in Luther's career. There are certain crises which mark this stage more or less definitely.

1. There was the debate about indulgences and its issue in the nailing up of the ninety-five theses. In the latter part of the year 1517 John Tetzel, a Dominican friar with considerable gifts as a popular preacher, was appointed by his superiors in ecclesiastical authority to preach and to sell indulgences. The use of the indulgence already had a long history in the Church. To the principle upon which its use was originally projected Luther had no particular objection. But it now began to be very seriously abused and to constitute one of the most grievous of all the corrupt ecclesiastical practices of the time. The Elector of Saxony had forbidden the sale of the indulgences within his dominions, but Wittenberg was not far from the border and Luther found some of his own parishioners in possession of them. They had come to him showing the "papal letters" they had bought and demanding "priestly

absolution in due form without either confession of sin or showing any signs of real sorrow." He was not slow to discern the real character of the abuse. He could see further than the people could see, and had a duty to protect them from so palpable an imposition. The Pope proclaimed the indulgence with all the prestige of his great authority, and commended it as a great boon. To the common people it meant "that on the payment of certain specified sums of money, spiritual privileges, including the forgiveness of sins, could be obtained by the purchasers." Those who bought the tickets were assured of the "complete forgiveness of sins, participation in the grace of God, and freedom from purgatory." Full remission and release were provided for those already in purgatory if the price were paid. "The soul flies out of purgatory," Tetzel shouted to the crowds, "as soon as the money rattles in the box."

On All Saints' eve, October 31, 1517, a time chosen so as to catch the attention of the crowds who would come to the church for the special commemorative exercises on the next day, held according to an annual custom, Luther nailed to the door of the Castle Church in Wittenberg ninety-five theses challenging the sale of indulgences and all the abuses connected with the same. As Lindsay says, they were "ninety-five sledge-hammer blows directed against the most flagrant ecclesiastical abuse of the age." He had unwittingly sown the seed that should revolutionize the world. Within two weeks the publication of the theses had been blazoned through nearly all of Germany, and within two weeks more they had gone far beyond its borders. Immediately it was beyond the power of popes or opposing princes to stay the tides of the coming reformation. Instantly the theses were taken up and everywhere they either awakened earnest advocacy or aroused violent opposition. The first thesis raised the whole issue between scholasticism and Scripture, between ecclesiasticism and conscience, between *repentance* and *penance*. It contained the principle of all the rest and read as follows: "When our Lord and Master, Jesus Christ, says, 'Repent,' he means that the entire life of believers should be a repentance." No more needed to be said. There was the very essence of evangelical theology. *Pœnitentiam agite;* that is what the Vulgate makes John the Baptist say at the first opening of his mouth to preach. What does it mean? Is it an act of the will and the conscience, proceeding out of the deepest purposes of man's moral nature as wrought upon by the Spirit of God? Or is it a series of ceremonial and ritualistic performances accomplishing a satisfaction as legal as the performances themselves, and the worth of which is capable of being measured exactly by a priest? There the whole issue hung, for these two positions are not agreed and cannot live together. The man who in the Church of that age said what Luther had said must either recant or go on his way.

The publication of the theses by Luther pledged him to defend them—which also he was not slow to do. Tetzel, chief salesman of the indulgences, and Prierias, a Dominican of distinction, entered the lists against him. He was at first terrified at the attack of the latter upon the theses, because of his high rank; but on reading it he concluded that the best answer he could make to it would be to republish it. The defense he was compelled to make only made him bolder in his position and deepened his conviction of the truth of the stand he had taken. Controversy cleared his thinking, and he was driven further and further from medieval principles—an experience which is by no means unusual with honest and earnest advocates of contested positions and principles. But he had no intention of breaking away from the Church and its institutions. He even went so far as to write a humble letter of apology to the Pope, but without showing any disposition to yield his ground. His enemies raged; but "the more they rage," he said, "the more I go forward." The Pope himself stepped into the waters which Luther had stirred for the healing of the nations, but without stilling them. He cited the troublesome monk to appear at Rome within sixty days, but the Elector of Saxony, Luther's steadfast friend, interposed his authority against the citation and demanded that the trial should take place on German soil.

In the midst of the controversy Philip Melanchthon, the comfort of whose friendship stayed Luther all his days, came to Wittenberg to take the chair of Greek. He had just passed his twenty-first birthday, and his youthful and unpretentious appearance, with the diffidence of his manner, started serious misgivings. But the ability of his inaugural address cleared away all doubt and established him at once with authority in his position.

2. Since Luther could not be compelled to answer the Pope at Rome, he was summoned to appear at Augsburg and defend himself before the papal legate, Cardinal Cajetan. Many of his supporters regarded his journey to Augsburg as his death-march, but he answered them with the assurance that even in Augsburg Jesus Christ reigned. "Let Christ live; let Martin die," said he. Cajetan was disposed to deal with him in a very summary manner. He demanded of him in the name of the Pope that he should make a recantation of errors, that he should give a promise to refrain from them in the future, and that he should avoid all other acts which might disturb the peace of the church. These demands, indeed, if complied with, would leave him little to do unless it might be to sit quietly down and smoke a pipe of peace.

He asks to know what errors he is required to recant. The cardinal indicates as containing specific errors certain of the theses which involved both the formal and the material principles of Protestantism. He adduces to prove the error a bull of one of the popes of which he seems to think Luther is ignorant. But Luther is a better monk than Cajetan is a cardinal. He not only shows his acquaintance with this particular bull, but also points the cardinal to a similar statement by another pope. These and other points of greater or lesser importance the discussion covered, while Luther repeated from time to time that he was ready to concede everything else, but that he could surrender nothing that was a matter of conscience. Cajetan was uncertain of his course and delayed his answer. In the meantime Luther appealed "from the Pope ill-informed to the Pope better-informed," and left the place by night through a small gate in the city walls opened for him by a trusted friend. It was learned afterwards that the papal court had prejudged the case and had communicated secret instructions to the legate to deal with Luther as a notorious heretic, and that he was to be forthwith excommunicated if he did not recant his errors.

3. Miltitz, a Saxon nobleman and representative of the interests of the Elector at Rome, was now dispatched as papal nuncio to Germany to seek by political or any other means to effect a reconciliation of the entire situation. The gravity of the undertaking far exceeded anything that he had anticipated. His efforts led to nothing more decisive for his cause than Luther's disputation with Eck at Leipzig. In this disputation the primacy of the Pope and the authority of councils were the principal points at issue. Eck was one of the shrewdest opponents Luther ever pub-

licly encountered, and he really had the better of the debate.

Luther left Leipzig with a heavy heart. A momentary and more or less personal discomfiture prevented his seeing that his cause had been drawn out to its long and final issues. Eck had forced him to the logical results of his premises and this could only be his gain. He had been compelled to define to himself more definitely than he had ever done before his true religious position, and to see that there was no going back. He saw as never before what lay in his opposition to indulgences, and others saw it too. He began to be more and more definitely the leader of a movement, and to gather into himself the interests of the German nation. As time went on "it became more manifest," as Principal Tulloch says, "that the real question was Germany or Rome—national independence or hierarchical bondage; and still more deeply, Scripture or Church, conscience or authority."

4. After Leipzig came the Pope's bull of excommunication. The connection between the two was one of cause and effect as well as chronology, for really it was Eck who instigated and hastened the Pope's action. The bull demanded the public burning of the works of Luther, and this demand had been complied with at Louvain, Cologne, Mayence, and perhaps elsewhere. Luther's answer to this demand was to try whether the bull itself would not burn, and he left its ashes to the winds and the weather in the streets of Wittenberg. In the fire he also burned the last bridge behind him, and retraction or retreat was less and less possible. Papal bulls had been burned before, but only by great monarchs who had arms and armies to support their action. But now an unpanoplied monk, unsupported save by his own manhood, has disregarded and burned the revered papal document. All Europe was thrilled as the

tidings went forth, and there was the dawn of a new day in the sky.

But fire was not the only weapon Luther had against the promulgation of papal decrees. In the very year of the issuance of the bull of his own excommunication he issued the three great treatises which constitute his chief reformatory writings—namely, his "Address to the Christian Nobility of the German Nation," "The Babylonian Captivity of the Church," and "The Freedom of a Christian Man." "In the first," says Köstlin, who is credited with having written the best life of Luther, "Luther calls Christendom, in general, to the battle against the outward abuses of the Pope and of the estate that boasted of being the only one possessing a spiritual and priestly character. In the second, he exposes and breaks the spiritual bond, whereby this estate, through its means of grace, kept souls in bondage. In the third, he reaches the most profound and important question concerning the relation of the Christian soul to its God and Redeemer, and the way and nature of salvation."

5. By the use of the arts of a diplomacy which would have been more worthy of the politics of a ward than the policy of a church the young Emperor Charles V, who had been chosen the head of the Holy Roman Empire, was won to the support of the papacy, though before the election Rome had expressed its preference for another. Thus there issued for Luther the Diet of Worms. He was summoned to appear. But the summons itself was a triumph; for a Catholic sovereign is compelled thus to deal with a heretic who is already under condemnation by the Pope. Perhaps even the influence of the papacy could not prevent Charles's feeling the truth of Erasmus's reply to the Elector when he had asked whether Luther had really erred. "Yes," answered Erasmus, "in two things: he has attacked the Pope in his

crown, and the monks in their bellies." The publication of
the theses had greatly decreased the sale of indulgences, and
the revenues of the Church were in that measure dimin-
ished.

Luther could but be aware in coming to Worms that
empire and papacy concentrated there their combination
against him, with designs as sinister as could well be conceived. Upon the most unequal terms he must plead his
cause. The whole setting of the scene and the fixing of the
plan of procedure was in the hands of his enemies. And
yet it was not as completely so as it seemed. For the
people were with Luther, and his opponents had the chagrin
of seeing a heretic have a triumphal entry into Worms.
Indeed, his journey thither had all the way been a triumph.
He came more as a conqueror than as one already condemned. Standing there in his own defense before the
Diet he looked upon a pile of his books lying on a table
which stood between him and the Emperor, sitting in state
beyond. He must answer, in the first place, whether he
had written these books and others published under his
name; and, secondly, whether he would recant or abide
by them. He wishes and asks for a day's delay, and obtains his request. He thus secured a postponement until
the next day, and what he really desired and his opponents
wished to avoid, an opportunity for debate.

There is an old tradition that as he was entering the
hall the next day a doughty German warrior cried out to
him: "My poor monk! my poor monk! thou art on thy
way to make such a stand as I and many of my knights
have never done in our toughest battles. If thou art sure
of the justice of thy cause, then forward in the name of
God, and be of good courage; God will not forsake thee."

Being confronted with the same demands as on the day
before, Luther spoke for two hours, it was said, and then,

at the request of the Emperor, who did not understand German, he spoke again in Latin. When he had finished the Emperor told him through Eck—another John Eck and not the Ingolstadt professor—that he was not there to debate matters which had been settled by General Councils, that he must give a plain answer "without horns" whether he "would retract all that he had said contradicting the decisions of the Council of Constance; if so, then he would be dealt with leniently with regard to what else he had written." "Since your Imperial Majesty requires a plain answer," said Luther, "I will give one without horns or hoof! It is this: that I must be convinced either by the testimony of Scripture or by clear arguments. I cannot trust the Pope or Councils by themselves, since it is as clear as daylight that they have not only erred, but contradicted themselves. I am bound by the Scriptures which I have quoted; my conscience is thirled to the Word of God. I may not and will not recant, because to act against conscience is neither honest nor safe." Having said this both in German and in Latin, he added, after a pause, in the speech he drank from his mother's bosom: "I can do nothing else; here I stand; so help me God. Amen." The Emperor asked him through Eck whether he had really said that Councils could err. Luther "hardened himself like a hard rock" and stood to what he had said. After a brief parley on the point between him and Eck the crowd grew noisy and restless, and the Emperor himself became impatient and dismissed the Diet. Further efforts made in a more private way were all unavailing and left Luther immovable in his resolve that he would not submit himself to any authority except the Scriptures. Through the whole ordeal he had borne himself with unexampled manliness and courage. Coming first before the diet in the character and habit of a simple monk, he was ignorant of the proprieties of the occasion, was visibly embarrassed, and had not known how to conduct himself. But true manhood has its own manners and makes its own code. Set as the entire occasion was amid circumstances of such shrewd and studied opposition to himself and his cause, he at length bore himself with such composure of demeanor and grandeur of spirit as is rarely given to a man who stands in a crisis of the world's moral life and fights for freedom of conscience and the untrammeled future of the race.

Consolidating and Constructive Period

On Luther's return from Worms under imperial denunciation as a heretic he was seized by his friends and given an asylum in the Wartburg at Eisenach. His disappearance spread consternation throughout Germany, and some time elapsed before his whereabouts was really known. Even in his retreat, with his monastic habit changed for that of a knight, with a full beard upon his face and a sword by his side, and with the secret of his name known only to his host, he still fought the battles of the Reformation. Through his constant appeal to the testimony of the Scriptures in all the contest he had waged with opposing errors he had felt the need of an accurate translation in the speech of the people. Other considerations inclined him in the same way, and so his own work of translation began. While in the Wartburg for ten months he translated the New Testament, though hardly more than one-third of that time was occupied in actual work upon it. It was not published until after revision under the superintendence of Melanchthon, who was a much better Greek scholar than Luther. At length he gave to the German nation his translation of the entire Bible, a literary achievement which awakens admiring comment

until this day.   It has proved itself to have entered as a
formative factor into the very genius of the German
language.

Luther left the Wartburg in March, 1522, under an
urgent demand for his services at Wittenberg, where
under the leadership of Carlstadt and through the influence of the Zwickau prophets radical measures of reform had been instituted to the serious detriment of saner
measures. After a series of eight sermons of a remarkably
effective and vigorous sort the unrest was quieted, and
Luther resumed his teaching in the university. An incident of the time which is characteristic both of the man
and of the times is thus described by Stoddart in "The
New Testament in Life and Literature": "The clocks of
the city of Leipzig were striking noon on 3 December, 1521,
when a traveler, accompanied by his servant, dismounted
at the door of one of the inns. The stranger, a bearded
man of middle age, wore a gray riding costume, and
under his traveling hat he had a close-fitting red 'Schäpli,'
the cap which kept the head warm and protected the hair
from dust. It was noticed that he did not remove the
red bonnet when he sat down to table, and a sharp-witted
woman, who had probably attended the Leipzig disputation of 1519, hazarded in private conversation the bold
guess that the stranger was Dr. Martin Luther. . . .
The landlord when questioned later on as to his culpable
act in entertaining the arch-heretic who lay under the
Empire's ban, was able to assure the magistrates, with a
clear conscience, that the visitor was unknown to him."

In June, 1525, Luther made one of the most decisive of
all his breaks with medievalism by his marriage to Catharine von Bora, a nun who had spent ten years in a cloister
reserved for members of families of the nobility. Luther's
writings had penetrated to her retreat, and she and a num-

ber of her companions in the cloister were convinced of their error and wished to escape. This design they were not able to effect until finally they were assisted by Luther. Husbands were to be furnished them, and all of them seem to have acquiesced in the choices made severally for them except Catharine. No, she would not marry the man selected for her; she would like to marry Amsdorf or Luther. And Luther it was. The marriage was as fortunate and as happy as could be, particularly for Luther. He was of a tender and affectionate nature; Catharine was every way worthy of him, and his home was a haven amid the outward storms of an eventful life.

At the Diet of Speyer, 1526, in the face of the division of Germany into a Protestant and a Roman party, an agreement was reached which was interpreted by the Lutherans to mean that they might organize their ecclesiastical affairs according to their own mind, provided the terms of the agreement were not violated. This they proceeded to do. But at the Diet of 1529 the Roman majority sided with the Emperor against the Protestant minority in his repeal of the rights granted by the Diet of 1526. A portion of the Lutherans drafted a legal protest in which the signers declared their intention to abide by the decisions of 1526 and their refusal to be bound by the contrary action of 1529. From this circumstance the name *Protestant* arose.

Centering about the year 1527 there was a period of unusual literary activity, together with a visitation of the Saxon churches, with a view to their settlement on the basis of the order and principles of the Reformation. Luther not only bore the principal burden of all this, but did most of the work, whether literary or administrative. He issued new volumes of sermons, and prepared and published two catechisms possessed of very high religious and educational value. His literary output was enormous—

"a volume large or small on an average every fortnight of his active life." The administrative work of the Reformation grew to be both heavy and extensive; but there was never any haste about any formal attempt to construct a new ecclesiastical system or to organize the movement according to any predetermined plans.

The Diet of Augsburg, meeting in 1530, promulgated the great confession of the Protestant faith, known from the place of its origin as the Augsburg Confession. This Confession was prepared by Melanchthon in close consultation with Luther, who, from prudential reasons, was not present.

In 1537 articles were drawn up and presented to a gathering at Smalkald of electors, princes, and states which were designed to show how far the Protestants were willing to go in order to avoid a final rupture with Rome, and hence called the Smalkald Articles. They bear witness that the early Protestants were not schismatics.

All too soon divisions appeared among the Protestants themselves, and Luther was not permitted to see and to preserve the unity of the evangelical movement. The Germans were against the Swiss, and the Swiss were against the Germans. Luther and Zwingli could not agree upon the nature of the Sacrament of the Lord's Supper; though in a meeting designed to effect an agreement Zwingli displayed the better temper.

Luther was impulsive and had in him besides an element of coarseness. He left a permanent stain on his name in the matter of his attitude toward the Peasants' War. True, Thomas Münzer had charged the peasants "not to let the blood cool on their swords." But this could not justify the pamphlet of Luther in which he "hounds on the ruling classes to suppress the insurgents with all violence." Like-

5

wise in the matter of the bigamy of Phillip of Hesse he was
not blameless.

Luther's last days were filled with incessant toil and
care which had to be borne upon a margin of strength continually depleted by ill health. His efforts were often
thwarted by headaches, insomnia, and by symptoms of
heart trouble. On more slender resources of physical
strength an equally prodigious amount of work has rarely
been done. And it was that varied and arduous labor
without which all that had gone before would have come
to naught. He died at Eisleben, the place of his birth,
on February 18, 1546. His funeral services were held in
the Castle Church at Wittenberg, on the doors of which he
had nailed up the theses, and beside the pulpit where he
had so often preached he was buried. There he and
Melanchthon rest side by side.

A New Epoch in Preaching

One of the facts of finest significance about all the life
and work of Luther is that preaching was the chief instrument in his promotion of the interests of the Reformation.
It was a new epoch in preaching, and he was himself the
maker of the epoch. "It was he," as Garvie truly says,
"who put the sermon in Protestantism in the place held
by the mass in Roman Catholicism; and made preaching
the most potent influence in the churches of the Reformation." He held preaching to be the most important part
of public worship, and even placed it above the Bible, not
as to its authority, but in the sense that it gives life and
application to the Bible. As a matter of fact a large part
of the new emphasis he gave to preaching was due to the
fact that he and his associates and disciples, on whom he
exercised so potent an influence, made preaching much
more directly dependent on the Bible than it had been in

Roman Catholicism. This high view of preaching became one of "the distinctive notes of the Reformation." These three items of incalculable import stand to the credit of Christian preaching, that by it above all other agencies Paul planted Christianity in the Roman Empire, Luther effected the Protestant Reformation, and John Wesley effected the great revival of the eighteenth century.

1. The fact of first significance about the preaching of Luther is that it had its springs in his own experience. He advanced to his great achievement as a preacher along the way of a certain and incontestable experience—through the hard experience of his early life; through the severity of the experiences of his monastic life, so barren of any immediate fruitfulness, yet showing profoundly what monasticism and all its observances could not do; above all, through his happy experience of God's grace in Christ; and, when he had begun to preach, through his confident experience of what God could do to sustain his own cause.

First of all, his experience gave him Christ. He had ceremonies a plenty, excelling all others in the use of them. But he found them no better than the rags of his own righteousness. He had tested to its foundation the scholastic principle "that a man becomes just by doing just acts." What he learned was that "we must first be just, and then we shall do just actions." Without faith in Christ men can no more become holy "than a crab apple can become a fig." He had seen his hopes die down in ashes on every other altar, and then, there stood the Christ. How different from a rigid ceremonialism and a hard and fast legalism it all was.

"O Saul, it shall be
A Face like my face that receives thee; a Man like to me,
Thou shalt love and be loved by, forever: a Hand like this hand
Shall throw open the gates of life to thee! See the Christ stand!"

The very subject of preaching to Luther came to be "the glory of God in Jesus Christ." And of Christ in his singular and personal devotion he could say, "Thou, Lord Jesus, art my righteousness while I am thy sin."

Again, his experience gave him forgiveness and peace. Whereas he had not been able to *attain* salvation by his own efforts, he now *obtained* it through Christ. He was freely forgiven and had nothing to pay.

> "In my hand no price I bring;
> Simply to thy cross I cling."

Here was the doctrine of justification by faith on which his whole Christian life and ministry was based. "For this cause it is of faith, that it may be according to grace." Salvation does not begin in us by any act or merit of our own: *it is the gift of God*. Luther only found peace when the forgiveness of sins became a fact of his own experience, clearly and completely expressed in Christ.

Again, his experience gave him freedom. His mind had been bound. His soul had been shackled. His conscience had been intolerably burdened. Christ burst all these bonds, and so not only set him free from let and hindrance by them, but also established his soul in life in the power of that liberty wherewith Christ alone sets men free. He had a sense of the reality of moral freedom which no man in this world ever yet had save as it came to him through Christ and his grace. When this divine sense of freedom in Christ asserted itself as an immovable fact in the experience of this unknown Saxon monk the Reformation was free to be born. It was born first in him, and then in the world.

Again, his experience gave him the Scriptures. Through his experience the Scriptures ceased to be scholastic and became evangelical. We have already very definitely seen what the Scriptures had to do with the creation of his experience, how he wrestled for an understanding of Paul until Paul's gospel by God's grace quickened him into life. Harnack says that until Luther "no one in the Church really understood the Epistles to the Romans and to the Galatians." Be that as it may, the Scriptures became evangelical to him. He grounded theological verity itself solely on the Scriptures. But it was in his preaching that they came to new life. It was with his knowledge of the evangelical content of the Scriptures that he "confounded and silenced all his adversaries." He rediscovered and re-vivified the apostolic gospel. He grasped God by faith, and God grasped him in redeeming mercy. He knew God, not as the God of canons and ceremonies, but the God of grace, and of a realized and vital experience. He was evangelical in thought and faith as opposed to all that was ceremonial, or legal, or priestly, or ecclesiastical, or scho-lastic, or ascetic. His religion could not mean anything to him that was apart from the grace that was in Christ: in its essence it was "simply the personal and continual giving of the heart to God, a daily regeneration of man." His common sense enlightened by his experience enabled him to escape the two religious extremes of the times—on the one hand the conception which lost vital religion in ceremony, and on the other the confusing of high religious attainment with the morbidly and tenuously and, too often, immorally mystical.

2. His power to deliver his preaching to the understand-ing and the conscience of his hearer was a marked element of his effectiveness. For so preaching is to be delivered. It is not delivered until it reaches the understanding of the hearer; and it is not preaching until it reaches the conscience. And Luther made a hearer of the humblest man present. "When I preach," he said, "I regard neither

doctors nor magistrates, of whom there are in this church about forty; but I have an eye to the multitude of young people, children, and servants, of whom there are about two thousand." He taught in pictures, and described what he saw; and this was to his advantage in preaching. Instruction and impression, though these might vary in their proportion, were the preacher's sole concern. He was to be a *dialecticus* and a *rhetor* as these represented the work of instruction and impression; but he was not to care for literary or any other kind of personal fame. "Clearness and simplicity of style is what he insists on." And these are the qualities which his own style achieved. When he preached there was no lost motion of the mind in the effort to understand what he meant. And it was also understood that he not only meant to be understood, but that the word of the gospel must issue fruitfully in the lives of those who heard. "He had a singular lack of self-control," says Lindsay, "in the use of violent and incendiary speech." But this vice had its contrary virtue, when he was self-controlled, in a remarkable power of public utterance.

3. His homiletic axiom, "Step boldly forward, open your mouth well, stop soon," might be enacted into a perpetual pulpit ordinance. But this was an axiom of delivery, an axiom for regulating the conduct of the preacher before his audience. Back of it were his prayers and his preparation. His praying was his hardest and most forceful work. His prayers were mighty wrestlings with God; they were stern contests with himself; they were mighty conflicts with his foes; they were the trumpet blasts of the Reformation; they were the overtones of his pulpit. When he had prayed he could win at Worms. And when he had prayed he kindled in his pulpit the fires of a holy reformation.

It is difficult to judge of his homiletic method. We have

his sermons as they were taken down by others and hardly ever seen by him before they were printed. His method in the main was extemporaneous. How else could a man as busy as he have done? He chose his text, or subject, meditated upon it, arranged his thoughts in outline, and perhaps jotted down some of his illustrations. But after all you cannot find just how he did prepare to preach. His praying could never be omitted. He prepared himself. He prepared his sermon. He preached. Dr. John A. Broadus thought his preaching had a great advantage in being all of it bound around the great central and controlling idea of justification by faith. Doubtless this is true. The preacher who does not have some great and central and controlling theme will hardly have a theme at all. He will never build a temple, but only scatter stones. The stones may be of good quality, but they would be much more serviceable and valuable if they were given some structural form. Luther, of course, in making justification by faith central in his preaching did not do so in a mere didactic or doctrinal way, but so as to make Christ central in man's redemption. And he was very humble about it all, as his own words testify. "When you are about to preach," he says, "speak with God, 'Dear Lord God, I will preach to thy honor and speak of thee. Thee will I adore, and praise thy name, although I cannot do it as well as I could wish to do.'"

Nor did he learn to preach Christ all at once, nor yet for a long time, as he himself again has said. The devil, he said, was his best professor in the chair of apologetical, and exegetical, and experimental, and dogmatical divinity. "It was my temptations," he declares, "and my corruptions, and my transgressions that ultimately made me a true minister of the New Testament." And he adds that "without incessant combat, and pain, and tears, and blood, no stripling of a student ever yet became a great preacher."

4. His preaching grew with the greatness of the issues he had to meet. He says in his Table Talk in a manner characteristic of that itself characteristic book that he was, as it were, tugged by his hair to the office of preaching. And then he continues in his frank and hazardous way: "But had I then known what now I know, ten horses should scarce have drawn me to it." And as if that were not enough, he says still further: "Moses and Jeremiah also complained that they were deceived." This reluctance we have seen in him before. And in a great nature it is a fine thing. And his frank way of expressing it is not altogether a bad thing. There is in it a seed of submission to the will of God. There is in it a sort of premonition that the human will really wishes the divine will to prevail.

This was never more strikingly true than in the case of Luther. There developed in him a rare submission to the will of God. Each new responsibility brought with it a new demand for submission, and whatever his struggle might be, at the last he did not fail. He could have been a petty priest, going upon such a priest's trivial round, and never have gotten outside his Augustinian cloister. But what sort of preacher would that cloister have made of him? It took all Germany to make him a preacher. It took the continent of Europe to make him a preacher. It took the corruptions of a world to make him a preacher. It took the decadence of the Church and the prostitution of the priesthood to make him a preacher. This is not to say that all these things existed that he might be a preacher. But since they did exist and he took the burden of them as a charge upon his own soul he was thereby made a preacher. His conversion made his soul too big for a monastery. He went out and his preaching opened the

gates of a new epoch. The Church and the world required
a reformation, a reformation in practice, in manners, and
in morals, a reformation in their very thinking, and in the
principles by which they were guided. It was a task great
enough for God. And that is just why Luther could under-
take it. He took it up as God's task and not his own, and
so he could do it. Said he in his great prayer preserved by
tradition from Worms, and from the affliction which lay
there upon his soul: "Almighty and Eternal God, how is
there but one thing to be seen upon earth! . . . Do
Thou, my God, stand by me, against all the world's
wisdom and reason. O, do it! Thou must do it! Yea,
Thou alone must do it! Not mine, but Thine is the cause.
For my own self, I have nothing to do with these great
earthly lords. I would prefer to have my peaceful days,
and to be out of this turmoil. But Thine, O Lord, is this
cause; it is righteous and eternal. Stand by me, thou true
Eternal God." And truly did the Eternal God stand by
him the next day and lead him on to a great victory.

Coleridge in his "Aids to Reflection," speaking of the
manipulation of the purgatorial system by the Church of
Rome, says of Luther substantially what Harnack has
said: "As the encysted venom, or poison-bag, beneath the
adder's fang, so does this doctrine lie beneath the tremendous power of the Romish hierarchy. The demoralizing
influence of this dogma, and that it curdled the very lifeblood in the veins of Christendom, it was given to Luther,
beyond all men since Paul, to see, feel, and promulgate."
There was the making of the preacher. There were these
incalculable issues involved in the situation and in the system, and it was given to him *to see, to feel, and to promulgate.*

5. The full potency of his personal force comes to its
finest issues in the preëminence of his preaching. By whatever variety of processes or whatever combination of

causes there was at length evoked in him one of the most potent personal forces in modern history. It was the man who preached above all that he had to say. And so the man does always preach, either above or below what he has to say. Moral truth can never be made an abstraction. This is the very secret of the Incarnation. In a sense the truth may save, and does save; but it is the truth in Christ, and he is himself the Saviour. Others might, according to their capacity, hold the truth, as Luther held it. But who else could hold it as he held it, or do with it what he did? All this was conspicuously true of Erasmus. But more was true of Luther. He was a consummate example of Phillips Brooks's idea of preaching as truth expressed through personality.

He was an instrument fitted beyond the wisdom of men for the task assigned him. Elemental to his nature, and nobly developed in their masterly employment, and so joined together by God that the machinations of men could not put them asunder, were the two great qualities required alike by the preacher and by the reformer—the daring of the bravest of prophets and the conservatism of the wisest of priests. Dr. John Ker thought there had been nothing like his preaching since the day of Pentecost. "He has not the majesty of Howe," says the same authority, "the spiritual fervor of Baxter, the searching spiritual insight of Jonathan Edwards, the ideal beauty of Vinet, the concentrated rush of Chalmers; but, for his own work, Luther was the man chosen of God, and the Church of Christ bears the mark of his personality as of none other since the canon of Scripture was closed." James Anthony Froude goes still further, and says: "In mother wit, in elasticity, and in force and imaginative power he was as able a man as ever lived." His own countryman, Heine, thought that "the fine discernment of Erasmus and the

gentleness of Melanchthon had never done so much for
us as the divine brutality of Brother Martin."

6. Luther was a poet as well as a preacher. Coleridge
said he "did as much for the Reformation by his hymns
as he did by his translation of the Bible." Some doubt
has been raised as to whether he was really the author of
the great hymn, "A mighty fortress is our God," or only
adapted it from its original sources. Anyway it was so
well adapted to his purpose as to have been called "the
Marseillaise hymn of the Reformation." And certainly
more explicit proof will be required before it is severed
from its putative authorship. "Luther composed it,"
says Stead in his "Hymns That Have Helped," "for the
Diet of Spires, when, on April 20, 1529, the German princes
made their formal protest against the revocation of their
liberties, and so became known as Protestants." Tradition has it that it is the prose of his prayer preserved from
the night before the contest at Worms translated into
poetry. Many translations have been made from the
German into English. Thomas Carlyle's is generally regarded as the best. His first two stanzas read as follows:

> A sure stronghold our God is he,
>   A trusty shield and weapon;
> Our help he'll be, and set us free
>   From every ill can happen.
>   That old malicious foe
>   Intends us deadly woe,
>   Armed with might from hell,
>   And deepest craft as well,
>   On earth is not his fellow.
>
> Through our own force we nothing can,
>   Straight were we lost forever;
> But for us fights the proper Man,
>   By God sent to deliver.

Ask ye who this may be?
Christ Jesus named is he.
Of Sabaoth the Lord;
Sole God to be adored,
'Tis he must win the battle.

Says Stead further of the hymn: "Luther sang it to the
lute every day. . . . Every one sang it, old and young,
children in the street, soldiers on the battle field. . . .
When Melanchthon and his friends, after Luther's death,
were sent into banishment, they were marvelously cheered
as they entered Weimar on hearing a girl sing Luther's
hymn in the street. 'Sing on, dear daughter mine,' said
Melanchthon; 'thou knowest not what comfort thou bring-
est to our heart.'" Gustavus Adolphus and his troops
sang it at Leipzig. It was sung at Lützen. Time and time
again it was sung by German troops in the Franco-German
War. "'Tis He must win the battle" might well be the
refrain of every Christian contest with the forces of this
world's ill and evil.

In times more recent some have said that "modern
critics have dethroned Luther from the pinnacle on which
his worshipers placed him," or that "there has been a
shrinkage in his posthumous personality." The enormous
literature which his name and fame have evoked in the
nineteenth and twentieth centuries would seem not to
support the allegation. All this interest in the man would
hardly seem to tend to the diminution of his personality,
or to dwarf him "into one of a crowd."

Out of the noisy centuries
The foolish and the fearful fade;
Yet burn unquenched these warrior eyes
Time hath not dimmed nor death dismayed.

III

RICHARD BAXTER

(1615–1691)

An Unpropitious Parish

To prognosticate the propitious or the unpropitious in a field of Christian endeavor might well be counted a matter of considerable difficulty. More good may come out of Nazareth than the tattlers think. Less good may come out of Jerusalem than the priests propose. Some roots do well in a dry ground. Others are less prosperous in a more promising soil. An investigator charged with the task of proposing the time, the place, and the conditions of an eminently successful ministry could hardly have settled upon the middle of the seventeenth century in England as the time, or upon Kidderminster as the place, or upon the dissoluteness and depravity preceding, and running concurrently with, and continuing after the Cromwellian wars as furnishing the requisites of such a ministry.

Upon Kidderminster in particular, if any place was to have the bad eminence, the ignorance, the grossness, and the vileness of the times had settled. If evil found not here a new, it found certainly a congenial, habitat. "If I were asked," says Dr. John Brown in his "Puritan Preaching in England," "what, in the year 1646, was one of the most unpromising towns in England to which a young man could be sent, who was starting his career as preacher and pastor, I should feel inclined at once to point to the town of Kidderminster in Worcestershire. With a population at the time of between three and four thousand, mainly carpet weavers, it had been, morally and spiritually, so

(77)

grossly neglected as almost to have sunk into practical heathenism. . . . The majority of the people were ignorant beyond the ignorance of the time, debased beyond its defilement, disorderly beyond its rudeness." When one saw the town there was no beauty of situation that it might be desired. It "lies in the lap of a shallow irregular basin scooped out by the Stour, a sluggish tributary of the Severn which it joins four miles away." Several roads descending from higher ground form a junction of traffic tending naturally toward the formation of a town, and for fifteen hundred years settlers have been attracted there.

In Baxter's time the town suffered more from a sluggish ministry and sluggish religion than from any "sluggish tributary of the Severn." Time, for too much of the long period of the town's existence, had been made accessory more to evil than to good. Evil had taken deep root and flourished. Usmore, signifying a place of "broad waters," had formerly been the name of the town. But it had gotten a new name when it got a church, as the second half of the name Kidderminster indicates. But there had vanished the glory and the dream. The luster of the new name had faded. The devotion which had built a new minster had waned. The very priests at the Lord's altars were corrupted. The Long Parliament, when it came, instituted measures for the reformation of the clergy. The fact itself is sufficiently ominous: the state has to become sponsor for the morals of Christian ministers. Under the new regulations Kidderminster proceeded against its vicar. He was charged before the Committee for Scandalous Ministers "as being in character and attainments utterly unfit for his position." Though his ignorance itself was not elementary, it extended to the very elements of Christianity. He preached but once a quarter, and then "in so feeble a fashion as to expose him alike to the ridicule and pity of the people who listened to him." His own wife only escaped exposure to this temptation to ridicule and pity him by leaving the church when he preached. She could bear the burden of his incompetence in private, but not in public. She would for shame, says Baxter, "go out of the church." It was also definitely alleged against him that he was a frequenter of alehouses, and that he had been seen drunk.

His curates were no better. One of these labored in the town and was associated with the vicar in the charges brought against him before the committee. The other had a charge in a distant part of the parish. His isolation seemed only to give license to his evil disposition and deeds. He was ignorant, more ignorant of religion than even a child ought to have been, and a profaner of the very decencies of the religious life. He was notorious as a railing quarreler. He was a common tippler, and a drunkard. He had his gain chiefly by celebrating unlawful marriages. He would corrupt any fountain if there might flow to him a stream of filthy lucre. Turning to either side of their own parish, the people found ministers no more worthy nor capable than their own. On one side the curate got his living by cutting fagots; on the other, by making ropes—their abilities in either case being judged to be "answerable to their studies and employments." Parish after parish in the England of the time was thus depleted of true pastoral service through the inefficiency and wantonness of the clergy themselves. Many of the best preachers had been virtually driven out, and had gone into other countries, some of them as far away as into New England in the United States of America, in order to find the liberty to be religious, and at least to exercise their ministry in terms of its indubitable decency.

An Unpromising Preacher

As things appear to the human understanding Richard Baxter was scarcely the man to be selected for such a parish as Kidderminster. Again Dr. Brown has said: "If I were asked, who of all men—taking merely physical reasons into account—would seem to be the most unlikely man to be sent as pastor to this most unlikely and unpromising place, I should have said that man was Richard Baxter." He went there when he was twenty-six years of age. He had lived out a little more than one-third of his extended life. He had still a long lease of years before him, but none could have known it. The probabilities all seemed to turn in the other direction. There was but the slightest promise that there was before him any such career as he achieved. And there was a long journey before him before he came to the turn in the road where there was a brighter prospect ahead.

Baxter was born at Rowton, not far from Shrewsbury, on November 12, 1615. His ancestors of one remove or more were gentle folks. But his own father had led so loose a life as to reduce the affairs of the family to a very low estate. His great weakness had been strong drink; and he had been addicted, too, to gambling. But at about the time that Richard was born there came a great change in him. "It pleased God," said Baxter, "to instruct and change my father." Mother and son had lived apart at the mother's original home at Rowton. There was no alienation between husband and wife. Their temporary separation seems to have been due to the fact that the Baxter estate at Eaton Constantine had been encumbered by the gambling debts of the elder Baxters. The father's reformation improved his temporal condition and his wife and son returned to their own home.

This father proved after all to be his son's best teacher. The instruction he gave him in the Bible was especially valuable, most of all in that he taught him so to read it as to love it. This was the beginning of that fine devotion to the Bible and usable knowledge of it which so characterized Baxter in the days of his maturity. Otherwise his means of an education were worse than negligible. His schooling, if by any stretch of charity it could be called schooling, was had at the hands of the ignorant and generally incompetent clergy of the parishes round about under whose care from time to time he haplessly fell. To their obvious intellectual incompetency there had to be added the notorious delinquencies of their moral life. A provident man could not have wished to commit his pigs to such keepers.

Near the beginning of his fifteenth year Baxter had a better school at Wroxeter kept by a man of some real ability and character, and able to exert some formative influence upon the mind and character of those intrusted to his charge. Baxter wished to go on to one of the universities, preferably Oxford; but when the time for a decision came his master "drew him into another way" by persuading him "to accept the offer of Richard Wickstead, Chaplain to the Council at Ludlow," who was on the outlook for "a scholar fit for the university, and, having but one, would be better to him than any tutor in the university could be." This plan met the approval of his parents, who, having but the one child, wished to have him near them. But Wickstead neglected him entirely; though not so much by direct and malevolent intention as by the fraudulent nature of the man himself. He was ready to "speak much for learning," but really cared little for it; and "thought more of pleasing 'the Great Ones' than of doing his duty by his pupil." These same "Great Ones" loomed so large in the eyes of the poor sycophant that the

6

only really great one around him, in the person of his young pupil, was obscured entirely to his consciousness. When the little seem great and the great seem little it is as if evil were called good and good were called evil.

His stay at Ludlow, however, was not to Baxter all loss and no gain. He had free access to the books of the Castle library, and time to devote to them; so that, though he had no "considerable helps," neither had he any "considerable hindrances" from his negligent master. He turned the time he spent there—about a year and a half—to the finest account in the way of substantial self-improvement. He held in long remembrance the influence of one intimate companion, unnamed, whom he had there, whose assistance had been the principal means of his escape from the evils which else had sorely scathed him.

Though for a while at home, Wickstead's sinister influence sought him out still and was near to making a common courtier out of him. He was counseled to lay by all his purpose and preparations looking to the life and work of a Christian minister, and "to go to London and get acquaintance at Court and get some office, as being the only rising way." It was a temptation which later could have found no joint in Baxter's Puritan armor. But for the time he was nearly seduced. Again his parents approved. He was to stay at Whitehall with Sir Henry Herbert, whose younger brother George likewise tried "the painted pleasures of Court life," and had his own waverings back and forth before he turned to the ministry of the Church. A month sufficed for Baxter. When he had seen a stage-play instead of a sermon on the Lord's day, and "saw what course was there in fashion, and heard little preaching but what was, as to one part, against the Puritans," he was glad to be gone. The wines which were poured into the chalice of Court life could neither lure his lips nor stupefy his soul.

He was glad of an opportunity which his mother's illness afforded him of returning home.

FINDING FREEDOM THROUGH RESTRAINT

For four years, from 1634 to 1638, Baxter lived at home, working as the occasion required, but also carrying on his studies with the greatest diligence. In May, 1635, his mother died, and he set his heart more resolutely than ever upon the ministry. His father married again, and his stepmother, for whom he had an "extraordinary reverence," lived to the age of ninety-six, and spent her last days in his house.

The greatest obstacle, however, to his studies, and to all his purpose to prepare for the ministry, was his ill health. During the last four years spent with his father, carrying on the while his studies, he was "much hindered by the miserable state of his health." From the age of twenty-one till near twenty-three, he says, his weakness was so great that he expected not to live above a year. His life was one long conflict with disease. He had more than one kind of illness which caused him pain, oftentimes incessant. "I had at several times," he says, "the advice of no less than six and thirty physicians, by whose order I used drugs without number." Modern medicine will not wonder that he did not get well. More times than could be easily numbered it was thought that he should die. "Again and again he was brought to the very gates of the grave, and again and again he returned to life through the long and wearisome ascent of slow and difficult recovery." It has been said that if he had done nothing but take care of himself as an invalid he might have been excused.

Nevertheless, there were ways in which he counted pain itself to be a gain. "For it greatly weakened Temptations," he said; "it taught me highly to esteem of Time . . . ;

it made me study and preach *things necessary* and a little stirred up my sluggish heart, to speak to Sinners with some compassion, as a dying Man to dying Men." Most of all he regretted the time he lost by his illness. "For all the Pains that my Infirmities ever brought upon me," he said, "were never half so grievous an Affliction to me as the unavoidable loss of my time which they occasioned."

Again, the very expectation which he had that his life was to be short was one of the most decisive promptings he had toward the ministry. A natural argument against his contemplated action was turned into a moral argument in its favor. Said he: "My own soul being under serious apprehension of the matters of another world, I was exceedingly desirous to communicate those apprehensions to such ignorant, presumptuous, careless sinners as the world aboundeth with."

Other obstacles he regarded more seriously than his ill health. Most of all was he deterred by his "want of Academical honors and degrees." These acquirements were especially counted in the opinion of the time as requisites for the ministry; and Baxter felt that without them he would be "contemptible with the most." But the call was too clear to be quenched. He had "a thirsty desire for men's conversion and salvation"; he thought that he had "some competent persuading faculty of expression which fervent affections might help to accentuate"; and there was added again "a conviction of his fast-approaching death." All reasons to the contrary were beaten down and he "resolved that if one or two souls only might be won to God, it would easily recompense all the dishonor which for want of Titles he might undergo from men."

Then there opened a door at which he had not knocked; but he knew it was opened for him. He could go to Dudley as a schoolmaster, and at the same time would be unre-

strained in the opportunity to preach. He thought it not
an inconvenient condition of his acceptance that he might
preach up and down in places that were most ignorant,
before he took a pastoral charge. "So to Dudley I went,"
he continues. His ordination followed at the hands of the
Bishop of Worcester, and he had his license to teach school
and to preach.

All this occurred, of course, within the Church of England. But he was thrown immediately into circumstances
which raised all the issue between conformity and the
Nonconformists, who had begun to be pretty numerous.
He found himself compelled "to set upon a serious impartial trial" of the whole matter in dispute. The merits of
episcopacy were not directly involved. Neither were the
Nonconformists identical with the Presbyterians. Baxter
has been called a Presbyterian. In the strict sense he never
was, either in principle or practice. More than once he
signified his assent to a moderate episcopacy. He was a
nonconformist within the Church of England; and he became more and more straitened in his opposition to prelacy.
He was a Puritan. All else clings merely to the perimeter
of the man. That stands at the center. It has been said
that he "is perhaps the greatest single force in the history
of English Puritanism." He had further to go, of course,
in the development both of his nonconformity and his
Puritanism. But what he was to be is already determined.
Such a man as he, taking these directions, never turns back.

For the time the matter in dispute between the Nonconformists and the Church was no more than the Puritan
protest against particular ceremonies. To these points
Baxter applied himself with the result that in some things
he was ready to conform and in others not. To subscribe
everything in the Book of Common Prayer as he had done
at the first, were it to be done again, he certainly would

not do. Most of this, however, as he himself says, he kept to himself. His excuse for his silence was the implacable temper of the local nonconformists. They were censorious and bitter in their language against the bishops and were likely to go to the extreme of separation from the Church. This idea Baxter could not tolerate. But he had already great difficulty in steering a peaceful course. He labored continually to keep disturbers within bounds. But he says, "their sufferings from the bishops were the great impediment to my success." He coined a proverb: "He that will blow coals must not wonder if some sparks do fly in his face."

He was as much against sectaries as against prelates, and labored between the two for the peace and unity of the Church. All forms of Church government he regarded as subservient to the true purposes of religion. He would not have his nonconformists become sectaries and separatists. He strove to restrain them, but not always with the success he deserved. The fatefulness of the issues involved were yet to be more fully declared.

After Dudley, where he had less than a twelvemonth, Baxter became a full-time minister at Bridgnorth, though only in the capacity of an assistant. The pastor's name was Mastard, whom Baxter describes "as a grave and severe Ancient Divine"—though he lived in all to be only forty-one; and as "very honest and conscionable, and an excellent Preacher, but somewhat afflicted with want of Maintenance."

"I had," says Baxter, "a very full congregation to preach to and a freedom from all things which I scrupled or thought unlawful." More than all *full congregations* he prized his freedom. *A very full congregation* does not make preaching. Freedom must prepare the way if there is to be preaching. Any constraint of the merely human will laid upon the pulpit, any restraint of a merely material or fleshly design or desire, anything of the mere frippery of ritual, any mere assertion of the will of an outworn ec-clesiasticism, anything of the will of man seeking to act as a restraint upon the will of God is fatal to preaching. Christianity must cease within the Church and go outside to find a place where it can be free, if preaching is to be shackled.

Richard Baxter had a great passion for preaching; and in proportion to the loftiness of his conception of preaching he valued his freedom as a preacher. He asked for no freedom as a mere assertion of self-will; but he would be free as God's grace and his Spirit are free. If the preacher is to be bound at all, it is baser that he should be bound by a false assertion of self and the pseudo-liberty of self-will than that he should be bound by some false assertion of ecclesiastical authority. Others he may escape; but how shall he escape himself? "Here I stand," said Luther at Worms. He could do no otherwise. He could not have done otherwise without forfeiting freedom itself, his free-dom as a man and as a Christian, his freedom to think, freedom of conscience and of action. And where freedom falls all of us fall, and preaching and the pulpit are doomed. There at the base of Pompey's statue, which itself all the while ran blood, not Cæsar, but freedom itself lay bleeding to death. There "great Cæsar fell." But a greater than Cæsar fell.

> "O, what a fall was there, my countrymen!
> Then I, and you, and all of us fell down,
> Whilst bloody treason flourish'd over us."

This was one of the greatest of all the great elements of his soul, and one of the most masterful features of Baxter's preaching. The worst of the ills of his checkered career was to be silenced from his preaching, as happened in his later life. But it were better to be denied his pulpit and keep his freedom than to keep the pulpit and lose his freedom.

At Dudley Baxter labored "among a poor tractable people, lately famous for drunkenness, but commonly more ready to hear God's word with submission and reformation, than most places where I have come." Bridgnorth was less docile. There he had "a very ignorant, dead-hearted people"; with many inns and alehouses in the town, and little settled employment of the people; so that his labors were "not so successful as they proved afterwards in other places." With the generality, he says that an applause of the preacher was most of the success of the sermon of which he could hear.

An Epochal Pastorate

Then Baxter came to Kidderminster. It was as if God had said to him: Go join yourself to this town. The man's very nativity was transferred to the town. He is no more Baxter of Rowton, but Baxter of Kidderminster. "There have been three or four parishes in England," said Dean Stanley, speaking at the unveiling of a statue to Baxter in Kidderminster nearly two hundred years after his death, "which have been raised by their pastors to a national, almost a world-wide fame. Of these the most conspicuous is Kidderminster: for Baxter without Kidderminster would have been but half of himself; and Kidderminster without Baxter would have had nothing but its carpets."

The complainants of the town of Kidderminster against their vicar before the Parliamentary Committee for Scandalous Ministers were so far successful in their action as to bring the accused to an agreement that sixty pounds of his annual allowance of two hundred pounds should be allotted to the maintenance of a lecturer or preacher who should come as the choice of a committee provided for the purpose, to be responsible for the preaching without official reference to the vicar himself. He was to have the liberty to preach "whenever he pleased."

Under this arrangement Baxter came. The plan itself was a reversal of the policy of Archbishop Laud, who had aimed "at a complete suppression of the Lecturers as a mischievous Puritan institution." The reversal of policy under which Baxter came to Kidderminster was but the beginning of some reversals of policy which he himself was to effect. "There is no parallel in the annals of any other Protestant State," says Sir James Stephen in his "Essays in Ecclesiastical Biography," "of so wonderful a concentration, and so imperfect a diffusion of learning and genius, of piety and zeal." He is speaking in very definite terms, and continues: "The reigns of Whitgift, Bancroft, and Laud were unmolested by cares so rude as those of evangelizing the artisans and peasantry. Jewell and Bull, Hall and Donne, Hooker and Taylor, lived and wrote for their peers, and for future ages, but not for the commonalty of their own." But it was to the commonalty that Baxter was coming. Christianity was not to be bereft in England of her privilege of the poor. That decision was sealed when Baxter settled among the drunkards at Kidderminster.

The parish at the time of his coming had a total population of about 4,000, a little more than half of which lived in the town. The total area was about thirty-one square miles, with a circuit of about twenty-one miles. There was trade, but no wealth. It is said that there was not a wealthy resident there in Baxter's time.

At first, as was expected, Baxter did nothing but preach. He had "the Puritan estimation of his office as the highest possible." This was "their vital point of difference from the ceremonialists." Not by ritual primarily, nor even by sacraments, is the grace of God imparted; but through personality. And there is no higher exercise of the gifts and power of personality than in preaching. Baxter did not make the other parts of his service barren. He gave due place to the ordinances. He made much of prayer and praise and the sacraments. But the office and function of the preacher was with him supreme. "Christ maketh them (his ministers)," said he, "the chief instruments for the propagation of his truth and kingdom in the world, for the gathering of Churches and preserving and defending eontradicted truth."

Old things began to pass away in Kidderminster, and all things to become new. The church itself, though already capacious, had to be several times enlarged, gallery after gallery being added in order to care for the increasing congregations. The center of interest was the sermon. Some come for the crowds. But Baxter's congregations came to the preaching. There in the pulpit was "the tall young man in black gown, which set off the paleness of his already pain-worn face—upon whom all eyes were fastened." The sermon was never less than an hour long, and was often read; but the vehement intensity with which he delivered it kindled a fire in sermon and in audience alike; and accomplished the preacher's aim, "first to convince the understanding and then to engage the heart." He began with a careful unfolding of the text, proceeded to the removal of possible difficulties or objections, made an application of the uses of the text, and came at last to a fervent appeal for obedience of the heart and conscience to the word and will of God. For all his passion for the gospel, and the vehemence of his delivery, he was not in the ordinary sense an emotional preacher. Rather he kept his own emo-

tions under that fine restraint which gives the speaker so
sure a power over his audience.   There was in him a clear
and intense heat, but no conflagration.

Measuring his early preaching by his maturer judgment,
he condemned his style of the earlier time as being "more
extemporate and lax."   But "by the advantage of *affection*," he says, "and a very familiar moving voice and
utterance, my preaching then did more affect the Auditory
than many of the last years before I gave over preaching;
but yet what I delivered was much more raw, and had more
passages that would not bear the trial of accurate judgments; and my discourses had both less *Substance* and less
Judgment than of late."   A man who is capable of exercising so just and severe a judgment as this upon himself
and his work can always grow from less to more, and from
more to most.

Converts at first were comparatively few and he could
know them all.   But later there were so many that he
could not take note of them.   They were of all ages, but
"most numerous among the young."   Says he: "In the
place where God most blessed my labors my first and
greatest success was upon the Youth."   Then when the
heart of the young had been touched the "parents and
grandfathers who had grown old in an ignorant worldly
state, did, many of them, fall into liking and love of piety,
induced by their children, whom they perceived to be
made by it much wiser and better, and more dutiful to
them."

His success, however, was not uniform.   Sometimes the
rabble was raised against him.   Once a slander, "too gross
for credence by any decent person," was started against
him.   Sponsored by a sot, it ran the round of the alehouses, and "soon all the drunkards had got it in their
mouths."   In self-defense he applied to the magistrate,

and his calumniator confessed his wrong and said he "spoke it as a jest."

Neither did he always escape the censure of somewhat better people. He was railed at as he passed through the streets for some of his preaching on the state of infants. Dr. Powicke, his latest biographer, declares that "the ignorant Rout were for once nearer the truth and wiser than their teacher." Baxter himself was constrained to admit that once he had been young, and "of small experience and no great reading"; that he had been but a novice in knowledge, and his conceptions uncertain, shallow, and crude; that in some mistakes he had been confident, and of some truths very doubtful and suspicious. Surely in all this he was a man after God's own heart.

In this period of his ministry he passed through a siege of doubt concerning the most vital matters of his faith. But he acquired thereby a surer background of experience for his faith, and was also led to write and preach with more reference to the rational character and grounds of Christian belief.

CROMWELL SHIFTS THE SCENE

Baxter had been only a short while in Kidderminster when the quarrel between King and Parliament reached its culmination and he was forced to declare for one side or the other. He would of course go with Parliament, though he did not believe that side to be immaculate nor the other to be wholly reprobate. The details of the situation belong to the history of the times, and only incidentally to Baxter's personal life. He was a patriot; but he hoped for the prosperity of the country only as the true status of the Church should be preserved and the religious standards of public and private life should be maintained.

In some of the rioting in Kidderminster in the early

days of the conflict he had felt that his life was in danger.
Worcester was for the King, and he withdrew to Gloucester
—"a city as thoroughly for Parliament as Worcester was
for the King." After a short stay he suffered an entreaty
to return to Kidderminster; but "only to be driven forth
again by the still raging fury of the rabble." He witnesses
some fighting, but not of a very brave or well-ordered sort,
and remarks upon "the vanity of armies and how little
confidence is to be placed in them."

His situation was really a very difficult one. He had
neither money nor friends, nor anywhere to go. At last
he went to Coventry, with whose minister he had had some
previous acquaintance. His purpose was "to stay there
till one side or the other had got the victory, and the War
was ended, and then to return home again." But his expectation had little effect upon the course of events, and
there was no sign of peace. In the meantime he was desired
by the city authorities to accept lodging with them and
to preach to the soldiers. He would not yet accept a commission as a Chaplain. In addition he preached on the
Lord's Day to the people. In these circumstances he continued for about a year, preaching as indicated and following his studies as quietly as in a time of peace.

He had his opinions about the conflict which was raging
through the land. The great cause of the Parliament's
strength and the King's ruin "lay in the resentment and
disgust evoked by the treatment of all that were called
Puritans"—that is, of all that were of a strict and pious
life. This it was he was certain "that filled the armies and
garrisons of the Parliament with sober, pious men."
Otherwise many of them would have been only too glad to
remain at home.

He was in Coventry and thereabouts for two and a half
years. He was drawn from there into the army. After

the battle of Naseby he went to the front to learn the fate of two or three intimate friends. When he had found them, and had stayed with them a night, he understood the state of the army better than he had ever done before. In the quiet of Coventry he had felt that in reality he might be for both King and Parliament; and that the War was only to save the Kingdom from Papists and Sectaries, leaving King and Parliament to rule amicably. But when he came to the army he said he found a new face of things which he never dreamt of—plottings and evil intentions to subvert both Church and State, and to give the ascendancy to the enemies of both. And so into the army he went himself as a Regimental Chaplain, but as much to contend against the sectaries there as to be a spiritual benefit to the soldiers. And against them he did contend, both in season and out. Once in a sharp public contention debate went on from morning until almost night. His opponents, who greatly outnumbered him, hoped to wear him out and see him leave. But "I knew their trick," he characteristically says, "that if I had but gone out first, they would have prated what boasting words they listed when I was gone, and made the people believe that they had baffled me, or got the best; therefore I stayed it out till they first rose and went away."

Moving up and down the land with the army, his ministry assumed perforce an itinerant aspect. This gave him the opportunity to preach in many counties and parishes which in the ordinary course of events he would never have entered. Whatever came of it afterwards he did not know; but at the time "they commonly seemed to be much affected."

A haven amid the tumult of war he found in the home of Lady Rous, of Rous-Lench, where he was as cordially received as if he had been already known, and treated not as a soldier but as a friend. But whether amid martial or domestic scenes, his health still could not be counted on. There came at last a complete collapse in his physical strength; but he welcomed it as a divine interposition by which he might get out of the army. Out of the travail of this season of unwonted affliction there came the classic, "The Saints' Everlasting Rest," described in the Encyclopedia Britannica as being "charged with a robust and manly eloquence and a rare and unsought felicity of language that make it a masterpiece of style."

Baxter felt during these months of enforced retirement, though he did not wish it, that he probably should die. "Being conscious," he says, "that my time had not been improved to the service of God as I desired it had been, I put up many an earnest prayer to God that he would restore me and use me the more successfully in his work."

All along his old flock at Kidderminster had desired and expected his return. They knew of his being at Rous-Lench, and elsewhere. In the meantime they had renewed their complaints against their old vicar and his curate. The committee had vacated the place, but put no one in it. Baxter might now himself be vicar, and he was implored so to become. But he would not. He would only return in his former relation. He had the promise of more than the sixty pounds of his former compensation, but this expectation was but slightly realized. All the time he was at Kidderminster "he received but eighty pounds per annum or ninety at most, and house-rent for a few rooms in the top of another man's house." This ninety pounds per annum he preferentially accepted over five hundred pounds offered him elsewhere.

When he had returned—it would be about June, 1647— his trustees, fearing certain contingencies which might arise to disturb their arrangement, had Baxter privately appointed as vicar. For more than three years he knew nothing whatever of this action. His treatment of Dance, the old vicar, still present within the parish, was truly admirable. "All this while that I lived at Kidderminster," he could nobly say, "did I never remove the old sequestered Vicar so much as out of his Vicarage House, no, nor once come within the doors of it; so far was I from seizing on it as my own or removing him out of the town. But he lived in peace and quietness with us, and reformed his life, and lived without any scandal or offensiveness, and I never heard that he spake an ill word of me." And though it was a requirement that a minister in his ecclesiastical state should remove without the parish where he had been vicar or forfeit his "fifths," Baxter still allotted that to him in the amount of forty pounds a year.

A MARVELOUS MINISTRY

On his resumption of his work at Kidderminster Baxter was still hindered by ill health. Still he took it with a beautiful devotion: "I humbly bless his gracious Providence, who gave me his treasure in an earthen vessel, and trained me up in the school of affliction." Yet his physical suffering was an impediment to his effectiveness, and in some ways to his usefulness; and it greatly increased the strain under which he accomplished what he did accomplish. One is amazed at the amount of work he did, considering these hindrances. Let his prodigious literary product for the moment be passed by. How could he, his labors being thus impeded, meet the requirements of his pulpit and his pastorate? He could not brook the least neglect of either. In both the intensiveness and the extensiveness of his pastoral care he far exceeded his earlier period. At first he catechized only at specified meetings in the church appointed for prayer and conference. He talked to individuals only "now and then." He found, however, "that his preaching, to be rendered fruitful, must be followed up by direct personal converse with every family and every member of the family." Accordingly he arranged that he should be at home all the afternoons of two days of each week "to a certain specific number of families from the town; while his assistant should spend all the mornings of the same two days in visiting an equal number of families in the outlying parish."

Other meetings also were held—meetings for what he called Parish Discipline, a monthly ministers' meeting for Discipline and Disputation, a weekly meeting for local ministers at his own house mainly for lunch and an afternoon of social intercourse; and one hardly knows what else. How could a sick man do it? How could any man do it? His labors in themselves are one of the marvels of his ministry. But the success which attended them is more marvelous still. His own often-quoted account of his success is in part as follows: "On the Lord's day there was no disorder to be seen in the streets, but you might hear a hundred families singing Psalms and repeating sermons, as you passed through the streets. In a word, when I came thither first, there was about one family in a street that worshiped God and called on his Name, and when I came away there were some streets where there was not one family in the side of a street that did not so; and that did not by professing serious godliness give us hopes of their sincerity. . . . We had 600 that were communicants, of whom there was not twelve that I have not good hopes of, as to their sincerity." When he established his custom of personal conferences there were few families that did not come; "and those few were beggars at the town-ends, who were so ignorant that they were ashamed it should be manifest." "And few families went from me," he con-

7

tinues, "without some tears or seemingly serious promises for a godly life." Some of the poorer men "were so able in prayer that very few ministers did match them in order and fullness and apt expressions and holy oratory, with fervency. . . . The temper of their minds, and the innocency of their lives, was much more laudable than their parts."

Lamenting his unfitness in the very midst of his rejoicing, he breaks out: "O what am I, a worthless worm, not only wanting academical honors but much of that furniture which is needful to so high a work, that God should thus abundantly encourage me, when the reverend instructors of my youth did labor fifty years together in one place, and could scarcely say they had converted one or two of their Parishes! And the greater was this mercy, because I was naturally of a discouraged spirit; so that if I had preached one year and seen no fruits of it, I should hardly have forborn running away like *Jonah*, but should have thought that God called me not to that place."

He notes a wider benefit of his labors in that some Independents and Anabaptists who had the conceit that the Parish Churches were the chief obstruction to Church order and discipline were convinced by what they saw done at Kidderminster that it was the fault of the ministers that the parishes were not more prosperous; and that it was a better work to reform the parishes than to gather other Churches out of them unless there were a great necessity.

Baxter's own statement of the causes of his success deserves careful consideration:

1. He accounts as the first factor of all, "apart from which nothing else could have availed," the fact of the freedom guaranteed through the Cromwellian settlement of religion for the Commonwealth. This was not all that he

desired, but it far surpassed anything of the kind in the days of Laud.

2. He came to a people prepared for his ministry in the sense that they had not hardened their hearts by turning away from a pure gospel. No such gospel had been preached to them, and so they had not trampled down its impressions. They were much like the virgin soil of heathenism, which offers no artificial hindrances to the entrance of the good seed.

3. He had from the first a few faithful and influential helpers. Among these were several honest and diligent assistants who could travel and preach and catechize.

4. The character of his converts availed him much. They so maintained the integrity of the Christian character as to act "as a constant silent reënforcement of the minister's influence."

5. The comparative poverty of his people he counted as a condition favorable to his success. They were not proud and obstinate as he thought the rich were wont to be. Moreover, his people were weavers and had some leisure, even while at work, to turn their thoughts and conversation toward religion. Along with these advantages he thought that the very "quality of the sinners of the place" helped him too. They were so bad none could wish to be like them. They were so debauched that they served as a warning to others, and sometimes perchance even to themselves.

6. Several other advantages he enumerates as follows:

(1) His single life (he had not yet married). "I could the easilier take my people for my children, and think all that I had too little for them, in that I had no children of my own to tempt me to another way of using it."

(2) His changed method of pastoral care after 1653. This involved two things in particular: first, the work of

personal conference by families; and second, "the exercise of Church Discipline."

(3) His habit of adapting his teaching to his congregation "in a suitableness to the main end, and yet so as might suit their dispositions and diseases." And yet he would not have them think that they knew more than he did: "I did usually put in something in my sermon which was above their own discovery, and which they did not know before." He thought this was necessary in order to keep them humble, and to enable them still to perceive their ignorance, and to preserve in them a teachable temper, and to prevent them from the temptation of turning preachers themselves and railing against the pulpit.

(4) His long pastorate. "It much furthered my success that I stayed still in this one place (near two years before the War, above fourteen years after): for he that removeth oft from place to place, may sow good seed in many places; but is not like to see much fruit in any, unless some other skillful hand shall follow after him to water it." He thought also that his own hands could best mature the grain which he himself had planted.

(5) Even his public disputations he thought were an advantage to him. He claimed that by means of these he had confirmed his own people and kept them united.

It were vain to say that his work was complete. He did not succeed throughout the parish as in the town; and the town itself was not made perfect. Differences and discords of one sort and another did not entirely cease, and wickedness was not entirely eliminated from the life about him. But there is his work. And it will never grow less.

EXPOSTULATION EXTRAORDINARY

That Baxter himself was extraordinarily faithful and efficient as a pastor has gone without gainsaying through

23446

the long period of time since he labored. But there are
other means of ascertaining his estimate of the pastorate.
His famous book, "The Reformed Pastor," is first of all
an expostulation with pastors themselves concerning their
office. It was produced and published in relation to the
general ministerial efforts he promoted. He interested
himself and took the lead in the formation of the ministers
of Worcestershire into an association for the common advantage, with an especial emphasis upon the principle of
the unity of the Churches, which was one of the real passions of his life. His opposition to prelacy on the one hand,
and his distaste for sectaries on the other, grew alike out of
his dislike for all that provoked discord in the Church, or
tended in any way to disrupt it. He wished for peace and
prayed for peace all his life long, though often seeming to
others himself a brand of discord. In forming his ministerial association he had reference especially to the four
outstanding church parties of the time—Erastian, Episcopal, Presbyterian, and Independent.

Having an engagement for an address before this Association on the occasion of one of its stated gatherings and
being unable to be present, he formed the substance of
what he had intended to say into the "Reformed Pastor."
The conditions under which the obligations of the pastoral
office must be met have greatly changed since Baxter's
time. His work can no longer be done in his way. But
for the probing of ministerial motives, for searching the
ministerial conscience, and as a challenge to ministerial
character and conduct there is still no other book like it.
"It drives home the sense of clerical responsibility with
extraordinary power." Dr. Alexander Whyte supposes
"that Paul is the only minister that ever lived who could
have read Richard Baxter's 'Reformed Pastor' without
going half mad with remorse, and with a fearful looking

for of judgment." The very first chapter, in which he discusses the nature of the oversight which ministers are to have of themselves, is as solemn as if it had been delivered from Mount Sinai. This is his outline:

I. See that the work of grace be thoroughly wrought in your own souls.
II. See that you be not only in a state of grace, but that your graces are in vigorous and lively exercise.
III. See that your example contradict not your doctrine.
IV. See that you live not in those sins against which you preach in others.
V. See that you want not the qualifications necessary for the work.

In answer to the objection that he should not have spoken so plainly against the sins of ministers, he says: "If the ministers had sinned only in Latin, I would have made shift to admonish them in Latin, or else have said nothing to them. But if they will sin in English, they must hear of it in English." Powicke thinks the "Reformed Pastor" the best written of all Baxter's books.

Royalty Returns

Affairs moved on until the King came back. Cromwell had mightily shifted the scene on the political stage, but he could give no guarantee that it would not shift back again. Meantime Baxter was not quiescent. Even in dull times he could not have been inert. He had his interest in public affairs, and his share in shaping the direction they should take. Private affairs alone would have sufficed to keep him busy. He carried on an enormous correspondence, which for the most part was not of his own seeking, but his response to all sorts of people who brought their troubles and perplexities to him. This was in addition to the more formal and public aspects of his ministry.

He was much in London during the Protectorate, observing the course of events and taking a turn at them himself. He preached in Westminster Abbey and had for the principal part of his audience Cromwell and "many honorable members of Parliament." His theme was "Divisions and Distractions of the Church," with marked emphasis upon "how mischievous a thing it was for politicians to maintain such divisions for their own ends, that they might fish in troubled waters, and keep the Church by its divisions in a state of weakness." This was an anomalous proceeding in so far as it was aimed at Cromwell; for he was seeking even then, and no doubt with sincerity, to promote the unity and tolerance which Baxter desired. But he did not like Cromwell, and he did not understand him. No doubt if he had understood him he would have liked him better; and if he had liked him he would have understood him better. If the truth must be told, in the matter of their relations Cromwell made a better showing than Baxter. "There were forces around him, mighty and malignant, which would have made short work of Baxter and his like, but for Cromwell's strong hand; and, if Cromwell had been vindictive, he would himself have made short work of Baxter. But he let him alone, and compelled others to leave him alone." It seems to be one of the great perversions of history that so often men who should have assisted have only hindered each other.

In April, 1660, fourteen years after he had first gone to Kidderminster, Baxter was called by influential agencies to London. A long story may be made short by saying that he and some of his closest friends were won over to the support of the proposal to invite Charles II to return to the throne. They gave their assent not without serious misgivings. The outbreak of licentiousness which they already saw in the streets of London bore the unmistakable marks of a calculated revolt from Puritan strictness.

Another fear of even a graver nature, based upon signs which could not be concealed, was that "the High Prelate's party were plotting to get the upper hand and were likely to succeed."

The King got his throne again, and Baxter led a determined effort to make secure the cause of religious freedom against prelatical intolerance. The King gave a fair promise, but the Bishops were not long in winning their way. Baxter had been made a Chaplain to the King and was commanded to preach before him at Whitehall just when the Bishops had repulsed all proposals for a just agreement. "After listening to such a sermon as he can never have heard before," the King ordered that it be printed.

The King drew up a Declaration concerning ecclesiastical affairs which seemed favorable to Baxter's contention. Nevertheless, all efforts toward an understanding were unavailing. In a meeting where there were present the King himself and other distinguished persons, some of them for position and some of them for ability and character, Baxter spoke with such directness and plainness as to injure his own cause. "Probably this speech . . . did more to cool the King's zeal for a fair settlement and play into the Bishops' hands, and alienate the Independents, etc., than anything else."

Baxter was offered a bishopric and at first was inclined to accept, not seeming to sense the bribe concealed in the offer. But maturer consideration led him to a firm refusal. How could he have been a bishop under the new order which was to prevail? He did wish, however, if the matter might be arranged, to return to his charge at Kidderminster. The determination of his request was held up indefinitely, while he was held in London, striving still as the head of those ministers who could not go with the

Bishops to save some ground on which they could conscien-
tiously stand in the service of Christ. In the course of
events a meeting was held in the official residence of the
Bishop of London and called hence the Savoy Conference.
The Archbishop of York and twelve bishops represented
the Episcopal side, while Baxter and ten other Nonconformists represented the other side. At the very start
the Bishop of London stated that the meeting was not of
the seeking of his side and that they had nothing to say
until the other side presented in writing their desire for
alterations in the liturgy. Adjournment was had that this
demand might be carried into effect. But when the matter was again submitted to the Bishops they were indis-
posed to accept any of the changes proposed. "The chief
good that resulted from the Savoy conference was the pro-
duction of Baxter's 'Reformed Liturgy,' a work of remarkable excellence, though it was cast aside without
consideration." This conference, says Stephen, "was the
scene of Baxter's triumph and defeat—the triumph of his
promptitude, subtlety, and boundless resources—the defeat of the last hope he was permitted to indulge, of peace
to himself or to the Church of which he was then the
brightest ornament."

Baxter had throughout to bear the brunt of these contentions. By ability, character, courage, and zeal he was
set apart to the task of leadership.. But he did not complain of being the one by far the most blamed by the opposing party of all who were of his party. "For myself,"
he said, "the reason why I spake so much was because it
was the desire of my Brethren, and I was loth to expose
them to the hatred of the Bishops; but was willinger to
take it all upon myself." And he had too to learn that
debate and controversy were not as persuasive and useful
as he had once wished to believe. "I have perceived," he

says, "that nothing so much hindereth the reception of the truth as urging it on men with too harsh importunity, and falling too heavily on their errors; for hereby you engage their honor in the business, and they defend their errors as themselves and stir up all their wit and ability to oppose you. In a learning way men are ready to receive the truth, but in a disputing way they come armed against it with prejudice and animosity."

EJECTMENT AND EXILE

Baxter had once more had a brief stay at Kidderminster, but he was never permitted to return there again as pastor. Without knowing it, his leaving in that relation had been permanent.

On May 19, 1662, fell the foul Act of Uniformity on the liberty and the living of two thousand of the bravest and best men and ministers in England. It was an act of positive ejectment and of virtual exile, not from their country to be sure, but from their pulpits and from their livings. And they were not men to love their country more than their pulpits. If they had, then they had loved their country less.

The Act required holders of church livings to be ordained by a bishop; to assent to the Prayer-book; to make an oath of canonical obedience; and attendance to some other matters purely political. Baxter was the first to declare his dissent, though others were not less prompt in either decision or courage.

Baxter had already been deprived of Kidderminster and forbidden to preach in the diocese of Worcester. He still had had license to preach in the diocese of London. Now he might not preach at all. For thirty years the bravest and most powerful preacher in England was silenced by an act of Parliament. "In the forty-seventh

year of his age, bowed down with bodily infirmities,"
writes Stephen with pathetic truth, "he was driven from
his home and his weeping congregation, to pass the remainder of his life in loathsome jails or precarious hiding
places; there to achieve, in penury and almost ceaseless
pain, works without a parallel in the history of English
theological literature, for their extent, or their prodigality
of intellectual wealth." Naught can atone for such an act.
Its evil effects take fast hold on coming time. This Act,
says Benjamin Jowett, Master of Balliol College, Cam-
bridge, "was the greatest misfortune that has ever befallen
this country, a misfortune that has never been retrieved.
For it has made two nations of us instead of one, in politics, in religion, almost in our notion of right and wrong;
it arrayed one class of society permanently against another,
and many of the political difficulties of our own time have
their origin in the enmities caused by the rout of August
22, 1662, called 'Black Bartholomew's Day,' which Baxter strove vainly to avert."

On September 10, 1662, Baxter was married to Margaret
Charlton. This did not come about by anybody's deliberate calculation. When a young girl Margaret had
unwillingly followed her mother to Kidderminster, whither
the latter had gone to put herself under the ministry of
Baxter. Later they also, as had Baxter, had gone to London.
Margaret found an arrow in her heart from Cupid's bow.
All along she had been drawn to Baxter; and now in the
obloquy of his age, all the more. He was nearly fifty, and
she, scarcely twenty. She was beautiful, refined, winsome,
and of high social position. She was not rich, but had more
means than Baxter. She delicately offered herself to him;
whereupon he himself was smitten, and they were married.
Margaret was no ordinary woman, and made him a lovely
wife.

From 1662 to 1687, when some indulgence had been granted him, Baxter suffered still such treatment as justice could not have visited upon a proved malefactor. He retired to Acton, hoping at least to be allowed to pursue his writing in peace. But he was dragged thence to prison on the charge of keeping a conventicle. At length he was hailed for trial before the court of the infamous Lord Chief Justice Jeffreys on the absurd charge of libeling the Church in his "Paraphrase of the New Testament." He was convicted and fined, and sentenced to prison until the fine should be paid; being bound over also to good behavior for seven years. Jeffreys binding Baxter to good behavior— could comedy in a court room go farther? He was at the time in his seventieth year. He went to prison and stayed two years, when the King remitted his fine. It was said that but for the resistance of the other judges Jeffries would have ordered him to be whipped through the streets in addition to the sentence of imprisonment.

Prodigious Literary Production

Baxter acquired the rank of the most voluminous author in the field of religion and theology in the English language. He is credited with one hundred and sixty-eight separate works. These were largely the fruit of his solitude. The period of his long oppression and injury, when he was also sorely afflicted in his body, was marked by his greatest literary activity. He undertook too much. But there is a certain majesty about the performance anyway. "From the recesses of the library in Red Cross Street they lower, in the sullen majority of the folio age, over the pygmies of this duodecimo generation—the expressive, though neglected, monuments of occurrences, which can never lose their place, or their interest, in the history of theological literature." Having characterized the Puritan authors in general, Sir James Stephen goes on about Baxter: "Such, above all the rest, was Richard Baxter. Intellectual efforts of such severity as his, relieved by not so much as one passing smile—public services of such extent, interrupted by no one recorded relaxation—thoughts so sleeplessly intent on those awful subjects, in the presence of which all earthly interests are annihilated—might seem a weight too vast for human endurance; as assuredly it forms an example which few would have the power, and fewer still would find the will, to imitate. His seventy-five years, unbroken by any transient glance at this world's gayeties; his one hundred and sixty-eight volumes, where the fancy never once disports herself; a mortal man absorbed in the solemn realities, and absolutely independent of all the illusions, of life, appears like a fiction, and a dull one too. Yet it is an exact, and not an uninviting, truth."

The extent of Baxter's own reading would seem to be matched only by John Wesley in the life of any other so busy a minister. The man who thinks he has read may look over Baxter's list and count the books he himself has never heard of. To one who spoke to him in his old age of the usefulness of his writings, he said: "I was but a pen in God's hands; what praise is due to a pen?" Though it remains a marvel that a bleeding bough should bear such abundant fruit, there is still this suggestion by Stephen, that "his ailments were such as, without affecting his mental powers, gave repose to his animal appetites, and quenched the thirst for all the emoluments and honors of this sublunary state."

Permanence of His Place in the History of Preaching

1. There were elements of endurance in the man himself which were bound to make his ministry endure. Adversity only chastened and hardened these elements into a

manhood against which nothing that was contrived to his disadvantage could prosper. Unjust opposition can only stiffen the integrity of such a man into more resolute resistance. When duty called him into the lists, and the will of God, as he believed, lay upon him to set forth the requirements of righteousness, or to expose and denounce all the opposition of the wrong to the right, his fearlessness as a preacher rose to all the demands of the occasion, whether the issue concerned Kidderminster alone, or his brother-ministers of a county, or the judges and lawyers of the country's courts, or the Lord Mayor and Aldermen of London, or Cromwell in Westminster Abbey, at whose bosom his shots went point-blank, or Charles II returned again to the fancied security of Whitehall, listening perchance for two hours without hearing "one courtly phrase" to relieve Baxter's censure of the vices of the great. He wanted to enter the *Saints' Everlasting Rest*, and that was ultimately a state beyond the turmoil that racks us here. But for him heaven meant primarily not the attainment of a condition, but of a character, a character in Christ and formed by fellowship with him, the attainment of that "perfect fellowship with God which comes through perfect moral likeness to God." He might be too quick to speak, he might be too ready to contend, he might sometimes defeat his own purpose, he might be drawn too much into side issues; but on the main issues he was clear, and he was unshakable; and character was certain in the long run to prevail over temperament and bring him back to a straight course.

2. Nowhere else did the qualities of the man come out so clearly as in his preaching. In the pulpit he was supreme. There all his powers burst into their best. There his very frailty acquired a certain magnificence. Of the orator's natural equipment he had only the eyes, roving, ranging

eyes that transpierced an audience; and the voice, "a
familiar moving voice," carrying the accent of uncon-
strained conviction. His eye kindled his audience like a
fire; his voice swept it as the wind in a cornfield.

He put all his might into his preparation and his preaching. "In the study of our sermons we are too negligent,"
he would say. "We must study how to convince, and *get
within men*, and how to bring each truth to the quick, and
not leave all this to our extemporary promptitude. . . .
How few ministers preach with all their might! There is
nothing more unsuitable to such a business than to be
slight and dull. What! speak coldly for God and men's
salvation! Let the people see that you are in earnest.
Men will not cast away their dearest pleasures upon a
drowsy request. A great matter lies in the very pronuncia-
tion and tone of speech. The best matter will scarcely
move men if it be not movingly delivered. See that there
be no affectation, but let us speak as familiarly to our
people as we would do if we were talking to any of them
personally. We must lay siege to the souls of sinners. In
preaching there is intended a communion of souls and a
communication from ours unto theirs. I have observed
that God seldom blesseth any man's work so much as his
whose heart is set upon success." This consuming sense
of responsibility throbs all through the "Reformed Pastor," and in every accent of Baxter's own pulpit.

His idea of hell might be too terrific. But at any rate
it was not sublimated into moonshine on a field of ice.
He accepted the Scriptures, and based his belief of the
great moral antitheses on them. It did not occur to him
that he could invent a new theology in matters upon which
Christ had spoken. And he obtained some sanctions and
got some motives for his ministry big enough to control
the consciences of men. Christian preaching has but little

of the transient time motive. If its sanctions cannot raise eternal issues, it accomplishes but little. Whatever may have been the excess of literalism in some of Baxter's thinking, he got down to the great motives, and his grasp of the eternal issues which are involved in preaching, if it is to be really Christian, were unerringly sure and effective. "O that there were no cause to complain," he exclaims, "that Christ and salvation are made light of by the preachers of it!"

3. His purpose was so plain that it made his preaching plain. His own experience led him to cultivate a plain and even diffuse style rather than the more precise style which would have been more according to his taste. The more he had to do with the ignorant sort of people, the more he found that he could not speak too plainly to them. He found in general that "the plainest words are the profitablest in oratory in the weightiest matters. Fineness is for ornament, and delicacy for delight: but they answer not *Necessity*."

The same concern for plainness led him to repeat essential truths. He liked "to hear a man dwell much on the same essentials of Christianity. For we have but one God, and one Christ, and one faith to preach; and I will not preach another Gospel to please men with variety, as if our Saviour and our Gospel were grown stale."

He discovered, what many another preacher has discovered, that most hearers are displeased with what they most need, that men in general like to have the sins of others roundly denounced, the poor those of the rich, the rich those of the poor, and so forth. But he was determined to be so plain that every man should have his own.

4. He found that he himself profited as his hearers profited. The Quakers had charged that he carried on his ministry for his own profit. He repels that charge in a

passage which is both pathetic and indignant. And then
he declares what his real profiting had been. So far as his
flesh was concerned he might take it for the happiest hour
he ever saw if he might lay aside his calling. "But do I
approve of this," he asks, "or grudge at my employment
and the disposal of my God? No, I bless the Lord daily,
that ever he called me to this blessed work! It is but my
flesh that repineth at it. God hath paid me for all these
sufferings a thousandfold. O the sweetness of sacred
studies and contemplations! They are the recreations of
my spirit, though a weariness to the flesh! O the consolations I have in the very opening of his Gospel Mysteries,
and in revealing the hopes of the saints, and the unseen
glory of the life to come! O how the Lord doth sweetly
revive my faith and love and desire and joy and resolution
and all graces, whilst he sets me on those thoughts in my
studies, and those persuasions in my preaching which tend
to revive the graces of my hearers!"

5. He acquired a value for preachers which stands in
principles so permanent that that value does not lessen.
This is indicated in many ways, both direct and indirect.
But aside from all that has been said, or could be said,
he touches the very quick of the preacher's life in his
"Narrative of His Own Life." The gist of this narrative lies
in the last few pages of the first part where he examines and
sets out his own gain in self-knowledge and self-improvement.
It is an illuminating delineation of his own understanding
of himself and of his capacity for improvement, or, as Bushnell called it, "the talent for growth." Dean Stanley relates that Sir James Stephen in terms of peculiar solemnity
once recommended him to read that part of Baxter's
"Narrative" without delay. "Lose not a day," said he,
"in reading it. You will never repent of it." "That very
night," says the Dean, "I followed his advice, and I have

8

ever since publicly and privately advised every theological student to do the same."

Through incessant study, and varied and heart-searching experience; through sorrows that ran like an anguish through his soul; and through unsparing self-observation he grew until he knew that he had grown, and could trace definitely many of the most important steps of his progress. One of the most important of the acquisitions of his advancing life was a knowledge of his own ignorance. Very frankly he says: "Formerly I knew much less than now, and yet was not half so much acquainted with my ignorance." Many things he had not understood as well as he thought he did; and therefore now he has far meaner thoughts of his own understanding, "though it is better furnished than it formerly was."

He had learned to be more tolerant than when life was young and undisciplined and he himself untrained to charity. He had come to see that good men were not as good as he had supposed them to be, and that bad men are not as bad as their enemies would have them be.

He has less confidence in a mere multitude of controversies than when he was raw and zestful for debate; and would influence young men "to study and live upon the essential doctrines of Christianity and godliness." Controversies were better if they had *right stating* rather than mere *debating*.

He has a broader view of Church communion. "I am not so narrow in my principles of Church communion as once I was. I am not for narrowing the Church more than Christ himself alloweth us, nor for robbing him of any of his flock."

Maturer thinking had brought him to a deeper sense of sin. Once it had been his sins that troubled him, now it is his sinfulness. "I was once wont to mediate most on my own heart, and to dwell at home, and look little higher; I was still pouring either on my sins or wants or examining my sincerity. But now I see more need of a higher work; and that I should look oftener upon Christ and God and heaven than upon my own heart."

The conclusion of the whole matter for the whole life and ministry of the man is that he got his help and his power and the cherished effectiveness of his ministry from God and the moving of his grace through the deep travail of his own soul. So runs the substance of the concluding part of the "Narrative."

Some Easing of His Sorrow Ere the End

Relentings toward Baxter began with the King's remittal of his fine. Not even this was an act of pure charity, but rather a belated attempt to win the persecuted but still influential old man to the support of the government and its measures involving ecclesiastical regulations.

After his release from prison he lived in London, and preached occasionally. His long fidelity began to have its reward and friends and comfort came to him. Some of the clergy even of the Church of England deplored the injustice which had been heaped upon him, and gave him their sympathy. In other unmistakable ways he had tokens that character and courage can triumph over all adversities.

Cotton Mather, of New England, came to see him the day before he died, and asked him how he did. "I have pain," he replied; "there is no arguing against sense, but I have peace, I have peace." He died in London, December 8, 1691, and entered upon a heritage even in this life which many an adverse circumstance sought to deny him while he lived.

On the pedestal of the statue erected in Kidderminster to his memory are inscribed these words:

"BETWEEN THE YEARS 1641 AND 1660
THIS TOWN WAS THE SCENE OF THE LABORS OF
RICHARD BAXTER
RENOWNED EQUALLY FOR HIS CHRISTIAN LEARNING
AND HIS PASTORAL FIDELITY.
IN A STORMY AND DIVIDED AGE
HE ADVOCATED UNITY AND COMPREHENSION
POINTING THE WAY TO THE EVERLASTING REST.
CHURCHMEN AND NONCONFORMISTS
UNITED TO RAISE THIS MEMORIAL, A.D. 1875."

IV

THOMAS CHALMERS

(1780–1847)

Assessing the Assets of a Church

A Church has material assets—buildings, endowments, legacies, varied equipment for its varied service, the financial pledges and will to give of its constituency, and others which might be enumerated. But its real assets, quite unreal in a material sense, consist in what cannot be so easily estimated—the virtues of the saints, the consecration of its people, access to the throne of God's grace, the Christian fellowship of the ages. These are just those imponderable things of which no exact account can be made. If they could be measured, they would themselves become material.

The fruit of all the Church's resources is found at last in Christian character, and the power of that character to be a savor of life to the world. By the character it can create Christianity must at last stand or fall. The world will never willingly dispense with an institution which can produce saints. It may not wish to have them canonized; but it does wish to have them created. If the Church can raise the fallen, cheer the faint, heal the sick, and lead the blind, it still has a task. While sickness, sorrow, sin, and death abide, religion will remain. And there need not be anticipated the too speedy advent of a material civilization which will eliminate these casualties from human life.

The accumulated sainthood of the centuries does constitute a treasury of merit, but not to be dispensed as the Romanists assume. The saints constitute the great reserve assets of the Church, ever to increase as the ages increase, and, as to the past, secure. But their virtues and achievement are to be appropriated by aspiration and imitation, and not by any artificial ecclesiastical transfer. They have value only to those who "follow in their train."

This is where Chalmers comes in. He is one of those who have enriched and endowed the Church for all time. The Church which has produced one such man as he can never be counted poor. Moreover, he had the distinction of being a great preacher. Now, with all God's giving he gives nothing else to his Church quite like a truly Christian preacher. "Christ's last resource," as Principal C. T. Edwards was wont to reiterate, "is a great preacher." Who that could have known what was coming in Scotland could have done better than to produce Thomas Chalmers?

"A Lad o' Pregnant Pairts"

"The little fellow is named Tom," said his father, announcing by letter to a relative in London the fact of his birth, which had occurred four days earlier, on March 17, 1780, in Anstruther, Fifeshire, Scotland. He was the sixth of fourteen children, and the fourth son in a total of nine born to his parents.

His father was John Chalmers, who, in 1771, married Elizabeth Hall, the daughter of a wine merchant at Crail. John Chalmers succeeded to the business of his father, who was a "dyer, shipowner, and general merchant." He was a burgher, member of the town council, and an elder in the Church. "Ye'll be wanting Dr. Chalmers' house," said the women of the village to Mrs. Oliphant when she went there and surprised them by asking for an old tenement which had once belonged to an ancestor of her own. They thought she must be mistaken about the house she wanted. It was a tradition among some in the village that when the herrings came in shoals to their coasts Providence arranged it that the new potatoes were ready at the same time.

Among so many children none too much attention could be bestowed by the mother upon any one of them. Nor did they fare any better at the hands of their father. He was not without concern for his family; but amid the multiplicity of his secular affairs, which perchance he allowed to become needlessly secular, he was kept very busy. At two years of age Thomas was committed to the care of a nurse "whose cruelty and deceitfulness haunted his memory through life." In order in part at least to escape her cruelties he went away of his own accord to school at the tender age of three years. Still he received little personal instruction from his parents; and his teacher, alas! was little better than his nurse. In his almost blindness the tyrant used to creep up behind the bench on which his pupils sat and mercilessly whack them for any least semblance of disorder which he thought he could detect. An assistant having been put in charge of the younger children they found themselves better situated.

The ability to read which through his schooling he so early acquired little Tom Chalmers turned to immediate collateral account. "Pilgrim's Progress" in particular took a strong hold on his mind. The Bible, too, very early made a profound impression upon his mind and imagination. One evening when he was but three years old he was discovered alone in the nursery greatly excited and absorbed, and pacing up and down, while he repeated to himself the lament of David, "O my son Absalom! O Absalom, my son, my son!"

When he seemed still too young to form or announce a decision he declared that he would be a minister. He saw and heard much of ministers, and the suggestion doubtless came to his mind in that way. A sister of one of his schoolfellows at Anstruther once came upon him closeted with her brother, while from a chair he preached vigorously to his single auditor below.

When not yet twelve years of age he was enrolled as a student in the United College of St. Andrews. He had but one contemporary there who had entered the college at an earlier age than he. He was at the time not only very young, but "volatile, and boyish, and idle in his habits." He made no notable progress in his education during his first two sessions. In his third year, however, his mind seized as if by native predilection upon the study of mathematics. This was the signal of his intellectual birth. Was it better that he had not obtained an earlier intellectual development, that the growing mind of his childhood, virgin and unexhausted, should have been stirred to its first intensive interest and endeavor by so exact and stimulating a science as mathematics? Hanna in his "Life of Chalmers" hints at this view of the case. At any rate he was fortunate in the instructor he had in the subject, whom he rated as one of the best he ever had. Though for the time mathematics was his favorite science, there were other subjects which elicited his attention. Ethics, political science, and natural theology were especially included among these.

In his fourth college year he was enrolled as a student of theology. The subject but slightly won his interest. He preferred to read the higher branches of mathematics in French, a language which he had sufficiently acquired to enable him to do this. The orthodoxy of his teacher he questioned, thinking that it was "formed in conformity to the standards, rather than as the truth most surely believed." The professor had advised that Calvinism need not be brought forward too distinctly in pulpit address lest it should prove repulsive to the hearer. "If it be truth," said Chalmers, "why not be above-board with it?" A student referred to a very able lecture the professor had delivered. Chalmers said he had not heard it. "Why," said the student, "did you not attend to a disquisition so able?" "Because," answered Chalmers, "I question the sincerity of the lecturer." Though not yet a Christian by experience, he could not tolerate insincerity.

The only permanent profit he had in divinity at this time was through his study of Edwards on the Will. This he did with such ardor "that he seemed to regard nothing else, . . . and one was almost afraid of his mind losing its balance." Still his grasp of religion consisted of hardly anything more than sublime ideas of the attributes of the Godhead. Writing in his journal twenty-four years afterwards of this period, he said: "I remember when a student of divinity, and long ere I could relish evangelical sentiment, I spent nearly a twelvemonth in a sort of mental elysium, and the one idea which ministered to my soul all its raptures was the magnificence of the Godhead, and the universal subordination of all things to the one great purpose for which He evolved and was supporting creation." This conception of God, however, whatever its limitations, was amazingly present to his mind. He told a member of his family "that not a single hour elapsed in which the overpoweringly impressive imagination did not stand out bright before the inward eye."

He could always impress others as far as he himself had gone in allegiance to Christian truth. Morning and evening prayers were conducted daily at St. Andrews by the theological students. Chalmers in his turn made an almost startling impression upon his audience. The people of St. Andrews flocked to the hall when they knew he was to pray. He was then only sixteen years of age, "yet he showed a taste and capacity for composition of the most glowing and eloquent kind."

For the cultivation of the art of composition he was largely indebted to debating societies conducted by the students. One of these societies was formed entirely of divinity students. The themes discussed were appropriate to the purpose of the body, and Chalmers's part in the deliberations was both prominent and profitable. A part of one of his college compositions on enthusiasm he reproduced in an appeal to his brethren when they faced the issues of the Disruption many years afterwards, "and no passage he ever wrote," it is said, "was uttered with more fervid energy or a more overwhelming effect."

Having some time at his disposal before his entrance upon his eighth and final session at school, which itself was restricted as to time, he essayed the work of a tutor in a private family. He could report only dissatisfaction with his situation.

Soon after his return at the beginning of January, 1799, for the completion of his work at college he applied to the Presbytery of St. Andrews for his examination as a candidate for a license to preach. He was only nineteen and under the prescribed age. But there was an old statute which made an exception of such as were of "rare and singular qualities." A friend in the Presbytery urged this statute in his behalf, and pleaded for his reception as "a lad o' pregnant pairts." The plea was admitted, and he was licensed on July 31, 1799.

The Power of the Ministry to Appropriate Preparation and Talent

The Christian ministry is so remarkable a form of service and capable of so wide an application to the conditions and needs of human life that nothing a man has learned, nothing he has experienced, no stage of preparation through which he has passed seems ever finally to escape its place in the development and serviceableness of the minister's career.

What had Chalmers's love of mathematics to do with his
being or becoming a preacher? What had his reveling in the
higher mathematical abstractions to do with his preparation
for the pulpit? What has chemistry, studied so ardently by
Chalmers, to do with city missionary work? A man said
the other day, trying to point the way to preachers, "If I
were a minister, I think I would study economics." But
who would have thought in Chalmers's time of political
economy as a proper subject of the preacher's study?

On looking deeper into the matter, might it not be conceived that preparation has more to do with making the
man and his mind than it has to do with pouring into the
man and his mind something from the outside? The preacher has to be a learner, to be sure. He has to be an inquisi-
tive and perpetual, an indefatigable learner. But it is not
more important that he should learn than that he should
acquire the ability to appropriate and apply what he does
learn. The best study is assimilation, and not mere accumulation. Accumulation may fill the mind: but assimilation builds it. Assimilation is more vital: it is the finishing
process. Our bodies assimilate naturally. So to some extent do our minds. "And things vegetable make a success
of it," says Burton in his "Pulpit and Parish." "A live slip
set into the ground is as cunning in the matter as is an old
wise tree." This is what the preacher at any cost has to
learn.

Chalmers learned it. Somehow he got his mind vitally
set on this process. What does it matter if it was by means
of the study of science that he did it? True, he was to be a
preacher and not a teacher. But who is a teacher more than
the preacher? And he is a preacher besides. It is a part of
the foolery, not the foolishness, of preaching to assume that
the preacher does not need a trained and an assimilative
mind.

The significant thing about the early preparation of Chalmers was that it trained his mind. If science does it, if philosophy does it, if language does it, if literature does it, if theology does it, why, then, it is done; and it is a precious thing when it is done. Chalmers had first to make his mind, and then the mind, submitted at last to God's grace, made the preacher. John Wesley comes out of Epworth and Oxford; and Charles H. Spurgeon comes out of the fens of Essex. Wesley transferred the university to his saddle, and never left school. Spurgeon thought that to go to college would be but a form of self-seeking, and never went to school in the academic sense. But he could never be counted an unprepared man except in the veriest technical meaning of the term. Each man after all, whether in the schools or out of them, made his own preparation. And right wondrously was the preparation of both the one and the other appropriated to the great ends of the Christian pulpit and pastorate.

Though now he was licensed, Chalmers did not concern himself much about preaching. His first sermon he preached twice over. He applied for a teaching vacancy in Edinburgh, but was not successful. The winter after he was licensed he spent there, and began mathematical studies again. In January, 1900, he wrote his father that he had preached only once since coming to Edinburgh, and that out of town. He formed a class in mathematics, and says that he finds himself so profitably employed that he "would be sorry of any interruption for the winter."

The kind of interruption he dreaded was a possible call "to ministerial employment." He returned for another winter to Edinburgh, and attended lectures in moral and natural philosophy, and in chemistry. Strange to say that though he is still dodging the active work of the ministry, he is preparing for it. But "science still swayed it over theology." He had an uncontrolled thirst for literary distinction. To fill the chair of mathematics in one of the universities was his highest ambition. This he would count no interference with his work as a minister.

KILMANY AND THE CRISIS OF HIS MINISTRY

With reference to a vacancy in the parish of Kilmany, Chalmers wrote: "I have been as vigorous in my application for the Church as possible, but cannot state with any certainty what will be the issue." This living he obtained as his first regular pastorate. Previously he had served a few months as assistant at Cavers. But he did not live in the parish, and "satisfied his conscience with a weekly visit for the purpose of preaching the sermon that was required of him."

He came to Kilmany with a divided heart. In connection with his pastorate there he held an assistant professorship in mathematics at St. Andrews, about nine miles away. But it was his leisure and not his active time that he counted as belonging to his parish. He had not yet awakened to the importance of his ministerial labors. His serious employment was his professorship. "He believed that after the satisfactory discharge of his parish duties he might have five days of the week uninterrupted for the prosecution of any scientific work to which his taste might incline him."

At the end of a year he lost his professorship, the action by which he was deprived of it being due, as he thought, to the jealousy of the head of the department. He had invested mathematics with an interest not ordinarily supposed to attach to the subject; and in the proportion that he aroused the enthusiasm of his students he stirred a feeling on the part of other members of the faculty that he was a disturber of college routine. Under the circumstances Chalmers pursued the unusual, but he thought justifiable, course of setting up an independent and outside class in the place of the work of which he had been deprived. There was opposition: but "no hostile influences could quench the admiration which kindled around such a lectureship." He organized also a class for lectures in chemistry. Still he held on to Kilmany to the extent that he filled the services on Sunday, going out generally on Saturday to the manse, and returning early on Monday.

His course in these circumstances could but increase the concern which his father had long felt about him. He had looked forward with anxiety to the commencement of his son's ministry. He feared that science had usurped the place which the Gospel of God's redeeming love should hold. Chalmers wrote to justify himself in his course, but doubtless his father felt that his explanation did not explain.

Hostile influences also arose behind him at Kilmany. Some of his brethren of the ministry thought he should be checked in his double course; or that at any rate some censure should be inflicted. The matter at last reached the Presbytery, but Chalmers won the day.

He repeated the chemical lectures at St. Andrews the next winter. There was further remonstrance, but the lectures went on. He is ever on the lookout for a professorship. He applies for a vacancy in mathematics at Edinburgh, and in natural philosophy at St. Andrews, and obtains neither. His father writes to James, another of his sons, referring to Thomas: "I should feel more comfortable were he to cultivate his present situation." In the meantime Chalmers himself published a pamphlet in which he said: "The author of this pamphlet can assert, from what to him is the highest of all authority, the authority of his own experience, that after the satisfactory discharge of his parish duties, a minister may enjoy five days in the week of uninterrupted

leisure for the prosecution of any science in which his taste
may dispose him to engage."

Kilmany was to witness the complete reversal of all these
attitudes on the part of Chalmers toward the work of the
Christian ministry. There was to come to him there the
great and transforming crisis of his life and ministry.

He was first brought into wide and prominent attention
by his maiden speech in the General Assembly, delivered in
1809. The subject had to do with an act regulating clerical
stipends and in itself was sufficiently dry. But Chalmers
warmed and vivified it exceedingly. "Do you know anything of this man?" said a prominent member to his neighbor; "he is surely a most extraordinary person." Many
others were asking the same question, and answering it in
the same way. The speech won him attention for its unusual ability, its humor, its Scotch "canniness," its clear
indications of genius and power. Dr. Andrew Thomson,
than whom there was not a more influential man in the
Church, asked him to write for the *Christian Instructor*. Dr.
Brewster invited him to write for the "Edinburgh Encyclopedia," and the article on Christianity was assigned him.

The article on Christianity for the encyclopedia, at which
he labored most assiduously, conspired with certain intimate personal experiences to bring him to Christ with his
heart as well as with his head. He had lost both a brother
and a sister by death. When he had followed each of them
to the disquieting edge of eternity, as it proved to be to him,
and had found that he could not look across with any of the
confidence of a certified Christian faith, he asked himself
some very serious questions. A long and serious illness of
his own, during which for four months he did not leave his
room, and by which he was kept a still longer time from his
pulpit, drove a sense of disturbance even more deeply into
his soul. It only needed the reading of Wilberforce's "Prac-

tical View of Christianity" to complete his conversion to Christ.

All along he had been firmly persuaded intellectually of the truth of Christianity. This was so well known that none could doubt it. "He unhesitatingly believed that the Scriptures are the Word of God, and that the Christian system is divine." But his belief had not become a religion. "It could not stand the scrutiny of the sick room; it could not bear to be confronted with death"; it could not even bear the test of reason, "for surely, even reason taught that if man have a God to love and serve, and an eternity beyond death to provide for, toward that God a supreme and abiding sense of obligation should be cherished, and to providing for that eternity the whole efforts of a lifetime should be consecrated." Convinced of fatal errors in matters so vital as these, he resolved to seek the necessary change. He had in truth but the religion of "Butler's Analogy." In fact, he once said that it was "Butler's Analogy" that "made him a Christian." Now he is made a Christian through faith and conscious spiritual renewal. From that moment his whole life and character, both personal and ministerial, were transformed, and transfigured as well.

He had been in Kilmany seven years before his conversion, and remained five years afterwards. Previously he had naturally cared little for personal contact with his people, and had not known what real pastoral work was. He cared but little more about the preparation of his sermons. His ministry had been both unpopular and ineffective, and his church but poorly attended. Now all this was changed. The first use he made of his returning strength after his illness "was to visit all the sick, the dying, and the bereaved in his parish." The obstacles which "extreme delicacy of feeling and his own great reserve" had thrown in his way were swept aside, and he became a diligent and devoted pastor. The catalogue of his pastoral activities reads like the program of a modern institutional church.

The change in his preaching was even more profound. Even now his pulpit surpassed his pastorate in power. The Kilmany pulpit had had a change of preachers as the Kilmany parish had had a change of pastors. The last three years at Kilmany "supplied as many, as elaborate, and as eloquent discourses, as any other three years in the whole course of his ministry." This was in good part due to his renewed interest in his Bible. He had a friend who, though of an order of gifts much inferior to his own, had been admitted to a good deal of intimacy with him. "I never came in before," said this friend, "but I found you busy; yet never at your studies for the Sabbath. You said, 'O, an hour or two Saturday evening is quite enough for that'; but now I never come in but you are at your Bible."

His sermons, now prepared with the greatest care, were closely read from manuscript in their delivery. Sometimes, however, leaving his manuscript, as a hearer said, "he would bend over the pulpit, and press us to take the gift, as if he held it that moment in his hand." The gift he so earnestly pressed upon his hearers was Christ, Christ in his gospel offering his great salvation. It was done with a fervor, and a power, and an effectiveness which the history of Christian preaching has rarely witnessed.

"The whole aspect of the Sabbath congregations in Kilmany church was changed." The change in the preacher wrought the change in the people. Preaching in the Kilmany church had been exalted to the standard of a transaction between the preacher and God. The people who transacted business with that preacher transacted business with God. Aside from this changed aspect of the whole congregation there were remarkable instances of individual conversion.

9

In his last address to the inhabitants of Kilmany, Chalmers bore his own explicit testimony to the profound change wrought in his ministry there:

And here I cannot but record the effect of an actual though undesigned experiment which I prosecuted for upward of twelve years among you. For the greater part of that time I could expatiate on the meanness of dishonesty, on the villainy of falsehood, on the despicable arts of calumny; in a word, upon all those deformities of character which awaken the natural indignation of the human heart against the pests and diturbers of human society. Now, could I, upon the strength of these warm expostulations, have got the thief to give up his stealing, and the evil speaker his censoriousness, and the liar his deviations from truth, I should have felt all the repose of one who had gotten his ultimate object. It never occured to me that all this might have been done, and yet the soul of every hearer have remained in full alienation from God; and that even could I have established in the bosom of one who stole such a principle of abhorrence at the meanness of dishonesty that he was prevailed upon to steal no more, he might still have retained a heart as completely unturned to God, and as totally unpossessed by a principle of love to Him as before. In a word, though I might have made him a more upright and honorable man, I might have left him as destitute of the essence of religious principle as ever. *But the interesting fact is that during the whole of that period, in which I made no attempt against the natural enmity of the mind to God;* while I was inattentive to the way in which this enmity is dissolved, even by the free offer on the one hand, and the believing acceptance on the other, of the gospel of salvation; while Christ, through whose blood the sinner who by nature stands afar off is brought near to the heavenly Lawgiver whom he has offended, was scarcely ever spoken of, or spoken of in such a way as stripped Him of all the importance of His character and His offices, even at this time I certainly did press the reformations of honor and truth and integrity among my people, but *I never once heard of any such reformations having been effected among them. If there was anything at all brought about in this way, it was more than I ever got any account of.* I am not sensible that all the vehemence with which I urged the virtues and the proprieties of social life had the weight of a feather on the moral habits of my parishioners. And it was not till I got impressed by the utter alienation of the heart in all its desires and affections from God; it was not till reconciliation to Him became the distinct and the prominent object of my ministerial exertions; it was not till I took the Scriptural way of laying the method of reconciliation before them; it was not till the free offer of forgiveness through the blood of Christ was urged upon their acceptance, and the Holy Spirit given through the channel of Christ's mediatorship

to all who ask Him was set before them, as the unceasing object of their
dependence and their prayers; in one word, it was not till the contemplations of my people were turned to these great and essential elements in
the business of a soul providing for its interests with God, and the concerns
of eternity, that I ever heard of any of those subordinate reformations
which I aforetime made the earnest and the zealous, but I am afraid, at
the same time, the ultimate object of my earlier ministrations. . . . You
have at least taught me that to preach Christ is the only effective way of
preaching morality in all its branches, and out of your humble cottages
have I gathered a lesson which I pray God I may be able to carry in all its
simplicity into a wider theater, and to bring with all the power of its sub-
duing efficacy upon the vices of a mere crowded population.

THE GLORY THAT WAS GLASGOW

Chalmers was installed as pastor of the Tron Church,
Glasgow, on July 21, 1815. When the call was in process a
suggestion was made to him that since he had never preached
in Glasgow he should make an early opportunity to do so,
as members of the Town Council, who because of the State
connections of the Church had to authorize the call, wished
to hear him. An effort was also made to obtain from him
beforehand some intimation of the acceptance of the call in
case it were given. He firmly refused to do either the one
or the other. A letter written from the Kilmany manse
deals with the principles he conceived to be involved in the
proposals. Nowhere does the unalloyed nobility of the man
appear to better effect:

When I first heard of the Glasgow business, I resolved not to help it
on by any step or declaration of mine. . . . If, in spite of this reserve,
the Town Council of Glasgow shall call me, I will take it up, and think
of it, and pray over it, and view it in a far more impressive light than if
any interference of mine had contributed the weight of a feather to such
a result. To fetter myself with a promise previous to my appointment,
compels me to accept of it; and upon what principle? upon a principle of
obligation to man. To keep myself uncommitted, is to leave room for the
only principle upon which a call should be obeyed; the commitment of the
cause to God, the openings of whose providence we are bound to pay
respect to, and the good of whose Church should be our paramount consideration. But, you may think, cannot this commitment be made now?

No; I will not consult God about my conduct in a particular situation, till he brings me into that situation. I will not decide upon my acceptance of any appointment till the appointment is before me, for then, and not till then, will the reasons for and against have fully developed themselves.

No small stir was made about the call in Glasgow. "No small stir, I'll assure you," said one, "has been in that city, and no such stir has been there since the days of John Knox, it is said, about the choice of a minister." Chalmers was strongly evangelical, and the Moderatists, whose name indicated their preference for a state of quiescence as against any grave concern about doctrines, or discipline, or evangelism, opposed his coming. But his friends prevailed, and he won the election in the Council by a vote of fifteen, to ten for one of the other candidates, and four for still another.

His brother James strongly advised against his going. But he thought he had a surer guide, and said: "I cautiously abstained from giving any encouragement to the electors, would not tell them whether I would take it or turn from it, but left it a question quite undecided till Providence brought it to my door; then, if there is no intimation of the will of Providence here, it must follow either that events afford no interpretation of that will, or . . . God has no share in the matter at all."

There were two chief obstacles to his going: first, he dreaded the drudgery of what he regarded as extra-pastoral labor, and feared its secularizing effect upon his ministry; and, second, the pain of his breaking away from Kilmany. There was a promise from Glasgow that he should have the relief he wished at that end, though he could but wonder whether this could be realized. The other difficulty none could remove. Waving his staff toward the Kilmany hills, he said to a friend: "Ah, my dear sir, my heart is wedded to these hills." In his journal he records a prayer against his grief: "Preached as usual. A great crowd. O my God, sustain me against tenderness."

In Glasgow he was to write a new and permanent chapter in the history of Christian preaching, and a new and formative record in parochial achievement. The city really did not know how remarkable a man was coming to them. He had preached in a pulpit there on an occasion previous to his permanent settlement, and a critical observer had described his impressions of his personal appearance:

> Immediately above the extraordinary breadth of this region, which, in the heads of most mathematical persons, is surmounted by no fine points of organization whatever, immediately above this, in the forehead, there is an arch of imagination, carrying out the summit boldly and roundly, in a style to which the heads of very few poets present anything comparable, while over this again there is a grand apex of high and solemn veneration and love, such as might have graced the bust of Plato himself, and such as in living men I had never beheld equaled in any but the majestic head of Canova.

The distractions which he had feared would attend upon his ministry in Glasgow were all too surely realized. There was an incessant demand for the personal attendance of ministers upon every occasion, long or short, grave or gay. "They must have four to every funeral, or they do not think that it has been genteelly gone through." In one solemn meeting he "sat nearly an hour in grave deliberation with a number of others upon a subject connected with the property of a corporation, and that subject was a *gutter*, and the question was whether it should be bought and covered up, or let alone and left to lie open." Another such occasion he describes in his best style:

> Some of the gravest of the city ministers and some of the wisest of the city merchants had been summoned to the conclave, when the weighty and perplexing question was propounded, whether pork broth or ox-head broth should be served to the inmates of the hospital. Opinions differed, the debate waxed warm, and at last it was resolved to subject the matter

to actual trial. A quantity of both kinds of broth was produced, each
sitter tasting it as it made its circuit of the Board. The judgments were
then collected and compared, when the sapient decision was given forth—
that sometimes there should be served the one kind of broth and sometimes
the other.

This sort of thing he soon saw would be disastrous to
the highest ends of his ministry, and was resolved that it
should not continue. His liberty was never made complete;
but a part of his bondage, at any rate, he was able to shake
off. It was more difficult to regulate the number of persons
coming to him. Much of this was necessary, and what he
desired. But much of it also was pure waste, and he groaned
to be delivered.

How could trivialities such as these be attached to a great
preaching ministry? Yet Chalmers reached the height of his
fame as a preacher in Glasgow. From there his pulpit sound-
ed through all Scotland and into England. When he came
to the city it was the custom that the ministers of the city
should preach in rotation on Thursdays from the Tron
Church pulpit. On Thursday, November 23, 1815, Chalmers delivered the first of his famous "Astronomical Discourses," and intimated that there would be a series on the
theme thus begun. It was at a time when science was ex-
panding the heavens into hitherto unsuspected immensities
of space. As man's conception of the universe was extended his own importance seemed relatively to shrink. A
prejudice was raised against the Christian revelation on
this ground. The magnitude of the world outside the mind
of man tended to minify the world within. The object of
the sermons on astronomy was to combat these erroneous
tendencies, and to turn the force of the argument in the
other direction. Immense enthusiasm was aroused by the
delivery of the sermons. Long before the hour for the service streams of people poured along the ways leading to the

Tron Church. Busy merchants deserted their desks at one of the busiest hours of the day, clerks and apprentices were permitted to drop their tasks, coffeerooms ceased their mid-day clatter, and standing room itself failed many who came eager to hear. The expectant throngs await the arrival of the preacher. The service begins. There is a hush of the soul which is deeper than the strained outside silence. The following contemporary description has been preserved as being characteristic not of these services only, but of Chalmers's preaching in general at the time:

Every countenance is up, every eye bent with fixed intentness on the speaker. As he kindles, the interest grows. Every breath is held, every cough is suppressed . . . ; every one, riveted himself by the spell of the impassioned and entrancing eloquence, knows how sensitively his neighbor will resent the very slightest disturbance. Then, by and by, there is a pause. The speaker stops to gather breath, to wipe his forehead, to adjust his gown, and purposely too, and wisely to give the audience as well as himself a moment or two of relaxation. The moment is embraced; there is a free breathing, suppressed coughs get vent, postures are changed, there is a universal stir, as of persons who could not have endured the constraint much longer. The preacher bends forward, his hand is raised, all is again hushed. The same stillness and strain of unrelaxed attention is repeated, more intent still, it may be, than before, as the interest of the subject and the speaker advance. And so for perhaps four or five times in the course of a sermon there is the relaxation and the "at it again," till the final winding up.

In a little more than a year this series of sermons was announced as ready for publication. Their sale was extraordinary. In ten weeks 6,000 copies had been disposed of. Nine editions were issued within a year, and nearly 20,000 copies were in circulation. They "disarmed even the keen hostility of Hazlitt," and he said of them:

These sermons ran like wildfire through the country, were the darlings of watering-places, were laid in the windows of inns, and were to be met with in all places of public resort. . . . We remember finding the volume in the orchard of an inn . . . and passing a whole, and very delightful morning in reading it without quitting the shade of an apple tree.

"No student of English preaching," says Broadus in the "History of Preaching," "must fail to read the magnificent Astronomical Sermons, nor at least a part of the expository Lectures on Romans."

In the midst of the rapture raised about him by his preaching Chalmers went to London to preach for the London Missionary Society. A Scotsman heard him and wrote back to Glasgow:

> Dr. Chalmers has just finished the discourse before the Missionary Society. All my expectations were overwhelmed in the triumph of it. Nothing from the Tron pulpit ever exceeded it, nor did he ever more arrest and wonderwork his auditors.

Wilberforce wrote in his diary: "All the world is wild about Dr. Chalmers." Everybody now called him *Doctor Chalmers*. Glasgow had given him the degree of Doctor of Divinity. Afterwards Oxford made him a D.C.L., and he was made a member of the Royal Society of Edinburgh, and elected to membership in the Institute of France.

Parish organization and management in his time he regarded as being specially defective with respect to the spiritual and temporal care of the poor. Let their temporal care, he contended, be provided for through voluntary contributions made at the Church, and not through a provision enforced by the state. Artificial and enforced assistance could only make them poorer and more dependent. When he went among them and found their interest leaning to the merely temporal side of his assistance he speedily allowed them to know that he "only dealt in one article, that of Christian instruction, and that if they chose to receive him on that footing he should be glad to visit them." He would not have the spiritual issues confused by the temporal, the major by the minor.

State assistance and ecclesiastical neglect were, he thought, the twin evils which impoverished the poor, and lowered not only their standards of living, but their standards of life as well. "His object was not to keep his poor people fictitiously comfortable, but at any cost, even of discomfort, even of complaint, to keep them independent, to preserve them by every strenuous art from becoming poor in the technical sense of the word, or depending on charity at all." With these principles in mind he set out to visit every family of the large population of his parish, both at the Tron Church and later, at St. John's. The visit would be brief, but very earnest. And he left an elder to invite every family to a meeting to be held at some convenient place in the neighborhood on a specified evening. Dr. Chalmers in these evening meetings was the highest style of a pastor, gathering his people as a shepherd would gather his sheep, and pouring out upon them floods of compassion and eloquence never surpassed in his address in his crowded churches. The children of the poor he gathered into Sabbath evening classes and provided suitable instruction for them. When these schools were looked upon by some with a cold dislike he warmly defended them and persevered in their promotion.

Glasgow might at this time have lost him to Sterling, whence there came to him a most attractive offer, providing a personal freedom and a security which he could not have as he was situated. Nevertheless, he thought it not well to go.

In August, 1819, Dr. Chalmers was transferred from the Tron Church to the parish of St. John's in the same city. The situation was virtually created for him as a means of enabling him to test to the fullest extent his theories and plans for the poor. The new parish was established by the Town Council to contain a population of at least 10,000, composed almost entirely of operatives. "In St. John's Church," says Taylor in his "Scottish Pulpit," "he inaugurated and superintended what was perhaps the greatest and most effective parochial organization which the Christian Church has ever seen in operation."

He had for an assistant at St. John's the gifted but erratic Edward Irving. Their relations were amicable, and even cordial. However, there was a sharp though unexpressed protest when Chalmers opened a new chapel for Irving in London, and the latter, who had kindly proposed that he would assist in the service, "chose the very longest chapter in the Bible, and went on with his exposition for an hour and a half." "When my turn came, of what use could I be in an exhausted receiver?" asks Chalmers.

Chalmers had a strange idea about the social structure. He thus expressed himself:

Whatever political convulsions may await us, through whatever stormy and adverse seasons of tumult and destruction and disturbance this land may have to pass, it cannot fail to settle down at last, both in this and in every other nation, into an economy of men of affluence who compose the minority, and men of labor and artisanship who compose the great majority of every commonwealth.

Yet his devotion to the poor of his parish, or wherever and in whatever condition he found them, cannot for a single moment be questioned. Again in Edinburgh, as he had done in Glasgow, he is found turning to them.

AMONG THE ACADEMICIANS AT ST. ANDREWS

Chalmers was not of a temperament which easily bears up under strain. Early in his Glasgow ministry he complains of "the fatigue of preaching." His church was "in a confined situation, and crowded to excess," and this oppressed him. He preaches "louder and longer" than he used to do, and is determined "to make the diminution of his fatigue a serious object."

Furthermore, he was of a sensitive and self-accusing temperament. "He walked among the elements of inconstancy and distrust." His journal is full of complaints against himself. He is not satisfied with his sermon. He fears that "personal distinction" is one of his idols; charges himself with "vanity"; prays that God would "sweep away these corruptions," and enable him to struggle with them. He is distressed and perplexed. He finds that fatigue lays him open to the power of evil thoughts, and takes this as proof that his labors are not spiritual. "O my God, give me to grieve not thy Spirit," is the cry that rends his heart. There are ways in which Glasgow fatigues him. His Sundays are fatiguing. He laments his deficiency in such soul exercises as distinguished Thomas Boston, and many others.

These are just the kind of exercises that wear a man down. There is no heavier burden than human self-consciousness exposing its uncleanness to God. It is that Jacob-like wrestling with God which leaves its mark on a man. It is a struggling with self which is very wearing. The leonine Chalmers was lamblike in his humility before God. He was a man who was forever straining himself in the ascent to higher things. He found,

"That rare track made by great ones, lone and beaten,
    Through solitary hours,
Climbing past fear and hate and sin, iron-eaten,
    To godlier powers:
A road of lonely morn and midnight, sloping
    O'er earth's dim bars;
Where out at last the soul, life's pinnacles topping,
    Stands with the stars."

The continuous strain of the work in the pastorate began to wear down his strength, and he was the more inclined to accept the chair of Moral Philosophy in the University of St. Andrews when it was offered him. The ambition, too, which he had early had to seek academic and literary distinction had no doubt only slumbered in him, and was never dead. But though he had not killed it, he had conquered it; and he might now gratify it in the form of a godly desire. He went to St. Andrews and remained from 1823 to 1828.

Still it was hard to break the bonds that held him to Glasgow. His parting words from the pulpit of St. John's were as pathetic as any psalm:

If I forget thee, O Jerusalem—if I forget thee, O thou Church and city of my God—let my right hand forget her cunning. If I do not remember thee, let my tongue cleave to the roof of my mouth: if I prefer not Jerusalem above my chief joy.

Of the sum of his ministry there it was written that, when he came,

by the great body of the upper classes of society evangelical doctrines were nauseated and despised: when he left it, even by those who did not bow to their influence, these doctrines were acknowledged to be indeed the very doctrines of the Bible. When he came . . . in the eye of the multitude evangelism stood confounded with a driveling sanctimoniousness, or a sour-minded asceticism: when he left it, from all such false associations the Christianity of the New Testament stood clearly and nobly redeemed. When he came . . . for nearly a century the Magistrates and Town Council had exercised the city patronage in a spirit determinately antievangelical: when he left it, so complete was the revolution which had been effected, that from that time forward none but evangelical clergymen were appointed by the city patrons.

Chalmers's work as a professor was not of the usual academic sort any more in moral philosophy than it had been in mathematics. More than double the number of students who had ever attended in the days of his most famous predecessors were soon gathered into his classes. Students who had passed beyond that stage of their curriculum returned to him. So high was the strain of eloquence attained in the lectures that applause spontaneously burst forth from his classes. This "pedestrian approbation" he did not much appreciate. Response he thought might far better "come from the heads than from the heels of the rising generation." As his powers matured he naturally became more promi-

nent in the councils of the Church. On the side of the
evangelical group in the Church as it began to be felt in the
General Assembly he was a strong influence. When he entered the lists of debate he was sure to bear a conspicuous,
though not always a successful, part. There was an unfor-
gettable incident of debate which intimately concerned him.
The question pertained to pluralities—should a minister,
for instance, be allowed to hold a city pastorate and a university chair at the same time? Chalmers was opposed to
the arrangement. An opponent in the debate quoted from
the pamphlet in which he had taken just the opposite part.
The publication had been anonymous, but Chalmers was
well known as the author. All eyes turned to him. He
arose amid breathless silence and spoke as follows:

> Sir, that pamphlet I now declare to have been a production of my own,
> published twenty years ago. I was indeed much surprised to hear it
> brought forward and quoted this evening. . . . But since that gentleman
> has brought it forward in the face of this house, I can assure him that I
> feel grateful to him from the bottom of my heart for the opportunity he
> has now afforded me of making a public recantation of the sentiments it
> contains. . . . I was at that time, sir, more devoted to mathematics
> than to the literature of my profession; and feeling grieved and indignant
> at what I conceived an undue reflection on the abilities and education of
> our clergy, I came forward with that pamphlet to rescue them from what I
> deemed an unmerited reproach, by maintaining that a devoted and ex-
> clusive attention to the study of mathematics was not dissonant to the
> proper habits of a clergyman. Alas! sir, so I thought in my ignorance and
> pride. I have now no reserve in saying that the sentiment was wrong,
> and that, in the utterance of it, I penned what was most outrageously
> wrong. Strangely blinded that I was! What, sir, is the object of mathe-
> matical science? Magnitude and the proportions of magnitude. But
> *then*, sir, I had forgotten *two magnitudes*—I thought not of the littleness of
> time—I recklessly thought not of the greatness of eternity.

As the greatness to which Chalmers had grown challenged
and recanted the error of his immaturity the effect was overwhelming and sublime.

There arrived a time when he found his position at St.

Andrews uncomfortable. A question arose about Church attendance. Should the parents of students be allowed to select for them a Church outside the Establishment? Chalmers thought they might; and that in doing so there was no hostility to the Church of Scotland. He was sure that he himself was loyal to the Church; and he announced emphatically the principle upon which he stood. "I have no veneration," he said, "for the Church of Scotland merely *quasi* an Establishment, but I have the utmost veneration for it *quasi* an instrument of Christian good."

Again he was in a hopeless minority over a more distressing difference of opinion. Certain college funds were subject to administration by the faculty, and these had been used to supplement faculty salaries. Chalmers could not consent to this, and was left painfully standing alone.

He had interested himself in efforts for the improvement of theological education, and had so far succeeded that the requirement of at least one year's attendance at the Divinity Hall on the part of students for the ministry was made. In 1887 he declined an offer of the chair of Moral Philosophy in London University.

No academic employment could strip him of his character as a Christian minister. St. Andrews students when Chalmers went there, according to Hanna, were "a singularly Godless, Christless class." But he did not begin too directly upon them. Selecting a neglected district of the town, he began religious work there with a zeal and a success which would have been worthy of a man laboring in the pastorate alone. But the most lasting results of his labors were among the students themselves. There was a marked revival of religious interest in the school, and men went out under the constraint of his remarkable influence to the pastorate of the churches in the homeland and in the distant mission fields to incarnate that influence in their own spheres of

labor. Not a nobler name among them all was there than
that of Alexander Duff, who in India raised for all time the
standards of missionary devotion and endeavor.

An Educator in Theology in Edinburgh

Dr. Chalmers was professor of theology in Edinburgh
from 1828 to the disruption of the Church in 1843. Previously he had been offered the parish of St. Cuthbert's in
the same city, "one of the most desirable livings in the
Church of Scotland." But he declined. He was convinced
of the superiority in point of usefulness for himself of a professorship to the pastorate, and in this conviction he remained unshaken. The vacancy at the university he would
not seek any more than he would seek a vacant pastorate.
He says privately that he will accept the place if it is offered
him, but he will give no public intimation. Not even Dr.
Thomson, who was deeply interested in the matter, could
persuade him to commit himself in any public way. Nevertheless, he obtained a unanimous election. He had a year
of preparation before beginning his active work. He continued meanwhile at St. Andrews.

He began at Edinburgh in the autumn of 1828. The aid
of the police had to be invoked to restrain the crowd that
sought admission to his first lecture. When it was delivered
it was received with "rapturous applause." Nor was there
any sensible abatement of this interest throughout the entire session. He was upon "favorite and familiar ground."
He could now form into a system the results of his prolonged study and mature reflection.

There faced him from time to time an audience "altogether unique," gathered in part from beyond university
circles, and composed of distinguished members of the civic
and professional life of the city. So great was the appreciation of this non-professional attendance that at the end of

the school year they presented to him a sum sufficient to a little more than double his regular stipend.

His strength as a teacher lay not so much in his ability to impart instruction as in his power to awaken interest and stir enthusiasm. "He was not so much an instructor as a quickener." The other professors "laid the material in the minds of the students"; he set it on fire. He did do some teaching. His *viva voce* method with his classes at the end of a lecture was in its way very effective. But his main business was to be the inspirer of men. He became Professor of Theology to the Free Church at the Disruption, "and to the end of his days he had around him a circle of loving and devoted students, all of whom were fired with enthusiasm which they had caught from his lips."

At this time he had occasion to declare himself concerning the repeal of the Catholic Disabilities Act. He had but one mind on the subject. He would not impose civil disabilities on account of religion. Protestantism itself was weakened by it. Some of "the most unconquerable principles of human nature were enlisted against such a measure." It had "transformed a nation of heretics into a nation of heroes." He would trust in the power of truth alone to prevail over error. Lord Jeffrey heard him in a speech on the subject in Edinburgh and said that "never had eloquence produced a greater effect upon a popular assembly, and that he could not believe more had ever been done by the oratory of Demosthenes, Cicero, Burke, or Sheridan."

Again he had an attractive offer of a parish—the West Church in Greenock, "the most lucrative ecclesiastical living in Scotland." He declined, having now a firmer conviction than ever of "the superior importance of a theological chair to any church whatever."

Exposition of the Epistle to the Romans

During his academic years Chalmers kept his pen busy. He had an unquenchable craving for composition. The way in which he could snatch a moment from his already overburdened time and apply it to composition may excite admiration if not emulation. This is one of the revelations of his journal. After his prayers he records nothing so much as his composition. The recurrent word "composed," "composed," "composed" stamps a sort of proprietorship upon its pages. Much of the product of his pen found its way into print. Perhaps none of this has a greater permanent value than his "Exposition of the Epistle to the Romans." Well has it been said that he wrote for the ear and not for the eye. Though he read his sermons, he was a speaker and not a writer. Nevertheless, much of the power of his thought, the grandeur of his imagination, and the forcefulness of his utterance are found in what he has published.

His expositions on Romans were prepared first for his pulpit, and the most of them used there, though the volume had to be completed after he left the pastorate.

In an introductory lecture he has a passage on the possible—and evidently he thinks probable—means of adapting the eye to the light it receives:

One can imagine that, instead of the light being made instantaneously to burst upon us in its highest splendor, and, instead of the faculty being immediately bestowed upon us in full vigor to meet and to encounter so strong a tide of effulgence—that both these processes were conducted in a way that was altogether gradual—that the light, for example, had its first weak glimmering; and that the eye, in the feebleness of its infancy, was not overcome by it—that the light advanced with morning step to a clearer brilliancy; and that the eye, rendered able to bear it, multiplied the objects of its sight, and took in a wider range of perception—that the light shone at length unto the perfect day; and that the eye, with the last finish upon its properties and powers, embraced the whole of that variety which lies within the present compass of human contemplation. We must see that if one of these processes be gradual, the other should be gradual

10

also. By shedding too strong a light upon weak eyes, we may overpower and extinguish them. By granting too weak a light to him who has strong eyes, we make the faculty outstrip the object of its exercise.

He was strong on the singleness of Paul's principle of justification:

He would admit of no compromise between one basis of acceptance and another. This were inserting a flaw and a false principle into the principle of our justification; and to import the element of falsehood were to import the element of feebleness. We call upon you, not to lean so much as the weight of one grain or scruple of your confidence upon your own doings—to leave this ground entirely, and to come over entirely to the ground of a Redeemer's blood and a Redeemer's righteousness.

Christian belief must constrain to obedience:

An article of belief may lie up in our minds, without any change or any transition; and such a belief can have no footsteps. But when it is a belief that carries movement along with it—when it is a belief in one who both bids and blesses with his voice at the same time, . . . when it is belief in a God who so manages this intercourse with his creatures, as to cheer them by his promises, and guide them by his directions at the same instant—there is a dependence that will issue from such a faith, but there is an obedience also; and the successive parts of that practical history which it originated at the first, and animates throughout afterwards, are the footsteps of the faith.

Christian hope must lead to holiness. Christians

will know themselves to be strangers and pilgrims; and their affections will be kindred with the country to which they travel, and not with the country through which they pass. They will sit loose to this world's cares and this world's pleasures; and thus a patience under all earthly discomforts, and a self-denial to all earthly gratifications, will be to them the discipline that shall at once inspire the hope and qualify for the enjoyment of higher gratifications.

On the Spirit of God's interceding for us he says:

When He comes into contact, and especially at the first, with a soul before dead in trespasses and sins—when he has to operate on that mass of carnality, where he finds naught but one inert and sluggish mass of resistance—when, instead of doing the work separately and by himself, he does it through the opaque medium of a corrupt human soul—we should not marvel, though the prayers that even he hath originated, be tinged with the obscurity of that dull and distorted medium through which they have to pass. . . . This imperfection is not because of himself, in whom there is perfect and unclouded splendor. It is only because of the gross and terrestrial mind upon which he operates.

He fears that there is a certain metaphysical notion of the Godhead

which blunts our feelings of obligation, for all the kindness of his good will, for all the tenderness of his mercies. There is an academic theology, which would divest him of all sensibility; which would make of him a Being devoid of all emotion and of all tenderness; which concedes to him power and wisdom and a sort of cold and clear and faultless morality, but which would denude him of all those fond and fatherly regards that so endear an earthly parent to the children who have sprung from him.

He puts a volume in a sentence and says:

The main anxiety of a truly Christianized heart is for its own integrity.

CHAMPION OF THE CHURCH'S FREEDOM

The Church of Scotland as distinguished from the Church of Rome had the roots of its existence in the Reformation and the labors of John Knox. The Free Church of Scotland as distinguished from the Establishment had its origin in the Disruption of 1843. A ground of agreement between the contending ideas of a free or an established Church had never really existed in Scotland. It was only the acute form of this contention which manifested itself at the Disruption. There were ten years of open conflict before the break. This conflict assumed the form finally of contests at civil law between the claims of the State and the rights of the Church. The State stood for the right of patronage. A minister presented to a church according to the law must be accepted even against the will of the congregation. Leaders of the Church held that no minister should be intruded into any parish "contrary to the will of the congregation." Decisions of the courts unfavorable to the Church

were sustained by Parliament. The courts at last made it
clear that the Church in their opinion held its temporalities
on condition of rendering such obedience as the courts required. Again their decision was sustained by the government. A final and peremptory negative was given to the
Church's claim of spiritual independence. Chalmers, Welsh,
Cunningham, Candlish, McFarlane, and others led for the
Church, contending that as to the essence of its existence
the Church could have no head but Christ. Parliament
might sustain, but could not create, the Church. No state,
no bishop, no ecclesiastic of whatever rank had any independent or original right in her government.

Chalmers himself never ceased to believe in the propriety
of the establishment of the Church by the State. He had
gone up to London in 1838, and before one of the most
brilliant audiences the metropolis could assemble, Lords of
the realm and members of the House of Commons constituting its major part, had delivered a series of lectures not
overmatched in brilliance by the audience itself, on the
principles upon which a state establishment of the Church
might stand. The whole city was stirred into admiration
of both the lecturer and the lectures. His position was made
very clear. Establishment was just "a legal provision for
the support of a Christian ministry." In return the State
received the spiritual nurture of its citizens. He would have
the Church established by the State; but not one iota of her
spiritual freedom would he yield. For this he contended
as for the very existence of the Church as a spiritual institution.

It was inevitably seen that disruption was pending. The
situation narrowed itself down more and more to the ascendancy of the State over the Church in the matters which
were in dispute. Several notable steps had been taken by
the movers of the opposition to state encroachment. The

General Assembly of 1838 pointed explicitly to the fact that it was declared in the Confession of Faith of the Church that Christ is "the only spiritual King and Governor of his Kirk." Attention also was called to the fact that in the Act of Patronage itself it was stated that the Church had "full power to put order to all matters and causes ecclesiastical, *according to the discipline of the Kirk.*"

In a speech which occupied three hours in its delivery Chalmers in the General Assembly of 1839 endeavored to make clear the precise footing upon which the Church enters into that alliance with the State by which it becomes a National Church. He declared that "she did not make over her liberties to the State; . . . she only made over her services. . . . Her subsistence came from the State; but her formularies, and her doctrine, and her discipline, and the methods of her ecclesiastical polity, and her articles of faith, and her methods of worship and of government were all her own."

Ample warning was given that the submission demanded was impossible. In a speech in Edinburgh Chalmers said unequivocally: "Be it known, then, that we shall not retract one single footstep—we shall make no submission to the Court of Session. . . . They may force the ejection of us from our places: they shall never, never force us to the surrender of our principles. . . . We shall give place by subjection, no, not for an hour—no, not by an hair-breadth."

All the while the Moderate party in the Church stood with the State. The evangelicals had come into the ascendancy as far back as 1839; and thereby the Church had greatly profited. But the Moderates had wealth and social prestige, and political advantage. Differences grew more intense. Lines were more sharply drawn. State and Moderate action became bolder. The evangelical party became more determined, Chalmers leading all the while. Sir Robert Peel from his eminent position as Prime Minister had spoken against the Church. Chalmers replied. His moral indignation might well have raised the temperature even of the House of Lords. Said he:

I ask, Is it well for Sir Robert, from his elevated station and seat of silken security, to deal forth such a lesson to the Church and people of Scotland; while he spares the patrician, the lordly feelings, of all in rank or in office who have leagued to bear us down, to make no allowance for the consciences of men who, though humble in condition yet high in sentiment are, like their fathers before them, prepared to renounce all for the integrity of that Church which is at once the glory and the bulwark of our nation?

The clerical conscience lay at the root of disruption, and there could be no withdrawing from the steps already taken. "Be it known unto all men then," said they, "that we have no wish for a disruption, but neither stand we in the overwhelming dread of it." "To the very last," Chalmers avowed, "we shall assert a government in the Church distinct from that of the civil magistrate. . . . We are not dealing in threats, but in remonstrances. We are not making an experiment on English courage. . . . We are making an appeal to English justice."

Disruption was more and more seen to be inevitable, and measures were taken in anticipation of the event, most notable among these being the raising of a fund for the support of a ministry for the new Church to be formed. Then came the General Assembly of 1843. When the Church of Christ shall construct a new calendar for the great deeds done outside the New Testament this day will go in it. Much public incredulity had been expressed concerning the actual event of disruption. If the resisters of government went out, "they could not carry on the Church." Less than one hundred "would cover the whole secession." An eminent London divine had said that he "*was not sure that any would secede.*" It became the favorite subject of betting at the clubs. "Mark my words," said a sagacious citizen of Edinburgh, destined to lose some of his reputation for sagacity, "not forty of them will go out."

The Assembly met in Edinburgh. Dr. Welsh was Moderator. He arose from the chair. "We protest," he said; and having stated his reasons he proposed that all who were of his mind should go out. Laying his protest on the table, he turned and bowed respectfully to the Royal Commissioner, left the chair, stepped into the aisle of the Church, and proceeded toward the door. Chalmers, who was standing near by, awoke as from a revery, seized his hat, and followed him. Then followed an elder; then another minister. In all there were more than four hundred ministers, and a still larger number of elders who went out. They were leaving most of the wealth and aristocracy of the Church behind them. As they went out into a world empty alike of churches, manses, and provision for their own, they might well have asked,

> "Why should hard-favoured grief be lodged in thee,
> When triumph is become an alehouse guest?"

Outside the Church as the procession moved "a loud and irrepressible cheer" rent the air. Elsewhere in the city Lord Francis Jeffrey, none too sympathetic with the attitude of the seceders, sat quietly reading. A messenger burst in upon him and said: "Well, what do you think of it? More than four hundred of them are actually out." Flinging his book aside and rising to his feet, he exclaimed: "I'm proud of my country; there's not another country upon earth where such a deed could have been done."

Proceeding to a hall which had been prepared for them, the men who had dispossessed themselves of their ecclesiastical livings and treasured religious connections organized the Free Church of Scotland. Chalmers was called to the chair as the first Moderator of the new Church. He had been its chief creator; and while he lived he was to be its chief guide.

The Elemental Qualities of the Man

Few men attain to the eminence of the elemental in character development and practical efficiency. Most men must be content to make their contribution to the sum of the world's good on a lower level. Chalmers belongs among the elemental men. Both in character and achievement he goes back to the primary stuff of which great men are made. The greatness which time does not disturb—that alone is elemental. Eternity is set in its heart. Centuries only lengthen the calendar of true greatness, and increase the dimensions in which it is measured. Shakespeare is greater by every mentionable dimension. Millenniums only raise Plato higher. His greatness is infused with the elemental and cannot perish. Socrates is more majestic than when he drank the hemlock. Luther still rolls the tides of his influence through the ages. Cromwell still rules England. Washington still rules America. Henry Ward Beecher is assailed. He had faults. But he also had qualities by which the race has its sustenance; and it will not let him die. "A solar man, of ample nature," was Thomas Chalmers.

1. The deepest sources of his strength must be sought in the constraint under which he was brought to the consciousness of God. "Events are God's," he said. He had a native consciousness of God which indicated in him the potency of extraordinary achievement. He was consumed with a consciousness of the God who, as he came to know, had always been conscious of him, and was ever seeking to take deeper hold on his consciousness. His journals and private letters abound with the conviction that he had to deal with God. "The very sense of being made by another,"

he says, "how it should annihilate the sovereignty of self."
"O do thou, the very God of peace, sanctify me wholly,
and enable me to cut off the right hand, or pluck out the
right eye." "Here is a man," said Lord Rosebery, "bus-
tling, striving, organizing, speaking, and preaching with the
dust and fire of the world on his clothes, but carrying his
shrine with him everywhere."

2. Pivotal in his experience both as a man and a preacher
was his profound and conscious conversion. Men may say
what they will about the psychology of conversion, but
Chalmers writes his own. The depth of the evangelical impression made on his soul was marvelous. The saintly Andrew Fuller visited him soon after his conversion and was
brought under such constraint to the force of the fact to
which Chalmers testified that afterwards he wrote him:
"After parting with you, I was struck with the importance
which may attach to a single mind receiving an evangelical
impression." The sagacity of the remark had an admirable
illustration in the whole life and ministry of Chalmers. This
evangelical impression he lavishly poured out in his preaching. The fervor with which he thrust forth the call of the
gospel had its springs in those deep centers of his being
where his conversion first of all so finely registered its effects.

3. The control of action by the Christian conscience came
to be established in him as a token of the total integrity of his
nature. Why should he say beforehand whether he would
go to Glasgow? Why should he give an intimation whether
he would accept the chair of theology in Edinburgh? Why
should a man bound as he was to God and his own conscience put himself at the disposal of tentative proposals?
Let the whole matter be openly laid before him and then he
would decide. He had a conscience that kept sleepless
watch over every mood of his soul. How then could he
create moods by anticipation? This may be said by some

to be spinning a very fine thread; but it was the very soul
of the action of Chalmers. His conscience kept watch over
him, and he kept watch over his conscience. He is ever
charging himself to keep a good conscience. "Do I seek the
glory of God?" he asks himself after he has preached. "Have
I no secret longings after my own glory?" He is unconsciously his own best witness to the high-toned integrity of
his conscience.

4. The power of intellect he had to apply and did apply
to the tasks of his life does not require to be exhibited.
When he turned away from all the paths of human preferment and laid the unmaimed gift of his intellect on an altar
of burnt-offering raised through God's grace by his own
hand, he performed a service for Christian preaching the full
measure of which men are still endeavoring to take. What
with a gift for both mathematics and metaphysics, for both
natural and moral philosophy, for both natural and revealed
religion, and with a gift of imagination worthy of a poet, he
had much to offer. But he had nothing which he had not
received; and few could ever have given humbler recognition of this fact than he.

He had a remarkable power of mental abstraction, of
withdrawing a subject, even though it were itself a subject
of the most abstruse kind, from all other subjects and setting
it apart in absorbed contemplation. There was in his mind
at the same time a rare power of concentration. These two,
abstraction and concentration, made the mental act complete. None of this did he withhold from the humblest
task. Not content with his settled employment in Edinburgh, he went into the Westport, one of the most abandoned districts of the city, and established Christian agencies for the uplift of the population. He made a tanner's
loft his preaching place, and there poured forth upon the
untutored people a flood of eloquence which he never sur-

passed in the high places of the great city's religious concourse. Nowhere does his greatness appear greater, nor the
benignity of his soul more benignant, than in that tanner's
loft where men came in their common attire as in an interval
of evil or sorrow or toil they hearkened to his voice. A poor
woman of the place was asked if she ever went to church.
"Yes," she answered. "Where?" "O, just to the tannery
hall ower by—ane Chalmers preaches—I like to encourage
him, puir body!"

He never underestimated the opportunity which called
to his own or to another's gifts. When Thomas Guthrie had
come from beautiful Arbilot to St. John's in Edinburgh he
was standing one day on George IV Bridge overlooking the
poor, neglected, and noisome brood of the Cowgate which
constituted his charge, feeling discouraged, doubtless, over
the prospect as contrasted with what he had left, and wondering how he should do. He felt a heavy hand laid on his
shoulder, and heard the gruff voice of Dr. Chalmers say,
"A magnificent field of operations, sir—a magnificent field
of operations!"

5. The prodigious power of his delivery and the effect of
it in his sermons all but surpasses our later credence. He
read his sermons. There was not wanting a rather plentiful
sprinkling of such terms as "vesicular properties," "un-
bridled appetency," and the like. His physical action was
awkward and inadvertent. There was, as John Caird said,
"a continuous sawing the air with one hand whilst the other
followed the lines of a closely read manuscript." But he
made that manuscript somehow a marvelous conductor of his
own earnestness and energy to his audience. His action
would become at times so intense that he would foam at the
lips; and, having exhausted himself, he would have to sit
down in the midst of a discourse to rest before proceeding
to a finish.

The effect of his sermons was profound. Gladstone long remembered having heard him, and said: "I never heard any one preach who more completely conveyed his own moral character through the medium of every sentence he spoke." It was said of his first sermon in Glasgow that "tears fell like raindrops on the manuscript" as he spoke. A hearer of a General Assembly sermon said: "Probably no congregation since the days of Massillon ever had their attention more completely fixed, their understandings more enlightened, their passions more agitated, and their hearts more improved."

He liked, and yet did not like, the crowding of the people to hear him. "Preached in the forenoon to an immense crowd. . . . Preached to another very immense crowd." So runs the journal of a single day. He would not have been human not to have been gratified. Yet he came to have "a most nervous repugnancy to crowds." It was not easy to preach to twenty-six persons in a pew intended for fourteen, or to three thousand in an auditorium built for seventeen hundred. Once at least he had to go through a window to get to his pulpit. Sometimes the crowds outside would crash the doors in when the inside was already full. Once when this had happened at an afternoon service Dr. Wardlaw was present. Chalmers chafed under the confusion and disorder. Complaining to Dr. Wardlaw as they left the church, he explained that he had preached the same sermon in the morning; and with the very purpose of preventing the annoyance of a crowd, he had intimated that he would preach it again at the afternoon service. Turning naïvely to Wardlaw, Chalmers asked him, "Have *you* ever tried that?" Wardlaw did not remember that he had.

6. Chalmers was an establisher of Scottish pulpit standards. He was, says Cadman, "the primate of a preaching ministry which has maintained the highest average in the

world." He touched the Scottish pulpit and bade it see
what it had not seen and hear what it had not heard, bade
it bound into a power the glory of which it can never lose.
He took up the Scotch pastorate and sent it into the slums,
turned it into the Cowgate and the Westport, and bade it
expand to the needs of the nation. He took the Scottish
ministry as it came to him in the schools and sent it to the
ends of the earth. He blessed Scotch preaching as God
blessed him. His qualities, says Taylor, "so finely balanced,
were all sublimed by genius, and heated to a constant in-
candescence by the consecrating influence of the Holy
Spirit." This preaching was his bequest to the Christian
pulpit.

He commanded all audiences from the tanner's loft to St.
Giles. He had incarnated the old prophetic word that "every
valley shall be exalted, and every mountain and hill shall
be made low." Preaching once in the Tron Church in the
interest of a provision for the poor, the magistrates of the
city being present, he had taken the "Dissipation of Large
Cities" for his theme. Urging the duty of abstention from
the unclean convivialities of fashionable social life, he was
insisting that there could be no compromise. One who gave
his countenance to them at all was guilty of all. Clenching
his right hand and bending straight across the desk, he
looked full in the face of the Town Council and said:

It is quite in vain to say that he has only sanctioned one part of such
an entertainment. He has as good as given his connivance to the whole
of it, and left behind him a discharge in full of all its abominations; and,
therefore, be they who they may, whether they rank among the proudest
aristocracy of our land, or are charioted in splendor, as the wealthiest of
our citizens, *or flounce in the robes of magistracy*, it is his part to keep
as purely and indignantly aloof from such society as this, as he would
from the vilest and most debasing associations of profligacy.

It was difficult to tell which was the more startled, the
audience or the magistrates.

His sermon on the "Expulsive Power of a New Affection"
serves well to exhibit his method in sermon construction.
Having seized the true idea of the text as expressed in the
theme, he proceeds to present the idea as the continually re-
curring thought of the entire discourse, this idea being con-
structively set forward in argument, illustration, application
until the dullest hearer could hardly fail to be impressed
with the preacher's purpose. The preacher is not less noble
than the poet who on the same theme has sung,

> "The rich, golden shaft
> Hath killed the flock of all affections else
> That live in her."

Best of all the descriptive tributes to his preaching which
have been preserved is that by young John Brown, author
afterwards of the immortal "Rab and His Friends." He
was in the country on a school vacation, and "heard that
the famous preacher was to be at a neighbor parish church."

Off we set, a cart full of irrepressible youngsters. . . . As we entered
the kirk we saw a notorious character, a drover, who had much of the
brutal look of what he worked in. . . . He was our terror, and we not
only wondered but were afraid when we saw *him* going in. The kirk was
as full as it could hold. . . . The minister comes in, homely in his dress
and gait, but having a great look about him, "like a mountain among
hills." . . . He looks vaguely round upon his audience, as if he saw in
it *one great object, not many*. . . . He read a few verses quietly, then
prayed briefly, solemnly, with his eyes wide open all the time, but not
seeing. Then he gave out his text; we forget it, but its subject was, 'Death
reigns.' . . . He told us how death reigns—everywhere, at all times, in
all places; how we all knew it, how we would yet know more of it. The
drover, who had sat down in a seat opposite, was gazing up in a state of
stupid excitement; he seemed restless, but never kept his eye from the
speaker. The tide set in; everything added to its power; deep called to
deep, imagery and illustration poured in, and every now and then the
theme—the simple, terrible statement—was repeated. . . . How astonished and impressed we all were! He was at the full thunder of his
power; the whole man was in an agony of earnestness. The drover was
weeping like a child, the tears running down his ruddy, coarse cheeks, his

face opened out and smoothed like an infant's, his whole body stirred with emotion. We had all insensibly been drawn out of our seats, and were converging toward the wonderful speaker; and when he sat down, after warning each one of us to remember who it was and what it was that followed Death on the pale horse, and how alone we could escape, we all sunk back into our seats. . . . How he poured out his soul before God in giving thanks for the Abolisher of death! Then a short psalm, and all was ended.

We went home quieter than we came. We did not recount the foals, with their long legs, and roguish eyes, and their sedate mothers; we did not speculate upon whose dog *that* was, and whether that was a crow or a man in the dim moor. We thought of other things—that voice, that face, those great simple, living thoughts, those floods of resistless eloquence, that piercing, shattering voice, that "tremendous necessity."

Chalmers was stormy, but he made the "irrepressible youngsters" quiet.

Dr. Chalmers reached the age of sixty-seven in the year 1847. On the evening of May 30, in that year, he left the family circle in one of his most cheerful moods and retired to his room. In the morning they found him in that posture the most care-free and reposeful of any they were ever accustomed to see him assume, resting upon his bed, in the calm and unterrifying embrace of death. He had fallen upon that endless repose some hours before. He had obtained the last grace of the Spirit of whom he wrote, that he is "still to meet the promise of help to the infirmity of our understanding with a prayer for that help."

His funeral "seemed truly a national act, and the holy catholic Church might be said to follow in the train." The end must come to all. But:

> "Death makes no conquest of this conqueror;
> For now he lives in fame, though not in life."

V

JOHN HENRY NEWMAN

(1801–1890)

A FORECASTER CONFOUNDED

WILKINSON in his "Modern Masters of Pulpit Discourse" expressed explicitly the opinion that the fame of Newman would decline. "On the whole," said he, "I conclude that, *unless the English-speaking world shall become Roman Catholic,* Newman's fame, whether as preacher or as writer, is destined not to wax but to wane." His "phenomenal reputation" was due, "in chief part, to two accidentally coöperative influences." One of these was "a personal or traditional comradeship working in his favor," particularly through the contacts he had had at Oxford. The other was a popular reaction toward him on account of the unjust treatment from which he had so long been conceived to suffer. "When these two influences have ceased," Wilkinson said, "as with mere lapse of time they will cease, to work in favor of Newman, his fame will gradually decline from its present rank as a star of the first magnitude in the English literary heaven to the rank of a luminary still bright indeed with a pure and steady ray, but not particularly distinguishable in the great and growing galaxy which zones that intellectual sky with light."

Well, let this sky now be scanned, by whatever watcher, for the waxing or the waning of those lights which the English pulpit of the nineteenth century thrust upon its screen, and let him tell us which have waxed and which have waned. Not the dearest friend or admirer Newman ever had, whether it were Ambrose, St. John, or the Pope who made him a

(160)

cardinal, or Keble, or Hurrell Froude, or Dean Church, or Father Ryder could wish for a surer increase of his fame. The two latest writers on the subject are Garvie in "The Christian Preacher," and Cadman in "Ambassadors of God." The former says: "There can be no hesitation about the place to be assigned to Cardinal John Henry Newman." Cadman names him among seven of the greatest British preachers of the nineteenth century. None of the others he names—Chalmers, Hall, Robertson, Dale, Spurgeon, Mc-Laren—approaches Newman, he says, "in his analysis of the human spirit, his exquisite English, his tender if indignant fervor." And yet it is just this "exquisite English" which Wilkinson selects for his merciless and pedantic dissection. There were here and there faults of expression in Newman, no doubt, as there may be faults in a beautiful face, but the faults need not obscure the beauty.

DIM AND UNDISTINGUISHED DAYS

An autobiographical memoir records that John Henry Newman was born in London on February 21, 1801, and that he was baptized in the Church of St. Benet Fink on the 9th of April following. There was in those days a garden in London hard by Bloomsbury Square where he and Benjamin Disraeli used to play together when they were boys nine or ten years old. His father was a London banker, though not in opulent circumstances. His mother, whose name was Fourdrinier, was of French Protestant extraction, a member of a family which fled to Holland at the time of the revocation of the Edict of Nantes, and settled in England a generation later. There is nothing to show, as has sometimes been suggested, that there was anything Jewish in the Newman ancestry. Mrs. Newman was a moderate Calvinist and trained her children in that way. She instructed them in Scott, the commentator, in Romaine, and Newton,

11

and others of that school. Beyond anything that she knew she was influencing the mind of the child destined to be the most distinguished of all her group. Newman declared that to the effect produced upon him by Scott he almost owed his soul.

The children of the Newman household were divided equally between boys and girls. John Henry was the oldest of them all. He was devoted to his mother, tender and sympathetic toward his sisters, and attentive to the servants to whom he read and explained serious books. Law's "Serious Call" was one of his early adventures in literature, though it is not clearly indicated whether he used it in his school for the servants. Between him and his brother Francis, who was himself a brilliant man, there were not in later life any cordial relations.

From a child he was characterized by that undue personal sensitiveness which so afflicted him amid the stress of after years. He had a very active and vivid imagination, and a strong tendency to superstition. His mind dwelt on "unknown influences"; on "magical powers and talismans"; he used "to wish the 'Arabian Nights' were true"; and "used constantly to cross himself on going into the dark." In his earliest childhood home he thought there had appeared to him those angel faces which he had "loved long since and lost awhile."

He was never in a public school, but was eight and a half years in a private school in Ealing. He was hardly known to take any part at all in the games of his schoolmates, but in more sober ways was influential among them.

His early home training made him familiar with the Bible, but left him without definite religious experience. He had a wish "to be virtuous, but not religious." There was something in the idea of religion which he seemed not to like; and he declared that he did not "see the meaning of loving God." In his sixteenth year his conversion came, profoundly changing his life. From the Rev. Walter Mayer he received deep religious impressions which bore immediate fruit in the beginning of a new life. There was no marked disquietude of feeling, none of the "special Evangelical experiences," as he himself described it, but "a return to, a renewing of principles under the power of the Holy Spirit which I had already felt and in a measure acted on when I was young." His matured verdict on his conversion he gives in the "Apologia": "I believed that the inward conversion of which I was conscious (and of which I am still more certain than that I have hands and feet) would last into the next life, and that I was elected to eternal glory." This experience, and the Calvinistic aspect which it assumed to his mind, confirmed him, he says, "in my mistrust of material phenomena, and in making me rest in the thought of two, and two only, absolute and luminously self-evident beings—myself and my Creator."

Again he says in the "Apologia," speaking still after the manner of his feeling about his conversion: "If I am asked why I believe in God, I answer that it is because I believe in myself, for I find it impossible to believe in my own existence (and of that fact I am sure) without believing also in the existence of Him, who lives as a Personal, All-seeing, All-judging Being in my conscience."

At the early age of sixteen, in truth, when he was only about midway his sixteenth year, he reached the conclusion that it was God's will that he should lead a celibate life. This conviction was but slightly shaken from time to time until he was twenty-eight, after which it "possessed him without a break."

Newman was entered as a student at Trinity College, Oxford, on December 14, 1816, and went into residence the following June. He entered in a transport of expectation, and was awed at the thought of the reality of his opportunity. The extent and variety of the college dinners surprised him; but from the wine-parties he promptly revolted. He was very glad to go to prayers after the party, for he was sure that he "was not entertained with either the drinking or the conversation."

Two years after his entrance he obtained a scholarship the proceeds of which alone and naught else enabled him to continue in school. In June, 1819, he was entered as a student in Lincoln's Inn and destined to the law. The direction his life was now intended to take awakened fears within him that he was "too solicitous about fame." He found himself physically unable to sustain with too great fullness of application the tasks laid out for him, and the character of some of his work produced a disappointment which no subsequent success could ever completely erase from his mind. He was obliged, too, to hasten his work because of financial pressure arising from the failure of the banking house with which his father was connected. The difficulty he had had with his studies led his father to doubt whether after all the more or less contentious life of the lawyer was desirable for him; and Newman's own profound religious tastes gave the final determination of a vocation in favor of the ministry.

In 1823 Newman won a scholarship in Oriel College, then the most distinguished in the University, and felt it a partial compensation for his earlier failure. He had deprecated any harboring of a desire for repute or wealth, but now found himself "perpetually praying to get into Oriel and to obtain the prize for my essay." He fears that he is inconsistent. Nevertheless, he was greatly elated over his success. "The Oriel fellowship," says Wilfrid Ward, author of "The Life of John Henry Cardinal Newman," "was the turning point in Newman's early life. Not only did it give him an assured position, but, to use his own words, 'it opened upon him a theological career, placing him upon the high and broad platform of University society and intelligence, and bringing him across those various influences personal and intellectual . . . whereby the religious sentiment in his mind which had been his blessing from the time he left school, was gradually developed and formed and brought on to its legitimate issues.'"

The directing of his course from this time onward lay not with the school alone. In the same year that he entered Oriel he read Butler's "Analogy," and there encompassed his mind ever afterwards two of the most important principles of his thinking. One of these was that the less certain aspects of natural religion should be interpreted in terms of revealed religion, and not on the contrary principle. And the other, in Butler's own language, was that "probability is the guide of life." This of course was to be taken in the sense in which Butler uses it.

Newman's extreme shyness and almost unconquerable sensitiveness left him strangely open to personal influence. He suffered in society, fearing the proprieties which he might violate, and grieving afterwards over those which he felt he must have committed; and yet he profited much above the ordinary measure by his personal contacts, as if it were a sort of counterpart of his shyness. His rigorous Calvinism, too, drove him into isolation of thought and solitariness of soul and increased his need of contact with others. Had it not been for the channels through which personal influence operated upon him he must inevitably have suffered a much more severe separation from his fellows. But these channels were open both ways; they were open both to receive and to give forth personal influence. In a reference to Newman's sermon on "Personal Influence" Dr. Alexander Whyte remarks that "all his days he was his own best ex-

ample of that kind of influence, both as experiencing and
as exercising it."

Richard Whately, afterwards archbishop and author of
well-known treatises on logic and rhetoric, was Newman's
first and one of his foremost influences at Oriel. His mind
matured slowly and Whately rendered him a great service,
both here and in the matter of his excessive shyness. Whately was a great talker "who endured very readily the silence
of his company," and Newman was willing to make his contribution to silence. "While I was still awkward and timid
in 1822," says Newman, "he took me by the hand, and
acted the part to me of a gentle and encouraging instructor.
He, emphatically, opened my mind, and taught me to think
and use my reason. . . . He had done his whole work toward
me, or nearly so, when he had taught me to see with my own
eyes and to walk with my own feet." Their cordial relations did not continue through life, but Newman's sense of
gratitude never abated.

Dr. Hawkins, afterwards provost of the College, communicated to Newman his finer care in the use of words,
delicacy in discriminating between cognate ideas, and that
habit "of obviating mistakes by anticipation," which to
Newman's surprise was taken "to savor of the polemics of
Rome." From the same source he also learned "the doctrine of tradition," and had his mind quickened in the direction it was naturally prone to take. By the time he wrote
his "Arians of the Fourth Century" he was ready to give
"full expression to his confidence that dogma is the backbone of religion."

More powerful in determining the final direction of his
life than any of the other influences which wrought upon
him at this critical time was that of Hurrell Froude. It was
not only the high tone of his character and the fine quality
of his intellect which told upon Newman, but he taught him

"to look with admiration toward the Church of Rome, and in the same degree to dislike the Reformation." "I never, on the whole," said Newman, "fell in with so gifted a person. . . . I cannot describe what I owe to him—as regards the intellectual principles, the philosophy of religion and morals."

No accounting of the personal influences to which Newman proved himself so susceptible can omit John Keble, author of the "Christian Year," a noble book which in the very fineness of its qualities is but a mirror to the fine qualities of the mind and heart of its author. "Having carried off as a mere boy," says Newman, "the highest honors of the University, he had turned from the admiration which haunted his steps, and sought for a better and holier satisfaction in pastoral work in the country." But the country could not conceal him. He was brilliant, but lowly-minded. He had the finest prospects opening before him, and became a country curate. He was very devout, and yet a High-Churchman. He was a composite of the influences to which Newman was most susceptible, and perhaps did as much as Froude to carry him to Rome.

Newman served diligently in the curacy of St. Clements for two years, dating from 1824, the year of his ordination. He was made a tutor of Oriel and resigned his curacy.

DESERVED AND UNDEBATABLE DISTINCTION

In 1828 Newman was made Vicar of St. Mary's, Oxford. The distinction he won there, more particularly as a preacher, cannot be disputed or debated. The output of that pulpit under his administration has been published in eight volumes of "Parochial and Plain Sermons," in one volume of "University Sermons," and in one volume entitled "Subjects of the Day." Whether these sermons be taken for their religious, their intellectual, their doctrinal, their ethical, their literary, or their homiletical value, they must be ranked very high. They have a value arising out of the very restraint under which their author labored ere the time elapsed when he should become a Roman Catholic. They show a great mind in unconscious struggle with itself, and in conscious struggle with the world about it. And a great mind under strain and in process of finding its own release is always vital and productive. The Oxford sermons have this value which the later Roman Catholic sermons do not have, while the latter have a certain value which attaches to the product of a mind which has at last come to rest on its own ultimate issues.

Everybody in the University and its community and from beyond came not so much to the services as to these sermons. The congregations, which met in the afternoon, numbered "probably two or three times the whole population of the parish." It came to be, said Lord Coleridge, "as remarkable a congregation as I should think was ever gathered to hear regularly a single preacher. There was scarcely a man of note in the University, old or young, who did not, during the last two or three years of Newman's incumbency, habitually attend the service and listen to the sermons." Deans of colleges changed the dinner hour, "so as to make the hearing of Newman's sermon and a dinner in Hall incompatible transactions." It was said that "one Dean certainly, who had changed the time of his College dinner to prevent others going, constantly went himself; and the outward interest in the teaching was but one symptom of the deep and abiding influence which Cardinal Newman exercised." Though at the time he was of course not a cardinal.

A single sermon might change a career. R. W. Church heard the sermon on "The Ventures of Faith," and felt himself profoundly arrested by its demand for something really ventured for Christ, for some real constraint laid upon the

life by faith in Him, and some real alteration in conduct and
its ventures in proportion to the greatness of this faith. He
counted the occasion as in some sort a turning point in his life.

Gladstone was an undergradute at the time and describes
Newman's manner in the pulpit: "Without ostentation or
effort, but by simple excellence, he was constantly drawing
undergraduates more and more around him. His manner
in the pulpit was one about which, if you considered it in
its separate parts, you would arrive at very unsatisfactory
conclusions. There was not very much change in the in-
flection of the voice; action there was none. His sermons
were read, and his eyes were always bent on his book; and
all that, you will say, is against efficiency in preaching. Yes,
but you must take the man as a whole, and there was a
stamp and a seal upon him; there was a solemn sweetness
and music in the tone; there was a completeness in the figure,
taken together with the tone and with the manner, which
made even his delivery, such as I have described it, and
though exclusively from written sermons, singularly attractive." This judgment has the greater value in that it
came from Gladstone in his maturer life in the form of an
address on preaching.

Another sketch of the remarkable impression made by
the man in his pulpit is drawn by Principal Shairp: "The
look and the bearing of the preacher was of one who dwelt
apart, and who, though he knew his age well, did not live
in his age. From his seclusion of study, and abstinence, and
prayer; from habitual dwelling in the unseen, he seemed to
come forth that one day of the week to speak to others of
the things he had seen and known in secret." Speaking of
the sermons rather than of the preacher, Dean Church has
said: "Dr. Newman's sermons stand by themselves in modern English literature: it might even be said, in English
literature generally. There have been equally great master-

pieces of English writing in this form of composition, and there have been preachers whose theological depth, acquaintance with the heart, earnestness, tenderness, and power have not been inferior to his. But the great writers do not touch, pierce, and get hold of minds as Newman does, and those who are famous for the power and results of their preaching do not write as he does. We have learned to look upon Dr. Newman as one of those who have left their mark very deep on the English language. Little, assuredly, as their writer originally thought of such a result, the sermons have proved a permanent gift to our literature, of the purest English, full of spring, clearness, and force."

Dr. Alexander Whyte, the great Edinburgh Evangelical, was so great an admirer of Newman that his admiration only enhanced a certain disappointment which he felt in him. He greatly admired the homiletics of the sermons. "The very titles of Newman's sermons," he said, "are a study in homiletics. . . . A carpenter friend of mine once told me that sometimes on a Sabbath night he took down the selected volume of Newman's sermons just for the benefit and the delight of reading over their titles." Just to read over the catalogue of his publishers he thought was "in itself a great lesson in pulpit literature." But Newman was not sufficiently evangelical for him. "Looked at as pure literature," he said, "Newman's St. Mary's sermons are not far from absolute perfection; but looked at as pulpit work, as preaching the gospel, they are full of the most serious, and even fatal, defects. . . . They are not, properly speaking, New Testament preaching at all." None could be more exacting of the evangelical element in preaching than Dr. Whyte. Something of truth has to be allowed in what he says. Nevertheless, none could be more earnestly desirous that men should be sincerely religious than Newman. He was as antagonistic to the shallow religion of the day, wherever he found it, as Dr. Whyte himself could be. In a sermon on this very subject, "The Religion of the Day," he asks whether the state of the world is not that to which it might be brought "quite independent of religion, by the mere influence of education and civilization," and then goes on to say: "I do not at all deny that this spirit of the world uses words, and makes professions which it would not adopt except for suggestions of Scripture; nor do I deny that it takes a general coloring from Christianity, so as really to be modified by it, nay, in a measure enlightened and exalted by it. Again, I fully grant that many persons in whom this bad spirit shows itself are but partially infected by it, and at bottom, good Christians, though imperfect. Still, after all, here is an existing teaching, only partially evangelical, built upon worldly principle, yet pretending to be the gospel, dropping one whole side of the gospel, its austere character, and considering it enough to be benevolent, courteous, candid, correct in conduct, delicate—though it includes no true fear of God, no fervent zeal for His honor, no deep hatred of sin; . . . in a word, no seriousness—and therefore is neither hot nor cold, but (in Scripture language) *lukewarm*. Thus the present age is the very contrary to what are commonly called the dark ages; and together with the faults of those ages we have lost their virtues. I say their virtues; for even the errors then prevalent, a persecuting spirit, for instance, fear of religious inquiry, bigotry, these were, after all, but perversions and excesses of *real virtues*, such as zeal and reverence; and we, instead of limiting and purifying them, have taken them away root and branch. Why? Because we have not acted from a love of Truth, but from the influence of the Age." And in the same sermon he utters those words so out of the fashion for his time which have been the occasion of suspicion to many, but which might better be taken as a challenge to a more genuine

Christian life: "Here I will not shrink from uttering my firm conviction, that it would be a gain to this country, were it vastly more superstitious, more bigoted, more gloomy, more fierce in its religion, than at present it shows itself to be. Not, of course, that I think the tempers of mind herein implied desirable, which would be an evident absurdity; but I think them infinitely more desirable and more promising than a heathen obduracy, and a cold, self-sufficient, self-wise tranquillity."

Dr. Whyte thinks that "Newman never was converted as John Wesley, say, was converted," and consequently Newman never preached any such sermon at St. Mary's as Wesley preached in the same place on the text, "By grace are ye saved through faith." And yet who can doubt either the depth or the genuineness of Newman's conversion? Perhaps after all God allows more for differences in men than men do themselves.

In December, 1832, Hurrell Froude went to the Mediterranean for his health, and asked Newman, who might well go for the same purpose, to accompany him. They came to Rome on the journey, and Newman thought it "the most wonderful place in the world." But he does not doubt that the religion it harbors is a "wretched perversion of the truth."

Returning from Rome to Sicily, he had a dangerous illness and was detained for three weeks. His attendant thought he would die, but he insisted that he would live, and from this crisis in his life dated a definite conviction that there was a work for him to do in England. In the stress of his illness he had an almost crushing sense of human frailty and sin, but there accompanied it a strong feeling of self-abandoning trust in God. He set out from Palermo in an orange boat for Marseilles. In the Straits of Bonifacio the boat was becalmed, the journey was delayed, and it was there that he wrote the familiar lines, "Lead, kindly Light," which have since found their way into the hearts of thousands whose lips have never called the name of Newman.

Newman reached home five days before Keble preached in the University pulpit the sermon on "National Apostasy," which event he ever afterwards considered and kept "as the start of the religious movement of 1833." From this circumstance, augmented by the influence which Keble otherwise exerted, Newman regarded him as "the true and primary author of the Tractarian Movement." It was a movement which was destined to create a great stir in English religious circles and to make itself a divider of many hearts. Newman conceived that he had a mission to make war against the Liberalism in thought which was menacing ancient institutions both in Church and State, and which he thought if left unchecked would not cease from its work till it had destroyed religion.

The Tractarian Movement had for its more immediate object so to strengthen the position and authority of the Church of England as to enable it to withstand the disintegrating forces represented by the liberal tendencies of the time. In order to do this its establishment upon apostolic foundations must be shown, and the catholic elements of its constitution must be reasserted. Again, in doing this special emphasis was placed upon the defense of Apostolic Succession and the integrity of the Book of Common Prayer.

There were ninety of the tracts in all, and Newman was the author of twenty-seven of them. A variety of authors contributed the rest. It will not be forgotten that Dr. Pusey joined the movement. Newman, however, was both its intellectual and religous leader, and it is said that but for interest in him the tracts would no longer be read. The issue of the movement was not at first foreseen, whether by those inside or outside its main currents. And yet that issue was hardly less than inevitable. Some would drift, or even be driven to Rome. Others would be driven into a deeper allegiance to the Church of England.

Newman's "University Sermons," except the first, which belonged to 1826, were produced during the progress of the Tractarian Movement. They were on the general subject of the philosophy of faith, and must be regarded as very remarkable sermons. It is said that they were regarded by Newman himself, as well as by some others, as "containing his best and most valuable thoughts." The last in the series upon "The Theory of Development in Religious Doctrine," and based on the text, "But Mary kept all these things, and pondered them in her heart," must in particular be allowed to be projected upon lofty levels both of thought and expression. Naturally, however, these sermons have not had the vogue of the more popular sermons preached at St. Mary's, or of his later Roman Catholic sermons, which were published as "Discourses to Mixed Congregations."

The village of Littlemore, not far out of Oxford, was attached to the parish of St. Mary's. From his early connection with the parish Newman had given catechetical instruction there on Sunday evenings. In 1836 he had built a chapel there and regarded the event as a landmark in his history. Eventually he had a home there, and his life there, as well as at Edgbaston in his later life, was according to Hutton "more than half monastic." He withdrew to continual and very retired residence there in 1842.

On the Road to Rome

Sarolea in his "Cardinal Newman," in "The World's Epoch Makers Series," gives the following reason why Newman became a Roman Catholic: "*Newman became a convert because Catholicism was adapted to his temperament, because there was a preëstablished harmony between his character and*

the Catholic system, because his soul was naturaliter catholica."
This may be regarded as conclusive in its philosophical com-
prehensiveness.   But certain details of his progress toward
Rome will throw much light on the transaction.

He started out, aided by the other Tractarians, to establish the apostolic connections of the Church of England.
As he began to doubt his being able to do this conclusively,
thoughts of the Roman Catholic Church as meeting the need
began to insinuate themselves into his mind.   As early as
1839 these misgivings as to the soundness of the Anglican
position began to disturb him.   In the pursuit of his Patristic
studies, in a review article by Dr. Wiseman, in one way and
in another these doubts were multiplied.   In 1843 he wrote
definitely to a friend that he believed the Roman Catholic
Church to be the church of the apostles.

No doubt it is also true that without entire consciousness
to himself he was moving in that direction from within.   Dr.
Whyte thought that no reader of his St. Mary's sermons
could fail to see his "Romeward footprints on every page."
If he had not gone to Rome, perhaps nobody would have
thought of this.   But once the journey was over everybody
could see the direction he was taking.

Then there came the proposal to establish an English bishopric in Jerusalem, the bishop to be consecrated by the
English Primate, and to be authorized to assume the spiritual and ecclesiastical care of any who offered themselves to
his jurisdiction, Lutherans, Calvinists, or any others.   This
seemed to Newman to cut the last ground from under the
claim of the English Church to be apostolic.

Again, his own position with respect to dogma was largely
determinative of the step he was destined to take.   He believed in a revelation from God as contained in the Scriptures if any man either in or out of Rome believed it.   But
he gave a large place, too large a place, to dogma.   Reve-

lation required to be supported, almost to be validated, by dogma; and dogma required for its definition and enforcement an authoritative Church. Hence, he came to regard both dogma, and an authoritative church, made necessary by the necessity for dogma, as important elements in the revelation itself. But the great object of Christ's incarnation was the revelation of God, and not dogmas concerning God. If there was to be a Church, there must be dogma, but the duty of defining the dogma which was to guard the revelation could itself only be secondary and subordinate. But Newman confused dogma with the essential content of the revelation, and virtually assumed the position that dogma was as necessary as the revelation itself. This was where he went wrong. Revelation was made to be dependent upon dogma in a way which no Protestant could admit. Having come thus far, he must either go on to Rome or find satisfaction in inconsistency.

There remains at least one very practical consideration which must have operated toward the determination of his Roman destiny. Wordsworth in a line has unwittingly described Newman. He was oppressed by

> "The heavy and the weary weight
> Of all this unintelligible world."

He came to believe that the weak and wavering ranks of mankind could never be steadied and instructed and guided and brought into subjection to the saving will of God except by the agency of some institution acting externally with authority to compass these great ends. Preaching on the text, "I came down from heaven, not to do mine own will, but the will of him that sent me," his theme being "God's Will the End of Life," he pictures the state of the world as he sees it: "The world goes from age to age, but the Holy Angels and Blessed Saints are always crying, Alas, alas! and

Woe, woe! over the loss of vocations and the disappointment of hopes, and the scorn of God's love, and the ruin of
souls. One generation succeeds another; and whenever they
look down upon earth from their golden thrones, they see
scarcely anything but a multitude of guardian spirits, down-
cast and sad, each following his charge, in anxiety, or in
terror, or in despair, vainly endeavoring to shield him from
the enemy and failing because he will not be shielded. Times
come and go and man will not believe, that that is to be
which is not yet, and that what now is only continues for a
season, and is not eternity. The end is the trial, the world
passes; it is but a pageant and a scene; the lofty palace
crumbles, the busy city is mute, the ships of Tarshish have
sped away. . . . O my Lord and Saviour, support me in that
hour in the strong arms of Thy Sacraments, and by the fresh
fragrance of thy consolations. Let the absolving words be
said over me, and the holy oil sign and seal me, and Thy
own body be my food, and Thy blood my sprinkling, and
let my sweet Mother Mary breathe on me, and my angel
whisper peace to me, and my glorious saints, and my own
dear father, Philip, smile on me; that in them all, and
through them all, I may receive the gift of perseverance,
and die, as I desire to live, in Thy faith, in Thy Church, in
Thy service, and in Thy love." It was but his own cry echo-
ing that of the angels and the saints, "Alas, alas! Woe,
woe!" And after all would a dying man better not go out
to meet his final account with God encumbered with all this
ceremonial luggage, as a good Protestant would call it, than
to go out with that fleshy confidence which has no consciousness that his soul was ever touched with any taint of evil
in all the experience of this life?

Preaching in his Roman Catholic days that remarkable
sermon on "The Salvation of the Hearer the Motive of the
Preacher," he exclaims: "My brethren, a large town like this

12

is a fearful sight." That expresses his feeling exactly. A large town with its woes, its sorrows, its sins, its degradation, its death, its stricken, staggering masses of human kind was to him an oppressive sight. To be in the world was to him almost like Dante's being in purgatory. He looked out upon the world with the compassion of Christ, but without His hope and confidence and courage. He fell back upon an infallible church by which alone his staggering hopes for mankind could be adequately sustained.

And so he went to Rome. He resigned at St. Mary's and retired to Littlemore while for two years more he tarried within the fold of the Church of England. He had sometime previously publicly retracted all that he had ever said against the Church of Rome. On October 8, 1845, he wrote to his sister Jemima:

> I must tell you what will pain you greatly, but I will make it as short as you would wish me to do. This night Father Dominic, the Passionist, sleeps here. He does not know of my intention; but I shall ask him to receive me into what I believe to be the One Fold of the Redeemer. This will not go till all is over.
> Ever yours affectionately,   JOHN H. NEWMAN.

Dr. Wiseman, at whose hands his confirmation took place, wrote of it: "He opened his mind completely to me; and I assure you the Church has not received, at any time, a convert who has joined her in more docility and simplicity of faith than Newman." There need not be any doubt entertained of the assurances he himself has given of the peace of mind and conscience he had in the change to the Church of Rome.

An offer of Old Oscott, which had been for a long time the property of the Church, was made to Newman and to others of the new converts, and was accepted. In course of time he went to Rome and received ordination to the priesthood, and had conferred upon him the degree of Doctor of

Divinity by the Pope. He accepted a place in the church
as an Oratorian, or member of a congregation of secular
priests—that is, priests who have taken no vows, who retain their patrimony, and contribute to the upkeep of the
oratory in which they live as a community. It is the only
congregation of priests in the Roman Church not molded
upon the monastic idea. Newman and his community was
settled at Birmingham. The details of his life hencefor-
ward it is impossible to follow in any contracted account.

The first product of his pen in his new ecclesiastical relations was "Loss and Gain." It is in the form of fiction
and contains some indications of the movements of his
mind after he was admitted to the Roman communion.
Next came his "Sermons Addressed to Mixed Congregations." The dedication, which was made to The Rt. Rev.
Nicholas Wiseman, is in Newman's best style. "These sermons," says Hutton, "have a definite tone and genius of
their own; they have more in them of the enthusiasm of a
convert than any other of Newman's publications, and altogether contain the most eloquent and elaborate specimens
of his eloquence as a preacher, and of his sense, if I may so
call it, of the religious advantages of his position as a spokes-
man of the great Church of Rome. They represent more
adequately Dr. Newman as he was when he first felt himself 'unmuzzled'. . . . than any other of his writings; and
though they have not to me quite the delicate charm of the
reserve, and I might almost say the shy passion, of his Oxford sermons, they represent the full-blown blossom of his
genius, while the former show it only in bud." In them is
distinctly seen the increasing ascendancy of the Roman
system over Newman's mind. This appears particularly in
the place assigned to Mary in the sermon on "The Glories
of Mary for the Sake of Her Son." Nowhere is he more incomprehensible to the Protestant mind than when he gives

expression to views such as these, or when he accepts the
dogma of the Immaculate Conception or the Assumption of
the Virgin, unsupported as they are by the least thread of
historic proof.

R. H. Hutton counts as a landmark in Newman's history
as a Roman Catholic the "Lectures on Anglican Difficulties,"
which he himself heard as a young man on the occasion of
their delivery in London. "I shall never forget," he says,
"the impression which his voice and manner, which opened
upon me for the first time in these lectures, made on me.
Never did a voice seem better adapted to persuade without
irritating. Singularly sweet, perfectly free from any dictatorial note, and yet rich in all the cadences proper to the
expression of pathos, of wonder, and of ridicule, there was
still nothing in it that any one could properly describe as
insinuating, for its simplicity, and frankness, and freedom
from the half-smothered notes which express indirect purpose, was as remarkable as its sweetness, its freshness, and
its gentle distinctness." Whether by calculated forensic intention or not the lectures avoided the most conspicuous
Roman Catholic difficulties.

Out of these lectures grew the Achilli suit for libel against
Newman. Achilli was a renegade Roman priest who had
been cast out and had taken to lecturing against the Church.
There was no doubt of the utter profligacy of his life, but
Newman in his reference to the case had taken his proof
secondhand, and Achilli by the connivance of the court, or
rather by the leaning of the court toward Protestant prejudices, gained the case. It cost Newman bitter heartache,
as well as £12,000 in money, an amount which he was only
able to pay through the voluntary generosity of his friends.

In 1852 Newman was sent to Ireland to lead a movement
for the founding of a Roman Catholic University there. He
had no gifts for this kind of administration and the under-

taking did not succeed in his hands. But lectures which he
prepared and delivered as an aid to the enterprise were collected into one of his rarest volumes called, "The Idea of a
University."   His contention that a true university cannot
exist and exclude the science of theology is theoretically incontestable.   Dr. Whyte with characteristic enthusiasm says
the book is "the universally accepted masterpiece on the
whole subject."   The chapters on "Literature" and on
"University Preaching" lead all others in permanent value.

"Callista," also done in Ireland, is one of the most delicate pieces of all the fine products of Newman's prolific pen.
It reaches its climax of interest and power in Agellius's offer
of marriage to Callista, who charges him with a certain
baseness in his love, else he could not have loved her better
than he loved Christ. And loving her better how could he
win her to Christ? "The reproaches she heaps on Agellius"
—again it must be Hutton who is quoted—"for not clearly
discriminating between his love for her and his wish for her
conversion, which she calls 'speaking one word for his Master and two for himself,' and the deep disappointment with
which she discovers, or fancies she discovers, that Agellius
after all is a good deal more taken up with her and her
beauty than with the faith which she had hoped to have
found the one great reality of his existence, seem to me in
many respects better expressions of the true passion and
significance of Newman's own unique and single-hearted
life, than anything else which he has written." Callista was a
heathen and Agellius a Christian, and she had thought that he
wished most of all to win her to Christ. "O Agellius,"
she cries, "you have stood in the way of Him, ready to
speak of yourself, using Him as a means to an end."   And
she continues: "Here is a man who, so far from feeling himself blest, thinks I can bless him; comes to me, me, Callista,
a herb of the field, a poor weed exposed to every wind of

heaven and shrivelling before the fierce sun—to me he comes to repose his heart upon. But as for any blessedness he has to show me, why, since he does not feel any himself, no wonder he has none to give away." The book in the highest kindling of its passion is but a transcript of Newman's own devotion to Christ.

Apologia Pro Vita Sua

In January, 1864, Charles Kingsley in a review of Froude's "History of England," published in *Macmillan's Magazine*, used the following language: "Truth for its own sake had never been a virtue with the Roman clergy. Father Newman informs us that it need not be, and on the whole ought not to be; that cunning is the weapon which Heaven has given to the saints wherewith to withstand the brute male force of the wicked world which marries and is given in marriage." The basis of the charge, as Kingsley afterwards stated, was Newman's sermon on "Wisdom and Innocence" in the volume on "Subjects of the Day." Newman wrote to the publishers stating what he regarded to be the gravity of the offense committed by the publication of such a charge. Kingsley wrote to Newman replying to his communication to the publishers. Several letters passed between them without much progress toward a settlement of their differences. At length Newman made a rejoinder in which he published the correspondence and gave a witty and ironical summary of the course it had taken. This summary is in some of the best and most effective qualities of his style and is in part as follows: "Mr. Kingsley relaxes: 'Do you know I like your *tone*. From your *tone*, I rejoice, greatly rejoice, to be able to believe what you said.' I rejoin, '*Mean* it! I maintain I never *said* it, whether as a Protestant or as a Catholic.' Mr. Kingsley replies, 'I waive that point.' I object: 'Is it possible? What? Waive the main question? I either said

it or I didn't. You have made a monstrous charge against
me—direct, distinct, public; you are bound to prove it as
directly, as distinctly, as publicly; or to own you can't!'
'Well,' says Mr. Kingsley, 'if you are quite sure you did not
say it, I'll take your word for it, I really will.' My *word!* I
am dumb. Somehow I thought that it was my *word* that
happened to be on trial. The *word* of a Professor of lying
that he does not lie! But Mr. Kingsley reassures me. 'We
are both gentlemen,' he says; 'I have done as much as one
English gentleman can expect from another.' I begin to
see: he thought me a gentleman at the very time that he
said I taught lying on system. After all it is not I, but it
is Mr. Kingsley who did not mean what he said. *Habemus
confitentem reum.* So we have confessedly come round to
this, preaching without practicing; the common theme of
satirists from Juvenal to Walter Scott. 'I left Baby Charles,
and Steenie laying his duty before him,' says King James
(in Scott) of the reprobate Dalgarno; 'O Geordie, jingling
Geordie, it was grand to hear Baby Charles laying down
the guilt of dissimulation, and Steenie lecturing on the turpi-
tude of incontinence.'" This refined kind of sarcasm did not
much soothe the feelings of Mr. Kingsley, and he injected
a pamphlet into the controversy. And Newman wrote
the "Apologia."

"*Apologia Pro Vita Sua*" is the full title of this remarkable specimen of personal defense. It is remarkable in many
ways, but most of all for the tone of sincerity, of self-evidenc-
ing honesty with which Newman defends himself and his
associates of the Roman priesthood against Kingsley's
charge. Let a man think what he will of the Roman Catholic Church. The question here is, What does he think of
Newman? That he was but a crafty and shrewdly calculat-
ing casuist, insinuating his way where he dared not proceed
openly, is what no fair-minded Englishman believed after

this book. The acceptance of his plea on his own behalf by the great straight-thinking English public left nothing further in that direction to be achieved. And what pleased him still more was that he had opened the way for a fairer judgment of his co-religionists.

The book cost him infinite pains. It had to be prepared under pressure for serial publication in weekly installments. To open the secrets of his soul to the public gaze down to the very motives which filled him either with darkness or with light, as he himself judged, as they on their part must try to judge, cut square across the grain of his sensitive nature. There were times when he was "found with his head in his hands crying like a child over the, to him, well-nigh impossibly painful task of public confession." During a part of the writing he himself said he "could not get on from beginning to end for crying." Parts of it he wrote so many times over that his labor was immensely increased. "I am writing from morning to night," he said in a letter to Keble, "hardly having time for my meals. I write this during dinner time." No other time than for his meals would he suffer himself to take from the task. He would write for hours at a stretch, as many as sixteen hours being noted at one time, and at another he went on through the whole night. With such pains and tears did he seal his devotion to his own honor.

The only serious adverse criticism of the "Apologia" held that he had been "unduly sensitive and personally bitter toward Kingsley." He himself admitted that a casual reader might think that his language denoted anger, but he insisted that it did not. This was his last word on the subject: "I said mass for his soul as soon as I heard of his death."

Chafing and Constraint

Newman did not obtain at once nor for a long time all that he wished for in his change to the Church of Rome. Not

that there was anything sordid in his going. He had no
secular aims. He entertained no ecclesiastical ambitions.
Desires such as these he had stifled at their birth in his soul.
He had kept them far from his purpose and had fought
against them in his prayers. Manning, himself a recruit to
Rome from the Church of England, was made a cardinal
when Newman might have been. But nobody knew whether
he would have accepted had the office been offered him.
He kept his soul free from these entanglements, for he was
fighting another warfare.

But he did desire to get into a position from which he
might do something for the causes which lay nearest his
heart. After the supreme judgment of God he desired the
favorable judgment of those with whom he was associated
for the advancement of God's kingdom. He would labor
for God, but in and for the Church he had now made his
deliberate choice. This desire he was long not able to attain.
There were sad days and hardly any end to the weariness
of his waiting. Ward sets down the whole period 1859 to
1864 as a time of sadness and despondency. And again
there were peculiarly sad years from 1875 to 1879. He was
morbidly thin-skinned and sensitive and many a time was
the skin torn off down to the very roots of his sensitiveness.
"His own nature enhanced the effect of untoward circumstance." Most of all he was afflicted by the feeling that
justice had not been done him. He was never much praised,
nor very much appreciated until it was so late in life that
it seemed he never should be. The very joints of the scales
of justice seemed to be rusted in the world. And yet he
loved justice as if he carried her captive in his bosom. It
grieved him to think that men could so thwart the will of
God, that injustice could thrive in a world where the will
of God should be done. Rome and the Italians did not understand him. Pius IX seemed not to understand, and cer-

tainly did not appreciate him. He was not fully trusted even among English Catholics. He thought that sycophancy ought not to be a path to recognition and preferment in the Church. He was not the subject of a disappointed ambition. But he felt "a scorn and a wonder at the injustice shown me," he says, "and at the demand of toadyism on my part, if I was to get their favor, and the favor of Rome." He could not

> "Crook the pregnant hinges of the knee
> Where thrift may follow fawning."

He had abundant opportunity to prove by practice the greatness of patience. "Had he died directly after his sixty-third birthday," says Ward, "his career would have lived in history as ending in the saddest of failures."

GREAT POWERS RELEASED AND REALIZED

And yet the Hand he so trusted was on the helm of his life was really there. After all he had practiced a wise passivity. There was yet

> "Something ere the end,
> Some work of noble note may yet be done . . .
> 'Tis not too late to seek a newer world . . .
> Made weak by time and fate, but strong in will
> To strive, to seek, to find, and not to yield."

At last all the gloom of his sky cleared away and he had a serene and happy old age.

Under whatever stress of circumstances he may have labored, by whatever obstacles he may for a time have been thwarted, there were at length released in him those conspicuous capacities and powers which had in the final course of his life their lofty realization.

1. There are men who are developed in part by restraint. This was true of Newman. Under what severe if not studied restraint did he hold his remarkable literary powers,

say in the time of the composition of the "Parochial and Plain Sermons," or the "Tracts for the Times." Who could have suspected at the time that there were such powers in him, and that in due time they should be released for such an unwonted realization? But they were not to be released to any lower service. He could hardly ever have deliberately said so to himself, but they were to be reserved for the service of religion. "I am writing on my knees and in God's sight" is one of the arresting records of his diary. It was as if he all but unconsciously held his powers in leash until the time of their showing unto the world. There were those gifts and qualities in him which could only be released and come to their proper realization through his obedience to the high resolves of his nature. His great literary gifts were not to be used primarily for literature, but only for those ends of which literature itself must be the servant. How could such a man barter his powers and seek mere literary eminence? How could he flee from his high task for refuge in the temple of some lower intention? How could he cast such pearls as he kept in the treasuries of his mind and heart into the mire of some lower design? How could he prostitute these gifts committed of God to him for high and holy purpose to ends which to him at least, whatever men might say, would be base? It is scarcely to be said that he reasoned in this way. No; he acted in this way, and therein lay one of the sure signs of his greatness. It was as if he had an intuition how to reserve his gifts and use them for their destined end. The very restraint which he put upon his powers ere the time of their full release should come gave him the ability to shape more surely the ends which at last they should serve. He simply kept his powers under the constraint of the consecration to noble endeavor which he had put upon himself and upon them.

2. Another source of Newman's strength and effective-

ness of achievement is but the complement of his resolution, whether it were ever definitely taken or not, to release his powers, only in the service of tasks of the highest and most serious import. His practical purpose in life cannot be better stated than when it is said that it was that "of winning his fellow countrymen from their tepid and formal Christianity to a Christianity worthy of the name, in spite of obstacles in the way which he has recognized with a candor and a vivacity that have strangely led some of his critics into imagining that he appreciated even more the obstacles to belief than he did the spiritual power by which these obstacles were to be surmounted." He had no signal success, perhaps, in the immediate achievement of this aim. But his success in directing his powers to those high ends to which he would devote them has very rarely been surpassed. What he said of his writings might as justly be said of all his other work—namely, that while in a long course of years he had made many mistakes, that though he had nothing of the high perfection which belongs to the writings of the saints, still he trusted that he might claim that in all he had written there was to be found "an honest intention, an absence of private ends, a temper of obedience, a willingness to be corrected, a desire to serve the Holy Church, and, through Divine mercy, a fair share of success." This he said in reviewing his life on becoming a cardinal.

The "Dream of Gerontius" is his highest literary achievement in poetry. But who can detect in it any literary aim at all? His aim was not to write a poem, but to make a serious impression. And the singular thing about it is that the didactic aim does not detract from the literary excellence. The canons of literary criticism are reversed, and it is the spiritual interest which enhances the poetic beauty.

Making a gift of his violin to Mary Church, a daughter of Dean Church, on hearing of the engagement of her twin sister Helen to Francis Paget, afterwards Bishop of Oxford, he wrote as follows, addressing his letter to Dr. Church, who was one of the original donors of the violin to himself: "I said mass for Helen and her husband elect this morning. So did Fr. Neville. Of course it is, however glad an event, a very trying one for all of you, and not the least for Mary. I don't suppose she will find a fiddle make up for Helen, but it has struck me that you and Blachford will let me give the beautiful instrument you and he gave me, to Mary. I don't think she will refuse it; I hear much of her proficiency. You gave it me in 1865, and I had constant use and pleasure in the use till lately—but I find now I have no command of it; nay, strange to say I cannot count or keep time. This is a trouble to me; one gets an affection for a fiddle, and I should not like to go without getting it a good master or mistress. . . ." This is an exquisitely beautiful letter, to be sure, but again it is the practical purpose which prevails.

Who has rivaled him in holding gifts marking him for such eminence so steadily and so confidently to those high ends to which the best literature can never be more than an end? "If the English language," says Dr. Whyte, "has an angel residing in it or presiding over it, surely Newman is that angel. Or, at the least, the angel who has the guardianship of the English language committed to him, must surely have handed his own pen to Newman as often as that master has sat down to write English. No other writer in the English language has ever written it quite like Newman." But his genius was first religious, and then literary.

3. He has left an ineffaceable impression as a preacher. In that character he is best entitled to be known and to be longest remembered. His practice of the principles of homiletics is not to be sought too much in the technique of the sermon. He was not an orator. He was not a speaker, but a reader of his sermons. He was more a master in the science

than in the art of preaching. But he was too deeply steeped in the science to be devoid of the art. He was too great to end as a mere artist. He was too great to be swallowed up in the mere machinery of his art. But if one wants to know what the aim is in preaching, what, indeed, it may be in the single sermon, if he wishes to know how the preacher can find his way into the secret of the great spiritual realities, let the hindrances be what they may, if he wants to know what can be extracted for preaching from the fundamental simplicities of the Christian revelation, what place pathos has in the pulpit, what service the most intimate knowledge of our torn and distressed human condition may render, what worth a superb mastery of the English language may have as an instrument of expression, what directness, clearness, and energy of speech may profit both the speaker and the hearer, if he wants to know how the sermon ought to be free and progressive in its structure, above all, if he wants to know how reality in the man must support reality in the preacher, how earnestness in the preacher must sustain earnestness in the preaching, how sincerity in the man is the very pulse of sincerity in the preacher, how detachment from the world may aid devotion to God, and how serious and lofty and timeless is this whole business of Christian preaching, let him give his days and his nights to Newman.

4. The man and his life are summed up in seriousness of purpose and loftiness of charcter. The Christian in him was "as deep as his character." He lived a "lonely and severe and saintly life." Rarely has there been a man so eminent in the attention which the world bestowed upon him and so preëminent in the interest men have felt in him who has so conspicuously separated from all compromise and set apart for such intensity of emphasis the great and validated spiritual elements of human character, human action, and human destiny. In an age prolific of the prod-

ucts of material prosperity he set them all aside as of nothing worth, and separated himself to a quest of the spiritual which won the mind of mammonism itself to an admiration of the singularity of his devotion.

FRUITION AT THE FULL

Few lives have been more justified in their final issue than Newman's. After all he was to be a cardinal. This eminence he did not reach till he was seventy-eight. But he had eleven years still to live. Death came and spread its calm over his wonderful face in Birmingham on August 11, 1890. He had come by a strange course to his final preferment in the Church. He had opposed the proposal that the Vatican Council should issue the decree of papal infallibility. He had thought it both untimely and extreme in the way in which it was proposed that it should be declared. But it had been done, and he had acquiesced. Gladstone had attacked the action, and Newman had defended it. The principle of it he said he had all along accepted. Pius IX had died, and Leo XIII, more favorable to Newman, had come into his place. It was proposed that Newman should be made a cardinal and it was done. Cardinals who are not archbishops and so connected with a charge eleswhere must reside in Rome. Newman was too old to make the necessary change. A special decree was issued to cover his case and he was allowed to continue to live in Birmingham.

The Pope's action brought increased favor to the Roman Catholic Church in all England. Newman himself was lifted to the third heaven. The crown was set upon his whole career. Bitter memories and disappointments were swept out of his heart. He rejoiced in his elevation as a manifest token of God's unfailing love and good will toward him. Henceforth he was to be John Henry Cardinal Newman.

There shall come travailing after him through the centuries hard-pressed hearts singing after him his great and tender and strangely pathetic lines:

"Lead, kindly Light, amid th' encircling gloom,
  Lead thou me on!
The night is dark, and I am far from home;
  Lead thou me on!
Keep thou my feet; I do not ask to see
The distant scene; one step enough for me.

I was not ever thus, nor prayed that thou
  Shouldst lead me on;
I loved to choose and see my path; but now
  Lead thou me on!
I loved the garish day, and, spite of fears,
Pride ruled my will.   Remember not past years!

So long thy power hath blest me, sure it still
  Will lead me on
O'er moor and fen, o'er crag and torrent, till
  The night is gone,
And with the morn those angel faces smile,
Which I have loved long since, and lost awhile!"

VI

HENRY WARD BEECHER

(1813–1887)

Beecher Among the Biographers

Henry Ward Beecher's lot is still cast in the lap of the biographers. What is to be their final decree in the fixing of his fate is the occasion of some doubt among them. Anyway he is still prolific of biography. He is much to the biographical taste, and sets the biographical pen going afresh. Whether some of these biographers, as in other instances has been the case, do not play the game with loaded implements is not an unprovoked query.

There is a sort of inevitability about the man. He possesses a sort of ubiquity. Whoever begins with preachers and preaching sooner or later encounters him. There will not be one opinion about him. There never has been. There never will be. But there is no escaping an opinion. One of the severest tests that can be applied to the student of preaching is to know what he thinks of Beecher. And the stringency of the test is increased by insisting that he give an intelligent reason for his opinion. But whatever opinions come and go there still is Beecher in the acknowledged possession of incredible gifts and challenging an attention which some of the ablest men in the ministry have not been able at all to attract.

The annals of military aggression cannot neglect Napoleon; the annals of statesmanship and war cannot neglect Washington; the annals of statecraft cannot neglect Jefferson; the annals of diplomacy cannot neglect Franklin; the annals of world reconstruction cannot neglect Woodrow

13   (193)

Wilson; the annals of empire building cannot neglect Bismarck; the annals of parliamentary leadership and of oratory cannot neglect Gladstone; the annals of religious reform cannot neglect Luther; the annals of martyrdom cannot neglect Latimer; the annals of continental heroism cannot neglect David Livingstone; the annals of Christian preaching cannot neglect Henry Ward Beecher. He fills more space in the indices of books on preaching than any other American preacher. Look at this volume on homiletics produced by a German—he is there. This one is by a Scotchman—he is there. Here is one by an American; you need hardly look to know that he is there.

Comes now Mr. Paxton Hibben in a biased biography written forty years after Beecher's death and gives occasion to the mercurial Mr. Mencken to release against the famous preacher some of the well-stored contents of his treasury of iconoclasm, if, indeed, so mild a euphemism may be employed to express so overt an act. But this combination against the too great splendor of Beecher's fame, whether the militarists would call it a direct or flank movement, immediately arouses the concern of the editor of the Boston *Herald*, publisher of the attack on Beecher which he in turn himself attacks. "As we read Mr. Mencken's articles from week to week," says the *Herald*, "the impression deepens that he has lost control of his critical faculty. He has just put Henry Ward Beecher in the pillory—'on the operating table,' as he expresses it—using the opportunity afforded by a recently published life of the preacher to let loose his own estimate of the man whose career, he declares, 'provides the materials for another Elmer Gantry ten times worse than Lewis's." Continuing its challenge of Mencken's opinion the *Herald* says:

Now, is it not passing strange that a man should continue as pastor of a church for forty years, through sunshine and storm, if he were the kind of man that Mencken imagines? During the greater part of that forty years Beecher was the most famous preacher in America. He was constantly in the public eye. On the one occasion, when his bitterest enemy called his moral conduct in question, he was found innocent. His congregation stood by him then and during all the years after. Mr. Mencken prefers to believe the worst, as he does always when a minister or a priest comes up for judgment. His remarks about the quality of Mr. Beecher's preaching exhibit shocking ignorance. He calls him "a boob-toaster almost comparable to the late William Jennings Bryan." We don't quite understand what a "boob-toaster" is, but if it is a flamboyant orator, we can say from knowledge that nothing in the preacher's pulpit style suggested it. He rarely lifted a finger from one end of a sermon to the other. He spoke simply and deliberately, as though conversing, seeming to feel his way in his mind for *le mot juste*. His voice had an infinite power to express the depths of pathos or the heights of the sublime. But his touch was always true, always sure. If we were to compare him with any preacher now living, we should say that his style was much akin to that of Dr. George A. Gordon—an appeal to the reason, to the conscience, rather than to the emotions.

The trouble with Mr. Mencken is that, knowing nothing of the spiritual life, disbelieving in it, he suspects that every clergyman is a hypocrite only biding his time to become, the devil willing, another Elmer Gantry.

Thus it will probably go on, diatribe and defense, defense and diatribe, until there shall be a judgment which will possess all the elements of finality. It will be a judgment which will revise, and, perchance, reverse some of the judgments of men.

His Lineage Licensed Him to Greatness

Henry Ward Beecher has been an unintentional usurper of the family name. When an American writer of distinction says that "Alcott, Conway, Bryant, and Beecher came to see Whitman," there is no mistaking the Beecher who is meant even before the dates are looked up to see who was contemporary with Whitman. But this is to filch from his father's fame and do the elder man an injustice. Lyman Beecher was renowned in his own right, and not merely as the father of Henry Ward. He was a Congregationalist minister of eminent ability and character, and a leader in his Church. He was a theologian, too, a better one than Henry Ward ever was, and an earnest advocate of reform. He was particularly zealous and bold as a pleader for temperance, and his attitude and action gave great impetus to that cause. In his own Church he was a progressive in theology as against the rigidity of the older Calvinism. He brought on himself a trial for heresy which Henry attended. Before a table full of elders and ministers one day as they all sat at table Henry drawled out to his father: "I know you are plagued good at twisting. But if you can twist your creed on to the Westminster Confession you can twist better than I think you can." Any man might under the circumstances have been disconcerted. But his father tartly answered: "All my boys are smart, and one of them is impudent." Lyman Beecher in Boston, confronting the Unitarianism which prevailed there, was a conservative in his theology, contending valiantly against liberalism.

For all his dignity he was as a child among his children. He would play the violin, and in his stocking feet dance with them about the room until it was all the worse for the stockings. The boys he would set arguing about every kind of question, political, moral, and theological, until he had established a veritable school of polemics in the family. In this way as well as through the channels of heredity he transmitted much of his own thinking and character to his children.

Roxanna Foote, Cavalier in her ancestry as her husband was Puritan, became Mrs. Lyman Beecher. She was sensitive and of a great natural timidity. Unsuited as she was to the presidency of the woman's society, or even to lead its prayer meeting, her adaptability to the position of a pastor's wife in its traditional rôle was not complete. But she possessed a noble nature, a fine mind, and a peculiar strength of

Christian character. She was eminently fit to be the wife of Lyman Beecher and the mother of Henry Ward. "There was a moral force about her," says Mrs. Harriet Beecher Stowe, "a dignity of demeanor and an air of elegance which produced a constant atmosphere of unconscious awe in the minds of little children. She died when Henry was but three years of age, but the sense of her worth and influence never departed from him. He was accustomed to say that through his feeling for his almost unknown mother he could understand the feeling of a devout Roman Catholic for the Virgin Mary.

He venerated his stepmother, too, though he had a certain awe even of her religion:

> My dear mother—not she that gave me birth, but she that brought me up; she that did the office-work of a mother, if ever a mother did; she that, according to her ability, performed to the uttermost her duties— was a woman of profound veneration, rather than of a warm and loving nature. Therefore, her prayer was invariably a prayer of deep, yearning reverence. I remember well the impression which it made on me. There was a mystic influence about it. A sort of sympathetic hold it had upon me; but still, I always felt, when I went to prayer, as though I was going into a crypt, where the sun was not allowed to come; and I shrunk from it.

Among his brothers and sisters, large as the number of them was, there was not a second-rate person. Harriet Beecher Stowe herself was not a satellite to anybody, whether to her father, her mother, or Henry Ward himself. She was a planet in her own right, swimming in her own ken, shining in her own light. Her "Uncle Tom's Cabin" was really a stroke of genius, and was one of the major weapons with which the institution of slavery was struck down in America. To one of his brothers Henry Ward used to go for his Hebrew when he was working on an Old Testament text. Another collaborated with others in the preparation of a life of Henry Ward. Of his Aunt Esther, half sister to his father, Henry himself said that she was "so good and modest that she would spend ages in heaven wondering how it ever happened that she ever got there, and that all the angels will be wondering why she was not there from all eternity." An American wit divided mankind into three parts—"the good, and the bad, and the Beechers." The family inheritance was in itself a license to greatness.

EDUCATIONAL EQUIPMENT

Beecher himself thought that a good part of his early education consisted in being let alone:

> I think I was about as well brought up as most children, because I was let alone. My father was so busy, and my mother had so many other children to look after that, except here and there, I hardly came under the parental hand at all. I was brought up in a New England village, and I knew where the sweet-flag was, where the hickory trees were, where the chestnut trees were, where the sassafras trees were, where the squirrels were, where all those things were that boys enterprise after; therefore, I had a world of things to do; and so I did not come much in contact with family government.

His early school days did not forecast a brilliant future. He was indifferent to his studies, and was even counted dull. He was diffident and extremely sensitive. He had a deficient memory, and had a thick and indistinct utterance. He did not have schools adapted to his requirements. Indeed, so far as the meeting of his special needs was concerned he might as well not have gone to school. He remembered going back to the schoolhouse where he *did not receive* his education. When he reached the district school, conditions were no better. He craved a larger liberty all around, and thought he might have been spared some of the punishment he received. Even in church he wanted to get out of the pew in which he had long been imprisoned and sit among the singers:

> My mother, in a day of unexpected grace, gave me permission, with many and multiplied charges of proper conduct; and I went into the gal-

lery with all the virtue of a dozen deacons, determined to behave well, and to earn the right of sitting there. . . . But, as I sat there, a martyr of propriety, on a hard seat, one of the roguish boys of the neighborhood gave me a shove, and pushed me off on the floor, and tore my coat.

His mother descried the rent in the coat, and no amount of pleading that it had been done in fun enabled him to escape the unhappy sequel. It was the town of Litchfield alone with its culture and fine breeding as an educational center which could have availed him much in these early days.

Restlessness and a natural love of adventure led him at last to a resolve to go to sea. His father agreed, but said he must have preparation that would make it possible for him to advance beyond the rank of an ordinary seaman. So he went to Mount Pleasant School at Amherst, Mass., and came under better influences. His intellectual and moral character entered upon sounder processes of development; and he began as a student to submit himself to the drudgery of his tasks. His father was now a pastor in Boston, and Henry had been for a time a student in the famous Boston Latin School. But his career there had at least not made it any more famous.

There was a revival in the Mount Pleasant School, and Henry united with his father's church in Boston. Even this action, however, was rather indecisive. He simply said that he "let them take him into the church." Constance Mayfield Rourke in "Trumpets of Jubilee" rather makes it out that at this stage of his life he had to be dragged into everything. He was "pushed into Amherst as a step toward the ministry." "He had been dragged in his father's wake to Cincinnati, and entered Lane Seminary." Even his love for Eunice Bullard was not allowed to be spontaneous. "In a rush of remorse he had fallen in love with her." But it is difficult to believe that he was ever so luckless or inert as all this.

He entered Amherst College in 1830, at seventeen years of age. His attitude is still one of indifference toward prescribed courses of study. He does only enough to get through on required subjects. He afterwards remarked that he was once next to head, but it was when the class stood in a circle. He did, however, throw himself with enthusiasm into the study of subjects of his own choosing; or it might be only such as appealed to the mood of the moment. He led prayer meetings, gave lectures on temperance, and there began with him the strange infatuation which the study of phrenology held for him for the rest of his life. He made ten dollars on a lecture, and invested it in an edition of Edmund Burke which formed the foundation of his library. He was regarded as the finest debater in the college debating society, and as an intellectual leader among his classmates. He was occupied in teaching in the long vacations, which were allowed for this purpose. He was graduated in 1834.

In the meantime his father had removed from Boston to Cincinnati, and had assumed the presidency of Lane Theological Seminary. It was a new and unformed institution, and a man from the East was sought in the hope that he might attract money from that source. It seems surprising that Lyman Beecher should have been attracted to the position. He said that there was not another place on earth that he would have opened his ears to for a moment. But he had been greatly interested in raising up ministers, and in the proper means of training them. The call to Lane "flashed through his mind like lightning." Henry Ward was now more definitely resolved upon the ministry. It was but natural that he should go to Lane for his training in theology. Still he did not care for the prescribed courses.

In truth, he did not care for theology. He never did. It must seem to many a strange confusion in the mind of a man of his understanding that he should virtually have flouted the idea of theological study. He could devote the whole of his third series of Yale Lectures to methods of using Christian doctrine in preaching and still seem not to care for theology. It may well be that the courses at Lane at the time required some defense and justified some neglect, but hardly to such an extent as to warrant Beecher's attitude.

He was not idle. He kept up a great deal of reading which, perhaps, to him did not seem as desultory as it did to others. He did a great deal of practical work which had in it the elements of preparation for preaching—the teaching of a Bible class, lectures on temperance, and some preaching on Sundays. He said in his Yale Lectures:

> I had the good fortune to be pitched into the ministry headlong, without anything to do but to make men better—for really my stock of *theology that I believed in* was very small. I have increased it very much since, but it was meager enough then. . . . I had nothing but the Bible to go to; and I remember times of deep water, when I took what I could get out of the Bible to help people with; and as I went out to help them, I felt something that demanded an idea of God; and I fell back on the Old Testament, as well as on the New, for my conceptions of him. In my early ministry I studied to preach God so as to touch the imagination, the reason, and the affections of men; and I learned to have great respect for that element in preaching which develops steadily and continuously the attributes of the Divine Being in such a way as to give men an idea of a Person that they could love as well as fear.

In the very midst of his theological studies he was in a state of skepticism and of profound religious depression. It seemed that he might abandon the ministry altogether. But there was one anchor that held him through all the flood of doubt and depression. In an address to the ministers of London in 1886 he referred to a profound spiritual experience through which he had passed the time of which is indicated as "when he studied theology." These are his memorable words:

I was a child of teaching and prayer; I was reared in the household of faith; I knew the Catechism as it was taught; I was instructed in the Scriptures as they were expounded from the pulpit and read by men; and yet, till after I was twenty-one years old, I groped without the knowledge of God in Jesus Christ. I know not what the tablets of eternity have written down, but I think that when I stand in Zion and before God, the brightest thing I shall look back upon will be that blessed morning of May when it pleased God to reveal to my wandering soul the idea that it was his nature to love a man in his sins for the sake of helping him out of them; that he did not do it out of compliment to Christ, or to a law, or a plan of salvation, but from the fullness of his great heart; that he was a Being not made mad by sin, but sorry; that he was not furious with wrath toward the sinner, but pitied him—in short, that he felt toward me as my mother felt toward me, to whose eyes my wrong-doing brought tears, who never pressed me so close to her as when I had done wrong, and who would fain with her yearning love lift me out of trouble. And when I found that Jesus Christ had such a disposition, and that when his disciples did wrong he drew them closer to him than he did before—and when pride, and jealousy, and rivalry, and all vulgar and worldly feelings rankled in their bosoms, he opened his heart to them as a medicine to heal these infirmities; when I found that it was Christ's nature to lift men out of weakness to strength, out of impurity to goodness, out of everything low and debasing to superiority, I felt that I had found a God. I shall never forget the feelings with which I walked forth that May morning. The golden pavements will never feel to my feet as then the grass felt to me; and the singing of the birds in the woods—for I roamed in the woods—was cacophonous to the sweet music of my thoughts. . . .

Time went on, and next came the disclosure of a Christ ever present with me—a Christ that was never far from me, but was always near me, as a companion and friend, to uphold and sustain me. This was the last and the best revelation of God's Spirit to my soul.

WINNING HIS WAY IN THE WEST

On the Ohio River about twenty miles below Cincinnati is the village of Lawrenceburg, Ind. Despite many obstacles to its prosperous existence, it is there still. But it has had to resign the most of its early ambitions in favor of Cincinnati. On his graduation from Lane Beecher went

there as the pastor of a struggling Presbyterian Church. He
was voted a salary of two hundred and fifty dollars, and was
paid all but one hundred dollars of it. Another one hundred
and fifty dollars was added from home mission sources. On
this stipend he married. He was already engaged to Eunice
Bullard back in New England. He wrote to her and suggested that after his ordination they should be married.
Waxing in his devotion he followed this suggestion with a
second which almost overtook the first in the mails that the
marriage need not wait on the ordination. What maiden
could resist the ardor of such a lover?

He and his bride "lived in two rooms over a stable at a
rental of forty dollars per annum." Miss Rourke says—and
being a woman she ought to know—that "a deal table, an
old bedstead, a husk mattress and pillows, some strips of
calico, a pair of plated candlesticks, comprised their household equipment." The bride eked out the scanty sums received on the preacher's salary "by work as a seamstress,
and took in boarders."

There were obstacles to his ordination. He held with his
father to the New School views in the Presbyterian Church,
and the Old School contingent was largely represented in the
Presbytery. He sustained his part very well in a prolonged
and hostile examination. Then it was proposed that he
should pledge his adhesion to the Old School General Assembly. This would take him contrary to his own convictions,
and also part him from his father. He would relinquish his
church and his salary rather than take such a step. His
church declared itself independent of the Presbytery, and
he remained.

Beecher's later fame reflected more glory upon Lawrenceburg than Lawrenceburg contributed to his future career.
He accomplished little there. The most valuable acquisition he made was a conviction that he had not learned to

preach. And he accumulated some very tender memories
of the place and people which were mellowed by the light
of twenty years thrown back upon them:

> I go back to the time when I first became the pastor of a church. It
> was twenty years ago. I remember that the flock which I first gathered
> in the wilderness consisted of twenty persons. Nineteen of them were
> women, and the other was nothing. I remember the days of our poverty,
> our straitness. I was sexton of my own church at that time. There were
> no lamps, so I bought some; and I filled them and lit them. I swept the
> church, and lighted my own fire. I did not ring the bell because there was
> none to ring. I opened the church before prayer meetings and preaching,
> and locked it when they were over. . . . And do I not remember every
> one of those faces? I think there were but two persons among them that
> did not earn their daily living by actual work; and these were not wealthy
> —they were only in moderate circumstances. We were all poor together.
> And to the day of my death, I shall never forget one of those faces or hear
> one of those names spoken without having excited in my mind the warmest
> remembrances.

After two years at Lawrenceburg Beecher came to Indianapolis to assume the pastorate of the Second Presbyterian
Church, an organization which had been created out of the
divisions between the Old and New Schools in the First
Church. Indianapolis itself was struggling up from the estate of a village to the condition of a town. Stumps still
stood in many of the streets and the wheels of vehicles had
their choice between running into these on one side or mud-
holes on the other. Beecher's salary was doubled. The
population to which he ministered was composed of the
early settlers, who were French Catholics, and immigrant
fortune seekers pioneering from the East. Life was primi-
tive and rough, and drinking, gambling, and brawling were
the accepted order of the day. Beecher came. He was as
unconventional in his sphere as any of them in theirs. He
showed them the first felt hat they had seen on a minister's
head. He painted his own house, and carried home his
groceries in a wheelbarrow. His success was immediate.

His church—as yet only a temporary meeting-place—was crowded from the first. The legislators came to hear him. Strangers heard him, from wherever they hailed. This was quite according to his taste. He always liked to preach to the world better than to the church, to sinners better than to saints. This pioneering was a fine school of preaching, and he prospered upon it. He began to realize the practical aim as a fundamental principle underlying all preaching. "I always aim at a mark," he said, "though I may not hit the mark I aim at."

He tells how he remembers the first real sermon he ever preached. He connects it with his early experience as a hunter:

I used to go out hunting by myself, and I had great success in firing off my gun; and the game enjoyed it as much as I did, for I never hit them or hurt them. . . . I recollect one day in the fields my father pointed out a little red squirrel, and said to me, "Henry, would you like to shoot him?" I trembled all over, but I said, "Yes." He got down on his knee, put the gun across a rail, and said, "Henry, keep perfectly cool, perfectly cool; take aim." And I did, and I fired, and over went the squirrel, and he didn't run away either. That was the first thing I ever hit; and I felt an inch taller as a boy that had killed a squirrel, and knew how to aim a gun.

Now he learns that he does not know how to bring down the game in preaching:

I sent for Dr. Stowe to come down and help me; but he would not come, for he thought it better for me to bear the yoke myself. When I had lived at Indianapolis the first year, I said: "There was a reason why when the apostles preached they succeeded, and I will find it out if it is to be found out."

Then having gone to the records and analyzed their sermons he said:

"Now, I will make sermon so." I remember it just as well as if it were yesterday. First, I sketched out the things we all know. "You all know you are living in a world perishing under your feet. You all know that time is extremely uncertain; that you cannot tell whether you will live another month or week. You all know that your destiny, in the life that is to come, depends upon the character you are forming in this life ; and in that way I went on with my "You all knows," until I had about forty of them. When I had got through that, I turned round and brought it to bear upon them with all my might; and there were seventeen men awakened under that sermon. I never felt so triumphant in all my life. I cried all the way home. I said to myself: "Now I know how to preach."

His ministry was at this period earnestly evangelistic. At one time he preached for seventy successive nights in revival effort. He was working at the same time editorially on a newspaper, and as a reformer and publicist. But above all he was preaching to the town and against all the vices that lifted their hydra heads in its streets. In Indianapolis his Lectures to Young Men were delivered. They scorched and burned and left the town in no doubt of the iniquities that abounded there. His style was ornate and rhetorical, but did not conceal his meaning or the object at which he aimed. His picture in one of these lectures of the progress of a gambler to his doom is not yet dimmed in its vividness:

Go with me into that dilapidated house not far from the landing in New Orleans. Look into that dirty room. Around a broken table, sitting upon boxes, kegs, or rickety chairs, see a filthy crew dealing cards smouched with tobacco, grease, and liquor. One has a pirate-face burnished and burnt with brandy; a shock of grizzly matted hair, half covering his villain eyes, which galre out like a wild beast's from a thicket. Close by him wheezes a white-faced, dropsical wretch, vermin-covered, and stenchful. A scoundrel Spaniard and a burly Negro (the jolliest of the four) complete the group. They have spectators—drunken sailors, and ogling, thieving, drinking women, who should have died long ago, when all that was womanly died. Here hour draws on hour, sometimes with brutal laughter, sometimes with threat and oath and uproar. The last few stolen dollars lost, and temper too, each charges each with cheating, and high words ensue, and blows; and the whole gang burst out the door, beating, biting, scratching, and rolling over and over in the dirt and dust. The worst, the fiercest, the drunkest of the four is our friend who began by making up the game.

Thus he preached against the sins that were running rampant in the streets, the saloons, and the gambling houses of the city. "Take it back," said a rough with an oath after one of his particularly caustic deliverances on Sunday as

Beecher met him in the street. "Take it back right here, or I will shoot you on the spot." "Shoot away," said the intrepid preacher passing calmly on.

Still his study of books is discursive, following his mood more than any particular method. Already he studied men more than books. In preparation for his sermon on gambling he inveigled a gambler to come to his study and spent ample time in drawing out of him the secrets of the gambler's life and habits of the game. A young man in the street asked him how he knew so much about a whisky saloon. "How do you know," replied Beecher, "if you have not been there?"

He did little regular work as a pastor. His reputation as a preacher extended throughout the State and beyond, and he began to receive calls from the East. His work in the West was a distinct preparation for the wider fields which awaited him.

Plymouth Pastorate

A Presbyterian Church in Brooklyn decided to sell their holdings and change their location. Several earnest Congregationalists thought the site to be abandoned a good location for a Congregationalist Church, and purchased the property. But they had only a location, and must have a preacher, a church membership, and a congregation. One of their number had heard Beecher in the West, and contrived to have him come to New York for an important meeting of the Congregationalists. Once he was there it was not difficult to secure him to preach for these brethren who were putting him on trial without his knowing it. Reverting to the matter when further events had developed its intention he said he had accepted the invitation to come to New York in order "to urge young men to go West, to show what a good field the West was, and to cast some fiery

arrows at men that had worked there and got tired and
come back. . . . I came East not knowing what I did; it was
a trap." But whether by direction or indirection, he came
to Plymouth Church. He had been eight years in Indianapolis. His public ministry in Brooklyn began on October
10, 1847.

The church was orthodox. It adopted a formula for the
reception of members which exacted of applicants only the
moderate avowal that they avouched the Lord Jehovah to
be their God, Christ to be their Saviour, the Holy Spirit
to be their Sanctifier, that they renounced the dominion of
the world over them and consecrated their whole soul and
body to the service of God. Beecher himself took the liberty
to depart at will from the standards of orthodoxy: not all at
once, but by stages which eventually put an interrogation
mark after his name in connection with the Atonement, and
issued in his denial of the fall and total depravity of man.
He certainly believed in the divinity of Christ, but he was
not a success in his theological statements of the doctrine.
He adopted quite freely the theory of evolution when it was
first propounded; and toward the end of his life was regarded by many as being so unscriptural in some of his
teaching that there was a perceptible waning of his influence. He did believe in the authenticity of the New
Testament, as he understood it; and in the reality of
miracles. He was neither naturalistic nor rationalistic. He
believed in "the deep sinfulness of universal man," and in
the "exceeding sinfulness of sin"; that "there is not one
faculty of the human soul that does not work evil, and so
repeatedly that the whole human character is sinful before
God"; that "every man that ever lived needed God's for-
bearance and forgiveness"; that "no man lives who does
not need to repent of sin, to turn from it"; that "turning from
sin is a work so deep and touches so closely the very springs

of being, that no man will ever change except by the help of God"; that "such help is the direct and personal out-reaching of God's Spirit upon the human soul."

His Plymouth pastorate was marked by zeal for revivals. He reacted in his early ministry against the theological controversy around him and said in solemn resolve to himself, "My business shall be to save men." Conversions were frequent in Plymouth Church, and there were many additions on confession of faith at the regular services. But he would have the revival too. In 1852 there was a noted revival in which there were nearly one hundred additions to the Church. Through his leadership and efforts his people shared in the widespread revival of 1858, more than three hundred persons having been brought into the Church on profession of faith. He did the preaching himself, and did it with all tenderness and simplicity. "The themes of his revival preaching," says Dr. Abbot, "might almost be summed up in the saying of Hosea: 'I drew them with bands of love.'"

The growth of the church under his ministry was quite beyond the ordinary. He began with twenty-one members. At the end of ten years there were twelve hundred and forty-one. At the end of fifty years, ten years after Beecher's time, it was reported that thirty-six hundred and thirty-three persons had come into the kingdom of God through its doors.

His success was not immediate. For six months the congregations were moderate. Then the crowds began to come. A new church was built. It was constructed for preaching and designed to gather the audience as closely and compactly about the speaker as possible. He would not have "one of these barreled pulpits" where there is no responsibility laid upon the preacher as to his body, and "he falls into all manner of gawky attitudes, and rests himself like a

14

country horse at a hitching post." Gothic pillars and other material hindrances to the effect of the sermon he did not count inconsiderable. But his *bête noire* was the boxed-up pulpit. "I tell the truth and lie not," he declared, "when I say that I would not accept a settlement in a very advantageous place if I were obliged to preach out of one of those old-fashioned swallows' nests on the wall." As a consequence of such care in design and construction Plymouth Church is well-nigh a perfect auditorium. Charles Dickens, when he had given a reading there, pronounced it perfect. It will seat a little more than 2,000 people; but by special seating devices and the use of standing room it was made to hold from 2,500 to 3,000 during Beecher's incumbency.

The church has the advantage of being located within five minutes' walk of the principal ferry to Manhattan. "How shall I get to Plymouth Church?" inquired a stranger in New York. "Cross Fulton Ferry and follow the crowd," was the ready answer. Edward Eggleston relates that when the street car would come on Sunday morning to the corner where the passengers landed for church the conductor instead of naming the street would call out, "Henry Ward Beecher," or perhaps simply say, "Beecher Station."

At Plymouth Church Beecher was still not a pastor according to the custom then in vogue of visiting from house to house. He did, however, give free opportunity at the close of the Friday evening meeting at the church to any who might wish a personal consultation. He had the heart of the pastor, though not the usual method. Neither was he a church administrator. He did not organize his church, but inspired others to take this kind of leadership. He preferred having influence, he said, to the mere exercising of authority.

He thought the professorship of pastoral theology the most important chair in a theological seminary; and that young preachers ought to be educated for life and not for seclusion. Some of the things still lingering in the theological curriculum he thought had been already "dead four days." He once conducted a mock examination of candidates for the ministry:

Brother, you may tell us what you have learned about the creation. . . . Yes, that is what you have been taught. . . . And you, brother, may tell us about Adam and the Fall. . . . Yes, that is in strict accordance with our belief here. . . . You, next, may state what you know about the Flood and about Moses. . . . Yes, that is correct. Your preaching will not fail to be sound. . . . So (he continued) they make ministers by taking a little foreordained dough, unleavened, and carry it to the seminary, and the professors within the dingy walls roll it, and roll it, and roll it, and pat it, and pat it, and pat it, and stick just so many little theological holes in it, each in exactly the right place, and then toss it up into the oven and bake it just twenty minutes, the prescribed length of a sermon—and out he comes a little cracker preacher. Do you know how I would proceed if I had the training and the examining of these young men? I'd ask them what they knew of the daily papers, I'd ask them what they knew of the lizardly sneaks that make up the New York City Council.

All this is, of course, one of his characteristic exaggerations. Nevertheless, he was striking at a need of the time in theological education.

In matters of health Beecher "coöperated with nature." He had a splendid physique and kept it unimpaired. "He used neither tobacco nor alcohol, until the latter years of his life, when he made occasional and rare use of the lighter forms of the latter. He did not use tea or coffee, and in his diet was never self-indulgent." He was a sound sleeper, could easily throw off cares, and kept Saturday for rest. He lived always as if he were in his pulpit, and had his reward when he actually came there.

His later Plymouth ministry was shadowed by the emergence of the now famous Tilton trial in which the plaintiff sought damages from the defendant on the charge of improper relations on the part of the latter with the wife of the former. The court proceedings occupied six months, and all the while were a newspaper and nation-wide sensation. Some one aptly remarked that "the episode had produced nothing short of the abolition of privacy." It shall suffice here to say that scant proof was offered of the truth of the charge. The only evidence which even seemed to incriminate Beecher were certain letters he had been led by designing persons to write when they made it appear to his sympathetic nature that he had acted hastily in advising Mrs. Tilton to leave her husband when she had applied to him as her pastor.

The verdict of the jury stood nine to three in Beecher's favor, and was reported to have been unanimously so until some diverting issue arose and the poll was recast. The chief counsel for the plaintiff was said himself to have been convinced of Beecher's innocence, and to have threatened to withdraw from the case. The judge who conducted the case later presided at a meeting held in Brooklyn on the occasion of Beecher's seventieth birthday in which a distinguished representative group of his fellow citizens passed resolutions certifying to him as "a man who by the integrity of his life and the purity of his character has vanquished misrepresentation and abuse, corrected and counteracted misunderstanding, and converted public alienation into personal affection."

Plymouth Church investigated the charges and found "nothing whatever in the evidence that should impair the perfect confidence of Plymouth Church or the world in the Christian character and integrity of Henry Ward Beecher." Dr. Lyman Abbot in his life of Beecher avers that "there was no proof at any time of any act of impropriety on Mr. Beecher's part toward Mrs. Tilton or toward any other woman." Speaking still further in an article in the thir-

teenth edition of the "Encyclopedia Britannica" he says:
"The largest and most representative Congregational Council ever held in the United States gave expression to a vote
of confidence in him which time has amply justified."

Most of those who know the facts and circumstances of
this case as they are set in the whole environment of Beecher's life and judged in the light of the motive and character
of the man will go a long way with Lyman Abbott before
they turn to follow the acrimonious disputings of some later
biographers and critics. If this be not a sane and edifying
course, then let us appeal to the desert to distil the dew,
to the clouds to drop down dust, to Mount Sinai to emit
whispers of mercy, and to the Garden of Gethsemane to
change its culture and its character and produce blasphe-
mies and hate.

Pulpit and Platform

Somewhat of the West clung to Beecher in the East. He
never became a highly cultured man in the sense that Phillips
Brooks or Horace Bushnell was. He at times offended good
taste, and was wanting in a certain delicacy of sentiment.
His very temperament, as he himself said, "necessitated
errors." His broad and ebullient humor would sometimes
take the reins out of the hands of a sound and refined taste.
It may be that it "was his humor that sinned." Still it
was an offense. "Entertainment superseded edification."
Thoughts as serious as death or eternity would fly away on
the wings of a sudden and apparently irresistible stroke of
humor. If we say that we sometimes wonder at what he
introduced into his pulpit, he might reply that we do not
know what he thought of and yet suppressed.

But for all this gainsaying he came from the West fashioned in a homiletic freedom which the more staid proprieties of the East could never cancel. On his coming to

Brooklyn some of his earlier excesses had begun to be "mastered and pruned." His early drilling in elocution had already "sloughed whatever stiffness and artificiality such drill might at first have produced." The foundations for his unsurpassed career in oratory had been laid. His public reading of the Scriptures was like setting up a school in the highest style of elocution. He would roll a torrent of indignation over the "scribes, Pharisees, hypocrites" in the words of Jesus taken from the Gospels, and turning immediately would make the same words a heart-moving lament.

In matching his gifts against the opportunities which came to him through the Plymouth Church and the constituency he gathered there he became one of the world's great preachers. He emphasized public speaking as his specialty. And by public speaking he meant primarily preaching. "A man who is going to be a successful preacher," he said, "should make his whole life run toward the pulpit." He was speaking with the emphasis of experience and the assurance of personal conviction. He lived and studied for his pulpit. He read that he might preach. He studied that he might preach. He read and reread Homer, Dante, Milton, Thackeray, Scott. All of it was knowledge and literature to be transmuted into the uses of his pulpit. "When that sheep bleats again," said he at a dinner of mutton, "it will be in my pulpit." He might have said, When that poet sings again, when that historian philosophizes again, it will be in my pulpit. He gleaned a book, not because he was interested in the book, but in something beyond it. "I never read a book through," he said; "a book is like a fish: you cut off the head, you cut off the tail, you cut off the fins, you take out the backbone, and there is a little piece of meat left." He said he owed more to Ruskin than to any theologian because he taught his eyes

to see and his ears to hear. It was the "new realms in the
universe of God" he was seeking, and not mere literary
treasures. He was seeking a pearl of greater price than any
of these. He studied nature, art, the manifold processes of
action and industry about him, he studied men, he studied
the Bible; and built his knowledge of all of them into his
pulpit. His "genius for acquiring" was as great as his
"genius for imparting." His intellectual genius fitted exactly into his genius as an orator.

He had a power of assimilation which operated like the
enthymeme in logic. There seemed to be no intermediate
steps between acquisition and assimilation. He seemed to
receive knowledge as the rose receives the warmth and color
of the sky. By a process too secret to be seen they pass as
if without process into the fragrance and beauty of the
flower. So the stamp of Beecher's homiletic genius was immediately impressed upon whatever he received. His was
the homiletic habit of mind *par excellence*. He would go
down to the Fulton Ferry on Saturday, and the gatekeepers
and the boatmen would appear in his pulpit on Sunday
morning in their native speech and habit, and not in un-
recognizable Sunday clothes. He said he had never found
a plain man who could not tell him many things he never
knew before. He would ride on top of an omnibus and talk
with the driver. He trusted his phrenology too far, and
said if he saw a man "with a large blue watery eye" he
knew he could no more be stimulated to action "than you
could a lump of dough by blowing a resurrection trump
over it." But in getting some things that were not true he
got a thousand that were. Brastow says he "was a most
notable example of this habit of mind among modern
preachers and indeed among all the preachers of the Church
in every age."

Out of considerations such as these the main features of

his method of preparation will readily appear. It was a
method so constant and wide-ranging as to be incapable of
exact exhibition. The books on homiletics call it *general* as
distinguished from *special* preparation. He wrote a good
deal when he began to preach, thus giving more time to
special preparation for the particular sermon and occasion.
Later his habit was to prepare his Sunday morning sermon
on Sunday morning and his Sunday evening sermon in the
afternoon, or, perhaps, even after tea. The text probably
would not be selected until the day it was used. But he had
always before his mind texts waiting to be used. He could
not take a text which had not gone through a drill of general
preparation. Even though the particular text may not have
been had under definite consideration, it still had been embraced in the constant scheme of his homiletic expectancy.
His general preparation was so constant and thorough that
he could not fail to relate his special to it. He thus describes
his method:

> I have half a dozen or more topics lying loose in my mind through the
> week; I think of one or another, as occasion may serve, anywhere—at
> home, in the street, in the horse-car. I rarely know what theme I shall
> use until Sunday morning. Then, after breakfast, I go into my study as
> a man goes into his orchard; I feel among these themes as he feels among
> the apples, to find the ripest and the best; the theme which seems most
> ripe I pluck; then I select my text, analyze my subject, prepare my ser-
> mon, and go into the pulpit to preach it while it is fresh.

The introduction and earlier portions of the sermon he
wrote in full. Then as the time was shortened he abbreviated and at last, as likely as not, he would go into the pulpit from an unfinished manuscript. But "he rarely if ever
in his ordinary preaching treated a theme until he had given
it weeks of meditation." A man of his mental aptitudes and
habits of observation and study could preach no sermon
which it had taken him only thirty minutes to prepare. No
man can tell by the calendar how long it has taken to pre-

pare a sermon; if he can, it is not well prepared.   It is related that Beecher once heard a young man preach a sermon which he recognized from beginning to end as one of his own.   "How long did it take you to prepare that sermon?" he asked the young man.   "About three hours," was the answer.   "Well," replied Beecher, "it took me forty years."

His facility in immediate preparation can only be explained in connection with the broader fact of his general preparation.   Dr. Abbott reports this incident:

On one occasion when he was to preach a dedication sermon he arrived rather late at the minister's house; after supper, and but a brief time before the service, he prepared his notes on the margin of a newspaper in fifteen or twenty minutes, preaching from them, as was represented to me, a sermon that held the almost breathless attention of the congregation from the beginning to the close, occupying more than an hour in delivery.

His first Yale lecture had to run the gantlet of extemporaneous preparation:

He had a bad night, as it happened, not feeling well; took the 10 o'clock train next morning to New Haven; went to his hotel, got his dinner, lay down and had a nap.   About 2 o'clock he got up and began to shave without having been able to get at any plan of the lecture to be delivered within an hour.   Just as he had his face lathered and was beginning to strop his razor, the whole thing came out of the cloud and dawned on him.   He dropped his razor, seized his pencil, and dashed off the memoranda for it, and afterward cut himself badly, he said, thinking it out.

He had not been ashamed to be a student of preachers and preaching, and had been a great reader of some of the older men of the English pulpit.   "I read old Robert South through and through," he said; "I saturated myself with South; I formed much of my style and my handling of texts on his method."   He had an early partiality for Barrow, too, and considering this he said he always regarded it as a wonder that he "escaped so largely from the snares and temptations of that rhetorical demon, the Adjective."   He read also Howe, Sherlock, Butler, and "Edwards particularly." He was "awakening his own preaching gifts," and learning what to emulate and what to avoid.

His platform was but an extension of his pulpit. Those who take it the other way around are perhaps not much in sympathy with preaching. Or perhaps they do not very much admire Beecher himself. He was not willing to neglect his pulpit or his church for any other interest whatsoever. The Tilton affair left him involved in debt. He began to lecture to make money, and did make a great deal. Major J. B. Pond was his business manager; or rather it should be said that he engaged himself to lecture for Pond. Once when Pond wrote him to go out—and the incident was not singular—he replied: "All the cities on the continent are not to me of as much value as my church. . . . When a deepening religious feeling is evident, to go off lecturing and leave it would be too outrageous to be thought of." He might very well say thathe had deliberately rejected many things that would have been consonant to his taste.

His chief public interest outside his pulpit was evinced in his attitude toward slavery. He believed that the institution was wholly evil, and its practice sinful. He believed that Christianity could be consistent with itself only by standing for its destruction. He would prefer to wait fifty years, and then have it go by the impact of the Christian motive and the Christian conscience rather than have it disappear through the operation of merely political and commercial considerations.

He was never an abolitionist. He did not hold with the extremists like Garrison and Phillips. He believed with leaders like Seward, Chase, and Lincoln that slavery was to be overthrown under the Constitution and within the Union. He threw himself fearlessly into the struggle. He created country-wide interest and gave a remarkable exhibiti onof his own platform ability by conducting an auction sale of two young Negro women in the Broadway Tabernacle, New York, where an audience was gathered especially in the interest of the freedom of these girls who were about to be transported to New Orleans to be put up for sale in the slave-market there. In the midst of an impassioned address he referred to the father of the girls, and dramatically stopped short.

"*The father!*" he exclaimed. "Do goods and chattels have fathers? Do *slaves* have *daughters?* The *father!* Would to God Will Shakespeare was living! He might make a drama out of that sentence more touching than any he ever wrote.

This affair was conducted hardly in the form of an auction. But in Plymouth Church he actually staged an auction—indeed, this was done more than once—with the subject of the sale present in the pulpit. An old negro woman in Baltimore had made an appeal for her grandchild, described as "too fair and beautiful for her own good," who was about to be sold "down South." The matter was brought to Beecher's attention, and he procured the child and brought her to the church. "Look at her!" he cried. "What do you bid for her? Who bids? Who bids?" The audience was raised to a pitch of most intense excitement, and the price of the child was oversubscribed. The girl, now an old woman, was very recently said to be still alive, the wife of a lawyer in Washington City.

As editor of the *Independent*, 1861-1863, he promulgated his anti-slavery views as vigorously as from his pulpit or platform, and attracted the attention of the thoughtful men of the country, both North and South. On one of his pronouncements John C. Calhoun, in his old age, is reported to have said, "He will be heard from again. He has gone to the bottom." He affiliated with the new Republican party, and "became indeed the outstanding ministerial figure of the country in the arena of political affairs."

He had not believed that the South would secede, but when it did he was in for the war. Going to England while hostilities were in progress, without any official authority whatever, he was led to defend the course of the North against the South. Much sympathy was felt for the South by the English aristocracy, and large business interests were involved in the same way. It was gravely suspected that England would recognize the Southern Confederacy. Beecher took the platform in Liverpool, Glasgow, Edinburgh, Manchester, and London. He faced the most hostile audiences, resolved and organized to beat down the speaker and not to allow him to be heard at all. A half dozen riots would be in progress in his audience at one time. His triumph was signal and overwhelming. If it took him an hour to tame his audience, he was ready to spend another hour in convincing it. There was not a little justification of the saying that he "achieved his largest fame in the realm of violence." Of these English addresses Dr. Abbott says: "The only parallel in public effect is that produced by Demosthenes' orations against Philip."

PRINCIPLES AND PRACTICE OF PREACHING

Aside from the impressiveness and power of his own preaching, the most valuable contribution Henry Ward Beecher has made to preaching is in the form of his Yale Lectures delivered before the faculty and students of the divinity school of Yale College in three annual series dating from 1872 to 1874 inclusive, initiating the lectureship founded by Mr. Henry W. Sage of Brooklyn, and named in honor of Lyman Beecher. The first series, the most valuable and important of them all, deals with the minister exclusively as a preacher, and seeks to define the secret of pulpit power as based upon personal elements. "The preacher is a teacher; but he is more. . . . He looks beyond mere knowledge to a character which that knowledge is to form." Therefore, it must not be the preacher alone who speaks, "but God in him."

The emphasis on personal power brings out the difference between the evangelical and the hierarchical churches:

Both hold to the indispensableness of divine power; but one believes that power to work chiefly through church *ordinances*, the other believes that it works through living men. . . . The man that preaches with power is an artist. He is a living creature. But the man who merely comes to administer ordinances on Sundays or Saints' Days, who goes through a regular routine, is nothing but the engineer who runs the machine.

Hence comes also a true view of the sermon

The highest conception of a sermon is that it is a prescription which a man has made, either for a certain individual, or for a certain class, or for a certain state of things that he knows to exist in the congregation.

The object of preaching must affect the style:

If a man can be saved by pure intellectual preaching, let him have it. If others require a predominance of emotion, provide that for them. If by others the truth is taken more easily through the imagination, give it to them by forms attractive to the imagination. If there are still others who demand it in the form of facts and rules, see that they have it in that form.

Preachers must show sympathy with men, not with sermons as an end. In order to do this they must themselves be human:

Christian ministers are to be, not men that pray four times a day, and wear black clothes and white cravats and walk with the consciousness that the whole universe is looking upon them. A minister is a live man. He is a large-hearted man.

Preaching has to be learned:

I shall have occasion to repeat every time I speak to you this thing: you have got to *learn your business*. It will take years and years before you are expert preachers. Let nobody puff you up by saying you are able preachers, because you can preach three or four good sermons. . . . You have not begun your education yet. You are but getting ready to study when you begin to preach.

There can be too much propriety in preaching:

I do not think that mistakes are *desirable;* but there may be a "propriety" in his preaching that will damn half his congregation, or there may occasionally be almost an impropriety that will hurt nobody, and, accompanied with the right manner, will save multitudes of men.

The sermon should leave something for the mind of the hearer to do:

That sermon has been overwrought and overdone which leaves nothing for the mind of the hearer to do.

He has a fine treatment of the art of resting audiences; and so the excellence of his exposition of preaching goes on from page to page. The second series of lectures deals with the Social and Religious Machinery of the Church; and the third with Methods of Using Christian Doctrines. Dr. Abbott expresses the earnest wish that the author before his death might have subjected these lectures to a careful revision. Nevertheless he concludes:

I do not know in the whole range of homiletical literature any other volumes as well worth careful study by any man of our time who wishes to understand the secret of pulpit power, and who is sufficiently catholic in his disposition, whatever his denomination may be, to take that secret from one whom history will regard as perhaps the most powerful preacher in American history, if not also in the history of the Anglo-Saxon people.

The Manifold Endowment of the Man

Beecher's strength in the comprehensiveness and totality of it lay in a rarely endowed personality. His genius was rooted more in a brilliant personality than in a profound mind. He was more an efficient personality than a proficient intellect, strong as he was in the latter. The intellect was brilliant, but the center of his brilliance was his acquisitive and radiating personality. He came one day into the home of one of his parishioners, greeted the mother, then turned and caught up her baby and said: "The Bible does not say, 'A man shall not covet his neighbor's children.'" That is undiluted brilliance. But is it not above mere intellect, above mere brain? In wit, too, he was brilliant, as in humor he was seductive. And these were of the mind. But was not his highest brilliance more of the personality in its comprehensiveness than of the mind in its sheer insight?

Dr. George Douglass, of Canada, whose position as a theological teacher compelled him to study the history of the pulpit through the ages, affirmed it as his solemn belief "that the ages have never produced a man so marvelously endowed as Mr. Beecher." Charles H. Spurgeon once called him "the most myriad-minded man since Shakespeare." The phrase won a wide approval and has been adopted by others. Such extraordinary judgments could not be expected to gain universal consent. Spurgeon is said later to have modified his own. But whatever diminution of his fame may be attempted or achieved, he remains one of the superlative men in the history of Christian preaching.

No analysis of mere qualities can completely exhibit personality. But Beecher's endowment, without straining after distinctions which the appropriate sciences will not warrant, may be said to be conspicuously three-fold—intellectual, moral, and motive.

1. His intellectual gifts require foremost consideration, whether or not they were most fundamental in the constitution of his personality.

(1) Foremost among his intellectual gifts was imagination, which in its true idea as the creative and constructive faculty of the mind is one of the highest human endowments. It might well be counted the faith faculty. In its high constructive capacity it is the faculty by which we see the invisible, by which God and all the unseen are made real. It is closely allied with the faith which "is the con-

viction of things not seen." Thus the imagination has its high moral uses; and these appeared in Beecher to a preëminent advantage. "We see in him as in the old preachers and prophets," says Hoppin, "the high moral uses of the imagination." "The real root and secret of power, after all, in the pulpit," he himself said at Yale, "is the preaching of the invisible God to the people as an ever-present God. . . . This power of conceiving of invisible things does not only precede in point of time, but it underlies, and is dynamically superior to, anything else."

This unveiling of the unseen and eternal world is the preacher's peculiar and distinctive function. It envelops all other aims. To this conception of preaching Beecher was deeply committed. Whether by precept or example, this was his unvarying dictum. Imagination he regarded "as the most important of all the elements that go to make the preacher." In him it made intuition superior to most men's logic, and contributed munificently to his originality in thought and speech.

(2) His intellect was resourceful in range and productiveness. The fertility of his mind was extraordinary. That high law of the fine mind that the more it produces the more it can produce was exemplified in him. Even in his earlier ministry when he was already taking on work outside the demands of his pastorate he once preached "through eighteen consecutive months without the excption of a single day." And yet he had no old sermons, and delivered no lecture twice in the same way. There was a fresh going forth of his intellect in every effort, a fresh and vital contact established with every audience and every occasion.

At a meeting of the Evangelical Alliance in New York, the assembly being divided into sections for the consideration of separate interests, he delivered an address before one of these sections, and passed immediately to another section and delivered effectively an entirely different address. "My sober impression is," said Dr. Joseph Parker, "that Mr. Beecher could preach every Sunday in the year from the first verse in Genesis, without giving any sign of intellectual exhaustion, or any failure of imaginative fire."

So wide was the range of his intellectual interests and effectiveness that there was realized in him a cordial intellectual catholicity. Criticized for speaking in Boston on Theodore Parker's platform and having in mind the intimation of the criticism that he agreed with Parker in religious beliefs, he said:

> Could Theodore Parker worship my God? Christ Jesus is his name. All that there is of God to me is bound up in that name. A dim and shadowy effluence rises from Christ, and that I am taught to call the Father. A yet more tenuous and invisible film of thought arises, and that is the Holy Spirit. But neither is to me aught tangible, restful, accessible. . . . But Christ stands my *manifest* God. I put my soul into his arms, as, when I was born, my father put me into my mother's arms. I draw all my life from him. I bear him in my thoughts hourly, as I humbly believe that he also bears me.

(3) He had a gift of knowing the ways of men and affairs which is usually called common sense. Practically all who have written about him attribute this quality to him. Dr. Storrs put it down as his second gift, after a "thoroughly vitalized mind" as first. The quality might be illustrated by his manner of preaching on slavery at Indianapolis. At first he did not do this directly at all, for there was not much sentiment on his side. But from time to time as if it were only casually done he would introduce into sermons on other subjects illustrations which opened out into his views on slavery, so that by indirection he was finding directions out. Without anybody's knowing it he was preparing for a full and open discussion of the subject. "Never before," says Wilkinson, "did so much common sense mate with so much genius, in any of the sons of men. . . . He never wasted

15

much time or strength in beating up against wind and tide. He felt for the current and found it." But there was nothing of the intuition of the coward in his doing it. He was not a mere opportunist refusing to beat up against wind and tide, being fearful of the results.

2. Moral and intellectual qualities hold together in the unity of mind and character. If we may provisionally separate them, there will appear in Beecher at least two conspicuously moral qualities.

(1) There was first his courage. He was cautious. But when he had to choose between caution and courage, caution was thrown down the wind. One morning in Plymouth pulpit when he was under threat of severe injury he read from the Acts about Paul's shaking off unharmed the venomous serpent. At the words, "felt no harm," he lifted his arm and hand and made a downward thrust as if in contempt of anybody's cowardly threat.

Congregations, he said, knew when their preachers were afraid of them "just as well as a horse knows that his driver is afraid of him." The moral was that they should not be afraid. On the contrary he advised them to cultivate the people who did not like them:

Young men, become very much attached to those who do not like you. Those who do will be your worst enemies generally; they won't tell you your faults. They will let you grow up into a little god; they will let you be the lump of sugar which all the brothers and sisters will stir around in the sweet cup of their meetings; and "our beloved pastor," and "what our dear brother has said," and all those little endearing phrases, will pass around, that do not do you half as much good as the rough-hewing of some old man or young man given to plain speaking.

But courage of character has deeper roots than courage in action sometimes has. It is in these deeper springs of character that the real man counts. Returning from England after his public addresses (when communication was slow and he had heard nothing), Beecher was wondering how the country looked upon his action. His reflections under these circumstances reveal the solitary and silent courage of the man's character:

> I had worked for my country, God himself being witness, with the concentrated essence of my being. I expected to die. I did not believe I should get through it. I thought at times I should certainly break a blood-vessel or have apoplexy. I did not care. I was as willing to die as ever I was, when hungry or thirsty, to take refreshment, if I might die for my country. Nobody knows what his country is until he is an exile from it and sees it in peril and obloquy.

(2) In none of the deeper and more intrinsic moral qualities did he more excel than in the breadth of his sympathy. Here was "a door at which every man might knock." And he had the power of so communicating himself that all knew they might knock. The moods of men stood out before him "like a procession passing in the street." He gathered up the sorrows, the distresses, the afflictions of men into his own bosom and poured them back in floods of compassion upon their recipient souls. He never merely heard, he said, the experience of others in sorrow, struggling, groping: "I do not *think* of it, but I *see* it."

3. Shall we say that there were emotional or motive qualities which without a too rigid insistence upon the distinction may be separated from the other elements which were mixed in him?

(1) He had an emotional tenderness which the very angel who presides over human distress could hardly surpass. Here his devotion to Christ was supreme. Christ's compassion for men he translated into terms of his own times and ministry. "He saw much people, and was moved with compassion toward them."

He was himself an acute sufferer, especially from the opposition and abuse of men. But suffering only strung his gifts to finer issues. It touched the chords of weakness and

pride and self in him, and these "past in music out of sight."
There were lines of suffering in the outward aspects of the
man which were but the outcropping of the inner conflict.
There are battle lines on all great faces, and he had his. But
suffering only dug deeper the channels of his own emotion
and opened them wide to the flow of his compassion for
others. "Somewhere," he said, "there must be that power
by which the man speaking and the men hearing are unified;
and that is the power of emotion." Sometimes he was carried
out of himself:

I have my own peculiar temperament; I have my own method of
preaching, I am intense at times on subjects that deeply move me. I
feel as though all the oceans were not strong enough to be the power behind my words. There are times when it is not I that am talking, when I
am caught up and carried away so that I know not whether I am in the
body or out of the body, when I think things in the pulpit that I never
could think of in my study, and when I have feelings that are so different
from any that belong to the normal condition, that I can neither regulate
nor understand them.

(2) His emotional receptivity did not exceed his power of
response. Out of the fountain of his replete emotions he
poured forth his concern for men who suffered, whether
they were far or near. "O Jerusalem, Jerusalem!" he would
cry, while his own eyes became a sea of tears, and floods of
emotion burst forth in all the audience. This mental sensibility or emotional responsiveness wedded him at once to
the occasion, put him *en rapport* with all centers of sensibility about him, and enabled him to pour back upon his
audience echoes of the eloquence which he had first caught
up from them. He was able, as Cadman says, "to browse
on his audiences as other men browse in books." Thereby
he won "the combined unconscious consent of many minds
who . . . listened approvingly as if to their own ideas."

A Prince of Preachers

Without doubt or just disputing Henry Ward Beecher was a prince of preachers. Phillips Brooks in the kingliness of his soul, himself as many will long believe fairly entitled to the rank he assigned to Beecher, said when the latter died that he was the greatest American preacher. Currier counts him "the prince of the American pulpit." Others have ascribed to him the same preëminence.

In a rare degree his natural endowment resolved its component qualities into preaching gifts. The qualities of the man cannot be considered but that the preacher is there standing in the foreground. If Julius Cæsar makes you think of war, Beecher makes you think of preaching. If Webster makes you think of the senate, Beecher makes you think of the pulpit. His name is as nearly synonymous with preaching as a name could be synonymous with a thing not itself. The closer the study made of him, the more surely it conducts us to this conclusion. Nevertheless, some of the emphases of his preaching require further consideration.

1. "What is preaching?" he asks in his Yale Lectures, and gives the answer in terms of his own practice. Preaching must have a practical aim. It cannot lose sight of its object and continue as preaching. That object must be to make the gospel effectual in the saving of men. If men are not saved, the gospel is not made effectual. This aim Beecher recognized and put his preaching unreservedly at its disposal. A purpose to be achieved dominated him, and that purpose was reconstructed manhood, manhood reconstructed by the power of Christ through his gospel in the individual, in the nation, in the world.

There may be some doubt as to the depth of his understanding of the evangelical aim, and as to his method of making it effective; but that he aimed to preach Christ, and

in what he regarded as the most effective way did preach
Christ, does not lie open to dispute.

He also sought to make his preaching a means of comfort
to men. "I have been blessed to an unusual extent as a
comforter," he declared. He held that "to be so placed
that you cannot suffer is to be so placed that you cannot
be educated." This view of suffering could but influence
his preaching. It is in the way that we are *exercised* by suffering which determines its value:

> Put the saddle of patience on your back, and say to suffering, "Mount
> and ride me"; and take the bit in your mouth and be "exercised." Be
> broken. Be trained. Be disciplined. . . . Bear your suffering till
> you know that you are master of it, as at first it was master of you.

He preached on "The Comforting God," and asks:

> Christian brethren, do you believe in the Holy Ghost? Do you believe
> that God's sun actually comes into contact with the lily, and pours it full,
> warms it, and changes it? So he believed the Holy Spirit came to men.

2. His interest in men was not less than his interest in
preaching. Indeed, his interest in preaching was sustained
by his interest in men. Preaching was made for men,
and not men for preaching. This conception of preaching
as an instrument and not an end gave him a power of
human appeal without the shadow of a suggestion of artificial or temporal distinctions among men. He reasoned
"to the depths of human nature, sinking shafts as it were
in the original soil of humanity," and appealed to men in
those aspects of their nature which externals do not change.

Every shop and every street was his study. He preached
"like a man who had gone through the city with his eyes
open." He could bring his intuitions down to the man in
the streets because he had lived and walked in those streets
as if they were his own habitat. He had fellowship with the
very children in the streets:

Is there anybody who enjoys as much as I do the little children on the street? They are a perpetual anthem to me. . . . They come to me like so many songs. And it is not that they are my own or my neighbors' children, but that they are God's children. The street is full of them; and no picture that was ever painted is so beautiful to me as the scene which they present.

Could there be a finer token of his interest in men?

Men gathered in audience were as fuel to his fire. His capacity was multiplied, his powers intensified. He mastered audiences as much by their consent as by his own desire. But whether they would or not he mastered them. "Probably he never stood before an audience which he did not master." Witness his triumph over hostile English audiences. Their very hostility, if it existed, aroused the combativeness in him. To oppose him was to loose the lion to ravage the lambs. Yet he was wise enough to be conciliatory. He was to lecture for Major Pond in Richmond in 1887. It was not an amicable time between the North and the South. The local promoter of the lecture telegraphed him and Beecher not to come, and said after their arrival, "It won't do for Mr. Beecher to speak here." A highly inflammatory circular against his being allowed to speak had been widely distributed. He and Major Pond determined to go on with the lecture. The legislature and other influential bodies resolved not to attend. But when the scene opened they were there, and the Governor too. Beecher arose. He was to speak on "Hard Times." There was a law of God, he said, a natural and common law, that brains and money controlled the universe. "This law cannot be changed even by the big Virginia Legislature, which opens with prayer and closes with a benediction." There were the legislators in a body, and the laugh went around on them. Within five minutes applause began. Pond said it was the most remarkable of the five hundred lectures he heard him deliver. Influential men in a large body visited

him at his hotel after the lecture and asked him to speak
again the next night. He arose and said: "Gentlemen, I am
a piece of artillery here that Mr. Pond pulls around and
touches off when he wants to." But Washington was billed
for the next night, and they had to go on.

Beecher was more persuasive than convincing and influenced the masses more than the cultivated. But he was
so persuasive as to seem convincing, and there were few
that could resist his power. A Southern slaveholder sits in
his church in Brooklyn. He pictures the escape of a dis-
contented slave:

> He portrays him stealthily creeping out from his log cabin at night;
> seeking a shelter in the swamp; feeding on its roots and berries; pursued
> by baying bloodhounds; making his way toward liberty, the North Star
> his only guide; reaching the banks of the Ohio River; crossing it to find the
> Fugitive-Slave Law spread like a net to catch him. . . . "Has he a
> right to flee? If he were my son and did not seek liberty, I would write
> across his name, 'Disowned'"—and he writes it with his finger as he
> speaks. The slaveholder catches his breath while he nods an involuntary
> assent. . . . As he walks out he says: "I could not agree with all he
> said, but it was great, and he is a good man."

3. Beecher was an artist in language, but not exact. It
was his not caring for a pedantic exactness that made him
so fluent and effective. "The price of literary perfection,"
says Dr. J. M. Buckley, "is the suppression of power"—and
that price Beecher would not pay. He was as far from being a
mere precisian in the use of language as Horace Greeley or
John Bunyan. He cultivated himself in *how* to say as well
as *what* to say, but the *how* never swallowed up the *what*.
He was both a user and an advocate of plain language.
There is a subtle charm in plain language. "It gives bell-
notes which ring out suggestions to the popular heart."

On these "bell-notes" he was himself wonderfully effective. "It is not easy to quench a fire that is fed with such
fuel as hers," says he on the Syrophœnician woman's prayer.

"One poor little thin servant-girl stopped" as an inquirer after one of his meetings. "She smelt of the kitchen and looked kitchen all over." He had effected a reconciliation between himself and a disagreeable neighbor: "I might have thrown stones at him from the topmost cliffs of Mount Sinai, and hit him every time, but that would not have done him any good. Kindness killed him." He says tersely: "The true way to shorten a sermon is to make it more interesting."

His gift in the use of illustrations contributed to his style one of its most effective features. None surpassed him here. For this alone he is worth his price to preachers. Vividness and variety are their chief characteristics. "If you choose to take a pole and stir up men from the bottom, you will find plenty of mud." Men's feelings in their conversion will be stirred according to their temperament. In some their feelings will surge as the ocean when a storm breaks upon it. "But suppose a well wanted to be stirred up, and mourned because it could not break and thunder its waves on the shore! A well has to be a well, and an ocean has to be an ocean."

He did not swallow all of Edwards:

I think that if the Angel Gabriel were sent down to this world, and should read "Edwards on the Affections," he would hang his harp on the willow, and think he was one of the reprobates, and had no right to be saved.

We must submit ourselves to suffering,

As a dove, supposing himself to be caught by the eagle, struggles to free himself, and then, looking up and finding that it is not the eagle but his master's hand that holds him, and knowing that it will not be hurt, ceases to struggle.

4. The number of the men, if there be any at all, who in all the history of speech have surpassed Beecher in power of speech must be very few. He had a voice which could soothe as a flute or startle as a trumpet. And he mastered

it on all its keys. He had spent as much as an entire hour at a time on the word *justice*, or on the single vowel *o*, until he had learned all the possible and most effective intonations, and all the highest and lowest pitches of voice. Yet he started with a speech so defective that his Aunt Esther said:

> When Henry is sent to me with a message, I always have to make him say it three times. The first time I have no manner of an idea, any more than if he spoke Choctaw; the second I catch now and then a word, and the third time I begin to understand.

But he had cultivated himself out of all this; and when he went into his pulpit or on the platform he swept all artificialities aside and wooed the zephyr and courted the storm, started a fountain of tears or waked anew the thunders of Sinai.

He was dramatic in delivery, but not violent in action. He assumed a communicative attitude toward his audience, and this requires the conversational or colloquial style. No man is ever a great orator who is a mere pyrotechnist.

His method of speech, after his early ministry, was extemporaneous. He had to come to this or miss his peculiar career. He had no verbal memory. He could not recite even a passage of Scripture correctly. By his own experience he was more and more committed to extemporaneous utterance. He thought he started Dr. Storrs, who found it so difficult, on this course. His own way of expressing it was that he had to cut the cord that tied him to his preparation. The secret of his success was as George W. Smalley says of Gladstone in his "London Letters," quoting Pascal: "You expected to hear a mere speech; you are astonished and delighted to find yourself listening to a man."

Beecher was on the program at a testimonial dinner given to Herbert Spencer in New York. The affair had drawn languidly on until the iron tongue of midnight was about

to strike the hour.   The room was full of tobacco smoke and
dead air.   "Not a vibrating note had been struck throughout the evening."   Beecher arose.   He beat successfully
against all the odds that threatened to thwart his endeavor
and came out into a clear field.

And when he ended, in what was, in all but its form, a prayer that God
would convey Herbert Spencer across that broader and deeper sea which
flows between these shores and the unknown world beyond, and that
there the two might meet to understand better the life which is so truly a
mystery and the God who is so much to us the Unknown here, the whole
audience rose by a common impulse to their feet, as if to make the prayer
their own, cheering, clapping their hands, and waving their handkerchiefs.

5. In pure homiletic value Beecher is disappointing.   He
lacked exegetical ability, and really had no taste for it.
He said: "A text is like a gate; some ministers swing back
and forth upon it.   I push it open and go in."   But he did
not do this.   Sometimes he climbed up another way.   Certainly he cared little for the relation of the gate to the land-
scape and the inclosure.

He did not arrange his material well.   There is no close
coherence of thought.   Sermons could be too thorough, he
said.   His own are not thorough enough.   He is guided in
his arrangement of his material too much by the feeling of
the immediate impression, and not enough by the thought
relations.   As a consequence his sermons are not easily analyzed.   Their immediate value exceeded what is found to
be their permanent value.   They may be read, and will be
read; but not as homiletic models.   He won a notable
homiletic freedom, and was an epoch-maker in American
preaching; but he used his freedom so lavishly as to detract
from his permanent homiletic worth.   His Yale Lectures
on Preaching make better reading than his sermons.

6. His preaching was born of the unquenchable passions
of the man.   He had a great passion for God and the realities
of the eternal world.   In that world he lived, not because he

abstracted himself from this, but because that world itself
was the reality of this world.   There had come One from
God who made himself the Great Reality both of that world
and this.   Of this Eternal Presence it was his passion to
preach and to bear witness.   "John beareth witness of him."
Brooks "beareth witness of him."   Beecher "beareth witness of him."   He poured out in his Yale Lectures his conviction of the value of preaching God.   But it is the personal sense and not the doctrinal conception of God of which
he is thinking.   It is not "merely analyzing God" that he
wants, but to "produce a sense of the personality of God."
He would none of the abstractions of God.   Jacob, he said,
did not say, "O my metaphysical Superior," but cried out
to the God of his father.

He had a passion for preaching Christ in his divine and
ultimate compassion for men.   He was resolved that "every
chime in his belfry should ring for Christ."

His passion for men was in his preaching.   He was both
priest and preacher to them.   He stood ever as "a preacher
and a priest making intercession for the people."   "Nothing," said Dr. Atticus G. Haygood, of Georgia, "was so perfectly satisfactory to us in the preacher's part of the service as the prayers."

No deeper secret of the sources of the fullness and power
of the man has been revealed than his own words about his
prayers for his people in Plymouth Church:

I can bear this witness, that never in the study, in the most absorbed
moments; never on the street, in those chance inspirations that everybody
is subject to, when I am lifted up highest; never in any company, where
friends are the sweetest and dearest—never in any circumstances in life
is there anything that is to me so touching as when I stand, in ordinary
good health, before my great congregation to pray for them.   Hundreds
and hundreds of times, as I rose to pray and glanced at the congregation,
I could not keep back the tears.   There came to my mind such a sense of
their wants, there were so many hidden sorrows, there were so many

weights and burdens, there were so many doubts, there were so many states of weakness, there were so many dangers, so many perils, there were such histories—not world histories, but eternal world histories—I had such a sense of compassion for them, my soul so longed for them, that it seemed to me as if I could scarcely open my mouth to speak for them. And when I take my people and carry them before God to plead for them, I never plead for myself as I do for them—I never could. Indeed, I sometimes, as I have said, hardly feel as if I had anything to ask; but O, when I know what is going on in the heart of my people, and I am permitted to stand to lead them, to inspire their thought and feeling, and go into the presence of God, there is no time that Jesus is so crowned with glory as then! There is no time that I ever get so far into heaven. I can see my mother there; I see again my little children; I walk again, arm in arm, with those who have been my companions and coworkers. I forget the body, I live in the spirit; and it seems as if God permitted me to lay my hand on the very Tree of Life, and to shake down from it both leaves and fruit for the healing of my people!

The Church where his great fame had been created and whence it had already spread to all the world closed its doors upon the last service he held within its walls on Sunday evening, February 27, 1887. On Tuesday morning, March 8, he was dead of apoplexy. A tablet in Plymouth Church, supporting his image in bas-relief, bears this inscription:

IN MEMORIAM. HENRY WARD BEECHER,
FIRST PASTOR OF PLYMOUTH CHURCH, 1847–1887.
I HAVE NOT CONCEALED THY LOVINGKINDNESS AND THY TRUTH
FROM THE GREAT CONGREGATION.

Such powers as he possessed cannot waste in eternal disuse.

"And, doubtless, unto him is given
A life that bears immortal fruit
In those great offices that suit
The full-grown energies of heaven."

VII

HENRY PARRY LIDDON

(1829–1890)

THE COMFORT OF THE INCOMPLETE

How keenly the infirmities of any man admonish and comfort every man. It only needs conscience in any case to find it so. In this community of infirmity there appears one of those ineffaceable touches of nature which make the whole world kin. Nowhere do the great come so near to us as in their weakness. They command us in their strength, but in their weakness they comfort us. None of their tracks quite so intimately assure us that we can follow on in the way they have taken as when they faltered, and when, perchance, they failed. This is not to compound for our faults, nor to convert immoralities into inevitabilities. But here is struck the chord of universal passion and infirmity. "Elijah was a man of like passions with us." That brings him near to us. But he prayed, and he prevailed. That brings us up to him. He was stronger for the contest he had with himself. Self-mastery made him clean and strong. We see men in their strength; but we see them also in their weakness. It takes both sides to make the shield a defense, both members to make the couplet complete.

A conspicuous instance of the incompleteness that inheres in human nature is furnished in Henry Parry Liddon. If we can see imperfection in him, why should we falter to find it in ourselves? If we can discover weakness in a soul so masterful as his, why should we shirk to acknowledge it in ourselves? If there were flaws in a mind so fashioned as his, why should we tacitly attribute infallibility to our own?

(238)

Across the shining foregrounds of Liddon's greatness there flit the shadows of his incompleteness. But may we not find comfort in the shadows which temper his brilliance? May we not gather courage where we sometimes see the faltering of his feet? Do not his faults bring his greatness down nearer to the level of our attainment? One who contemplates the nobility of his character, and the superb qualities of his mind, and the courage of his achievement, and yet presumes at this distance of time from him to delineate the gifts and qualities of the man feels constrained at the outset by reflections such as these to protect himself against the charge of partiality and extravagance. His physical and intellectual gifts and high qualities of temperament were such, said a contemporary, that "the dullest could not miss them, and the most richly endowed might covet them." Is that the verdict of the perspective through which he must now be seen? Does the tooth of time eat his fame away, or do his qualities defy the dingy process of the years?

Law of Diversity of Gifts as Applied to Preaching

"There are diversities of gifts, but the same Spirit." In none of its applications does this fruitful principle find a more congenial field than in the sphere of Christian preaching. The very diversity of gifts together with the diversity and frequency of the adverse conditions under which they have been exercised testify to the unity of the Spirit's action and the effectiveness of His endowment. Can a mere herdsman, keeper of a lonely flock of sheep in a wilderness, leave the austerities of his station there and challenge a priest at his altar and rebuke a king on his throne, and do all this in the name of the God who does nothing without making it known to his prophets? A solitary Tekoite is the answer. Could the narrowness of Jewish tradition and the training of a Jewish rabbi be made to have any fruitful relation to preparation for an illustrious career in Christian preaching, and the early ordering of the Christian conquest of the world? St. Paul is the answer.

Can any age be so dark and morally corrupt and the body of its clergy so lethargic as to quench the light and hush the voice of an assured Christian evangel? A Bernard of Clairvaux, a Francis of Assisi, a monk of Ferara is the answer.

Can a German slate-cutter's son, born to all the rusticity and limitations of a peasant's condition, hew a stone out of the mountain of all his adverse circumstance and shake the Roman ecclesiastical dominion to its foundations, and set the modern world in motion? A German monk is the answer.

Could an English university in the eighteenth century kindle a flame of evangelism which should leap over the barriers of oceans and of races, and spread through all the later time, burning the dross of moral inertia out of laggard nations and stirring afresh the flickering fires on the decadent altars of religion? A little Englishman named John Wesley is the answer.

Might an Arminian think that a convinced Calvinist could not make a Christian pulpit to become a fountain of evangelistic zeal and blessing flowing out to encompass the widest shores of the world? An English lad from the fens of Essex is the answer.

Can an uncompromising High-Churchman, vestments or no vestments, stand up in a Christian pulpit in the nineteenth century and preach Christ with a courage and a devotion which few rivaled and none surpassed? Henry Parry Liddon is the answer.

The Converging of His Paths upon Oxford

Liddon nearly missed Oxford. At any rate there was a chance that he should have done so; for when the opportunity came he was strongly dissuaded from that course by the curate-in-charge at Colyton where he had his first schooling. There was of course no mysterious dedication of his life to an Oxford residence. Nevertheless if there be a providence which watches over our lives in such matters we do not so easily lose the ends to which we may be more definitely destined than we have supposed.

At North Stoneham, in Hampshire, on August 10, 1829, the second of the ten children of Matthew Liddon and Ann Bilke was born and named Henry Parry. He bore the name of his two godfathers—Henry Bilke, his mother's brother, and Sir Edward Parry, his father's associate in the government naval service. His godmother was Miss Louisa Liddon, a sister of his father. She exerted over him a profoundly helpful influence from his earliest childhood to her death when he was twenty-eight years old. He was never married and for a long time this devoted aunt made almost the only home he ever had outside of his rooms in Christ Church College, Oxford.

His father attained to the rank of a captain in the British Navy and proved himself in this and in all other relations of his life to be a man of no mean worth and ability. His mother was a good linguist and a voracious reader, her knowledge of literature extending to several languages outside her own. Withal she was deeply evangelical in her religious sympathies and permanently influenced her son in the way of her own feeling and conviction. She was not pleased with the High-Church propensities which he began to develop after he went to Oxford, and was not unready to allow him to know the fact. Not long before her death she talked seriously with him and said: "You may be a good scholar, a good Churchman, and yet not a good Christian."

Henry Liddon's early life at school was hardly that of a normal boy. He played no games and engaged in no form

16

of athletic exercise except swimming. Later at King's College School, in London, entered in his sixteenth year, he displayed more fully the bent of his nature. He is described as "sweet, thoughtful, grave, complete"; and more particularly as having exhibited himself as "a priest among boys." Frederick Harrison, who makes these statements, says further: "His interests even then were entirely with Theology, the new Church Movement, and the teaching and preaching of the day. At seventeen Liddon was just as deep in Dr. Pusey and his work as at twenty-seven." Of this school Liddon himself said that it trained its pupils in only half of its motto—*Sancte et sapienter*. "Like many other schools, in spite of a large quantity of Biblical instruction, and of the high character of its teachers, it exercised practically no religious influence." His mind had already turned to the ministry, and on this account he refused an offer calling him to enter colonial service in India.

He matriculated in Christ Church College, Oxford, in June, 1846. He took but an indifferent part in undergraduate life, and mentions only one attendance upon a debate at the Union. Dr. Pusey had been at Oxford long before him, and R. W. Church, with whom he was afterwards to be so intimately associated at St. Paul's, was among the senior residents. Newman had gone out to Rome but a little while before. Liddon took his degree in 1850, and had more than two years to wait for his ordination. He obtained a theological scholarship the next year, but little is known in detail of the line of study he pursued. The Tractarian Movement, which had its seat at Oxford, a movement within the Church of England led by such men as Pusey, Keble, and Newman, and distinguished by a tendency to High-Church principles as against the prevalent tendency toward liberalism and rationalism, reached an acute stage about this time. Newman had gone to Rome, and others were

going. It was a trying time for many, Liddon among them.
He made no indecisive choice between the two sides to the
controversy. Nor was he irresolute when he had decided.
He set his face like a flint all his life long against liberalistic
and rationalistic tendencies. And he settled himself in
definite High-Church principles. For the practice of High-
Church forms he did not care except as they gave expression
to underlying principles. He was never a petty and mincing
ritualist. It was characteristic of the man to care first for
principles; though he knew not only that suitable practice
would follow principle, but also that principles without practice will lose vigor. They cannot be wrapped in an attitude of
unconcern and inattention without reaching at length their
own extinction.

Resisting the Attractions of Rome

Ere he was finally settled in his position Liddon proposed
some very definite questions to himself: "Could the Church
of England appeal to her children with all the strength
which belongs to the Catholic Church of Christ? Had she
ever in the past, or present, by any act of her own, forfeited
her claims to true Catholicity? What had the Church of
Rome to offer which the Church of England had not already?" As he moved toward the answer which he finally
gave to these questions the area of his sympathies was restricted. He visited Stirling Cathedral in Scotland and was
cold toward the memorials of John Knox. "I proposed to
the exhibitor," he says, "that Knox did a great deal of mis-
chief." He was also moved to thank God that the Church
of England was "very different from the Kirk of Scotland."

Traveling on the Continent of Europe at this time he felt
very keenly the attraction of the church life and services
there. In spite of himself there was something about the

Roman order and ritual which fascinated him. The impression never reached the point of an intellectual conviction, but the fervor of his emotional reaction to the appeal made to him, whether wittingly or unwittingly, cannot be doubted. He found the celebration of the High Mass at the Cathedral in Ghent very imposing. He felt "that it must have conveyed to the most uninitiated a semblance of the Supernatural." In Rome he saw Pope Pius IX in pontifical array proceeding with his part in a stately service, and thought "the most ferocious Protestant could not but appreciate" the beautiful expression he wore upon his face. On the same day he says: "Mons. Talbot took me into his oratory, which was beautifully lighted up, and begged me to be admitted into the Roman Catholic Church." He felt that the whole affair was an appeal to his imagination and feeling rather than to his conviction.

He had an interview with the Pope himself on the next day. "At length," he says, "I reached the apartment in which the Pope was sitting. He was at a desk, writing, surrounded with books and papers. I knelt first on entering the room, and a second time to kiss his feet. He was anxious to talk, and spoke for some minutes. He spoke in French; said that he hoped I had enjoyed Rome—of course I had—and then went on to express his hope that I should pursue my studies with constant recourse to prayer to God, without Whose aid nothing would be obtained, and Who would ultimately lead me into the truth."

On the day he left Rome "a final effort was made to win him." Again it is the accomplished Mons. Talbot, for ecclesiastical Rome is the shrewdest of propagandists; and Liddon would be a fine catch—nothing else like it except Newman. "He urged me," says Liddon, "with much importunity instantly to take the step. He had told the Holy Father, he said, that he was going to make a last attempt,

and the Pope gave his blessing. . . . Never do I recollect
having felt so much affected by a few words." He saw
Mons. Talbot early the next morning at Mass, had breakfast with him, and then finally left him. "I presented him
with a note," he says, "which I had written to close the
controversy; he was very melancholy, but quite touchingly
gentlemanly about it."

Twenty years later Liddon wrote to Pusey: "I too cannot become a Roman, because I entirely disbelieve the
Pope's infallibility and other things too." In the same year
he also could write this: "If the Creed (Athanasian) is muti-
lated or degraded, I retire from the ministry of the Church,
which, by such an act, will in my judgment so fatally impair
its claim to Catholic authority. Provincial Churches are
beneath the Catholic Creeds, not above them—to be judged
by them, but utterly incapable of judging them without
condeming themselves."

BROADER THAN HIS BELIEFS

Some men live with their convictions, and some live with
their fellow men. A man should, of course, live by his convictions, and live with his fellow men. That is a fine and
true word of Frederick Robertson's that, "It is not difficult
to get away into retirement, and live there upon your own
convictions; nor is it difficult to mix with men, and follow
their convictions; but to enter into the world, and there live
out firmly and fearlessly according to your own conscience,
that is Christian greatness." Liddon did not always easily
find this golden mean. He lived on strong convictions, and
did not readily understand the man who merely made shift
upon volatile opinions. But when he did understand he for-
gave the man everything except dishonesty. On the ground
of his convictions he refused Dean Stanley's invitation to
preach in Westminster Abbey because he was throwing the

pulpit there open to preachers of all schools, among them Frederick Denison Maurice, one of the noblest Englishmen of his time, and as brave a man as Liddon himself. And yet this same Stanley after his death Liddon warmly defended against imputations of disingenuousness and insincerity. "Stanley," he said, "had two intellectual deficiencies which flourished in his mind with a vigor that was extraordinary; he was hopelessly inaccurate, and he was more entirely destitute of the logical faculty than any highly educated man whom I have ever known. On the other hand he had a very strong will, and a very rich imagination which was under the guidance of an odd collection of impulses mostly negative, and which were incessantly capering all over earth and heaven. Under these conditions it was inevitable that he should talk and write in a manner which often seemed dishonest—which would have been dishonest in a person differently constituted. In these matters one cannot distrust one's own instinctive judgment of character. I have had many dealings with Stanley—most of them hostile; but it never occurred to me that he was or could be capable of writing or saying that which he knew to be untrue."

Liddon was a High Churchman good and stout; but for all that he cared more for the spiritual elements in the Church and ministry than for all temporal and ecclesiastical arrangements besides. He had been reading one of R. W. Dale's books, and could not subscribe to all it taught. Nevertheless he wrote to the author: "I do feel that we agree in our major premises much more nearly than I can with some others who, ecclesiastically speaking, are more nearly related to me. We neither of us have much heart for a Church polity which professes itself to be a matter of indifference, and does not claim the authority of our Lord; and this is my quarrel with that estimate of the Episcopate among ourselves which would keep it up for historical or social reasons, without feeling or professing any serious belief in its relation to the Divine Will. . . . And people will only understand the moving principle and the strength of the High-Church School (as it is called) when they see in it an effort to insist that the polity of the Church shall be a religious and not a worldly one. You would not agree in the Scriptural or historical considerations which appear to us to warrant this higher view of the Episcopate, but you would heartily agree in the necessity which all religious people must feel of seeing God's Will, and not some earthly substitute for it, in the laws and organization of His kingdom upon earth."

From the University pulpit at Oxford he delivered the following unaffectedly noble tribute to the evangelistic enterprise conducted by Moody and Sankey in Great Britain: "Last year two American preachers visited this country to whom God had given, together with earnest belief in some portions of the Gospel, a corresponding spirit of fearless enterprise. Certainly they had no such credentials of an Apostolic ministry as a well-instructed and believing Churchman would require, . . . and yet, according to the light which God had given them, they threw themselves on our great cities with the ardor of apostles; spoke of a higher world to thousands who pass the greater part of life in dreaming only of this, and made many of us feel that we owe them at least the debt of an example which He who breatheth where He listeth must surely have inspired them to give us."

A TRIAL OF THE PASTORATE

Liddon was ordained a deacon in the Cathedral at Oxford in December, 1852, and assumed a curacy at Wantage in the following month. He began by writing out all his sermons, but on the advice of Dr. Pusey, whom he had consulted about the matter, he applied himself to the extemporaneous method. He was not without "a splendid gift of extemporaneous oratory." Nevertheless in the long run he made no extensive use of it. Before he abandoned his manuscripts he had made a reputation "as a preacher of very long, very eloquent, and very impassioned sermons."

It soon became clear "that he was not strong enough for parish work." His health was not robust, and the climate of Wantage was not invigorating. "When he had been at Wantage exactly two months," says Johnston in his "Life and Letters of Henry Parry Liddon," "he had to leave it." A friend expressed the result by saying that "he was not up to Wantage requirements." Wantage itself might have been wiser; but perhaps Liddon also had something yet to learn. He gave up hope of regular parochial work. On the day he was ordained a priest he prayed, "My God, strengthen me for that to which Thou hast called me."

An Academic Habitat

Liddon gravitated again to Oxford. His life really had its geographical and mostly its intellectual center there. Samuel Wilberforce, Bishop of the diocese, designed the foundation of a college at Cuddesdon for the training of the clergy and proposed that Liddon should be its first Vice-Principal. The purpose of the college was to supply that devotional training for the clerical life which the universities did not profess to give. Liddon went with the work in education, but was resolved that as for himself the minister should not be lost in the teacher. The times were prolific of misgiving. Soon there were grave questionings of Liddon's general attitude, and his possible tendency toward Rome. At the end of five years he resigned. The enforced severance of his connection with the college touched his high-

strung and sensitive nature very deeply. His melancholy
temperament rendered him acutely amenable to suffering.
From his brightest thoughts, it was said, "a tinge of gloom
is never absent." He was now in a state of somber dis-
couragement and wrote in his diary: "I do not see any
future whatever. My first great attempt at work in life has
failed. This is, no doubt, good for my character." With
all the intensity of his desire for the priesthood—to him the
ministry was a priesthood in the best sense of the term—he
is left without a charge. For the moment "the most brilliant ecclesiastic in the Church of England found himself
without office, employment, or responsibility." He regarded his loss of his position in the college as the great disappointment of his life. "He was obviously," says Russell
on Liddon in the "Leaders of the Church" series, "unfitted,
both metally and physically, for the ordinary duties of a
parish, but his ardour for the Priesthood was intense, and
he was supremely happy in a sphere of work where he could
train men for the priestly life, stamping on young consciences
and wills his own high ideal of the Sacerdotal Vocation."

He thought he might go to India, which had just been
annexed to the British Empire. There were openings for
service there, both among the natives and the foreign residents. But his medical adviser told him that his constitution would not bear a single year of the climate there. There
was a vacancy in the Vice-Principalship of St. Edmund's
Hall, Oxford, and at length the place was offered to him.
He was attracted by the opportunity which the position
would afford him of working among the undergraduates.
He attended to the more formal part of his work, and busied
himself besides with the souls of everybody about him.
"Saw the messenger boy," he says, "and had a talk with
him about his prayers," etc. "A long talk with our Hall
messenger boy about his soul. He is sadly ignorant of Di-

vine Truth." It was a work which conspicuous talent, and even talent of a lesser sort, sometimes spurns. But Liddon had no bastard notions about the proper employment of his talent.

EXTENSION OF THE FAME AND POWER OF HIS PULPIT

Liddon began at this time to be more widely known as a preacher. To this his work in St. Edmund's Hall made its own contribution.

The sermons preached in St. Edmund Hall Chapel were mostly written out, like his earlier Cuddesdon addresses. But for most of his other sermons he made a few notes on an ordinary sheet of note-paper, and delivered them without any external aids to his memory. In 1861 he began the habit of writing out, at the earliest opportunity after delivery, a minute analysis of each sermon that he preached. There are two or three notebooks full of these analyses, written out in his clear handwriting, without any erasures. The elaborateness of the arrangement of these sermons, the fullness of the thought, the wealth and range of illustrations, the simple and ungrudged outpouring of his learning, the deep knowledge of the Bible and the clear grip of its inner meaning, and the fervor of his exhortations, strike the mind even more readily in looking over these analyses than in reading his printed sermons.

From 1858 onward he was regularly assigned the Lenten sermons at Oxford. It is significant to note that both in his development as a preacher and in his stated employment in the office of preaching his work was so definitely related to those great seasons of the Christian Year which draw out the faculties of a man upon the fundamental themes of the Christian religion. It is a fact which has its permanent value for preaching and the preacher.

The extension of Liddon's fame as a preacher as it emanated from Oxford now kept him busy either preaching or declining to preach all over the country. It was a kind of preaching that could not be confined to any less limits than those of the nation. A student of the time, afterwards himself a distinguished preacher and a follower of Liddon at St. Paul's, has written thus of those Oxford sermons:

Can we ever forget them? Could we tear the memory out of our heart? Can Liddon's life be written without a picture of that moving sight? The swarms of Undergraduates, herded in galleries, in deep rows, or crowded into every nook and corner of the floor; the lights; the unwonted fact that we were all in Church; the odd weird length of Burgon giving out the hymn in a shrill, piping tone; the young voices released, in their joy, to sing some old favorite like "Saviour, when in dust to Thee"; the mighty hush of expectation; and then the thrill of that vibrant voice, alive with the passion of the hour, vehement, searching, appealing, pleading, ringing ever higher as the great argument lifted him; the swift turns of the beautiful face, as he flung out over us some burning ironic phrase or quivering challenge; the beads on the brow that told of the force expended; the grace, the movement, the fire, the sincerity of it all. . . . We lived on the memory of it till next Lent came round, and then there we all were again; the same scene enacted itself, the same voice pleaded for our souls. So from year to year, in our weak, boyish hearts the flickering flame of faith was saved from perishing under the gusty tumult of the perilous times.

Beginning with 1861 he frequently preached in Westminster Abbey at the request of Dean Trench. He came to be the Select Preacher at Oxford University, and repeated the triumph he had won among the undergraduates. He preached first in St. Paul's, London, in April, 1863. The Dean told him that his sermon was an hour and ten minutes long, and that he had exerted himself too much to be heard. He was seriously unwell for thirty-six hours afterwards. The building itself was a great physical difficulty. Wilkinson in his "Modern Masters of Pulpit Discourse," speaking especially of Liddon's incumbency there, says:

St. Paul's Cathedral was too much for him; . . . too much for any man that tries to produce in it the just effect of preaching. Three-quarters of Liddon's never excessive physical force was absorbed and lost in the exhausting effort to overcome the pitilessly adverse conditions of the place and merely and barely get himself heard by his audience—if audience can fairly be called an unorganized multitude of people disposed and dispersed as people must be in that vast edifice resplendent for show and fatal for oratory. It was a cruel altar, however richly decorated, on which to sacrifice such precious gifts, gifts always so rare, as were Canon Liddon's.

During this period of Liddon's Oxford residence Bishop
Hamilton, of Salisbury, relations with whom influenced him
as deeply as did those with Pusey and Keble, first entered
the circle of his life. He became one of the Bishop's chaplains, and at his death preached his funeral sermon in the
Cathedral.

The Vicarage of St. Albans, Holborn, was offered to him;
but Dr. Pusey urged him to remain at Oxford, told him that
he thought intellectual development was his line, and that
he ought to concentrate upon resistance to rationalism. A
serious illness resulted in the resignation of his position at
St. Edmund's Hall. But he still had the right of residence
in Oxford, and moved into the rooms in Christ Church College which he retained until his death twenty-eight years
later.

The Bampton Lectures of 1866

Reluctantly Liddon decided when some progress toward
an election to the office seems already to have been made
to send in his name as a candidate for the Bampton Lectureship of 1866. At the election seven heads of houses voted
for him and seven for the rival candidate. The Vice-Chan-
cellor gave the deciding vote and Liddon lost. When only
four months intervened until the lectures were due to be
delivered the successful candidate resigned from ill-health,
and Liddon was unanimously elected in his place. There
were four months of terrible toil and strain, and much anxiety,
and then the triumphant delivery of the lectures.

There are those who owe to these lectures so deep and permanent a debt, such clearing of views and settling of convictions concerning the Person of Christ, that to speak of
them in studied moderation need hardly be undertaken.
Their full title is "The Divinity of Our Lord and Saviour

Jesus Christ." The Son of Man of whom he writes is the Archetypal Man:

Nothing local, transient, individualizing, national, sectarian dwarfs the proportions of his world-embracing character. He rises above the parentage, the blood, the narrow horizon which bounded, as it seemed, His Human Life; He is the Archetypal Man in whose presence distinctions of race, intervals of ages, types of civilization, degrees of mental culture are as nothing.

He is not the Christ of Arius:

Ascribe to the Christ of Arius an antiquity as remote as you will from the Incarnation, place him at a height as high as you can conceive, above the highest archangel, still, what, after all, is this ancient, this super-angelic being but a creature who had a beginning, and who, if the Author of his existence should so will may yet cease to be? Such a being, however exalted, is parted from the Divine Essence by a fathomless chasm; whereas the Christ of Catholic Christendom is internal to that Essence.

It is on the eternal Person of our Lord himself that Christianity ultimately rests:

It is not the miracles, but the Worker; not the character, but its living Subject; not the teaching, but the Master; not even the Death or Resurrection, but He Who died and rose, upon Whom Christian thought, Christian love, Christian resolution ultimately rest. The truth which really and only accounts for the establishment in this our human world of such a religion as Christianity, and of such an institution as the Church, is the truth that Jesus Christ was believed to be more than Man, the truth that Jesus Christ is what men believed Him to be, the truth that Jesus Christ is God.

Miracles are more than evidential:

Christ's miracles are physical and symbolic representations of His redemptive action as the Divine Saviour of mankind. Their form is carefully adapted to express this action. By healing the palsied, the blind, the lame, Christ clothed with a visible form His plenary power to cure spiritual diseases, such as the weakness, the darkness, the deadly torpor of the soul. . . . Such wonders as Christ's birth of a Virgin-mother, His resurrection from the tomb, and His ascension into heaven, are not merely the credentials of our redemption, they are the distinctive stages and processes of the redemptive work itself.

Already he has asked, "Where is Jesus Christ now?" Is
He possessed still of miraculous and creative power?

Does He reign, only in virtue of a mighty tradition of human thought
and feeling in His favor, which creates and supports His imaginary
throne? Is He at this moment a really living Being? . . . Does He reign,
in any true sense, either on earth or in heaven? . . . Is He present personally
as a living Power in this our world? Has He any certain relations to you?
Does He think of you, care for you, act upon you? Can He help you?
Can He save you from your sins, can He blot out their stains, and crush
their power, can He deliver you in your death-agony from the terrors of
dissolution, and bid you live with Him in a brighter world forever? Can you
approach Him now, commune with Him now, cling to Him now, become
one with Him now, not by an unsubstantial act of your own imagination,
but by an actual objective transaction, making you incorporate with His
life?

He is discussing the doctrine of Christ's divinity in the
writings of St. John, and asks why the Gospel of John has
been the subject of such vehement attack:

If St. John's Gospel had been the documentary illustration of some ex-
tinct superstition, or the title deed of some suppressed foundation, at best
capable of attracting the placid interest of studious antiquarianism, the
attacks which have been made on it might well have provoked our marvel.
As it is, there is no room for legitimate wonder, that the words of the
Evangelist, like the Person of the Master, should be a stone of stumbling
and a rock of offense. For St. John's Gospel is the most conspicuous
written attestation to the Godhead of Him Whose claims upon mankind
can hardly be surveyed without passion, whether it be the passion of ador-
ing love or the passion of vehement and determined enmity.

On the advantage of combining in Christ the two titles
Word and *Son* he says:

Yet the bare metaphors of "Word" and "Son" taken separately might lead
divergent thinkers to conceive of Him to Whom they are applied, on the
one side as an impersonal quality or faculty of God, on the other, as a
concrete and personal, but inferior and dependent being. But combine
them and each corrects the possible misuse of the other. The Logos, Who
is also the Son, cannot be an impersonal and abstract quality; since such
an expression as the Son would be utterly misleading, unless it implied
at the very least the fact of a personal subsistence distinct from that of
the Father; since the Father cannot be conceived of as subsisting without

the Eternal Thought or Reason Which is the Son. Nor may the Son be
deemed to be in any respect, save in the order of Divine subsistence, inferior to the Father, since He is identical with the eternal intellectual Life
of the Most High. Thus each metaphor reënforces, supplements, and pro-
tects the other.

Christianity as reposing on the Person and word of Christ is the absolute religion:

The Absolute Religion is introduced by a Self-revelation of the Absolute Being Himself. God has appeared, God has spoken; and the Christian
faith is the result. St. John then does not treat Christianity as a phase
in the history even of true religion, nor as a religion containing elements
of truth, even though it were more true than any religion which had pre-
ceded it. . . . St. John presents Christianity to the soul as a religion which
must be its all, if it is not really to be worse than nothing.

On the point of the unity of the Person of Christ in all the states of his existence as conceived in St. John and the Creed he asks:

Does it not seem as if both St. John and the Creed were at pains to make
it clear that the Person of Christ in His preëxistent glory, in His state of
humiliation and sorrow, and in the majesty of His mediatorial kingdom,
is continuously and unalterably One? . . . In order to heighten the ethical
import of the human life of Christ Nestorianism represents our Lord as
an individual Man, Who, although He is the temple and organ of the Deity
to which He is united, yet has a separate basis of personality in His Human
Nature. The individuality of the Son of Mary is thus treated as a distinct
thing from that of the Eternal Word; and the Christ of Nestorianism is
really a "double being," or rather he is two distinct persons, mysteriously
joined in one. But the Church has formally condemned this error, and
in so doing she was merely throwing into the form of a doctrinal proposi-
tion the plain import of the narrative of St. John's Gospel.

Deism he contends cannot construct an adequate or satis-factory theory of being without recourse to the idea of a Supreme Agent. But even so this being

is gradually divested of all personal characteristics, and is resolved into
a formula expressing only supreme agency. His moral perfections fall into
the background of thought, while he is conceived of, more and more exclusively, as the Universal Mind. And his intellectual attributes are in
turn discarded, when for the Supreme Mind is substituted the conception

of Mightiest Force. Long before this point is reached, deistic philosophy is nervously alarmed, lest its God should still be supposed to penetrate as a living Providence down into this human world of suffering and sin. Accordingly, professing much anxiety for his true dignity and repose, deism weaves around his liberty a network of imaginary law; and if he has not been previously destroyed by the materialistic controversialists, he is at length conducted by the cold respect of deistic thinkers to the utmost frontier of the conceivable universe, where, having been enthroned in a majestic inaction, he is as respectfully abandoned.

But he can be practical as well as philosophical. How did it fare with pagan Rome?

The fate of the great empire was not really decided on the Rhine or on the Danube. Before the barbarians had begun as yet to muster their savage hordes along the frontiers of ancient civilization, their work had well-nigh been completed, their victory had been won, in the cities, in the palaces, nay, in the very temples of the empire.

Pagan society in its alarm could not turn to the State, nor to philosophy, nor even to religion:

The Emperor was the State by impersonation; and not unfrequently it happened that the Emperor was the public friend and patron of the State's worst enemy. Nor could any reliance be placed upon philosophy. . . . Philosophy is much too feeble a thing to enter the lists successfully with animal passion; and, as a matter of fact, philosophy has more than once been compelled or cajoled into placing her intellectual weapons at the disposal of the sensualist. Nor did religion herself, in her pagan guise, supply the needed element of resistance and cure. Her mysteries were the sanction, her temples the scene, her priests the ministers of the grossest debaucheries: and the miseries of a degraded society might have seemed to be complete, when the institutions which were designed to shed some rays of light and love from a higher sphere upon the woes and brutalities of this lower world, did but consecrate and augment the thick moral darkness which made of earth a very hell.

"These lectures," says Wilkinson, "taken together, constitute what it is probably no exaggeration to pronounce the most exhaustive and satisfactory treatment of their subject existing in any language." Dargan in his "History of Christian Preaching" speaks of them as having been "recognized as one of the completest discussions of that sub-

ject in modern times." "Certainly one sees and feels various defects," he continues, "both in the thinking and the
expression, but, allowing for these, the treatise remains an
acknowledged masterpiece."

Many other judgments to like effect have been expressed.
But an article on Liddon in the "Encyclopedia Britannica"
pronounces another kind. There is a cordial recognition of
the author's character and gifts, but of the lectures the
writer says: "As a theologian his outlook was that of the
sixteenth rather than the nineteenth century; and, reading
his Bampton Lectures now, it is difficult to realize how they
could ever have been hailed as a great contribution to Christian apologetics." Why not as well say that the outlook of
the Fourth Gospel and the Epistle to the Colossians is that
of the first century, and express surprise that they should
ever have been thought to have any apologetic value? Is
there committed to the centuries but the Sisyphus task of
rolling the truth each up the heights of its own achievement
only to have it roll down again? Is an epoch of time born
to no truth, and must it bequeath none to posterity? If
each generation must make a fresh start in truth and God
must repeat himself over again, leaving nothing assured in
the minds of men, then indeed does he need to be eternal,
for his processes are very slow. Must there not have been
some truth here when the nineteenth and twentieth centuries lifted their radiant lines of development athwart the
portals of the East and lighted the earth with their coming?
There is a Life that is the Light of men. And is not this
the light in which all the centuries shine? Well, if any man
ever believed this, it was Henry Parry Liddon.

THE PREACHING THAT RESCUED A PULPIT

St. Paul's is the cathedral church for the diocese of London, Church of England. The building was designed by

17

Sir Christopher Wren. It is one of the famous churches of the world. But the building as a preaching place, till Liddon came, had hardly rendered more than a mediocre service. "Hitherto it had been a magnificent architectural monument, waiting, in dignified renown, for the discovery of its activities." Its very pulpit required to be rescued from the restraint which had circumscribed its usefulness. Dr. Blomfield, Bishop of London, driving one day up Ludgate Hill with Bishop Wilberforce looked toward St. Paul's and said: "I wonder what that great building has ever done for the cause of Christ?" This was the reproach that Liddon lifted; and to the building he left a character which all the genius of Wren could not confer upon it.

The Bampton Lectures firmly established Liddon's fame as a preacher. His work after that might add a certain splendor to his fame, but could hardly increase it. When Gladstone wrote to ask him whether he would accept a canonry at St. Paul's in case an arrangement should be made which would involve a vacancy there, he did not at once reply. At such a time he must needs write to Dr. Pusey. "The chief recommendation of St. Paul's," he says, "as of all that I hitherto have had to do in life, is that, if it comes to me at all, it comes without any effort on my part to get it." His appointment was announced early in 1870.

If consultation with Pusey went before the appointment, congratulations from Church, whom he had known at Oxford and who was to become his dean at St. Paul's, came after. The latter wrote him: "I hope the remembrance of those old times will excuse me for venturing to say how exceedingly glad I am that you are beginning, in place and outward function, to be something answering to what in reality you have so long been among us."

Liddon had long had an engagement to deliver a course of

Lenten lectures at St. James, Piccadilly, London. This he
did in the Lent of 1870. The sermons dealt in a closely
reasoned yet popular way with the fundamentals of the
Christian life. They were published under the title, "Some
Elements of Religion." One who had no acquaintance with
Canon Liddon might seek it by means of this book. He
might begin with the sermon on "God, the Object of Religion." Or he might select the sermon on "Prayer." Let
him attend to these sermons and see what the consequence
will be. Dr. Johnson and Boswell were dicussing Edmund
Burke. "Yes, sir," said the old Doctor; "if a man were to
go by chance at the same time with Burke under a shed, to
shun a shower, he would say, 'This is an extraordinary
man.'" Not less could the man say who had formed the
acquaintance, even though it were only casually, of the Liddon of the Piccadilly sermons.

In the same year that he came to St. Paul's Liddon was
elected to a professorship of exegesis in Oxford University.
This position he retained until Pusey's death in 1882. He
then resigned and devoted his time in a more concentrated
form to the work of his pulpit. The two positions in their
combined requirements had answered admirably both to his
talents and disposition—to his love of study and to his
passion for preaching.

His work at St. Paul's was truly epochal. That great
Cathedral, fittingly called a "center of the world's course,"
had found its voice. The personal factor in raising the great
shrine to its true dignity and prestige in the nation's religious life was the ministry and preaching of Liddon. "That
voice reached far and wide. It fixed the attention of the
whole city on what was going forward in its midst." Only
the eternal audit can assess the value of the twenty years
of his incumbency there. He was the first man to bring
the space beneath the great dome of the building within

the range of its pulpit. Hitherto the preaching services had been held in the choir. Thither now the multitudes came, three thousand or four thousand of them, to attend the Sunday afternoon services, which were customarily taken by the Canon in residence. "I have been hearing Liddon at St. Paul's," said Dr. Benson, afterwards Arshbishop of Canterbury:

He unites many charms. His beautiful look and penetrating voice are powerful over one, and then his reasoning is very persuasive. . . . All his physical and intellectual structure is quite swallowed up in spiritual earnestness. . . . One feels that his preaching in itself is a self-sacrifice to him—not a vanity nor a gain. . . . He does not look as if he were in pain, yet you can't help thinking of it.

At length death came and struck down the great priest at his altar. Canon Liddon died on Tuesday morning, September 9, 1890. In his own great Cathedral he was buried.

At the Burial Service at midday the vast area of the Cathedral was crowded, as for one of his Easter sermons in the preceding April. Every arrangement was as simple as possible. A guard of honor of the London Rifle Brigade, of which he had been the Chaplain, kept the line of the procession as the body was moved up into the Choir; the Altar was vested in white, nowhere was there any conventional sign of mourning. The Lesson was read by Canon Gregory; the Dean of St. Paul's—in a very few weeks about to follow his friend and colleague—uttered the Words of Committal; and the concluding prayers were said by Canon Scott Holland.

Preaching in the Cathedral on the following Sunday morning from the pulpit which the brilliance and devotion of Liddon had raised to such a height Canon Scott Holland said:

Can there be a better test of the spiritual sincerity of a man than this—that we feel no shock when he speaks to us the Bible language? And was it not this which was the entire secret of Liddon's power over us when he preached? As we listened, that inner world which lies before the spiritual eye was once more felt to be laid bare. Our world, . . . that world of shifting resolution, and bewildered doubts, and miserable timidities, and haunting hesitations; that world of ours was parted asunder! It was pierced through and through by that vibrating voice. . . . As I speak of him, . . . it is I who should be dumb. It is this silent pulpit which speaks to you.

Less than a month previously John Henry Newman had
died. On receiving tidings of the tragic event—for old as he
was it seemed tragic that such a man should die—Liddon
wrote in his diary, "Found it impossible to think of anything else throughout the day."

Should He Have Been a Bishop?

Liddon's character was so impressive and his ability so
conspicuous that insistently the question was raised whether
he should not be made a bishop. "There is danger in ostra-
cizing such a man as Liddon." So said so indisputable a
man as R. W. Church, writing from his position as Dean of
St. Paul's to the Archbishop of Canterbury. "He is a man
of strong opinions," he continued; "and he is a man who
has the courage of his opinions, and would, if the occasion
arose, make every sacrifice rather than surrender what he
held to be vital truth." He candidly admits some defects,
but still presses his point. Lord Acton also intervened in
Liddon's behalf; though he too was candid, saying that he
found in him all that he loved in the spirit of Oxford, and
something of what he disliked. He suspects Gladstone's
"ostensible preference for Divines of less mark," and urges
all the more the claims of Liddon. There would be some
objections. It would be said that he was "a decided partisan." There would be "much irritation on the thorough
Protestant side, and in quarters very near Downing Street."
He himself feels the force of some of these objections, but
by no means regards them as conclusive. "Assuredly," he
said, "Liddon is the greatest power in the conflict with sin,
and in turning the souls of men to God, that the nation now
possesses. . . . When I think of his lofty and gracious spirit,
his eloquence, his radiant spirituality, all the objections
which I might feel vanish entirely." Dean Church wrote
again, and having said that closely related as they were

Liddon had never made to him any sign as to any wish to be made a bishop, he continued: "I earnestly hope, for the honor of the Church of England, that it will be possible in some way, to recognize a man who is not only her greatest preacher, but, as I believe, her most learned theologian, and whatever criticisms may be passed on him, one of the most brilliant intellects and most attractive characters among her clergy."

Gladstone himself thought the Church of England had suffered heavily within his recollection "from the unnatural suppression of men who were in themselves great powers." He regarded Dr. Liddon as having been "nearly the first to associate a great thinking force with the masteries of a first-rate preacher." The Archbishop replied that there was nothing which he so deeply lamented "as the miserable policies of exclusion." He feared that Liddon's fighting spirit might sometime compromise the unity of the Episcopate: still he was sure that his gentle and winning nature would make for peace, and he felt that if it should at last be decided that it was right to appoint him "he would be one of the foremost undoubtedly of all English Bishops of all time."

Finally a proposal was made to Liddon in general terms as to whether he would accept a bishopric. "I should have had great and sore misgivings in answering *any* specific proposal," he said. This proposal he could only answer in the negative. Why should he be asked "to accept a bishopric *in the abstract*"? How could any high-minded man think well of such an offer? What would St. Ambrose have thought of it? or Dr. Pusey? or Mr. Keble?

Then there was brought to him a definite offer of the See of Salisbury in succession to his dear friend Bishop Hamilton: but he declined. He had engaged to write the life of Dr. Pusey, and if he became a bishop either the bishopric or the book would be neglected. Futhermore he had no belief that he had "the aptitudes for a useful Episcopate." Again, he did not think as a general principle "that an offer of mere preferment to higher dignity and larger income constitutes any claim upon the conscience." He had made up his mind, "with much misgiving and after long hesitation," that had Lord Salisbury offered him the bishopric of Salisbury when he came in as Prime Minister after Gladstone that "it would be his duty to accept." But this offer was not made. Henry Parry Liddon was never a bishop in the Church of England.

In 1886 he was elected Bishop of Edinburgh, but he did not accept. He thought "the Bishops of the Church of Scotland should be Scotchmen." In 1890 another bishopric in the Church of England was offered him. He travailed much over the matter, prayed, "Lord, guide me in Thy mercy!" and at last was led to decline. Within a few months death forever settled the question as to whether he should be a bishop. Francis Paget, Bishop of Oxford, who writes the concluding chapter in Johnston's life of Liddon, thought he should have been. He held that the responsibility and discipline of the office and the zest of its administration would have been an advantage to him. To this opinion G. W. E. Russell vigorously objects:

That Liddon would have been a chief glory of the English—indeed of the Universal—Episcopate is certain enough; but the effect of the Episcopal office on the character of even good men has not always been such as to make one wish to see the experiment tried in the case of those whom we love and honor. Of a certain Bishop who once "did run well," but, after his elevation took to persecuting Ritualists, Liddon wrote: "Popularity is his God, and all his higher chances in the way of character have been sacrificed at its shrine." As regards my loved and honored master, I feel assured that his spiritual temper would have been proof against all such base temptations; but still I am thankful that he was permitted to live and die in a position where he could testify for Truth without pausing

to consider the susceptibilities of worldliness and time-serving and misbe-
lief whether displayed at courts, or in newspapers, or on episcopal thrones.

CHARACTER AND CHARACTERISTICS OF THE MAN AND THE PREACHER

In aspect Liddon was "as ascetic as a monk." Beyond
his face he had no physical attraction. "He had neither
figure nor carriage." But in his face was a rare beauty—
such attractiveness as one finds also in the noble countenance of Savonarola, or Phillips Brooks, or Cardinal Newman. But besides his handsome face he did have "a
graceful action, and a ringing voice."

1. He possessed a richness and loftiness and potency of
personality which was easily one of his greatest assets in
preaching. Loftiness of spirit was in him in itself a quality,
and it tinged all his other qualities. Both in his personal
character and his preaching loftiness was his attribute—
loftiness of thought, of utternace, of tone, of style, of feeling.
The low and mean things of the world, aye, the low and
mean things which sometimes invade the Christian ministry
itself, came to him, and found nothing in him. Here he came
as near as any to his Master: "The prince of this world com-
eth, and hath nothing in me." No doubt he had his resist-
ances to make. He might find it hard always to be just to
those from whom he differed. He might be imperfectly
catholic ecclesiastically. But he was not imperfectly catholic spiritually. He humbly asked the great Nonconformist,
Dr. Dale, for his prayers. He cordially recognized the Christian character of Free Church ministers, though he doubted
the validity of their ministerial ordination.

He was "immovably convinced," when he was convinced
in both mind and conscience. A man never roots his convictions as Liddon rooted his, and does it in vain. Out of
such convictions courage arises as from its native soil. As-

saults of what he conceives to be error upon his convictions
only drive them deeper into the soil of the free and uncor-
rupted selfhood of the man. His convictions were religious
convictions and had the virtues of that essential quality.
In his devotion to Christ and in his sturdy and tireless contention for the honor due to His name there was an element
of the impregnably heroic. He was a Knight of the Cross
in the nineteenth century.

Yet in his greatness he preserved his simplicity, else he
had not been truly great. He possessed those gifts which
may well be counted perilous to simplicity. Yet his simple-
mindedness he never lost. He could not forego the solace
which simplicity brings to a sincere and a lonely soul. When
he was asked by a good woman, who could but greatly admire him herself, how it was that in the face of all the praise
and admiration which his gifts and his preaching brought
him he could still maintain a manner so unaffectedly simple,
he replied in effect that the responsibility of preaching was
alone sufficient to guard the simplicity of any serious man.

2. He gave the full consent of his mind, the deepest devotion of his heart, the most strenuous endeavor of his life
to the fact and the truth of God's revelation in Christ. "His
great strength was his undoubted faith in revelation." He
found dogma in the New Testament; and he could not himself hold the truth in leash. His sacerdotal and sacramental
teaching was extremely dogmatic. On the essentials as recognized by Christians generally he was more convincing;
and he stood his ground without hesitation or apology. He
considered "undogmatic religion insufficient for earnest
moral struggle." He was not, however, an ignorant dog-
matist. His bitterest opponent dare not call him that. He
could give a reason for the faith that was in him. He stood
for that dogma which, as Dr. P. T. Forsyth would say,
"creates the Church." His eager and melancholy mind—

and there was a strange potency even in his melancholy—could not live beneath the misty skies of speculation. He could make no separation between the ethics and the doctrines of Christianity, so that on all sides of his life he required some authority outside himself for the truth he held. "'The Word of the Lord came unto me, saying,' might have prefaced all his utterances." "The Christian believer," says Hardy in "The Religious Instinct," "holds the facts about Christ in a twofold sense. He holds them in a historic sense, and he holds them in a mystic sense. He holds them as having once happened, and he holds them as happening still." It is not surprising that, having said this, he goes on at once to quote Canon Liddon on the point. For Liddon himself said, "The Incarnation, the Crucifixion, the Resurrection are energizing facts from which no lapse of centuries can sever us."

3. Preaching was a travail and a toil to him; but he had put his hands to the plow and never turned back. In delivery he went on very rapidly, with all the passion in his utterance of Phillips Brooks or Thomas Chalmers. This was not only very difficult, but it rendered the articulation of even his rich and flexible voice indistinct. He was never robust in health anyway, and needed not to waste, but to husband, his strength. And he undertook work for which he was unfitted—as, for instance, the writing of the life of Dr. Pusey. Johnston says that beyond any other one cause this attempt led to his early death. Pusey himself chided him about a commentary he had promised to write. "You preach sermons an hour long," he said, "at St. Paul's, and nobody hears you, and you are knocked up for a fortnight afterwards. You have done nothing."

In preaching his subject consumed him as if in revenge for the grasp which he had first taken of his subject. He literally used up his subject in his passion to present it. A

completer, more comprehensive, more commanding grasp of
the theme of discourse than Liddon displayed can scarcely
be found in the literature of the pulpit. This was one of
his virtues which leaned to a fault. His treatment was too
complete. But as he consumed his subject and his subject
consumed him, so his preaching consumed the attention of
his audience. Russell describes the effect of a sermon
preached to the boys of Harrow School on Founder's Day,
1868:

"He looks like a monk," one boy whispers to his neighbor; and, indeed,
it is a better description than the speaker knows. . . . The spare, trim
figure suggests asceticism: the beautifully chiseled, sharply-pointed features, the close-shaved face, the tawny skin, the jet-black hair, remind us
vaguely of something by Velasquez or Murillo, or of Ary Scheffer's S.
Augustine. And the interest awoke by sight is intensified by sound. . . .
The vibrant voice strikes like an electric shock. The exquisite, almost
over-refined, articulation seems the very note of culture. The restrained
passion which thrills through the disciplined utterance warns even the
most heedless that something quite unlike the ordinary stuff of school-
sermons is coming. The text is announced—"Remember now thy Creator
in the days of thy youth." . . . Thirty-seven years have sped their course,
and the echoes of that sermon still quiver in the ears of memory. . . We
are listening, for the first time in our lives, to a man inspired. The scene
has transported the preacher. The sea of upturned faces, the graceful
architecture, the memorial windows flashing like jewels in the autumn sunshine, the handwriting of the names of saints and heroes speaking from
every wall and pillar—all combine to show him, as in a trance, the splendid
destiny of a Christian School. His eyes glow and flash, every line of his
face quivers with emotion, his gestures are so free, so expressive, so illustra-
tive, "that you might almost say his body thought." He leans far out
from the pulpit, spreading himself, as if it were, over the congregation,
in an act of benediction. "From this place may Christ ever be preached
in the fullness of His creative, redemptive, and sacramental work. Here
may you learn to remember Him in the days of your youth; and in the
last and most awful day of all may He remember you."

From the time of his coming to St. Paul's Liddon "began
to subject his genius to a more rigorous discipline." All his
sermons preached there, and at Oxford, where almost alone
he now preached outside of St. Paul's, were written out and

delivered from manuscript. This is very toilsome, both in preparation and delivery. How the reading of a sermon can be made as effective as he did it still remains inexplicable to many. But he did it. He would preach for more than an hour, and still the people would wish that he might go on. His last Bampton Lecture was an hour and forty minutes long. But the admirable structure of his sermons tended to diminish their length. Only the watch told how long he had preached, and not the sermon itself. He was a master of construction. Look at almost any one of his printed sermons; look at his first Bampton Lecture. What could surpass it for skill and strength in structure? Now the structure of a sermon has much to do with its being tedious or not. To walk down a long and unkempt warehouse is tedious. The distance increases instead of diminishing as the journey proceeds. But one traverses a gallery of art and wishes that the day were longer.

Here was one of Liddon's secrets. In lucidity of arrangement he was surpassingly effective. His own superb grasp of his subject, though it might involve some of the intricacies of both theology and philosophy, was so presented through his arrangement as to enable his audience to grasp it. The abstractions of philosophy he could argue as deftly as if they were but the commonplaces of thought. He is discussing the bearing of pantheism on the doctrine of the divinity of Christ. "Such divinity as Pantheism can ascribe to Christ is," he says, "in point of fact, no divinity at all. When God is nature, and nature is God, everything indeed is divine, but also nothing is Divine; and Christ shares this phantom-divinity with the universe, nay, with the agencies of moral evil itself."

4. The qualities of Liddon's style. apart from his lucidity of arrangement, and including this also, are manifest on almost every page he has printed—perspicuity in expression,

elegance of diction, vividness of imagination, felicity in illustration. With utmost patience he applied his keen and
discriminating mind to all the demands of his task. The
result is not a perfect style, but certainly it is one which
bears the impress of unusual fineness and culture. Often in
a single sentence, certainly in less than a paragraph, these
qualities will appear:

Christianity from the first has proclaimed herself, not the authoress of
an apotheosis, but the child and the product of an Incarnation.

Channing has said that the petition, "By Thine agony and bloody
sweat, by Thy cross and passion, Good Lord, deliver us," is an *appalling*
prayer. On the Socinian hypothesis, Channing's language is no exaggeration: the Litany is an "appalling" prayer, as the Gloria Patri is an "appalling" doxology.

We too have hopes embarked in the years or in the centuries before us;
we have duties toward them.

There was one Who had loved Israel as a child, and had called His infant people out of Egypt, and had endowed it with His Name and His
Law, and had so fenced its life around by protective institutions, that, as
the ages passed, neither strange manners nor hostile thought should avail
to corrupt what He had so bountifully given to it.

A religion which consecrated sensual indulgence (Mohammedanism)
could bid high for an Asiatic popularity against the Church of Christ.

The provinces (of Rome) were scarcely purer than the capital. Each
province poured its separate contribution of moral filth into the great store
which the increasing centralization of the empire had accumulated in the
main reservoir at Rome; each province in turn received its share of this
reciprocated corruption.

The Gospel came to her (Rome) unbidden, in obedience to no assignable
attraction in Roman society, but simply in virtue of its own expansive,
world-embracing force.

He (Renan) is keenly alive to the absurdity of supposing that such an
impoverished Christ as the Christ of Strauss, can have created Christendom.

Was that which He (Christ) believed to be knowledge nothing better
than a servile echo of contemporary ignorance?

The tremendous premise, that He who died upon the Cross is truly God,
when seriously and firmly believed, avails to carry the believer forward
to any representation of the efficacy of His Death which rests upon an
adequate authority.

It is His Divinity which makes His intercession in Heaven so omnipotent
a force.

5. His preaching was organically apologetic: that is to say, he had an eye out always for the tactics of the opposition. The thought of the defense of the Christian position was always present to his mind, and his reaction to the prevailing world view as he conceived it deeply colored his preaching. He had a profound distrust of the modern world. He thought its tendencies to be inevitably destructive, both in direct affirmation and in implication, of fundamental Christian truth. "German criticisms he abhorred." He felt himself called to be an apologist.

His method of refutation was just and sincere. He realized that in the long run truth has to be established by affirmation and not by mere negation. His published sermons might be fairly appraised as constituting an unusual body of apologetic divinity. So deeply does he meditate upon the issues of the present life that he finds in unmerited pain a pledge of immortality:

Reason perpetuates pain by committing it to the care of memory. To suffer with reflection upon the fact of suffering, is to suffer each moment with accumulating sharpness of agony. To suffer as men suffer, is to suffer, not as a mere disordered animal organism, but with the moral intensity of a submissive or reluctant will. What is such pain when unmerited, but the very pledge of an immortality which shall redress its unequal distribution?

The distinctive quality of timeliness in his preaching grew in good part out of his apologetic propensity. He preached to his own time, and did it on the basis of what is true for all time. He was an omnivorous reader of newspapers, tending to that excess in the habit which doubtless injuriously affected his style. But he knew what was going on about him. He did not look at the stars and step into a bog. He perceived that even the superficial aspects of an age arise from something deeper and more permanent. Back of his antagonism toward his age was his sympathy with it enabling him to understand its deeper tendencies. In the depth of his interest in religion and in the vividness of his imagination he could discern the ultimate needs of the human soul. In one of the University sermons he is speaking of the stoic philosophy as being a beautiful theory, but selfish at bottom; and he concludes with a single sentence which gives at once a fine example of his style and his effectiveness in the use of illustration. This philosophy, he says, "had as little effect upon the masses of mankind, as have the midnight speculations of an astronomer who is pacing the roof of his observatory upon the thought and habit of the sleeping cottagers around him."

6. Liddon was a preacher and not a philosopher. "You could not hear him five minutes," says Robertson Nicoll, "without perceiving that he was not a philosopher, not a speculator, but a messenger and proclaimer." Yet his subjection of philosophy to the uses of his pulpit is worthy of observation by all preachers who appreciate the worth to religion of a true philosophy. The same is true of his use of theology. He absorbed both the theologian and the philosopher in the preacher. There is to be found in his sermons not only the great forensic qualities, not alone apologetics, a distinct intellectual tone, moral uplift, spiritual illumination, and lasting instruction in the value of arrangement; but each volume is hardly less than suggestive of a system of divinity. Garvie thinks his theology was rigid, and his polemic vehement. But he subtracts nothing from his influence as a preacher. "His powers as a preacher," he says, "will continue to claim recognition."

Moreover, he was a preacher and not an artist. Master as he was of so much that is best in what both logic and rhetoric can contribute to Christian preaching, he yet held these in their subordinate place as instruments and means and never permitted his gift in the use of them to bring them in as usurpers of the true function of preaching. "Logic alone," says Pattison in the "Making of the Sermon," "can never hold an audience; but how much a congregation values a careful commingling of logic and rhetoric may be seen in the deep and powerful impression made on his hearers by Canon Liddon. His sermons are models of what such discourses should be, and his congregation at St. Paul's Cathedral was unsurpassed for intelligence." Liddon himself said in his Life of Pusey: "Good logic may remove difficulties which impede belief in sincere souls, but faith has its roots in a moral temper, and the absence of this temper reduces the most cogent arguments to silence."

7. Liddon has been aptly called "a debtor to the wise." "Among his congregations were always to be seen many of the guiding intellects of our time; and he had unique success with the most difficult of all audiences—educated young men." But he was also debtor to the simple. He possessed a marked power of popular appeal as is testified by the throngs at his afternoon services in a great London Cathedral. In few other instances has a preacher of academic tastes with an intellectual culture so high been so strong in his power over the masses. He was not only intellectual and scholarly; but through his vivid imagination he had the power to invest the commonplace with its true significance for life, and to move the multitudes, who saw the deeper intent of their own daily contact with the world transfigured before them. Here is the scene in St. Paul's on a Sunday afternoon:

The audience listening to Liddon was sacrcely less remarkable than was the preacher. All sorts and conditions of men gathered there, and they came from all parts of the London suburbs into the great silent city. . . . The tinge of sacerdotalism, the unconscious assumption of being in the apostolical succession, the priestly air of one who had little sympathy with the Protestant Reformation, and gloried in calling himself an ecclesiastic, the dogmatic insistence of the schoolman whose "typical abhorrence was a misty Teutonism," all these were minor matters, which might be blem-

ishes or might not. What was certain was that here was a preacher who
drew about him a vast crowd, thoroughly cosmopolitan and made up "of
many nations and of all varieties of creeds."

A clergyman in trouble with his bishop about some matter
of ritual, the episcopal rebuke having been ordered to be
recorded in the Archives of the Diocese, received from Liddon a comforting letter written in the following characteristic strain: "The 'Archives of the Diocese' do not matter
much; they contain a great many odd things, you may be
sure. 'The Lamb's Book of Life,' if through His infinite
mercy our names can only be found there at the last, is the
only 'Archive' worth fidgeting about." *The Archives of the
Diocese do not matter much:* that was a word written out of
the very fiber of his conviction, with the full tone of his un-
fretted soul. A man who in courage so calm as that can set
the *Lamb's Book of Life* over against the *Archives of the Diocese* need fear none of the revelations of the eternal world.

18

VIII

ROBERT WILLIAM DALE

(1829-1895) .

A Tale of Two Cities

ROBERT WILLIAM DALE was born in London on December 1, 1829. In the course of his life he traveled as far east as Australia and as far west as America, but not at any time did he have a fixed abode outside of London or Birmingham. For this feature of his life Dickens's famous title, "A Tale of Two Cities," might be adopted.

His parents were poor and undistinguished save for the distinction they had in being conspicuously blameless in their purpose and consistent in their life and character. His father was "not in any way noteworthy; reserved and retiring, shunning society rather than seeking it; without the enterprise and the vigor that are required for conspicuous success." His mother was more enterprising; more intense in her nature; full of energy and action; capable of enthusiasm, and able to impart her warmth to others. Both of them were members of the Tabernacle Church, Moorfields, which had been founded by George Whitefield. Whether from choice or supposed necessity, they were cut off from much social contact with their more prosperous neighbors.

The mother concentrated her affection upon "Bobby," not through any misplaced feeling of partiality, but rather through the force of hard circumstance, and perchance by the constraint of an unrecognized providence. By the cruel and untender hand of death the home was invaded while the children were yet young, and their number, which else had been six, was reduced to two. These were Robert and

Thomas. Robert had been his mother's sole care until Thomas came ten years later, a time quite sufficient for a frightened mother's heart to be very closely knit to the only child whom thus far the grave had spared. It need not seem strange if the dead whispered in her ears to be more tender to the living. With an ardent and peculiar desire she laid Robert upon God's altar that he might be a minister. "One impression remains with me to this day," said the Rev. James Key, "the passionately earnest desire of his mother that he should be a minister of the gospel of Jesus Christ." Little did she say to the child. But it might easily be that she said more by saying less. It is not the deep and silent currents which flow with the least force. And what if it be the will of God that stirs these currents and gives them the very direction which they take? Tarrying after the services at the church with a trusted friend, a neighbor, she would in their intimate conversation confide to her the unspeakable wish of her heart for her child. In ways such as these the deeper currents of the child's own life were set.

The sterner needs of the home left but a scant place there for books. It was one of those lacks which seem irretrievable. But "books must follow science, and not science books." Much more must books follow life, and not life books. This maker of books as he afterwards came to be was not made by the books of his early life, and yet by influences which run deeper than books that life was given its bent toward books.

The child does not emerge from the indistinctness which enveloped his early years until he appears as a pupil in his first school. Even here his individuality does not distinctly appear, though the school was a good one and fifty years afterwards he was still conscious of his indebtedness to the training he received there.

His next school was not a success. But on the removal of the family to another part of the city he found a school of considerable repute attended by the sons of both professional men and tradesmen. He began to learn from his contact from his school fellows as well as from his teachers. To two of these in particular he became a heavy debtor. Long years afterwards he wrote: "Neither of them knew at that time how much they were doing for me; but to those two school fellows of mine I am under far larger moral obligations than to any of my teachers." From the father of the same boys who on occasion would gather the children about him at his saddler's bench Dale received his first impulse toward literature and obtained lasting impressions about the preacher's work. "I should find it hard to say," he declared, "for how much of my own preaching he was responsible; his conversations with me about his two great preachers, Mr. Binny and Alfred Morris, made impressions on me which must have done a great deal to shape my whole way of thinking about the preacher's work." To his own church also, and to its pastor, Dr. John Campbell, he became a lasting debtor.

At fourteen he left home and began life on his own account. He obtained a position at Andover as an assistant schoolmaster, but found the vocation not suitable to either his taste or his talent. He continued in the position, however, for eighteen months, in spite of the drawbacks, and was not left wholly without compensation. His first year in the school brought him to a momentous crisis in his religious history. He had not been without earnest religious striving. A sermon he had heard when about thirteen had awakened him to insistent thoughts about God and his relation to him, and left him in a state of anxiety which continued for many months. His pastor's preaching had helped to keep alive the impression, but had not brought him peace. Then he had turned to James's "Anxious Inquirer," a book of the time which exerted a wide and very remarkable religious influence. "I read it," he says, "on my knees, and in keen distress about my personal salvation. Night after night I waited with eager impatience for the house to become still, that in undisturbed solitude I might agonize over the book which had taught so many to trust in God." Still he was much perplexed, and all but in despair. He was sure he believed in Christ, but not so as to win the assurance of salvation. He seems to have confused belief in Christ as a personal Saviour with belief in doctrines about Christ. The doctrines were important, but Christ was the Saviour. He sought help, a mere boy though he was, from Paley's "Evidences of Christianity," but discovered there no relief. "At last," he says, "how I cannot tell, all came clear; I ceased thinking of myself and of my faith, and thought only of Christ; and then I wondered that I should have been perplexed for even a single hour." He was received as a member of the Congregational Church at Andover, where he was teaching, being at the time fourteen and a half years of age. Forthwith he engaged in minor religious exercises. A year later he began to do some irregular preaching.

His first sermon was preached in a basket-maker's shop from the text in Ezekiel, "O house of Israel, are not my ways equal?" He defended Calvinism, but held at the same time to universal redemption. Evidently he was going to be his own theologian. But a theologian he was going to be. From the first he was not timid in making an assault with intent to preach upon the great texts. His preaching attracted attention. He had read and thought much for a lad of his age. But his training had been desultory, and he had still a long way to go. He had already made some immature attempts at literature, and now undertook efforts of this kind more systematically.

He had too sound an understanding to be unaware of his need of better equipment for the work of the ministry. Leaving off teaching he hoped to enter one of the colleges established by the Congregationalists to prepare students for the ministry. Dr. Campbell, of the Tabernacle, would be his and his family's almost sole reliance for the assistance which in their circumstances was indispensable. To their surprise and mortification their appeal to him only met with an immovable refusal. There seems to have been wanting on his part even so much as a word of sympathy or the lighting up of the future by a single ray of the hope of any help.

Dale was obliged to return to teaching. His hope that he had made his final escape from an uncongenial calling had vanished in bitter disappointment. Having gone back with a divided mind his work could not be highly satisfactory either to himself or to others. After a while, however, he found himself in more favorable surroundings and recovered his buoyancy and courage. He solaced himself with preaching in the villages round about, became an interested member of a debating society, and withal was making some progress. He occupied himself also with bringing out a small volume called "The Talents." It could not by any means have been faultless, but at the same time more or less creditable to a youth of sixteen. When Dr. Campbell saw it, he was inclined to think he had kept a firebrand out of the ministry.

In a crisis of his life precipitated by the financial failure of the school with which he was connected Dale was approached by his pastor with suggestions about his entering more definitely and decisively upon the work of the ministry, together with the advice that in order thereto he should apply for admission to Spring Hill College, Birmingham. Otherwise the way seemed clear, but the financial obstacles to such a course appeared to be insurmountable. But certain of his friends intervened and without his solicitation guaranteed the necessary amount. He was now not quite eighteen years of age.

The equipment of the college was scant enough outside its three professors. One of these at least, Henry Rogers, greatly influenced Dale, and shaped the intellectual interests and activities of all his other students. Edmund Burke, in particular, came in this way into his life. In his later life, not being a good sleeper, he kept a pile of books conveniently placed beside his bed, among which were always one or more of Burke's best. Others came and went as his mood varied, but Burke tarried always.

The city of Birmingham itself would naturally become one of the factors in his education. The variety of its activities and interests aroused his attention and were a constant stimulus to his work in and out of school. The great political orators frequented the city and had their day there, passing or permanent, as the case might be. To the churches of the city he had of course a natural and interested access. To Dr. James, with whom he was afterwards to be so closely associated, he was not immediately attracted. George Dawson was the preacher of his choice, and he heard him more frequently than any other. Dawson was both theologically and ecclesiastically irregular, but he was original, and had other gifts which appealed to Dale. Afterwards in his "Yale Lectures" and elsewhere he took occasion to say that Dawson was the only man he ever heard who could read the Bible supremely well in public worship.

His school work suffered from his previous lack of discipline, but he now had an appreciation of the value of discipline which he had won at a price, consequently he did not spare himself hard toil. He stood high in his examinations; won the prize offered for knowledge of the Bible; took a prominent part in the debating society; and was definitely advancing in nearly all the essentials of an effective ministry. He preached a good deal in the summer vacation, and obtained sufficient remuneration to go a long way toward meeting his school expenses.

Co-Pastor at Carr's Lane

When Dale went to Carr's Lane, John Angell James had been for forty-seven years its pastor. Dale when he first became acquainted with the situation had rather rawly expressed the opinion that the church would "go to pieces as soon as Mr. James goes to heaven." "In perfect unconsciousness of his own destiny," says his biographer—A. W. W. Dale, his own son—"he adds, 'God bless his successor!'"

His first invitation to Carr's Lane had been merely to preach in its pulpit by way of relieving Dr. James, whose health had not been good. He was now in his third year in college and had entered the theological class. It was arranged that during this year he should continue to give occasional help at Carr's Lane with a prospect of becoming assistant pastor when he had finished school. So it came to pass: and he entered upon the fulfillment of the terms of this more definite arrangement with much to encourage him, yet not without misgiving. He shrank from the very event to which success in the relationship would bring him. For who but he should come into the full pastorate if it should for any reason be vacated? His natural temperament subjected him to depression and struggle. Anyway he suffered distress at the possibility of proving "altogether unfit and unfaithful." "Give God thanks for your temperament," he said in his old age to his young assistant, George Barber. When he said it, he was thinking of his own. He felt keenly the disadvantage and the difficulty involved in his coming to Carr's Lane. "His ideal was, not to inherit history, but to make it."

He and Dr. James were very dissimilarly constituted. But considering the character and the good sense of each of them, it might very well be that they coöperated all the more effectively on that account. James fervently expressed to him the wish that a long, a holy, and a useful life might be his in coming into the relationship: "As it was in my case, so may it be in yours, and this church be your first, your last, your only love. Even longer, more happy, more useful may you be here than I have been. Rich in years, in honors, and in usefulness, may you come at some far distant day to your end; and then, after laboring in the same pulpit, come and lie down with me in the same grave, at the foot of it: so shall we resemble warriors resting on the field where they fought and conquered."

Dale's doctrinal and expository bent was made manifest very early in his ministry. Soon after his settlement in Birmingham he met one day on the streets an old minister, himself a preacher of remarkable power, who said to him: "I hear that you are preaching doctrinal sermons to the congregation at Carr's Lane; they will not stand it." "They will have to stand it," replied Dale. Passing by what might seem to be his brusque self-confidence, there still is found in the remark one of the secrets he developed as a preacher. An old Scottish lady being asked whether she thought the power of the pulpit was declining replied: "It depends on wha's in it." So it might be said in deciding on whether doctrinal preaching is declining. R. W. Dale was in the Carr's Lane pulpit. Pursuant to his purpose that he would do doctrinal preaching, he delivered a series of sermons on the Epistle to the Romans. But he advanced some ideas which contradicted some of the more severe tenets of Calvinism, and thereby involved himself in serious trouble.

As his exposition advanced excitement in the congregation increased. Matters at length came to a crisis. "The church was disturbed and divided; feeling began to run high. Anxiety and alarm were not confined to Carr's Lane. The sermons were gravely discussed at Board meetings of Spring Hill College, and among friends of the college elsewhere." In the meantime he was doing some warmly evangelistic preaching at the evening service. A friend, hoping to bring peace to the troubled situation, suggested that if he would preach a sermon of this sort at the morning service to the congregation which had been hearing the other sermons all might be well. But very decisively he replied: "That would be preaching Christ for my own ends; I could not do that." Finally Dr. James wisely intervened and said: "Now you leave the young man alone. He has the root of the matter in him. The young man must have his fling." All became quiet without Dale's knowing why until Dr. James's death. He went on his way and, as Dr. A. M. Fairbairn said, "ceased to be a Calvinist without becoming an Arminian." His greatest variation from the lines of the established orthodoxy was that in the course of time he came to accept the idea of the annihilation of the finally impenitent on the ground that immortality is not inherent to the nature of man, but is conditioned upon saving faith in Christ.

He continued to be more or less ill at ease in his position, and even went so far as to write to Dr. James saying that he had a growing conviction that he was "utterly useless at Carr's Lane," and that he was "standing in the way of somebody else who would do the work far better." He was sufficiently bound to the place, however, to continue there at the earnest solicitation of both Dr. James and the church when he had an attractive offer to come to the Cavendish Street Church, Manchester. He was now carried far afield in his preaching as invitations from the outside increased upon his hands, and was building his ministry on those solid foundations which should be able to bear the strain of the severer times which were to come. In the summer of 1858 the theological tutor at Spring Hill College resigned and he undertook the lectures on English, Literature, Logic, Philosophy, and Homiletics. He proved himself to be especially pleasing and helpful in the lectures on homiletics.

Sole Incumbent at Carr's Lane

Dr. James died in 1859 and Dale became sole pastor of the church after rather more than six years' connection with it in lesser capacities. One of the first results of his feeling of the responsibility of the unshared pastorate was the manifestation of an increased interest in young people and children. This interest he never willingly suffered to lag, though he was but an indifferent preacher to children. Somehow he did not know how to cause the grass to grow in its native fields for the lambs: he must needs cultivate it and cut it and cure it and lift it high in his pulpit where only the tall sheep could reach it.

He had never conserved his strength through any form of recreation or exercise, hence physical collapse was sooner or later inevitable. When it did come his whole nervous system suffered severe shock; and it is doubtful whether recovery was ever complete. His constitution was hardly sufficiently robust to sustain a complete collapse, no matter of how brief duration, without some measure of permanent injury. "He was still assailed by those shadowy fears which may be combated but cannot be controlled." Nevertheless, he returned to unremitting labor. He suffered nothing to divert him from his pulpit. But he undertook much besides. He wrote the life of Dr. James, became chairman of the Spring Hill Board of Education, and entered actively into a controversy raised about the celebration of the Bicentenary of the great ejection of 1662 when the Act of Uniformity drove two thousand ministers of the Church of England out of their parishes.   There was considerable divergence of opinion as to the way in which Nonconformist participation in the celebration should be defined.

Eminent Nonconformists opposed participation in any form.   Dale favored it.   He was asked to speak in its interest, and did so with remarkable force and effect.   More than once in the course of the evening when he first spoke he "brought the audience to their feet in tumultuous excitement."   This lecture as he himself said, [looking back on it, "fairly launched " him on his course of public service.

He had now reached the age of thirty-two, and was invited to accept the pastorate of a church in Melbourne, Australia.   There was some hostility to him at home, and the new field was inviting; but he declined to go.   A man of his temperament and wide range of participation in matters involved in controversy could not escape criticism and opposition.   And when there was opposition, whether excited against himself, his views, or his methods, his temperament led him to exaggerate both its nature and extent.   Also he gave offense unawares.   He was not selfish.   But he was apt to be self-absorbed, and so abstracted from what went on around him that he seemed distant and unfriendly.   Upon the whole he was committed to a laborious and lonely life.

In the spring of 1864 he was invited to take a place in a succession of eminent preachers who as the occasion required had delivered the annual sermon before the Directors of the London Missionary Society.   He preached on "The Living God the Saviour of All Men," and made a great impression.   Dean Alford in the *Contemporary Review* pronounced it to be one of the noblest sermons he had ever heard.   For two hours he "swept along with unflagging energy."   He was a frequent preacher of missionary ser-

mons, and his service in this field produced the following
story at his expense: "An old lady who for many years had
refused to subscribe to Foreign Missions heard Dale preach
at Surrey Chapel and at once became a regular contributor.
When asked why, she said that she had never thought much
of missions before; but when she saw what the grace of God
had done for that poor Hindoo, she could refuse to subscribe
no longer."

A series of sermons preached in the town hall of Birmingham while his church was undergoing repairs greatly enlarged and extended his fame, and really increased his
power. It was no occasion for trivial themes, even though
he had been a man addicted to such themes. He preached
on the Incarnation, Christ's Death, the Atonement, Justification by Faith, the Loneliness of the Soul, Individual Responsibility, and the Judgment to Come. There is no mean
measure of the man discoverable in the fact that he handled
themes such as these.

A volume of sermons published in the spring of 1866 under
the title, "Discourses on Special Occasions," won for him
another favorable criticism from Dean Alford. The book
had the additional advantage of being reviewed along with
three other volumes under the general title, "Recent Nonconformist Sermons." Dale's book was accorded the highest place, and was said to contain "some of the finest specimens of modern preaching."

He was elected to the chairmanship of the Congregational
Union in 1869, being not yet forty years old, and one of the
youngest men ever called to the position. The two addresses
required of him in the discharge of the duties of the office—
one at the spring and the other at the autumn session—and
the sermon before the same body two years later were of an
order so high that it was said that neither he nor any other
had ever surpassed them. Naturally he dealt with the vital

concerns of the ministry and the Church. He insisted upon
reality as over against mere artifice in worship. "We shall
never be able," he said, "by any artifices of liturgical arrangement, or by beauty of devotional thought, to charm
the impenitent into a sorrowful confession of sin, or the un-
devout into reverential worship." In the sermon as distinguished from the addresses he pleaded for a recognition
of "the supernatural qualifications required for the work
of the ministry," and of the fact of the presence of Christ in
his Church. He adverted to an impressive incident of a
previous time. "We were walking together," he said, referring to himself and a prominent Broad Churchman with
whom he had been intimate, "and he asked me, with an expression of astonishment and incredulity, whether I really
thought that if the shepherds of Patterdale—a dozen or score
of them—determined to constitute themselves a Congregational Church, it was possible for such a Church to fulfill
the purposes for which churches exist. To such a question
there could be but one answer. Great natural sagacity,
high intellectual culture, however admirable, are not essential: 'It is enough if, when they meet, they really meet in
Christ's name—but no man can say that Jesus is the Lord
but by the Holy Ghost.'" *Ubi Christus, ubi ecclesia.*

Publicist

Several years previous to this date he had begun to be
drawn into a very active participation in public affairs, particularly in the fields of education and politics. He was a
firm believer in a broad interpretation of the duties of Christian citizenship. He saw no reason why he should make
any secret of any of his political opinions or preferences.
He took an active part in elections and canvassed by public
speaking for the candidate of his choice. He was a Liberal in
his party affiliations, and numbered among his personal

friends Bright, Gladstone, and Joseph Chamberlain. He
became a sort of "Nonconformist conscience" within the
nation, and exerted a tremendous power over the Nonconformist vote. None knew better than the party leaders
what it meant to have his support. Mr. Chamberlain,
Member of Parliament for Birmingham, was tauntingly
referred to as "the member for Dr. Dale." He replied that
if Dr. Dale had such an influence in Birmingham it was
because he had built it up by the confidence of the people
in both his ability and the integrity of his character.

A prominent Roman Catholic priest with whom he was
intimate once asked him: "Dale, when do you mean to quit
politics and look after your soul?" But he did not understand that his political action was based upon any other
than the highest Christian principles. He would never himself become a candidate, but he acquired an enormous influence either for or against the man who was a candidate.
He did not preach political sermons; but he justified preaching on political subjects. He could not understand the principles of preachers who in the time of some great national
crisis or calamity would preach to the people about the
righteousness of God, and "yet think there is something
like profanation in attempting to show from the pulpit by
what political measures our legislation must be made more
righteous and Christian."

He could not escape criticism of a course involving such
conspicuous political activity. His great contemporary in
Manchester, Alexander McLaren, pursued a precisely contrary course. And hardly any will be found to doubt, in
the light of the remarkable influence he exercised there, that
for him this was best. Was Dale's course also best for him?
Says Dr. S. Parkes Cadman in his "Ambassadors of God":
"The breadth of his ambassadorship has been criticized,
but its scope was entirely harmonious with its depth and

vitality. He saw earthly affairs in the light of the Eternal and pitied the ignorance and deprivation of the people who suffer and toil, in whom he perceived the possibilities of a renewed common weal and the promise of a better day." And Dr. A. E. Garvie thinks, as he says in "The Christian Preacher," that "his civics and politics did not lower his standard, but increased his influence." At any rate all will agree that any day he would have regarded a seat in parliament as a descent from the Carr's Lane pulpit.

His activity in the field of education was scarcely less conspicuous: though it provoked less criticism as seeming to be an employment more proper to a Christian minister. He served for years on the Boards of the Birmingham schools and had much to do with extending and improving the educational system of the city. In the struggles of the Nonconformists for a more equitable settlement of the education of the nation he was a trusted and capable leader. His crowning educational achievement, however, consisted in the part he took in the removal of Spring Hill College from Birmingham and its establishment at Oxford as Mansfield College. This was done primarily in the interest of the Congregationalists and the education of their ministry, but it proved to be a service to Nonconformity at large.

OTHER EVENTS AND CONCLUDING DAYS AT CARR'S LANE

On declining an invitation to the Clapton Park Church, London, Dr. Dale said in renewing his ministry to his Carr's Lane people: "I have never feared and I have never flattered you; I have never shrunk from asserting any truth because I thought it might be unwelcome to any of you; I have tried to enforce most earnestly the duties which I thought you were most likely to neglect; but there is so wide a gulf between my idea of what the minister of Christ ought to be, and my actual work, that, though I thank God that during these last nine years your confidence in me has not been shaken, the expression of your affectionate loyalty and trust has given me pain as well as pleasure. You have told me what I desire to be rather than what I am." Whatever else they may have had at Carr's Lane, he had not fed them on blubber and soft fat.

Though not at all desisting from his diligence as pastor of his church Dr. Dale became for seven years editor of an influential magazine of his own denomination called *The Congregationalist*. This adventure, however, proved that he was not "born to the chair." His health required constant care, and not long after adding the burdens of this editorship to his already overstrained faculties he had a long and profitable journey to southeastern Europe, Egypt, and Palestine.

Moody came to Birmingham in 1875 on one of his evangelistic tours. His simplicity, earnestness, honesty, and spiritual fervor won the cordial coöperation of Dr. Dale, who at first had not been without some misgivings about the meetings. Most of all he was impressed with the "after meetings" and their results, and he labored in them with great zeal. From the meetings there came into his church one hundred and twenty members.

The Congregational Union Lecture—a series of lectures, really—for 1875 was delivered by Dr. Dale on the subject of the Atonement. The lectures contend specifically for that view of the death of Christ which makes it the objective ground upon which God forgives the sins of men. His reasoning at its best is massive in its proportions and full of grip and grasp. The subject was central both to his thought and utterance, and the book throbs with the ardor of his conviction. His conception of sin gave color to his view of the Atonement; and to him sin "was exceeding sinful." John Henry Newman rejoiced with his whole heart

19

"to see so important a defense of the cardinal doctrine of our Lord's Atonement, and such a straightforward recognition of his Divinity in this time and place, and from so distinguished a member of a School so divergent in many of its views from the teaching of the Catholic Church." Dr. Fairbairn described the lectures as "his most reasoned contribution to the theology of his time."

Controversies on the subject of religious equality as involved in the relation of the Free Churches to an Established Church within the same realm exposed Dr. Dale to special hostility. His idea of the relation of Church and State left no place for an Establishment after the order of the Church of England and he entered the fray for the freedom of all the Churches. "In the battle for religious equality," says Sir William Robertson Nicoll, "he took the foremost place, and no such champion of the cause has appeared in this country. He had every qualification—firm principle, an entire freedom from the angularity of mind often seen in those who are brought up to object to what is established, a deep, steady undercurrent of strong feeling, and, above all, a religious temper which helped him to preserve a certain aloofness even in the thick of war." Though he deeply regarded establishment as an obstacle to the realization of the true idea of the Church, he maintained at the same time a real appreciation of all that was worthy in the Establishment as an institution of Christ and not of the State.

He managed his own church without seeking too much to govern it, and preserved in the essentials a fine spirit of harmony during the long years through which he remained as the pastor of a single church. He attached much importance to the pastoral relation as directed to individuals, but found it impossible in his situation to fulfill in any considerable measure the tasks of the relation. Letter writing, in which he appeared to better advantage than in intimate personal interviews, made up to some extent the lack.

Dale became a Doctor of Laws by the generous action of the University of Glasgow. This title he freely used. But he rejected the title "Reverend," and was never willingly called by it. He declined also the use of the title of Doctor of Divinity conferred upon him by Yale. He was careful to explain that this was not because it was of American origin, but rather because he had a sentimental objection to divinity degrees.

Leaders of Congregationalism in Australia invited him to make a visit to them in 1887. Their wish was that he might strengthen the Congregationalists in their principles; "not to attack those who rejected what they affirmed, nor to spread dissatisfaction among members of other communions, but to convert Congregationalists to Congregationalism, to deepen their conviction, to fire their enthusiasm, to give them a larger and nobler conception of truths imperfectly understood or inadequately revered." His execution of this commission was abundantly satisfactory.

As a fruit of his pulpit work Dr. Dale published in the autumn of 1890 his "Living Christ and the Four Gospels." Stated briefly, his contention was that "faith in Christ is trust in a Person, not belief in a Book; that we believe in Christ, not because we believe the Bible to be supernaturally inspired, but we believe in the inspiration of Scripture because we believe in Him; that the ultimate foundation of faith is personal knowledge of Christ, and its originating cause the personal testimony of those who in our own time and before it have trusted in Christ and have found their faith verified in spiritual experience." The book would naturally fall into two parts—the fact of Christ, and the testimony to the fact. Dr. R. W. Church, Dean of St. Paul's, expressed his hearty approval of the execution of the task in both its parts. The book was produced directly out of Dr. Dale's own experience. While writing at his desk upon an Easter sermon the thought of Christ as being then and there actually alive came upon him with overwhelming effect. This is his own account: "'Christ is alive,' I said to myself; 'alive!' and then I paused; 'alive!' and then I paused again; 'alive!' Can that really be true? living as really as I myself am? I got up and walked about repeating, 'Christ is living!' 'Christ is living!' At first it seemed strange and hardly true, but at last it came upon me as a burst of sudden glory; yes, Christ is living. It was to me a new discovery. I thought that all along I had believed it; but not until that moment did I feel sure about it. I then said, 'My people shall know it; I shall preach about it again and again until they believe it as I do now.'" From that time onward he preached as never before the Living Christ, and his people were taught to sing in Carr's Lane Church an Easter hymn on every Sunday morning.

Notable sermons by Dr. Dale on special occasions came to be the rule rather than the exception. He himself regarded a sermon on "Christ and the State" as the best he ever preached. Dr. John Brown thought his sermon on "Genius the Gift of God" preached at Stratford-on-Avon on the occasion of the tercentenary of Shakespeare's birth to be one of his greatest. He testified also that thirty years afterwards he vividly remembered the profound impression created by his address delivered from the chair of the Congregational Union on "Christ and the Controversies of Christendom." "A friend of mine," continues Dr. Brown, "who heard him preach his great sermon on 'The Theology of John Wesley' in connection with the celebration of the centenary of John Wesley's death, told me that the effect of the sermon upon that great audience was, at certain points, simply overwhelming."

An International Council of Congregational Churches, the first of its kind, met in London in the summer of 1891. Dr. Dale was deemed to be the fittest person for its chairman. In the introduction which he wrote for the published proceedings of the Council he indorsed the suggestion, which had been more or less mooted in the Council, that the Congregationalists had a special mission to the intellectual and the cultivated. There was no question about the duty resting upon them of striving to reach "the lowest, the feeblest, the most ignorant, and the most vicious of mankind"; but there was reserved to them this *special* mission. The declaration could not pass unchallenged. The *British Weekly* "denounced it with unmeasured vehemence." It was not a wise, nor a safe, nor even a true thing to say. A church may in the course of its providential ordering find itself designated to a mission or a task more or less specific. But essentially a church built on New Testament principles and holding itself to New Testament standards can no more demean itself as a respecter of persons than God himself could do this.

In the meantime his health was more seriously impaired than ever before. He consulted Sir Andrew Clark and was reassured, though his illness was of the heart. He preaches again with great diligence and zest, but must have an assistant. He selects young George Barber, and finds him eminently satisfactory. His intellectual interests do not wane. He delights in the sermons of Dean Church and of Bishop Francis Paget, and recommends them to Barber. Newman, under whose spell he had previously fallen, holds him still. Flashy preaching he more than ever disapproves. Barber tells him of a sermon of the brilliant but flashy sort he had heard, and Dale replies: "Yes, I used to preach like that when I was a young man; but now, thank God, I have more sense."

Toward the end of his life Dale was driven both by his natural temperament and by what he conceived to be the force of inescapable circumstance into a state of great isolation. He withdrew from the Congregational Union on account of differences which arose over the policy of the government toward Ireland. Earlier he had withdrawn from the Liberal Association which had for its object the effecting of disestablishment. He objected to the formation of the Free Church Council, indispensable as such an organization seemed to others to be, because he feared it would make the Church too directly active in politics; and this attitude completed his isolation. He had much distress over it all, but if he had erred it was in his judgment and not in his conscience. His brethren had too much confidence in the integrity of his character and the purity of his motive to permit him to be isolated from their affection and esteem. Not being physically able to attend in person, he sent cheerful greetings to the Church Congress meeting in Birmingham in October, 1893, and gave assurance of the repose he enjoyed even in the midst of much which might have disturbed him. He severed the last link with the outside world when he resigned the chairmanship of the Council of the Board of Education of Mansfield College.

The suffering which laid so heavy a hand upon him in the last five years of his life mellowed him and gave him a power he had not had before. He found sources of comfort consonant with the change which had been wrought in himself. Sabatier's "Life of St. Francis" came out and awaked afresh the music of his own lyre. Dr. Westcott, whom he very greatly admired, wrote him about his "Lectures on Ephesians," saying: "I am not a patient reader of commentaries, but your lectures give me better than anything else the help which I welcome."

His book on "Christian Doctrine," issued late in life, also

met a welcome which greatly animated his heart. The
Bishop of Winchester, Dr. Thorold, wrote him that he
doubted whether there was another man living who could
write as he had written the passage in the lecture on the
Trinity in answer to the question, "For what does the word
'God' stand?"

YALE LECTURES

Dr. Dale delivered the seventh in the series of Yale Lectures on preaching for the scholastic year 1877-78. He was
the first Englishman invited to deliver them. His work
ranked with the best on this foundation, and indeed had
not a little to do with establishing the high character which
the lectures have almost uniformly maintained. Canon
Liddon, who was one of the most accomplished students of
the science of homiletics in his day and in whose hands the
art of preaching matched the science on which it is based,
"was most cordial in his praise."

Naturally the lectures reveal the man and also much of
his method. He sought "to strike hardest at the evils"
which had lessened the power of his own ministry. Characteristically he held back nothing which he thought he
ought to say. The preacher, he said, for purposes of discipline, should pursue some study which repelled him. There
can be little doubt that here he spoke out of his own experience.

His conviction with respect to the value of dogma finds
expression in the lectures. He thought that without giving
offense to the learned professors who had charge of other
departments he might "be permitted to utter an earnest
and emphatic protest against the disposition to speak dis-
paragingly and contemptuously of dogmatic theology—the
very queen of the sciences."

He believed in preaching on the great truths as being good

for the congregation as well as the preacher: "Occasionally it may do a congregation good to have their logical faculties strained to the utmost limits of endurance, like the muscles of a horse in a great race, and their whole intellectual life stirred to its very depths, by the defense, the demonstration, or the exposition of a great truth."

He thought that not to think of the congregation, and of the sermon as not being merely delivered but *preached*, was "treachery both to the Church and to Christ." He had heard while on a holiday an excellent man preach two sermons, a good man with real gifts, but who spoke as if all the requisites of preaching were present except a congregation. "Congregations soon discover," said he, "that their presence is not recognized by the minister, and they will leave him to do as well as he can without them." He recommended ward meetings to this kind of preacher. "It would do him a world of good to make twenty or thirty speeches at ward meetings, held night after night, in a hot municipal contest." He would have to do some persuading there which well might be transferred to his pulpit.

He instanced Mr. Moody as a fine illustration of the use of the imagination in preaching: "He talks as though Jacob had been an intimate personal friend of his; as though he had met the patriarch near Bethel the morning after he had seen the vision of the ladder and the angels; had been with him when his cruel sons brought to his tent the coat of many colors dipped in blood; had seen the old man's face when in later years these same sons returned from Egypt and told him how roughly the governor had treated them, that he had charged them with being spies, that he had made them promise to bring Benjamin down into Egypt to verify their account of themselves, and that meanwhile he had kept Simeon as a hostage of their faith." And so he goes on until you think his own imagination is as good as Moody's.

He warns young preachers against temptations to desul-
toriness in their habits and ministry; and advises the careful taking of notes as they read; and both these are warm
with the feeling of the loss or the gain which he has sustained
in these same ways in his own ministry.

The reading of treatises on preaching and on the science
and art of rhetoric he had found eminently useful. "I have
read scores of books of this kind," he said, "and I have
never read one without finding in it some useful suggestion.
I advise you to read every book on preaching that you can
buy or borrow. . . . Learn on what principles the great
preachers of other churches as well as of your own, of other
countries as well as of your own, of ancient as well as of
modern times, have done their work." He recommends the
study of sermons as well, and lists among his masters Chrysostom, Bossuet, Bourdaloue, Massillon, Lacordaire, Ravig-
nan, Monod, Bersier, Latimer, Jeremy Taylor, Barrow,
South, Tillottson, Howe, Owen, Watts, Chalmers, Edward
Irving, Guthrie, Robert Hall, McLaren, Spurgeon, Binney,
Parsons, Newman, Pusey, Archdeacon Manning, Robertson, and Liddon. Of American preachers he hesitates to
speak as counting them better known to his auditors. The
speeches of "the great secular orators" he thought should
be studied in the same way as the sermons of the preachers.

He challenged the preacher to a higher respect for the
language he uses. "You have no more right," he said, "to
injure the national language than to chip a statue or to
run a penknife through a picture, in the national museum."

If the preacher wished to be original, he should seek to
"pierce to the heart of things," to "get at the facts which
lie behind appearances." These are but gleanings from a
plentiful harvest of good things.

Preacher

Dr. Dale was distinguished as a preacher, an author, an educator, a statesman. But before all else he was a preacher. He believed preaching to be the loftiest of all vocations. No man could have preached as he did who did not believe in the supreme importance of the preacher's task. No man can make the pulpit a throne who does not believe in a certain kingliness about preaching. No cheap or vulgar notions could attach themselves to Dale's ministry. His was a dominant mind in a dominant man, and he devoted the mind and the man to preaching. He had his prominence elsewhere. But he had a larger place in the sphere of preaching. He eschewed "the perils of negative criticism," and preached the great affirmations of the gospel. He was "a supernaturalist of high degree," and this made his preaching a superlative act. He pursued a wide range of reading, and brought all its treasures back to his pulpit. As a corrective against too narrow a range of reading he advocated the use of books of "a merely ephemeral popularity," believing that this would not only relieve the preacher of the strain of severe studies, but that it would also keep him in closer touch with his hearers and what interested them. He never, however, relinquished his conviction that "the prophet of power must be a thinker, and in easy command of the problems that agitate men's minds."

He was preëminently a preacher of doctrine. But it was the way he did it that counted. Christian doctrine was not to him merely an intellectual system. If Christianity consists in part of a substantial body of truth, then, of course, that truth can be systematized. But to Dale the system was a means and not an end. He preached doctrine, not as an intellectual system, but as a means of conveying God's saving truth and grace to man through Christ. Doctrine in this sense was inseparable from man's salvation; not that he was saved by the doctrine, but that he was saved by truth as well as by grace. God's grace itself is a truth, one of the greatest of all truths. So understood doctrine cannot be set aside. These are not Dr. Dale's own statements, but they are pretty nearly such statements as he might have made.

Doctrinal preaching, then, in his hands was not remote or abstract, but personal and experimental. Doctrine was verified in Christian experience. What he preached he found verified in his own experience. What he preached he found verified in the experience of those to whom he preached. What he preached he found verified in "the experience of the commonalty of those who have received the Christian redemption, who, living the Divine life, are in contact with the presence and power of the Spirit of God." For the Spirit of God himself is the first of preachers of the doctrine of Christ and of God. To say that the Spirit of God can make the Christian redemption effective in the experience of the race and yet shy around the great Christian doctrines as some preachers do is a very rash assumption. This was not Dale's way. Writing to one who had been pleased with his "Christian Doctrine," he said: "It is a fundamental principle with me that Christian people who, like yourself, have known Christ for a long time . . . realize for themselves such great facts as those with which I deal in this volume; and if I found that my statements on these central glories of the Faith did not satisfy them. I should be troubled."

Nothing is more instructive for other preachers about his preaching than just this thing of the way in which he related Christian doctrine to Christian experience. If he preached on the doctrine of the Divine Existence, foundation truth as it is of all Christian belief, that was *belief*. But it may

come by tradition or otherwise to become mere belief and
not be vital and saving in its effect.   But let one who thus
believes be brought into personal contact with God—that
is to say, let his doctrine be translated into experience—
and he *knows* that God is.   The belief is the *doctrine*.   The
knowing is the *experience*.   But who could dispense with
either?

Again, he related doctrine to conduct.   The whole field
of life and of morals came within the province of the Christian gospel.   He was, therefore, profoundly ethical in his
preaching.   His "Laws of Christ for Common Life" afford
a rarely equaled example of the ethical element in preaching.
"The doctrines and the ethics of the Christian revelation,"
said he, "are really inseparable.   Christian morals are rooted
in the central mystery of our relation to God in Christ, and
God's relation to us in him; and we must believe in some of
the characteristic doctrines of Christ before we can discover
the possibility of obeying his commandments."

And yet his greatness as a preacher was not complete.
There was a stateliness about his style which more befitted
the study than the pulpit.   "His words," as Dr. Fairbairn
said, "though written to be spoken, are even more fitted to
be read than to be heard."   The study intruded upon the
pulpit.   In his church there had once been held a meeting
to consider what might be done to contribute to the greater
strength and efficiency of its agencies and activities.   A
paper presented by a layman had dealt with the pulpit.
There were those who had urged that Dr. Dale's preaching
"moved at a height—intellectual and spiritual—far above
that of the congregation generally."   It pained him a great
deal at the time, and kept him awake for many hours.   And
yet he came to feel on reflection that the criticism was just.
Furthermore, he feared that he had gone on so long in the
direction he had taken that he could not change.   "His de-

livery of the sermons was, as a hearer testifies, adversely affected by this mode of composition. It tended to monotony, and lack of pathos; the intellectual predominated over the emotional." So says Dr. Garvie. But Dr. Nicoll, writing at the time of Dale's death, attributes to him "one of the most perfect styles in the whole range of English literature."

The question is whether such a style is best for the pulpit. May not the very qualities which give a distinctive literary flavor be a hindrance in spoken discourse? Dr. Brown in his "Puritan Preaching in England" expresses the opinion that Dr. Dale with respect to this matter was excessively but not fatally affected by Burke, and refers by way of illustrating his point to the comparison which Hazlitt has drawn between Burke and his great contemporary the Earl of Chatham. Hazlitt says in substance "that while Chatham's wisdom was altogether plain and practical, Burke's was profound and contemplative; while Chatham led men to *act*, Burke made them *think*; that while Chatham's eloquence roused the multitude and enabled him to wield their physical energy as he pleased, Burke's carried conviction into the mind of the retired and lonely student; and that while Chatham supplied his hearers with *motives* to immediate action, Burke furnished them with *reasons* for action, which might have little effect upon them at the time, but for which they would be wiser and better all their lives after." John Morley's analysis of the powers and characteristics of Burke is equally suggestive and instructive; and in each instance there seems to be a remarkable justification of Dr. Brown's contention concerning Dr. Dale's style. And there would seem also to be a remarkable confirmation of the conclusion he reaches in the circumstance that, in an inquiry recently instituted in England, thirty and more years after Dr. Dale's death, to determine the names of those who were esteemed to be the leading Congregationalists of the country from the beginning, his name led all the rest.

THE CREATION OF A CHURCH

Carr's Lane Church existed, and existed not without its measure of influence and power, before Robert W. Dale came there, but it was he who made it a great church and expanded the influence of its pulpit to the measure of a world's demands. That his ministry might have been more widely diffused in its nearer effects as well as in those which were more remote none could have wished more devoutly than he. For he was great enough to recognize those defects which, though they subtracted nothing from his essential greatness, did detract more or less from the effectiveness of his ministry. But it was a great ministry, nevertheless. When young John Henry Jowett came into the pulpit which had echoed so long to the prophetic discourse of his great predecessor, it was no mean mantle which he gathered into his trembling hands, anxious and untried at such a task, and with which he struck out upon his own great career.

Dr. Dale died on Wednesday evening, March 13, 1895, and a great concourse of people poured out to him their tribute of admiration and affection while his body was borne to its burial in Birmingham. "No Nonconformist of the century," said Sir William Robertson Nicoll, "has left behind him a more splendid or stainless name."

IX

HUGH PRICE HUGHES

(1847-1902)

Ancestry, Childhood, and Conversion

A converted Jew changed his name from Levi to Phillips. His children, whether under their new or their old name, had all the advantages which he was wise enough to give them through his wealth and business as a banker. One of his sons was the father of Mrs. John Hughes. Being on a visit to Carmarthen, Miss Phillips met John Hughes, a young doctor just from the London hospitals. There was an affair of the heart between them which Miss Phillips at first refused to make mutual. But she had a head as well as a heart, and seeing that really there was no other such match available she at length succumbed. Of their union Hugh Price Hughes was born, at Carmarthen in Wales, in 1847.

Hugh Hughes, the father of John Hughes, was a preacher, and one of the founders of Welsh Methodism. One day in Breconshire a handsome and proud young girl, but of the soundest integrity of character and most earnest religious devotion, came to hear him preach. She lived to count it one of the proudest days of her life when Hugh Hughes asked her to be his wife.

John Hughes was a very devout Methodist as well as a skillful physician. When he would walk the streets with his grandchildren they would ask him: "Why does everybody here know you so well, grandpapa?" "Because," he would answer, "I see most of them into the world and out of it, my dear." According to this account the most of the

(303)

cordiality he received would be based on tradition and the rest on anticipation; but it seems to have been none the less genuine anyway.

Thus in brief is traced the lineage of Hugh Price Hughes. Whatever the influence of his environment upon him he could never have been what he was but for that admixture in him which was determined by heredity. He was a naturally delicate child, and to this physical constitution was added an exceedingly sensitive temperament. He was easily moved to tears, and when his mother cried he would cry too. Once when a little sister was ill he was found in the rain and darkness in the garden praying. He had a disposition to obedience so natural and strong as to amount to an instinct. And notwithstanding what seemed his brackish independence the instinct never forsook him.

Having been already in two schools, he was put at eleven in a boarding school at Swansea, chosen in part because it was not far away, but also, no doubt, because it was kept by a Methodist, who, with his wife and the school itself, was of the best repute. He assumed from the first a sort of unconscious, and certainly unsought, leadership, both in his studies and in play. His letters, however, indicate that in his general development he was backward rather than forward. It was noted that his spelling was bad. This is put down for the comfort of any to whom it may apply.

His father, listening and observing about the family fireside, had been struck with Hugh's argumentative powers, and decided upon making a lawyer of him. In this decision the boy himself seems to have acquiesced. But his ends were not to be thus determined. The number of brilliant men the ministry has stolen from the law, medicine, and merchandise has never been computed. And of course some of the wits will want to ask what became of the brilliance after they entered the ministry. But perhaps some judges

and juries think, and it may even be that some less official
folk think, that the ministry has not been guilty of all the
brilliance that has been snuffed out.

Along with her Jewish strain the mother of Hugh Price
Hughes gave him may of his traits of character. "I am a
Jew," he would say on some intense occasion. It was said
of his mother that she "wore herself out for her babies."
She longed for sons, and had three; though only Hugh was
spared to her. "Every day of my life since Hugh was born,"
she said, "I have prayed that he might do a good and great
work, and be aided in the doing of it."

One morning a crew of Cornish fishermen sailed into the
bay along the coasts upon which Swansea is situated. They
dragged their boat on the beach and went up to the service
in the chapel on the cliff where Mr. Colston and his pupils
were assembled according to their custom. After the more
regular service there was a prayer meeting, and these humble fishermen lifted their souls to the God of the mighty
waters which their little craft frequented. Their prayers
seized the very soul of young Hughes. He could shake off
neither the fishermen nor their prayers. Such a tossing up
of the depths of the soul, as they were swept by the power
of God, was new to him. It was as if the sailors had brought
the stormy life of the sea into this haven of prayer. Though
a boy of but thirteen, he was thrown into what he afterwards described as "a great perplexity, and distress of soul."
His eyes began to see "the King, the Lord of Hosts." But
like another young man standing on the threshold of a prophetic career, he could not see the Lord for seeing himself.
Certain impressions of the more rigid forms of Calvinism
had taken hold on his early life, and he had to battle with
these. A man might indeed come trhough them to God, but
not so readily as by some other paths.

He was never a success at concealing his feelings, and ob-
20

servant elders about him soon noted his condition. One of his teachers in particular, a white-haired old man as familiar with God as the fishermen themselves, a man of the first order of the Methodists of the time, read unerringly the scroll of the youth's soul. One day the venerable teacher and the young boy walked out, as had been their custom, and stood on the cliff overlooking all the expanse of the Swansea coast. His master turned to persuade the boy to yield to Christ. "I submit myself to Christ," at length he said, lightening both his own and his master's heart. But his conversion was not yet made complete. He had taken a very decisive step, but not the final one. He had entered the way of salvation, but did not yet know the power of a victorious, trustful life. His nature was ardent and impulsive, and his temper and his passions not easy to curb. He was "of the mettlesome order, easily irritated, and quicksilver throughout, swift to act and to speak."

Soon afterwards an American minister quite unknown to the neighborhood came to preach at the chapel. Not knowing into just what soil the seed should fall, he preached warmly of the love of God, and that love swept in tides of peace-giving power through the soul that had sought that peace and found it not. "I saw," he said, "that I had nothing more to do, only to receive the light and joy of Christ which was waiting for me all the time, only I was such a fool that I couldn't see it." He never ceased to remember the moment of his conscious transition into the kingdom of light and peace. "My heart danced within me," he would say, "and I scarcely knew how to contain myself as I sat shoulder to shoulder with my fellows."

His quickness over his companions, whether in games or studies, had given him an ascendancy over them which made him impatient and dictatorial. There had been disagreements between him and them. After his conversion there were no more of these. But his contests with himself never ceased. There began now in a new way "that long curbing and controlling of himself at which few guessed, and from which only death relieved him." He continued to excel in school athletics, though in more moderate ways than are found in more modern forms; and there was an early display of gifts in debate. He was able to pass the Senior Oxford examination in his junior year, and in general was without a close rival in the ordinary exploits of youth.

Preparing to Preach

At a very early age Hughes was induced to become a lay preacher. Among the Methodists, and not least among the Welsh people of that persuasion, preaching has been regarded as first of all a gift and a calling. Other aspects of the ministry have not been so much emphasized. They have started their ministers in ways which have seemed to others rather immature, and which must have come sooner to seem imprudent to themselves had not the seemingly immature instances turned out so often so remarkably well. Henry Ward Beecher had a very high opinion of the power of the Methodist system to make preachers. He lived right alongside the Methodists in his early ministry in the West, and he knew the system well. "I do not believe," he said, "there is any other system on earth in which you can take men in the state in which thay take them there, with as few aptitudes, and then work up as good ministers out of them by training, as they do. And I attribute their success to this simple fact, that they put the Bible into a man's hands and send him out among the people. It is the grinding of a man upon other men that makes him sharp. Of course, if you have men that are educated to begin with, it will be still better. But the Methodist brethren take men literally, right from the plow, from the flail, who cannot even speak good English. I knew good 'Old Sorrel,' as we used to call him, of Indiana; now a sound, well-educated, cultivated man, a man of great influence and power. But when he first went on the circuit in the Whitewater Valley, he didn't know enough to tell the number of the verse of the text. He had to count off from the beginning, 'one, two, three, four,' in order to announce "the fourth chapter and the sixteenth verse.' They take just such men, in the West, and put them into a field and set them at work; and they *grow* all the time. They are reading as they ride; their library is in their saddlebags; they are reading in their cabins. They unfold slowly, but the beauty of it is, that they are all the time bringing what knowledge they have to bear upon other men." Times change, of course; but the easier conditions of ministerial development do not always make the better preachers.

It is still quoted as a reproach against one branch of the English Methodists that they might have had Dr. Campbell Morgan if they had not too much feared his lack of early preparation and had not too closely considered the immaturity of his years. After all preaching is the best preparation for preaching. The best education a preacher ever has is that which comes by the doing of his task. But this is also true of every other calling. And haste, and inconsiderateness, and lack of preparation are certainly not the essentials of a strong ministry.

Hugh Price Hughes began to preach, or, let us say, began actually and experimentally to learn to preach, at fourteen years of age. He stood on a table in a little cottage on a cliff beside the coast while the waves brought in their murmurs from the infinite sea and announced his first text to an audience composed mostly of old women. Already, it is said, the prophecy was taking root in the breasts of his schoolfellows that he would be President of the Methodist

Conference. It is easier, however, to see what a man has been than to discern what he will be; and too ardent admirers sometimes get the two confused.

The currents of his life turned more and more toward the full service of the ministry. His gifts as a preacher was one of these. His desire to minister, and not to be ministered unto, was another. The verdict of the house, or the feeling of his fellows, as it used to be called in Spurgeon's Preachers' College, was still another. All about him it began to be said that he would be a Wesleyan preacher. Really his conversion had been decisive of the whole matter. It was another of the numberless instances in which conversion carried with it a decision for a life work in the ministry. The conversion of the man was the making of the minister. Change in the certainty of conversion mightily affects certainty in the call to preach. The method of conversion may be changed, but the fact must not be or the character of the ministry is changed at its very sources.

Having begun to preach Hughes continued, making excursions into country places round about, especially in the holiday seasons, and preaching in available chapels, often to the great surprise of the chapel-keepers at his youthful appearance, his Eton jacket, his unclerical collar, all so different from the garb he afterwards wore, and at his voice so unusual in the preachers they were accustomed to hear.

The final point upon his becoming a preacher having been at last definitely reached, he tersely wrote his father:

My dear Father: I believe it is the will of God that I should be a Methodist preacher. Your affectionate son,   HUGH.

Margaret, the gardener's wife, doing the duty of a maid, was sweeping the house when she was burst in upon by Mrs. Hughes in a state of great agitation and giving vent to the exclamation: "O, Margaret, such news!" "Indeed, now," said Margaret, expecting at the least to hear that somebody was dead. "Hugh is going to be a minister," Mrs. Hughes continued; "he wrote to the doctor this morning." "It is not for weeping, Mrs. Hughes; we must laugh," said Margaret; "there is nothing to weep about." But, indeed, weeping was only her way of laughing. For she knew that God had only answered her prayer, though more dramatically than she had expected. "My dear son," replied the father, speaking as tersely as the son himself had done: "I would rather you were a Wesleyan preacher than Lord Chancellor of England."

The enthusiasm of preaching seized Hughes from the first. It is not recorded that he was ever reluctant to preach anywhere the opportunity offered. Returning from school, he preached in his home church, the Welsh Wesleyan chapel, at Carmarthen; and then at the English Wesleyan chapel. These two sermons before his own people were occasions of a natural anxiety, and he is known to have made unusual preparation for them.

His health had now improved. His daughter who has written his biography says "he was no longer frail and undersized." His staid old grandmother did not like his cricket playing. She thought such a pastime "not fitting for a future Wesleyan preacher." His mother thought otherwise. "Whatever builds up the health of my son will build him up as a preacher," she said. Fresh mental activities had burst forth in him in his conversion. The range of his intellectual interests was widened. He had been early awakened to an interest in European affairs by one of his schoolmasters. He formed a habit which only grew with the years of searching the world's daily turn of affairs through the newspapers. He had opinions for which he stood ready to give a reason. His power in debate was inborn, and had only to be cultivated, not created. In theology and philosophy he read Butler, Pearson, and Watson. In history he read Carlyle and Motley. He favored the South in the American Civil War until he read Beecher's Liverpool speeches and faced about. He read "Uncle Tom's Cabin," and said: "Harriet Beecher Stowe abolished slavery!" He could never understand how ministers of Christ could stand for the retention of slavery. In these ways of study and reflection he was employed for two years while he remained at home in anticipation of his entrance upon a systematic course of theological study. His father's was the shaping hand in all this. His daughter thinks, however, that in his endowments he was "preëminently the child of the women of his race."

A Theological Student

Hughes passed a highly creditable examination and entered Richmond College, a theological institution of the Wesleyan Methodist Church, at eighteen years of age. A fellow-sufferer in the examination remarked to him: "If it is the will of God, I shall enter college this autumn." Hughes amended the pious statement by saying: "If you have passed your examination, my dear fellow." He was very happily situated in the college. Dr. W. F. Moulton, then about thirty years of age, one of the ablest all-round scholars British Methodism has produced, was there; and his character was not less excellent than his scholarship. What he did for Hughes is another of the incalculable debts of a student to his tutor.

Hughes in his politics is described as being at this time "the most ultra of conservatives." A change was due to come to him here, as also in respect of other matters; for Mrs. Moulton related how at her table "he would speak with strong disapproval both of revivalistic methods and teetotalism." In truth, it was said that "he could not see any reason why he should desist from drinking a glass of beer every night as he had been accustomed to do at home with his father." Habits of hard study, however, he did approve; and diligent application; and wide reading. He did not balance a prayer meeting over against his duty to his books.

His sermons of the time were intellectual, and it was predicted that his ministry would incline toward the tastes of intellectual and cultured congregations. His fellow students charged him with conceit; but he would only admit that he had just appreciation of his own ability. No doubt this is a good alibi, if it can be proved. In reality he suffered from periods of depression, and thought not too highly of either his gifts or his goodness. He had a facility for acquaintanceship when he wished it so, but he made few intimate friends. Before he got out of college there were one or two matters of current interest on which he was brought into collision with the authorities set over him. On one of these, which had to do with Conference authority and administration, he was resolute to the end. He never hesitated to contend for what he thought belonged to the progress of the Church and of the kingdom of God in the world. With respect to matters of this kind there is an inevitable difference of mind and opinion. But he was not afraid of the difference. He might be wrong, but he was not afraid. "Even the decisions of Conference are not infallible," he was reported to have said when he was not supposed to be heard at all.

There was at one time a movement toward having the Conference punish him for what was accounted to be a grievous indiscretion. His father wrote to Dr. Moulton: "Hugh tells me that in consequence of some impolitic observations made in a speech of his at the missionary meeting at Richmond, the Committee has resolved to recommend the district meeting to advise the Conference to take from

him one year of traveling which had been allowed him last
Conference—a punishment which, from the necessary pub-
licity which must be given to it, is certainly severe, though
it may be deserved." Hugh had recently been at home, but
had said nothing to his father about the matter. Even in
writing he had not specified the offense. "If he has deserved
this punishment," his father continues, "I have only to
regret it, and to submit to what is to me, I confess, a great
mortification." He escaped the proposed punishment, and
neither he nor the Conference was any the worse for it. But
there was a feeling aroused against him on the part of some
which did not readily abate. Dr. Moulton had advised him
to take a degree at London University, and this he accomplished with the B.A., in 1869.

Hughes took at Richmond College a course not prescribed
in the curriculum. The Governor of the College had a
daughter named Mary Katharine. She did not always go
across the campus alone. More frequently than mere convention required it was observed that she was accompanied
by Hugh Price Hughes. They had met when she was only
twelve. She distinctly remembered that she had felt from
the first that she had met some one who was going to influence her future life. She asked him to subscribe to her
missionary collection book. He at first refused because he
had promised another girl. But after a while he relented
and subscribed a penny a week. She had to go to his rooms
to collect it. And thereby a tale came to hang. Hughes
collected the fair young collector. They became engaged.
He went to the Governor, the very man most young lovers
have to go to. "She is very young," he said; "far too young
for such thoughts. She has much to learn—you both have,
I may say; but personally I would willingly trust her with
you—if God so will it." This was a virtual consent. But
Mrs. Barrett—the Governor was Reverend Alfred Barrett

—was not by any means so easily appeased. "Mr. Hughes had always alarmed her with his precocity, and here was precocity indeed." And so they waited. But they waited as "watchmen wait for the morning." Mary Katharine went away to school. They agreed not to correspond, and in general to hold the affair as much in abeyance as if it had not been. The waiting was long, and many a time it was weary. They were not married till his second year in Dover. But they were richly rewarded in a love and confidence which held them to the end.

Conditions and Directions of His Development

Hughes went at the age of twenty-two as pastor at Dover. He had still some notions about himself and the ministry which required settling. Mere revival preaching, pressing men to a decision then and there, he thought was a low type. He liked no extremes. Teetotalism was a fad. But Dover was reputed to be "dead." And Dover was to rescue his ministry from possible dullness and deadness. Mercifully and all but unasked the Lord of his ministry intervened. Eighteen penitents came to the front in the inquiry room when he had preached his first sermon in Dover. Nobody had seen it on this wise. He himself had not. Pale and spectacled, there he stood undergoing a great transformation. It may be said that the first Sunday night in Dover did it. It was the beginning of his ministry. It had now got its type, and was to expand, but not really to change again.

Again, at Dover he had lodgings looking out on the homes of the poor. Their condition sank into his soul. He took their burdens on his shoulders, their sorrows on his heart. "In the street, in the houses, in his own study, at the window, he drank in matter not only for his own learning, but for that of his Church and other Churches in addition."

Again, the type of his ministry was deepened and determined.

Once more, it was at Dover that the nonsense of teetotalism became sense to him. There lived in a humble quarter of the town an old sailor who had gathered a few disciples for the promotion of temperance. A young Wesleyan had been drawn into their circle. They had begun to organize Bands of Hope. This young man thought there should be one in Snargate Street Chapel where Hughes was pastor. He came with much misgiving. But Hughes received him cordially, and said: "Certainly, the idea is excellent. I will speak to my superintendent and see what can be done in the matter." An organization was effected and Hughes himself was the first to sign the pledge. Thenceforward his advocacy of temperance became more pronounced, extending to public measures and the public platform; though he opposed barring from official place in the church those who were engaged in the traffic in alcoholic beverages. This was one of the points at which he was charged with inconsistency. But of his advocacy of the main cause of temperance none was left in any doubt. A prominent public man came to remonstrate with him on the subject and said: "You must not upset the party with your teetotalism." With decision he replied: "What do I care for your party? I have to do with temperance and the cause of God."

It was also at Dover that he changed his political opinion and allegiance and became a Liberal. The change was indicated by the general enlargement of his ideas and sympathies at the time. Another instance to the same effect was his enlistment with Mrs. Josephine Butler in the Social Purity Movement.

Brighton succeeded Dover in the round of his pastoral assignments. His ministry here was more intellectual and less immediately fruitful than in Dover. Green's "Short

History of the English People" came from the press, and the reading of it profoundly impressed him. It seemed to chime with his idea that the world was made up mostly of people and not only of lords and great ones. The deepest and most permanent impression of his life at Brighton came through an incident, though surely not an accident. Some sane advocates of sane holiness came there, and a convention was held. The idea sought to be inculcated was that sin is not a necessary condition of existence, but that a searching work of God's grace through the Holy Spirit can produce holiness both in thought and act. The proposal was very congenial to both the mind and the desire of Hughes; and he also thought it soundly Methodistic. He had surrendered himself in his conversion and had thought of nothing further, nor conceived of any consecration more cleansing and profound. But now he did think. And in consequence he entered into an experience which cleansed all the secret and deeper intentions and purposes of his soul. Henceforth there lay upon his life the power of a singular and more unreserved consecration. He made no shibboleth of it, but there was no doubt of the change. Changes so profound and spiritual leave no doubt of themselves. They do not require to be published, any more than a new star requires to publish its presence in the sky.

It must be true, as Miss Hughes says, that "it is not natural to a gifted man to oppose a consensus of the educated, the influential, and the rich, as my father did, in openly espousing the causes with which he became associated—to wit, direct evangelical preaching, temperance, and measures connected with social purity." But in the Brighton experience the whole transaction was made complete, and there was no more glancing aside toward the allurements of what the world would have counted a more cultured ministry. Henceforth he was also able "to adjust more truly the difficult balance between the purely ministerial and those great public duties which it was part of that ministry to emphatically recognize."

Tottenham and Dulwich came after Brighton, and then Oxford. He was developing rapidly in the various directions of his many-sided ministry. His marked capacity for helping all kinds of people going through all kinds of struggle and sorrow was adding to his cares as well as to his usefulness. His health had been less than good, and in obedience to the advice of his physician, in whom he was fortunate to have his own brother-in-law, Dr. Howard Barrett, he had already taken several trips to Switzerland.

He came to Oxford at thirty-four. What rolls more grandly off the tongue than such a phrase as "ancient seat of British learning"? Well, here it was. And Hughes was not a man to be insensible to the finer issues of the occasion. Oxford had offered no fruitful field to Nonconformity, not even to the followers of John Wesley, easily one of the most distinguished of her sons. Hughes had serious thoughts about Methodism. He had already reached the conclusion that it must be reconstructed in some of its attitudes in order to come closer to the modern world. He now began to doubt whether its three-year system of appointments was suitable to all places alike. Could it meet the situation at Oxford, for instance? "If Methodism is to flourish," he said, "we must be continually adapting it to new circumstances. We lose more members than any other Church— that is our weakness. May God help us to remedy it."

At Oxford he remembered Newman. And he remembered Wesley. His Methodist critics should remember that—*he remembered Wesley*. How dull would be the soul to whom Oxford did not appeal! And Hughes was not a dull soul. He had the full time limit of three years there, and often regretted afterwards that he had not made more use of the peculiar opportunities for study which the place afforded. A good account of his preaching at the time is given by a young man who came up to stand an examination. "I heard him preach on a Sunday evening," he says, "and I must confess that the first impression was a little disappointing. Earlier in the year I had heard one of the last of Dr. Punshon's addresses, and superb rhetoric was not unnaturally the ideal of a schoolboy. Of rhetoric and fireworks there was not a trace in Mr. Hughes's businesslike method of speech. It was not till the end of the sermon that I noticed its *effectiveness;* I had not missed a single word. This quality of not only arresting, but keeping attention, was Mr. Hughes's most extraordinary mark as a speaker; and the effect was attained by the simplest means. There were no outbursts; no purple 'patches'; everything was plain and unadorned; but I do not believe that any speaker ever lived who had more thoroughly learned the secret of establishing a *rapport* with his hearers in his first sentence, and maintaining it unimpaired to the end." Some of this might be dismissed as consisting in youthful enthusiasm. But what shall be done when the *London Times* says that he was one of the six most popular speakers in England? or when a great religious editor says that this was rightly said?

Oxford culture was seductive; but it did not stupefy his conviction of the primacy of religion. What if he gained the whole world of culture and lost the souls of men? Passing down one of the streets of the city one day he noticed a member of the University walking on the other side. A constraint possessed him to cross over and speak to this man. He was not at all intimate with him, and had a difficulty to go. After a word or two he said: "Excuse me, but I am curiously constrained to come and ask you a question. What is your opinion of Jesus Christ of Nazareth? How does it stand between you and Him?" "Mr. Hughes," the

surprised man answered, "I have been waiting for twenty
years for somebody to ask me that question. Come to my
rooms and talk to me." This was an incident worthy of
John Wesley. "As for my friend Mr. Hughes," said Dr.
Parker, "he positively lies in wait for the devil at every
corner."

In many ways his ministry was not unfruitful in Oxford.
He organized and conducted a special mission there, as he
had done in Dulwich. He called to his assistance in effecting his organization a man whom he knew to be very capable
in business, and active in municipal and political affairs.
His service was very cordial and effective. He was of Methodist lineage, and came to chapel, but would go no further.
So now he wrote to Hughes and said he would not have him
rest under any misapprehensions. His part was now done.
He would have nothing to do with the "spiritual portion."
"But he would come to hear him preach," Hughes re-
sponded; "surely he would do that." "Well, he might do
that." Coming to chapel and seeing the man there Hughes
beckoned him into the vestry, and said to him: "You cannot imagine how lonely a mission preacher feels. Surely
you will sit in the front where I can speak to you if I require
anything." And so in front he sat and presently could
hardly believe the report his own ears brought him when he
heard himself called on to pray. But pray he did, and that,
too, as he said, with "a new tongue, a new brain, a new
heart." Of course one has to know his man in venturing
on that sort of thing.

On another point he and this same man seriously differed.
"You drink your water, and I'll drink my beer," said the
man. "Water pleases you, and beer pleases me." Hughes
had agreed to drop the matter. But the new converts
made in the mission were to be received and Hughes said:
"I am troubled concerning some of them. If they fall back

into old ways, it will be through drink. I hesitate to break my promise, but I do feel very strongly about it. Could not you, for their sake, and for example's sake generally, take the pledge as I shall ask them to do this evening?" "No, I cannot," was the vexed reply; "and I shall not come to the meeting this evening. What about promises, Mr. Hughes?" And he went away, but not without being ill at ease. Returning to Hughes' study, he said, "I have come to sign the pledge." "To sign the pledge, my dear sir!" "Yes, to sign the pledge. And as I am going to, I had better do it at once." And he had to be prevailed upon to wait until evening when the others would be asked to sign it too.

Hughes's work was notably successful throughout the extent of the Oxford Circuit. Dr. William Arthur, eminent among the Methodists of the time, and justly distinguished in all their annals since, came and saw what had been done, and published it in the *Methodist Recorder*, so that he began to be known throughout all the Connection. This immediately led the way into wider fields of denominational service. In the way particularly of addressing large meetings, and raising large sums of money, he was successful and correspondingly useful. His labor became more and more strenuous, while his strength had already seemed to be taxed to the limit. But he was ever a good sleeper and he did not brood too much over either inward or outward maladjustments.

LONDON AND ST. JAMES'S HALL

Hugh Price Hughes gravitated inevitably to London. Brixton on the edge of the great metropolis was the scene and center of his labors there. But the geographical bounds of his influence and action were continually extended. What came to be known as the "Forward Movement" in Methodism began to take shape. He was its principal leader and most decisive factor. Really he was at first almost the sole inspiration of the movement. The drift of it was that Methodism, first of all, that Nonconformity also, that the whole Church of God must arouse itself anew to the needs of the world, must adapt itself to effective ways of meeting those needs, though some of them may not have been tried before, and must go forward. Such a movement will always seem to many to run to excesses and one-sidedness. And generally it does. Not otherwise is a just balance easily established between progressive and conservative principles. One of the most frequently enacted tragedies of Church history has been that while both the progressive and constructive principles have been necessary to progress, the conservatives and progressives have tried to dispense with and to stifle each other.

Hughes saw with too much intensity, perhaps, to see broadly. He could see vividly certain points on the field, but he could not so easily see the whole field. He required the faculties of others as they required his. But he had his own way to go. The visit of Mr. Moody to Oxford had deepened his impression that "the Church was ruining herself with smugness." The thesis of his ministry in the main aspects of it was that Christ came to save society, and he saw all things, in so far as he saw them at all, in relation to this dominating idea.

The first distinctive result of the new movement was the *Methodist Times*, organized as an exponent and advocate of the movement, and destined to become one of its effective causes. Hughes started the *Times*, and edited it. It was able, fearless, and effective, and may be said to have given an especial welcome to an expression of *the contrary opinion*. Hughes desired and designed in particular that it might become the voice of the younger Methodism.

The paper had an influence and a following far beyond

21

the Methodists themselves. Robertson Nicoll said when he started the *British Weekly* that he wanted to make a paper "that Dale would read." Well, Dale read the *Methodist Times.* He writes to Hughes about what he has seen in it about one of his books: "It is a very great encouragement to me to learn, from your generous article in the *Methodist Times* of this week, that in your judgment my little book is likely to be useful." Hughes put himself about as completely into the paper as any editor ever does. A relative complained that he never wrote letters. "Read the *Methodist Times*," he answered. "They are my letters."

There was opposition to the establishment of London missions which were to become permanent appointments. The idea might be good, but to carry out the measures which were proposed might prove subversive of the Methodist system. Hughes loved Methodism, but did not consider that it was mainly a system. Anyway he thought it ought to be made more flexible. But to others "the itinerant ministry stood for a manner of life, and deeply ingrained associations, and to tamper with these was as distasteful to the average Wesleyan minister as Disestablishment would be in a different way to many Anglicans." This was the spirit opposed to him, and the spirit he opposed. It is not necessary to say that there was either duplicity or dishonesty on either side. It has never been a crime, though often made to appear such, that honest men should see differently when looking at the same thing.

After some hesitation Mark Guy Pearse joined Hughes in founding the West London Mission. "You shall edify the saints," Hughes said to him, "and I will pursue the sinners." By the time the project was matured in the minds of its chief promoters and presented to Conference opposition had well-nigh subsided. The obstacles to the enterprise seemed insurmountable. But this cannot be taken as an unusual circumstance. Hughes was asked whether he had considered the extent of the responsibility, financial and otherwise, which was involved. "No, my dear sir, I can't say I have," he answered. "I leave the full extent to God, nor should I presume to take part of it."

The mission, with continuing calls from the outside, was bound to keep him busy, and severely to try his strength. When once he had to go down to Bournemouth after an illness his wife rather pathetically said: "It seems so strange sitting at home with him in the evenings. For months we seem to have only passed each other on the stairs." Again his ability to command sleep was his surest guaranty of a return to strength.

With all the work of the mission upon his hands he gave up neither the *Methodist Times* nor his reading. "He would come in to meals with a book in his hand." Writing to a little niece, he asks her whether she has any sisters. "I think you have one," he says. "But I live so far off that I really cannot remember how many of you God has sent among us."

He organized all kinds of help for the Mission, and gathered efficient helpers about him. The center of his activities was in Piccadilly, and his headquarters were called St. James's Hall. All kinds of people came there for help, and a still greater variety came to the preaching services. They were there from Roman Catholic priests to all the varieties of London sinners, both respectable and outcast. A Sister was moved to speak to a young girl whom she had observed there Sunday after Sunday taking notes. "I often see you here," she said. "Yes," answered the girl, "I am learning shorthand, and as Mr. Hughes has a very good delivery, I like to come and practice myself in the way you see. What he says is quite indifferent to me, as I believe nothing religious, having been trained from my youth to think and to doubt." This girl was converted. A half-drunk soldier came in and was converted. Without the history of conversions the history of the Mission could not be written. These outcasts and middle class people came. And the gentlemen of the realm also came. Lord Roseberry came, and was shown to a front seat, from which vantage point he listened to a simple sermon for the masses.

The Mission greatly prospered notwithstanding all the obstacles it encountered and the burdens it entailed. Other missions modeled after it sprang up, and now these great central city missions are a feature of the work of the Wesleyan Methodist Church. Many of the great leaders of the Church have been the builders of these missions. Westminster Hall, so strategically located in London, was in contemplation before Hugh Price Hughes died.

His evangelistic method at the Mission seemed to some to make the way too easy. But there was no doubt either of his sincerity or the effectiveness of his method. There is no doubt of the simplicity or effectiveness of the New Testament method. And there is no doubt of the need in the modern church of more of the freedom and spontaneity of the New Testament method and principle. "Submit to the process—submit to Christ": this was the essence of Hughes's message and method. And he had rare skill in bringing men to a decision according to this method. But when it came to his insistence, at least as the implication of his method, that "a sense of sin in the deep sense was the fruit and not the germ of the spiritual life," he certainly was less close to the New Testament, whether judged by its message or its method. All the while, however, he was sound and even passionate in his contention that the Christian religion was not a mere ethic, and never could be. "The center of our religion," he would say, "is not a creed or a tradition, but a living Person."

The Mission, particularly when the later fruit of it is considered, was his most monumental piece of work. "I don't want to believe it," wrote Dr. Parker when he heard that Hughes might be laid aside by ill health.

The Mission is yours, and in the thoughts of Israel you are the one man to handle it. Have a colleague if you like, but do not give up your primacy. We hold you in loving honour, and for your great and precious ministry we thank the Head of the Church.

Ever affectionately yours,   JOSEPH PARKER.

"SOCIAL CHRISTIANITY"

Hughes published four volumes of sermons. The speed with which he did all his work characterized these also. Yet their very defect in this way gives them a certain value in that it brings them closer to the method of his pulpit. One of his volumes he issued just before leaving for his attendance upon the Methodist Ecumenical Conference in America in 1890. Dr. R. F. Horton wrote him concerning it: "One hurried 'God bless you' for your book. Anything more clear and pointed and hard pressing on the facts I have seldom seen. I do indeed thank God for it and you. Thou almost persuadest me to be a Methodist. But instead of that I hope that you may persuade all Methodists to be as yourself."

Of his volume on "Social Christianity," which as well as anything he could have published represents the man and his work, Dr. A. M. Fairbairn wrote him: "It is an admirable specimen of how the truth that does not change may be applied to the changed problems of our day."

These sermons were all delivered in St. James's Hall on Sunday afternoons and evenings, the most of them in the afternoon. Of the audiences gathered to hear them Hughes himself would say by way of warning to friends whom he might bring with him: "You may be startled, but my audience this afternoon contains queer brethren, who are accustomed to give vent to their feelings. They are quite ignorant of Christianity—most of them owing to our misrepresentations—so when they hear an exposition of it for the first time, they cannot resist showing rejoicing in the manner that is customary to them. You must not be startled. You may even find it somewhat exciting. Some have told me they do, but in any case there is no need for alarm, and I hope you will not resent it." At the same time he would tell them that if they would stay for the evening service they would find "a cathedral calm," and carry away a better impression of the place.

All of these sermons betray his bias toward the social aspects of Christianity. This statement he would probably himself repudiate. In him this attitude was ardent and positive, and not a mere bias. It was his conviction that this was the emphasis which Christianity required.

Subjects of the sermons under consideration were in part as follows: "Jesus Christ and the Masses," "Jesus Christ and Social Distress," "Christ the Greatest of Social Reformers," "Christianity Not a Doctrine or an Ethical System," "National Character Determined by the National Laws."

He is speaking on Christ and the masses and asks: "When you saw the crowd on Lord Mayor's Day, what was your feeling? If Christ had been in the window of some house in Trafalgar Square, his feeling would have been one of pity. When Jesus Christ saw a great crowd he was moved with compassion." And before he is through with his crowd in the Hall he brings to bear upon them the compassion of Christ as a present and compelling reality.

"You may be a large employer of labor," he says in the same sermon, "but what do you know about the men and women you employ? Between you and them there exists too frequently only what Carlyle, in his grim, vivid way, calls a 'cash-nexus.' They come on Friday or Saturday for their wages. They get so much money for so many hours' work, paid through a hole in the office window." Who would be likely to forget that "paid through a hole in the office window"?

"There is a great deal more of the sheep than of the wolf in sinners," he told them; especially in those who, humanly speaking, have never had a chance; who have been the victims from the very first of unfavorable circumstances; who, in the terrible language of Charles Kingsley, have been 'damned from their birth.'"

He has a sermon on the text, "Give ye them to eat," on which Bushnell and Martineau have also preached. It is certainly a study in the variety of homiletical talent to compare these three sermons. Hughes had not the gifts of either Bushnell or Martineau. But he had his own talent. This is the sermon on "Jesus Christ and Social Distress." The last Monday, he said, he had received a letter from an excellent Christian gentleman stating that he had gone from the service the preceding Sunday afternoon "very much grieved." Instead of "preaching the gospel" Hughes had talked about the duty of electing vestrymen (councilmen) who would close insanitary dwellings, etc. As a result it was only too possible that even then there were some who might have been saved who instead were "in hell suffering the torments of the damned." It is hard to believe that Hughes was not glad to get this letter. It was like a springboard to a diver, and he went down to bring up this brother. He admitted that twenty years ago he might have said that himself. But now he regards the opinion as "one of the most dangerous ever entertained by Christian men." "If every day of the week and twice on Sunday," he continued to his congregation, "we preach the gospel even to his satisfaction, may I not be permitted for this one brief hour, without neglecting any other duty of my sacred office, to deal with that public application of the gospel which has been so long and so perilously neglected by those who are the followers of Jesus Christ?" The people had deserted the places of worship on the Continent, and he feared that for this reason they would desert them in England too. He had not liked the spectacle presented in London sometime previously "when citizens of this so-called Christian city were rushing furiously through the streets . . . terribly afraid that they would be too late to secure shares in Allsop's Brewery."

The poor he declared were bitterly defrauded. An investigation had been made into their food supply in the East End. The result of this investigation was "that in some instances the sugar was not sugar, the tea was not tea, and the butter was not butter." There were those who wanted him to "deal with souls," but he said he might settle the whole issue by saying he had no disembodied souls in his congregation.

No sermon in the series need be passed over if this kind of material is sought; but some of them are more striking than others. In a sermon on "The Problem for Unbelief" he displays apologetic ability of a really high order. There are many, he argues, who do not know what Christianity is doing in the hearts of men, so they do not know what Christianity is. "If they would go to Christians as different in many respects as General Booth and Father Ignatius, or Spurgeon and Mr. Hay Aitken, or Canon Wilberforce and Mr. Moody, these experienced teachers would tell them of multitudes *now living* who had been saved by 'the power of the resurrection.'" There are documents of Christianity. But there are Christians too; and "the documents cannot be understood in our absence."

Throughout the volume he goes on very definitely and

concretely, not in softness nor by stealth, but specifying instances, and refusing to whitewash Allsop's Brewery itself. They were sermons which could but reproduce their own kind, and there is not an entire want of witness that they had an effect on the pulpit even in America.

RECOGNITION AND REWARD

Naturally Hughes had an active part in the formation and in the direction of the affairs of the Free Church Council. He was an advocate of the closer unity of Methodism, and had it followed his lead it would long ago have been an organic unity. None regretted more than he the divisions which had occurred in its ranks, and he desired with a fervent desire that they might be healed. Beyond this he believed in the closer unity of Nonconformity, and regarded the Free Church Council as a potent means to this end. He did not share with Dr. Dale the fear that it would tend too much to limit the freedom of the constituent Churches. He was elected to the presidency of the first fully organized meeting of the Council in 1896. Dr. Guinness Rogers, speaking at this session, said: "If it had not been for Hugh Price Hughes, we should not have been here at all." "One time," he continued, "everybody was speaking against him. Nobody seemed to agree with him, nor did I. But one Sunday night I went down to St. James's Hall, where he was preaching, and walked straight into the vestry, and I said, 'I have been reading and hearing all the things they are saying against you, and I don't see with you myself, but I want just to shake you by the hand to assure you.'"

Hughes had not yet been president of the Methodist Conference. Would he ever be? It was inevitable, thought some. Others shook their heads. To many he had been but a troubler of Israel. It had even been doubted whether he was loyal to the Methodists. More than once it had been rumored that he would leave them and go to the Anglicans. The Methodists themselves had not been universally esteemed. A lady of rank had reported to Hughes himself that once when abroad she had met a well-known Anglican clergyman of really high character to whom she had said that she meant to connect herself with the Methodists in England. The man had seriously replied: "Baroness, it is impossible! I assure you, no one belongs to the Methodists in England. They have no standing whatever."

But it was hard for such doubts about the man to live. And they did not live. He was elected President of the Conference in 1898. The great event of his presidency was the inauguration of the Twentieth Century Fund, first proposed by Sir Robert Perks, but ardently accepted and successfully advocated by Hughes. The fund was to consist of a guinea each from a million Methodists, and to be devoted to the extension of the work at home and abroad.

Though a more generous recognition had come, Hughes was not yet through with arousing opposition. At an earlier time he had opposed vaccination, and some of his friends in the medical profession could never be reconciled to him in that attitude. Later came the Boer War, and he was on the side of its defenders. To many of the best people of the country this position seemed an utter contradiction of the principles upon which he had opposed war in general. One morning a little while before he died a gentleman interviewed him in his study and proposed that he should have a quiet home in the suburbs, to be the gift of himself and other friends. It seemed to him an incredible thing. Nevertheless, it was done.

But it was too late for any creature comfort to prolong his life. He had at one time had eighteen months of almost complete silence, and the end now was not far off. On Friday morning, November 14, he came into London and drove to the Katharine House, where he conducted a service for the admission of probationers to the Sisterhood. His address made a remarkable impression. There was a Communion service, while around him were gathered "some who had gone with him, without resources, into the West of London fifteen years before."

On the Sunday evening in St. James's Hall he preached his last sermon, undying and quenchless still in the hope which had sustained his preaching through the years. Returning in the late afternoon of Monday from a meeting he had attended, and while walking through the streets attended by one of the Sisters, he was observed to be very ill. He was supported to a cab, and fell back unconscious. He had been stricken by apoplexy. In a little while he died on the sofa in his study without speaking again. It was the year 1902, and he had lived a little more than fifty-five years. It seemed too soon for him to die. But he had lived a laborious and consuming life. "The zeal of God's house had eaten him up."

From Wesley's Chapel, in City Road, London, his body was buried. He received the tribute of the streets through which the cortege passed, and of a crowded congregation in the historic church. The very shrine to which his body was brought was endowed anew by the heroism and devotion of the life he had lived.

The Man and His Measure

1. His high ethical sensitiveness was not the least potent element of his nature. Sensitive he was; and impetuous, too, almost to the point of rashness. Some one would say to his father that one day he would see him the President of the Methodist Conference. "Too rash, too rash," the old man would reply; "they'll never make him President." But impetuosity, if it is bound by high ethical qualities, has

something to gain, as well as something to lose. It may be as rash as the charge of the Light Brigade. But at any cost it is better than cowardice and sloth.

Impetuosity in Hughes was only a phase of his sensitive ethical nature. His boldness as a champion of the poor and oppressed, his insistence upon high moral qualities in civil magistrates, his outrage at the tolerance of iniquities in high places in the social system, his directness in bringing his speech down to the streets of London—all these were but an obedience to the demands of his own high ethical nature.

2. Of the intensity of his social consciousness the same may be said. What was wrong in its individual aspects and in the individual conscience was wrong in its social aspects and in the social conscience. The corporate conscience must be as clean as the individual conscience. He burned with indignation at social wrong because he had such a keen sense of personal wrong. After all there are not two consciences, but one—one for the individual and for society. And the man who does not recognize this, and first of all keep his own conscience clear, cannot be a social reformer. If he does not lay the law of his own deliberate will on passion, deed, desire, he cannot escape that short cut to humility which comes of the retort, not always courteous, "Physician, heal thyself."

3. Hughes had a marked instinct for practical effectiveness. Theorizing about conditions was not his strong point. But he vividly caught sight of conditions requiring to be relieved, and his action was as prompt as his seeing. He went into West London without equipment, and practically without resources, and left there all the agencies and equipment of the West London Mission. He went over the brook a very small company. He came back a great host. He saw a place for the *Methodist Times*, and started it when probably not another man in his Church would have

thought of it. He was interested in the elevation and in the widening of the sphere of woman, and as a part of the expression of this desire he had a well-organized Sisterhood at the Mission. If he could not go to meet a need himself, which in numberless instances was the case, he had at hands others who could go. Indeed, a large part of his practical effectiveness lay in the fact that he had the power to command the confidence, devotion, and service of others. "He had the gift of getting things done." Perhaps no other minister of the time had about him a more faithful band of helpers than he had at the Mission. And he was able also to draw from far beyond the circle of his people cordial appreciation of his work and a willingness to help.

4. He had conspicuous courage in making an issue of his convictions. He could permit no conviction to sleep in his soul. All things in him cried out for utterance and action. "I wish," he once said to a person associated with him in labors—"I wish we could start a guild to agonize over the sins and sorrows of London." That expressed the man. Not to find an outlet for his convictions was to imprison an agony in his soul. And its going forth was an agony too. His "chief resource, speaking from the human side, was the contagion of a great conviction." He led his own Church, and caught the ear of England. He led the way for his Church, and his Church led the way for others. He took an interest in politics, but had nothing of the mere politician in him. "Parties did not interest him as such; it was causes he cared for."

5. There came a certain stability and power of continuance and effectiveness to his ministry, both pulpit and pastoral, from the vital elements of his own experience. The two unshaken and unshakable supports of his life and work in the ministry were his clear and decisive conversion and the assured results of his deeper consecration at Brighton.

He never ceased to live on these experiences because they never ceased to live in him. With the confidence of Paul he could say, "I know whom I have believed." He perceived the need of social work by the churches. But one who knew him better than any can know him now said: "He never made the mistake of supposing that Christianity is to be subordinate to social reform."

His experience was crowned with his consciousness of Christ. His soul was beaten into the dust of humility before Him. His whole manhood was raised to heights of rare devotion and achievement by the sense of His power. When young ministers would come to him perplexed in their thinking, and there was much of this in his day, as there is now, he would say: "There is no cause for dismay, but feed upon Christ in your heart and go on studying and thinking." There was sufficient strength in his experience to keep him steady in his thinking.

His death itself was a devotion to Christ. "No river hurrying to the ocean was more bound and yoked to irresistible law than the desire of his spirit to Christ." He desired to have written upon his tomb the lines:

"Thou, O Christ, art all I want,
More than all in Thee I find."

6. His method of preparation for preaching was extemporaneous. That he employed the method of preparation by notes thrown into a form which might be extended or abbreviated at will is sufficiently testified by the remains of his last sermon which have been preserved in facsimile. His sermons he said "came" to him, so that he had no difficulty either in the genesis or planning of them. He had to prepare for his pulpit while he toiled for his parish. In doing this many would have given up the other, but not he. Some will give up the parish for the pulpit, as Dr. McLaren

was so strongly inclined to do. But Hughes did not do that.
"For some reason," he said, speaking again of his sermons,
"I never have any difficulty. God, I believe, suggests the
text to me, so I feel no anxiety on the matter, though I have
not the time often to prepare as others do."

On a day when he had utterly spent himself in committees
and other matters of tedious routine he came in the evening
to a meeting where he delivered "a peculiarly thoughtful
and beautiful address on the inner and mystical side of
Christianity." Dr. Lunn, who had been with him throughout the day, asked him how he had done it. "As I was walking with you up Gower Street this morning," he replied,
"the idea and outline of what I was to say flashed across
me."

He might begin a sermon by saying, "Last Monday I
received a letter," and end without conformity to any prescribed fashion. But every sermon had an aim and moved
in steady fashion to it. When he had finished nobody was
left in any doubt as to what he had been trying to do.

7. He was catholic in the breadth of his Christian thinking. He believed that there was a note of catholicity in all
the essentials of Christian belief and practice. He often
said: "If Cardinal Newman, the Archbishop of Canterbury, General Booth, and the President of the Methodist
Conference were locked up in a room and told that they
must not come out till they had arrived at a vital point of
agreement with regard to the Christian faith, they would be
released in two or three minutes." He could hardly have
believed this himself; but it was no discredit to him that he
wished it might be so.

Welcoming an Anglican deputation to the Wesleyan Conference in the year of his presidency, he said: "We know
full well no Church in Christendom has produced more

learned theologians or more eminent saints than the Church which you loyally represent this morning."

His fellows-in-arms in his own Church were Moulton, Pearse, Pope, Rigg, Watkinson, Lunn, Perks, and others. There was sufficient breadth of Christian mind and nobility of spirit among these alone to constitute an apostolic Church. To win the esteem which they accorded to him was one of the richest rewards of his life.

Dr. Pope said, writing to Mrs. Hughes: "His life and work have marked an epoch in the progress of Methodism. His influence will be a tradition that cannot die." Dr. Rigg's appreciation of him was very warm and very earnest; while the relation between him and Dr. Lunn was highly cordial and creditable on both sides. Dr. W. H. Fitchett, writing from Australia, said: "I told the Conference, what I believe profoundly, that not since John Wesley died has the Methodist Church possessed a man who was a more perfect embodiment of the central and imperishable characteristics of Methodism than your husband." A distant American Methodist writes in the same vein of appreciation: "I think, beyond all doubt, that he was the greatest man in all Methodism in the opening of the twentieth century."

Outside his own communion he had fellowship with many of the noblest men of the time—Dale, Horton, Parker, Spurgeon, Fairbairn, Nicoll, Gladstone, Stead, and others. He also sustained very cordial relations to Mr. Hall Caine, from whom he had letters from time to time. He made in one of them, as being of special interest to Hughes, the following communication: "Last night I dined with a group of Catholic ecclesiastics of various degrees, and the talk turned on Wesley. I described the expansion of Wesleyanism as indicated by the surprising chart which the *Methodist Times* published this week. Then I gave a little account of a prayer meeting of five old men in a disused chapel just under my house here at Greeba—the sincerity, the devotion, the fervor, the language of Scripture, the complete absence of the forms and ceremonies that usually accompany the approach to the Almighty. . . . I wish you could have heard what the priests said of it all—how they spoke of Wesley and the great man's great secret of employing the laity, and then that scene of the five old men."

When his shrouded figure lay in the fresh embrace of death Dr. Nicoll wrote in the *British Weekly:* "The Wesleyan Methodist Church has lost one of its most eminent and devoted leaders. But the death is almost the greatest bereavement that could have befallen Nonconformity."

Let a man be taken at his best, at the worth of his soul's deepest intent, let him be taken at his value to baffled and beaten men and women, and the struggling masses of mankind, let him be taken at the angle at which his manhood stood to honor and virtue and the truth and the justice which should rule the world, let him be taken as a man who had plucked out and cast from him all the lower ambitions—let Hugh Price Hughes be taken at values such as these, and he must be counted one of the best gifts of God to his people and his time.

22

X

CHARLES BETTS GALLOWAY

(1849-1909)

ON THE EVE OF GREAT EVENTS

TWELVE years after Charles Betts Galloway was born at Kosciusko, Miss., on September 1, 1849, the American Civil War was in progress. Other important events, some of them not directly connected with the War, were shifting the affairs of the nation and settling toward issues which were deeply to stir the whole people. Bishop Warren A. Candler in his "Bishop Charles Betts Galloway," a biography published in 1927 and already much prized among Bishop Galloway's own people, points in some detail to those events.

A little more than a year before the Bishop was born a treaty with Mexico comprised the terms upon which the war with that country was ended, and the territory of the United States greatly extended. A direct political effect of the migration which followed this extension was a revival of the agitation concerning slavery in the Territories and the enactment of further legislation upon the subject. Among these were the Fugitive Slave Law and the Kansas-Nebraska Bill. The turbulence of the times, the beginning of which was marked by these measures, portended more and more certainly the coming contest of arms.

Great moral issues have their inescapable political bearings and their inevitable political affiliations. In the decade preceding the War the Free-Soil and American parties came into a brief and troubled existence, and the Republican party, destined to a longer and more influential career, also arose.

(338)

Important events in the foreign relations of the country also marked the time. The Clayton-Bulwer Treaty of 1850 had to do with the control of a proposed interoceanic canal; and a treaty with Mexico in 1853 added to the United States the area known as the "Gadsden Purchase." A reciprocity treaty with Canada was effected in 1854.

Still further afield, but bearing directly upon the increase of influence and power which the nation was to attain, were the circumstances of Commodore Perry's visit to Japan in 1854, and the conclusion of a treaty with China negotiated by William B. Reed in 1858.

In ways which no mortal vision could have scanned both Perry and Reed had gone before the face of Galloway to prepare for his coming as one of the great missionary leaders of his Church. So are the strands of history interwoven and interlocked in ways beyond the ken of man.

With a bearing still more direct upon the trend of events there occurred in 1857 the famous "Dred Scott Decision" of the Supreme Court of the United States holding that slaves were property, and as a consequence that Congress was bound to protect slavery in the Territories. In 1858 John Brown made his historic raid on Harper's Ferry, then in the State of Virginia.

All unawares the stage was setting for the enacting of a career for which these events, without anybody's possible thought of such a connection, were preparing the way. The child sleeping in the arms of his mother in Mississippi, or else catching at his toys from his cradle, amid events so stirring and portentous as these, could not have been conscious even in his dreams of the career that awaited his coming in the great world beyond, so unheedful now of so much as his existence.

"During this most agitated and eventful period of our country's history," says Candler, "Charles Betts Galloway was a thoughtful child, growing up in a small town in Mississippi. Into the hospitable home of his cultured and honored parents came as guests many able men—prominent preachers of the gospel and conspicuous leaders in the political life of his native State. All these important matters and stirring events he heard discussed by them, and thus early he was being prepared for the great career which he fulfilled when the dreadful period of war was passed, the desolating era of reconstruction was ended, and the happier day of peace and prosperity came to pass after so long a night of deep distress."

THE BLENDING OF THE BLOOD OF MANY PEOPLES

Charles Betts Galloway, the future bishop, bore the full name of his father, who was a physician. Alfred Galloway, a native of North Carolina, was the father of Dr. Galloway, and of course the grandfather of the bishop. He was married to Sophie Ann Betts, whose brother, Rev. Charles Betts, was in his time a Methodist preacher of prominence in the Carolinas. For this uncle Dr. Galloway was named; and he in turn gave the name to his own second child and eldest son. In the father was blended English, Scotch, and Irish blood.

Charles B. Galloway, Sr., was married to Elizabeth Adelaide Dinkins. In her was blended Welsh, Irish, and Scotch blood. The Dinkins family was driven from Wales to Scotland in the sixteenth century, and emigrated thence to the North of Ireland, tarrying there long enough to receive a fresh infusion of Celtic blood. From Londonderry a branch of the family came to America and settled at length in North Carolina.

Blood so blended and infused as this suffered no diminution of its finer elements in the veins that took it over in the person of Charles B. Galloway, the younger. This was the blood that thrilled all but instantly to an audience when he faced it, whether in the pulpit, or on the platform, or in his official character before some great assembly of the Church. Who that witnessed it can forget the force and impressiveness of his action at the General Conference of the Methodist Episcopal Church, South, at Birmingham, Ala., in 1906 when a proposal looking to the revision of the Articles of Religion of the Church was under consideration? Some one had suggested that Bishop A. W. Wilson should be heard from. He had spoken briefly, but in his own incomparable way. Other bishops had been drawn into the discussion. There were those who doubted seriously whether there was either wisdom or propriety in bringing the bishops into a General Conference debate, particularly if legislative action was in any way involved. Then Galloway was called. He came forward modestly, but with a full appreciation of what he deemed to be the proprieties of the occasion. He said he thought the bishops should not be drawn into the debate, and that he could take no part in it. The whole atmosphere of the occasion was instantly changed, and the Conference proceeded with its deliberations in a calmer mood. It was a splendid exhibition of how the elements were so mixed in him that even the orator kept his poise.

Dr. Galloway and Miss Dinkins were married in October, 1845, and made their home in Kosciusko for sixteen years, Dr. Galloway being employed the while in the practice of his profession. Two generations are required to make the home complete. Or at any rate it used to be so before the companionate marriage people revised the ancient social and moral code. The second generation in this Galloway home consisted of eight children, four of them being daughters and four of them sons. Not one of them lived to go out into the world—and all but two of them went out, one daughter having died in her infancy and another in her sixteenth year—to whose garments, in Bushnell's fine phrase, the odor of the home did not cling. One other besides Charles became a minister of the Methodist Episcopal Church, South, and wrought honorably beyond the time limits of all the rest of his family.

One who out of an intimate knowledge of the home could vouch for its character has said: "Strict, but healthy, habits in the home were imposed upon both the sons and the daughters. There were regular hours for meals and other offices, and each member of the household was expected to conform to the parental rule. The sons were never absent in the evenings from the home circle. . . . Religion was taught by precept and example. Ministers of both the Methodist and Baptist Churches (Mrs. Galloway was a Baptist) were frequent and welcome guests in the house, which was given to hospitality."

A Difficult Era in Education

The Civil War fixed itself as a new date line upon the very memory of the South. A child born during or just after the dread and to him ill-understood time would bear ineffaceably in his memory the expression which none ever seemed quite able to fathom, "Before the war," or "During the war." Those four fateful years were a shock which severed as a cataclysm the time before from the time after. A Confederate soldier after four years in the field came back bearing the scars of battle upon him to find that he had nothing in the world but a wife and two baby graves, all innocent of the horrid conflict, in Monroe County, Ala. The eldest of his eight children, born after the war, remembers at least by proxy the hard pain and gloom of the bitter and distressful experience. The very vagueness of his understanding of it was but like a specter which magnified the horrors of the actual in his imagination.

Galloway was at just an age to receive the full shock of it all in his youthful bosom. He was sensitive to the sufferings of his people, and cognizant of the disaster which had fallen upon the land. The full measure of the devastation wrought could not be accurately known for many years. For instance, the taxable values in South Carolina according to the official returns did not again reach the figures for 1860 until 1910, or for a period of full fifty years. This but takes account of the actual loss, and leaves out of the reckoning the potential progress of those fifty years could they have been employed in accumulation and not in recuperation. It may be said that this is false reasoning, for it is based on the continued existence of slavery, and slavery had to go. Very well; let that be so. But this does not in the least alter the facts of the immediate economic situation. Congressman L. Q. C. Lamar of Mississippi, eulogizing in the House of Representatives Senator Charles Sumner of Massachusetts, described the South at this time as "prostrate, exhausted, drained of her lifeblood, as well as of her material resources."

When the glory of the achievement of the armies of Lee and Jackson, Longstreet, Hill, Stuart, and others whose names would maintain the equal honor of the list but make it too long—when all this, and the heroism of Southern women, and the loyalty of the plantation slaves had been committed to the fadeless and impartial keeping of history, as truly as such a thing may be done in this world, the facts of the situation had to be faced. Galloway's own early confidence in the outcome of the conflict of arms, as with a multitude of others, had suffered some reversal. When he had reached his fifty-second birthday and friends at his old home at Kosciusko sent him a letter of congratulation he incorporated this paragraph in his reply: "How vividly I recall the stirring scenes at the outbreak of the war, and how, as a boy of eleven years, I sharpened a knife in length like a bayonet, and determined to carve in pieces any Yankee who dared to invade the soil of Mississippi. I witnessed the departure of the first company, the 'Attala Minute Men,' under command of Captain Fletcher, and think yet that was as gallant a band as ever obeyed their country's call to arms. I remember how the preachers expounded the old prophecies and proved to my perfect satisfaction that the South was bound to win." We smile now; but had it not been for the depth of the people's resolves Jefferson Davis would never have been the President of a Southern Confederacy.

No other loss which the South suffered was more difficult of reparation, or bore more directly upon her power to recuperate, than that which affected her schools. They were left prostrate. Endowments were swept away. In many instances buildings had been burned. Faculties and students had been consumed by the war. The one chance there was to restore these schools of which scarcely a foundation was left lay in the self-sacrifice and devotion of the men who took up teaching in them when the war was over. Robert E. Lee was again the great exemplar of his people. Though he received the offer of a large sum for the use of his name as the head of a considerable business enterprise he promptly waved it aside, and went to a small college in Lexington, Va., to become the poorly paid instructor of the youth of his State, and of all the impoverished Southland. And yet he had his compensation. The South has been paying him that debt ever since. After all, this endowment of devotion and of character was worth more than all the money the South did not have, and could not expect soon to have. How incomparably richer is any community that has character than one which has money only. One of the problems of civilization is to change money into character. For character has power to sanctify money when money will submit to the ends and aims of character. But money alone has no power to cleanse the character of any people.

Galloway's means of an education were as favorable as any could have been under the conditions which prevailed. He went to his first school at six years of age. There, as he said, he "developed a good physique by much play and not excessive study, and had occasional strivings of an ambition to make something of life." Later he had a teacher to whom he was much attached, who was at the same time a devout minister of the Baptist Church.

When Charles was fourteen the family removed from Kosciusko to Canton. Here they were nearer to relatives on both sides of the house, and Dr. Galloway had a wider field of practice. Here also was a good school for boys, and Charles Galloway with such regularity as the circumstances of war permitted completed in two years the preparation which enabled him to enter the Sophomore class in the University of Mississippi at Oxford. He was as yet "just a genuine boy, full of life and good nature." He was very athletic. None of his school-fellows could excel him in the usual arts of running, jumping, swimming, wrestling, and the like.

The date of his entrance to the University was January 3, 1866, less than a year after Lee's army disbanded at Appomattox. He was only sixteen years of age, and seems to have been the youngest member of his class. Sixteen of the twenty-four men who were graduated with him in the class of 1868 had served in the armies of the Southern Confederacy. Fresh from their baptism of shot and shell, they took their work and life itself very seriously. There was too much sorrow outside for much of gayety within. "Jefferson Davis was then at Fortress Monroe; Federal troops were garrisoned in our principal cities; the Reconstruction Period had just begun; and Mississippi and the whole South were wrapped in mourning."

In the retrospect these boys seem a different species from the modern college set. But they have amply justified themselves and their course. "Wisdom is justified of her children." The first honor man of Galloway's class long afterwards wrote: "I suppose no body of students ever assembled at the State University that were more sober and thoughtful than those who attended the first three or four years after the war."

Not less serious was the attitude of the members of the administrative and teaching staff of the University. Dr. John N. Waddell, ranking conspicuously high as a teacher, and an eminently worthy minister of the Presbyterian Church, was Chancellor. Dr. L. C. Garland, afterwards Chancellor of Vanderbilt University, and one of the South's really great educators, was a member of the faculty. L. Q. C. Lamar, who does not need to be particularly characterized in Mississippi, or Georgia, or the South, or even to well-informed persons within the nation, was teacher of metaphysics and law.

Other members of the faculty were scarcely less able. Several of them had seen service in the army. They were set to do a reconstructive work which should be worthy of the hour, and of their own stricken people, and of the reunited nation that was yet to be. One of these very teachers, Lamar, was to speak across the gulf that divided the South from the North in the Sumner eulogy in the Senate in as brave and masterly a manner as such an occasion ever required. His greatness was that he could see the occasion while others could not. The speech was one of those great deeds which make a people great, and give to a nation its prestige, and make their call to impressionable souls like Galloway's. So he in his turn, like Henry Grady of Georgia, by the magnanimity of his spirit and the eloquence of his tongue, was to serve as few others could do in binding again South to North and North to South. In those sober University days he had lived and labored as if the impulse to these great tasks was already upon him.

The University itself in those days, though it was an institution of the State, was distinctively a Christian school. No errant and overworked cry for the separation of Church and State entered the ears of the men who guided its destinies. They were guiding the destinies of men, and not merely an institution. They would not, they could not sacrifice life and character to a political theory. Perhaps they could not understand how, if the State as ordained of God is to be an organ of the kingdom of God, it is to be separated in the deep and ultimate principle and purpose of the matter from that sister institution, the Church, which is ordained to be the primary organ of God's kingdom in the world. Anyway they did not go either furtively or dubiously about the matter of making their school Christian nor apologize for what they were doing.

Judge Edward Mayes, afterwards one of the most distinguished of his classmates, the author of a life of Justice Lamar, and himself a later Chancellor of the University, has written thus of the religious side of Galloway's school life: "Denominational colleges had not then been reëstablished, and many of the student body were young men preparing for the ministry, in which class young Galloway formed most of his close friendships. In 1867 a union protracted meeting was held in Oxford, in which the University faculty and students took part. Many were converted, among them Charles Galloway, who shortly afterwards united with the Methodist Church at Canton, under the pastorate of Rev. Charles G. Andrews; and so he began the long and unfaltering life of active piety which was his happy lot. He taught in the Sabbath schools; was a leading spirit in the students' prayer meetings, which were held on Sunday afternoons; and graduated with a settled determination to enter the ministry."

Mrs. Galloway has written of his conversion and decision to enter the ministry in the following intimate way: "My husband was converted at a students' prayer meeting, held in the room of his friend, Mr. Calvin Wells, at the University of Mississippi. He at once went to Canton and united with the Methodist Church at that place, his lifelong friend, Dr. Charles G. Andrews, being the pastor. Soon thereafter he decided that he would enter the ministry and wrote me of his decision. We had been engaged from the time we were thirteen and fourteen years of age, but it had never occurred to me that I would marry a preacher. After a night spent in tears I made my decision, which I have never regretted. My resolve was to do my utmost to make his ministry successful in every way, to be a helpmate and not a hindrance." The redemption of this tender and solemn pledge lived as the desire of her heart through all her life.

Rapid Strides in Pulpit and Pastoral Preferment

Immediately on his graduation young Galloway returned to the home of his parents at Canton and was licensed to preach. There were several months until the Annual Conference; and since there was nothing he could less wish than to be idle, or even to be merely shifting from one piece of work to another, he gladly accepted the invitation of Dr. W. L. C. Hunnicutt, president of the institution, to teach temporarily in the preparatory department of Sharon College, an enterprise of much importance for the time located in the same county as Canton.

Charles B. Galloway was admitted on trial into the traveling ministry of the Methodist Episcopal Church, South, in the Mississippi Conference, at its session which convened in Crawford Street Church, Vicksburg, on November 18, 1868. His first appointment read as follows: Sharon and Colored Charge, W. L. C. Hunnicutt, Charles B. Galloway. Dr. Hunnicutt was also appointed President of Sharon College; and the arrangement was designed to release him for that work, and to lay the responsibility of the pastorate upon the junior preacher. But through an emergency created by the ill health of a member of the faculty of the school Galloway found himself teaching again. He fulfilled the triple duty of preaching to the white and to the colored congregations and of teaching in the college, and his compensation from the Church expressed in commercial terms amounted to $300.

On September 1, 1869, Charles B. Galloway and Harriet E. Willis were married in the Crawford Street Church, Vicksburg. They lived for the remainder of that year in the home of his father in Canton. Then and thenceforth they were happy to live wherever the providence of God might lead them.

The next session of the Conference was held at Jackson, and Galloway was sent to the Black Hawk Circuit in the Yazoo District. The writer once heard him state to an Annual Conference that when he was read out to the appointment he did not know where the place was. Having gone as far as the railroad would carry them, he and his young bride set out across country for their destination. The season was December and the weather and the Mississippi roads conformable thereto. They arrived at the home of the chairman of the Board of Stewards of the charge and were cordially received. This gentleman expected to see the young wife weep when her husband left for one of his country appointments on the following Saturday. But if she did it was only in her heart, as these lonely preachers'

wives have often learned to do; for turning to her host she
began to ask him about the affairs of the charge.

Later the young couple obtained board for the year in a
home where they found friends who remained ever after
among the most cherished of their lives. Once more Galloway found himself teaching. A vacancy having occurred
in the presidency of the school at Black Hawk, he was called
to assume the position, and he held it in connection with his
regular work until the term expired.

Port Gibson Station was his next appointment. In view
of the fact that he had not yet been ordained an elder his
assignment to a charge of such importance was a distinct
promotion.

In the midst of the next year he was transferred from the
South Warren Circuit in the Vicksburg District, to which
he had been assigned at the preceding Conference, to the
Yazoo City Station. The circumstances were peculiar. The
preacher who had been appointed to Canton had stormed
the town, and kindled a quick blaze of popularity. But
after some spectacular expressions of devotion to the memory of his deceased wife he had surreptitiously departed the
town when a strange woman appeared on the scene and
made some suspicious inquiries about him. In this emergency Bishop J. C. Keener had telegraphed Dr. Hunnicutt
to go from Yazoo City to Canton, and Galloway to go from
his place to Yazoo City. When he arrived he found that
the people had protested the loss of Dr. Hunnicutt, and
were not in a very amiable mood toward him, toward Bishop
Keener, or anybody else. One very blunt man said to him
on the very first Sunday he was there: "Young man, I have
nothing against you personally; but if I could have my way
I would lock the door of the church and you should never
enter the house." "Well, I did not wish to come any more
than you wished me to come," replied Galloway; "but I

suppose we will have to make the best of it." "Young
man," said the same old gentleman again at the end of the
year, "you are going to Conference now. But you will come
back. We want you, and we will have you." And so for
that and still another year he was returned to Yazoo City.

From the session of the Conference of 1873 Galloway was
appointed to the church at Jackson. He was only twenty-
four years of age, had been preaching only five years, and
the church, located at the capital of the State, was the most
important in the Conference. He remained for four years,
rendering himself deservedly popular with his own people,
and much beyond their circle, both as pastor and a preacher;
and beginning the formation of those connections, religious,
social, personal, and political which so largely shaped his
life and career in the fruitful direction they should take in
after years.

From Jackson he went to Vicksburg, and had his dear
friend, Dr. Hunnicutt, for his presiding elder. Here he also
remained four years, and "fulfilled the most notable and
heroic pastorate of his life." The city is built on the Mississippi River and in the days when yellow fever stalked
unrestrained through the coast and other exposed cities of
the South was subject to the dread invasion of this disease.

At that time the Crawford Street Church of Vicksburg
was, perhaps, "the strongest Methodist Church in Mississippi." It was stronger in some ways than even the church
at Jackson, and Galloway's appointment there came along
in the natural course of events.

A reminiscence of his wisdom and fidelity as a pastor is
preserved from those days. Candler reproduces it from the
pen of Mrs. N. B. Harmon, Sr.:

A young man had engaged in certain worldly amusements, and some
zealous members of Crawford Street wanted him "churched." The pastor
gently asked if any one had tried to turn the youth from his evil ways.

On receiving a negative answer, "Brother Galloway" mildly requested them to leave the matter in his hands. The very next morning, after an early breakfast, he started forth to seek the young offender. Walking down town with him he talked of many things, save the matter uppermost in his mind. Before they parted the pastor casually remarked: "L., I haven't seen you at church since your return." The boy firmly replied: "No, Mr. Galloway; I don't care for such things any more." "Mr." Galloway saw that an argument would do harm, so, shaking hands, he went onward. Next morning again he met and walked with L., and likewise on the following day, which was Wednesday. This time as the two were separating the loving pastor remarked: "L., we are not having good singing at our prayer meetings, and the reason is that the people do not have books. I wish you would help me out a little. Won't you come to-night, get the books, and as persons pass in see that everybody is supplied?" The answer was cordial: "Yes. If it will be any accommodation to you, I will." The young man was on hand early at the prayer service, and saw that each comer had a songbook. After the meeting, which was good, linking his arm in that of the pastor and walking down the steps with him, L. exclaimed: "Wasn't that good singing to-night?" "Yes, indeed," replied our future bishop, "and it was all owing to your seeing that everybody had a book. Won't you come and help me out next Wednesday night?" L. did and from that time until his death, two years later, was always at prayer meeting, Church services, and Sunday school. He died an earnest, faithful Christian.

Galloway's courage in preaching the gospel and his zeal for its spread among his people were made abundantly manifest. There came to the church in Vicksburg during the first year of his pastorate a gracious season of the Lord's grace. The Church was strengthened in its life and faith, and sinners were converted. Many of the most prominent men of the city were brought under the power of the divine visitation, and many that were saved were added to the Church.

Then in 1878 there came to the city the dread scourge of fever. There were not wanting well-meant suggestions that with his family he should seek a place of safety. The children were sent away to relatives. But who that knew Charles B. Galloway could look back and find the shadow of a probability that he would flee? No more would his brave wife go away. When at last both of them were ill and it was thought that he would die, Mrs. Galloway was carried on her own bed to his bedside for what was supposed to be their last interview. When the distressed attendants returned, having left them for a while alone, they found he had not yet despaired of his own life. He said: "I am willing and ready to go; but I cannot think I will go at this time. I have much work yet to do."

But the report went out that he was dying. A letter written by Dr. C. K. Marshall to a friend in New York and published in the *World* said: "My wife and daughter are at the parsonage, where our gifted and useful pastor, Rev. C. B. Galloway, is dying of the plague, and his beloved wife, who has been very low with the fever, is now laid by his side to take perhaps only an hour's leave of each other till they reunite on the other side." So completely did the fact of his death seem to be established—a dispatch had even gone over the wires stating that "Mr. Galloway is dying"—that his warm personal friend, Major Barksdale, published in his paper, the *Clarion*, of Jackson, an obituary tribute. Speaking afterwards at Major Barksdale's own funeral Bishop Galloway said: "There is to me a striking coincidence, if not a strange Providence, in this hour. I have in sacred keeping a copy of the *Clarion*, issued during the fateful year of 1878, with a darkly-headed death notice of myself, and his tender tribute to his young friend and former pastor. That news proved erroneous. The death angel stayed his coming, and the one supposed to be at rest that day lives to reverently place a modest flower upon the honored grave of his Christian brother."

At the session of the Conference of 1881 he was returned for his second pastorate, of three years, at Jackson. This pastorate was even more notable than his first. The field was an eminently congenial one, both to his mind and heart. His God-given faculties found here a field for their

23

exercise as fruitful as if it too had been God-given. He did now but complete and set a seal to the work which he had formerly begun to do. After this second pastorate at Jackson there was no shaking loose the influence he was to have upon the whole commonwealth of Mississippi, nor the setting of any perceptible limit to the power for good which he was so widely to wield. He acquired an influence and a power which were so secure in Mississippi that easily his prestige began to extend elsewhere, and he began to be known throughout the South and the nation. And it was an influence and a power so manifestly free from all suggestion of chicanery, and scheming, and double-dealing, and so rooted in genuine worth, and so sustained by real ability as to challenge the admiration of all who were capable of looking up to the high standards by which he ruled himself.

When he came back to the church at Jackson it paid him a salary of $1,200; nor did either that or the church at Vicksburg ever pay him above $1,500 a year.

By the action of his *Alma Mater* he became a Doctor of Divinity in 1882. When he was more conspicuously advanced in his career the Northwestern University at Evanston, Ill., conferred on him the [degree of Doctor of Laws, as did also Tulane University of New Orleans, at another time.

ELECTED TO THE EPISCOPACY

Four editors in succession of the *New Orleans Christian Advocate* were elected to the episcopacy—H. N. McTyeire, J. C. Keener, Linus Parker, and C. B. Galloway. Galloway was elected editor to succeed Parker, who was elected a bishop by the General Conference of 1882. In course of time he enterprised a new church building for the ampler accommodation of his Jackson congregation, and organized a mission charge in West Jackson. All these editors of the

Advocate had been obliged to continue as pastors in order to keep the paper going financially; so that Galloway had only added to his already heavy burden. He had besides to travel continually between Jackson and New Orleans, giving constant attention to his widely separated charge. The next year he had the welcome assistance of the Rev. A. F. Watkins, who thus writes of the arrangement:

> In 1883 Dr. Galloway was the pastor of the First Church, or rather the Methodist Church, there being but one church in Jackson at the time. During that year he enterprised the new building, and by the end of the year we were able to use the Sunday school room for our services. At the session of the Conference in 1883 Dr. Galloway asked the bishop to appoint me to the Jackson Church in order that, in connection with his editorial work, he might address himself to the new mission that had been organized in the West Jackson engine house. Out of this West Jackson Mission came the present Capitol Street Church. He was nominally the pastor of the West Jackson Mission; and I was the pastor of the old Church. Practically I did the pastoral work, and we preached and held other services turn about in the two appointments. He occupied the parsonage and I boarded there.

He could now leave the work at Jackson in trusted and competent hands; so at the Conference of 1884 he was assigned to the lighter pastorate at Brookhaven, an arrangement which also placed him somewhat nearer New Orleans. Of his manifold labor at this time a friend at Brookhaven wrote:

> During the four years of his dual life as pastor and editor an account of his weekly work and travel would read almost like a story of romance. It began with two sermons on Sunday, in addition to regular attendance upon Sunday school in the morning and occasional preaching at a mission appointment in the afternoon. Monday morning early found him at his desk in the office of the *Christian Advocate*, where two laborious days were spent in getting out the paper, and Wednesday evening he was again in Brookhaven in time to conduct the weekly prayer meeting.
>
> Between Wednesdays and Sundays he found time for his pastoral visiting in Brookhaven and a lecture fifty or a hundred miles away in aid of some enterprise of the Church. Add to this the burden of leadership in

the great prohibition movement in the State and we have the record of a very busy life.

It is further recorded that "The Prohibition Handbook" and the "Life of Bishop Linus Parker" were written during the intervals of these labors.

At the General Conference of 1886, held in Richmond, Va., Charles B. Galloway, along with William W. Duncan, Eugene R. Hendrix, and Joseph S. Key, was elected bishop. He was the second of the four elected, his majority having been secured on the second ballot. No one was elected on the first ballot. He lacked about four months of being thirty-seven years old, and was the youngest man ever elected to the office in his Church. There were some who thought he was too young for so responsible a position. Dr. B. M. Palmer, of the Presbyterian Church in New Orleans, a wide observer of affairs and greatly distinguished as a pulpit orator, afterwards confided to a Methodist colleague that he had himself entertained misgiving on this ground. "Your Church has been fortunate in the selection of its bishops," he said; "but when you elected Dr. Galloway you did a dangerous thing. It is a dangerous thing to place an untried man in so important a position, and it is a *most* dangerous thing to place so much power in the hands of one so young. You were, however, again fortunate, for Galloway has demonstrated his worthiness for the high position and has not been tempted by the power placed in his hands, having risen above the temptation."

THE EFFICIENCY OF HIS EPISCOPATE

There were certain aspects of his episcopal administration which lifted it clearly out of the accustomed routine.

1. He was, however, not without skill in the requisite routine of the office. From the days of Wesley the minute business of an Annual Conference has been of vital im-

portance. The manner in which this part of the work of
the Conference is dispatched will have its bearing upon the
effectiveness of the whole procedure. Here Galloway was
alert in his attention to detail, and prompt and decisive in
his action. Few could surpass him as the mere business
president of a Conference.

Furthermore, he had a clear and unbiased insight into the
character and capabilities of men, and was wise in making
the appointments and in selecting men for responsible positions. A young preacher on leaving the Conference room
one day at a session where he presided turned in the vesti-
bule of the church and unexpectedly faced the Bishop.
Each extended a hand, but not a word of greeting was
spoken. Very intently he was searching the younger man's
face. The latter, thinking he was trying to recall his name,
simply called the two syllables of his surname. "O, I know
you," said he, as with a renewed pressure of the hand he
passed on. Two or three days later the same young preacher as the appointments were being announced was almost
thrown from his seat in the Conference room when he heard
his name called as the presiding elder of the district within
the bounds of which the Conference was sitting. Whether
this is a wise way to make appointments—though doubtless
in this very instance there was some inquiry in the cabinet—
may be debatable. But there is no doubt that one of the
indispensable qualities of a capable leadership is a sound
and not too tardy judgment of men and measures. The
action of the bishop in this case made a decisive break in
the administration of the affairs of a large Conference by
the appointment of a much younger man than was usual to
the office of presiding elder.

2. His first episcopal assignment consisted of the Indian
Mission, one Conference in Texas, and three in Arkansas.
At his Conference in Texas it was said that he had not yet

"found out that he was a bishop." Everywhere the Conferences acclaimed his coming, and on his departure wished for his return. But the first definite drawing out of his episcopal desire was toward the enterprise of missions. His first work was among the Indians and was so affectionately and effectively done as to stamp something of its character upon all his later episcopal labors.

He was assigned to subsequent labors among the Indians and displayed still all his early zeal for their welfare. He counted no inconvenience or discomfort of travel if only he might accurately know the state of the work among them and the more effectively plan for its progress. At one of their intertribal councils he heard a speech by an Indian which profoundly moved him. The following is his own account of the incident:

A speech by "Poor Buffalo," a Kiowa chief, impressed me as no other appeal I ever heard in my life. He was an elderly man, tall, with strong features, muscular frame, painted cheeks, and plaited hair decked with feathers. He wore a red shirt trimmed with yellow, beaded moccasins, elaborate leggings, and had his body wrapped in a scarf of muslin. He spoke with animation and emotion. His reference to their ignorance of our religion and his earnest desire that missionaries and teachers might be sent to his people as to the five civilized tribes, were eloquent beyond description. How I longed for men and money to go up and possess a land so white unto harvest. If the picture of that aged chief, with his facial expression, tone of voice, and pleading manner could be reproduced before every congregation in Southern Methodism, not a poor son of the forest would be denied the privileges of the gospel within the next six months. I became so interested in the chief and his people as to induce a friend, a prominent Creek, to interview him, and ascertain the facts of his history. Once a man of blood, he now pleads for a gospel of peace.

Missions among the Mexicans followed fast upon his interest in the Indians. Proceeding to the City of Mexico in advance of the session of the Annual Conference which had been assigned to his episcopal care he attended in various ways to the demands of the work, and held the first District Conference over which a bishop presided in the Mexican

republic. Speaking after all others in the love feast of the
Annual Conference on Sunday morning he said: "Brethren,
it was worth coming two thousand miles to see this meeting."

He presided over the Brazil Mission Conference held in
Rio de Janeiro in July, 1897. Concerning an incident of his
journey thitherward he wrote:

On the night of July 12, in latitude 12° north, we had the privilege of
seeing both the North Star and the Southern Cross. About ten degrees
above the horizon in the northern heavens "the sailors' delight" still held
his silvery throne, while to the south the beautiful cross hung in benediction just over the placid sea. The second evening thereafter the Star of
the North had disappeared, and the Cross of the South had been lifted
up the highway of the heavens. Whilst others on deck discussed these
astronomical phenomena, I thought of their spiritual suggestion—God's
great law of compensation. For every light that fades another appears.
Over the paths of every sea a lamp is hung out—either a North Star or a
Southern Cross.

On the adjournment of the Annual Conference he did not
obey a natural impulse to hasten homeward, but under the
constraint of his devotion to the work he turned his face
toward the interior, visiting many points of interest and
possible strategic importance, including Sao Paulo, Pir-
acicaba, Petropolis, Juiz de Fora, Barra Mansa, and still
others. As he journeyed he preached, visited the schools,
and intently studied the people.

Pursuant to appointment by his colleagues to assume the
official charge of the missions of the Church in China and
Japan, Bishop Galloway left his home in Jackson early in
January, 1894, for a circuit of the globe, as he himself designated the journey when he had assembled the letters
giving his account of it to the *Christian Advocate* and formed
them into a book. Dr. E. E. Hoss in introducing the book
said that no worthier series of communications had ever
appeared in the columns of the paper. "How my good
friend managed to keep up so high a level of thought and

style," said he, "amid all the difficulties and dissipations of almost incessant traveling, is a marvel to me. For fullness, for accuracy, for vivacity, he has few equals. I do not know half a dozen men who are so entertaining as he is with both tongue and pen."

In connection with his superintendency of the work in Japan he anticipated the necessity for the unification of Methodism there. "After a while—when we cannot yet prophesy," he wrote—"there will, and ought to be, but one Methodism in Japan. Now there are five bands, but we be brethren." Within thirteen years his forecast was realized in the organization of the Japan Methodist Church.

About two and a half months were occupied in Japan, and an equal length of time in China. On his final departure from the more immediate scene of his labors he said: "I leave China with unfeigned regret. I have become, in my feeling and faith, quite a part of our beloved missionary band. The vastness and importance of this mission field grow upon me with every day's observation and study. When these millions are turned to Christ the millennium will begin to dawn."

Four months still were employed in this then long journey. He visited other points in China, the Straits Settlement, Ceylon, India, Arabia, Egypt, Palestine, Syria, Asia Minor, Greece, Italy, France, and England. But the avowed and steadfastly maintained object of his "circuit of the globe" was "to inspect the work of Christian missions in other parts of the world," and outside his own Church.

On subsequent visits to these appealing lands of the Orient earlier impressions were but deepened, former attachments, personal and official, were but quickened, convictions of the power of the gospel to uplift the race were intensified, and his own missionary statesmanship was expanded. It was worth a trip to the East, he said, to witness a service he attended in Korea. He had "sweet fellowship" with his brethren of the mission of the Methodist Episcopal Church in Peking. There too he had a delightful renewal of his acquaintance with the Hon. E. H. Conger, the American Minister to China at the time of the Boxer uprising.

On these frequent journeys, made when travel was not by any means as comfortable as it is to-day, he went without murmuring and without complaint. Whether he traveled by horse-drawn vehicle in the Indian Territory, in an oxcart in Brazil, by canal boat, wheelbarrow, or sedan chair in China, on the back of a pony in Korea, by jinrikisha in Japan, or on board the "Empress of India" upon the imperial Pacific's expansive bosom, he went with equal willingness to the task assigned him. And he could but turn his back with reluctance upon his task when for the time it was finished.

3. The episcopal office afforded a fine scope to the exercise of his gifts as a leader. His very presence operated as a quickener of confidence, and his attitude toward great questions stirred in whole assemblies the courage of conquest. Of one of his Conferences in China he wrote:

As all the business had to be conducted largely in two languages, we had to move deliberately, but there was never a tedious hour from the opening hymn to the final adjournment, and the entire week was one of high fellowship. These Chinese brethren, especially, as I was assured by more than one of them, counted it the greatest occasion in their lives and went out to the work of another year in radiant hope.

But the inspirational qualities of his leadership were hardly less marked in the homeland. Men fully trusted in the integrity both of his knowing and his doing, so they followed him first of all by the high constraint of the character of the man himself. His gifts might solicit them, but his qualities constrained them. Who ever heard of his scheming to get a following? Or of his plotting to use his following after he got it? The practice of the mere chicanery of leadership his righteous soul detested. He would not, like Faust, lead his pupils around by the nose. But he challenged them to follow the light of their own high conviction, and first of all to be true to truth.

DISTINCTIVE FIELDS OF HIS ENDEAVOR

There are great causes to the advocacy of which the Christian minister by his very position is committed. If beyond the compulsion of his position he has a temperament inclined to an interest in such causes and talents suited to their promotion, the conditions of his activity become impelling. Charles B. Galloway's commission was first of all to the Christian ministry; but his ministry could not in any circumstances, and least of all in those in which he was placed, and considering the opportunities which were given him, be a narrow and restricted one. How could the convictions of the Christian and the sentiments of the statesman be so admirably mixed in him, and leave him absolved of interest in the education of his people, or his desire for the promotion of temperance in their lives and practice, or of his patriotic endeavor as a citizen, or of his obligation to lift the shield of his championship of the cause of the Negro in the South?

1. Inevitably he was drawn into educational work. The very conditions under which he was himself educated could but leave a deep impression on his mind. These conditions were neither local nor personal. Indeed, he was more highly favored in these conditions than the young men of the South in general could hope to be. He had received an education in trust, and the execution of that trust he never shirked.

Moreover, his own early experience as a teacher moved

upon him in the same way and strengthened the trend of his life. He could not be a Christian minister and not believe in Christian education. He could not be a Christian citizen and not believe in Christian education. He could not know the slenderness of the South's resources in education and not wish to augment them. When he came, therefore, to a place where the opportunities of his life answered back to its conditions he threw all the energies of his manifold nature into the great cause.

In his early episcopal administration of the work of his Church in Arkansas he discerned an urgent educational need. Assuming a wise and confident leadership in the enterprise proposed, he saw his own and the people's efforts crowned with the erection and equipment of Galloway College, at Searcy, a noble institution for women named for its chief promoter.

In his presidency of the Annual Conferences everywhere he gave the closest attention to educational conditions, and was called time and time again to participate in movements for the promotion of worthy and needy educational enterprises. There were those who thought that had he lived his personal and official influence would have prevented the rupture which lost Vanderbilt University to the Methodist Episcopal Church, South. At his death he was president of the Board of Trust of the University.

His educational monument, however, is the splendid Millsaps College at Jackson, Miss. Without the beneficence and statesmanlike character of Maj. R. W. Millsaps, for whom it is named, the institution could not have been. Without the wise administrative and inspirational leadership furnished by Bishop Galloway it could not have been. Others have been worthily named among its builders, but these two remain forever its founders.

2. Just as inevitable as his contribution to the cause of

education was his activity in behalf of temperance. He saw all the economic and moral blasting and hindrance of intemperance and the traffic in strong drink. He saw in particular the ravages of the traffic wrought upon his own section and people. How could such a man as he pass the great conflict by on the other side? He would go at least as far as the Irishman of whom he told in one of his speeches, he would cast a vote "for Peggy and the children."

He condemned lynching and all other forms of lawlessness, as a wise man naturally would. But there was an urgency about the call for temperance which affected the whole question of law observance and administration. He would allow no false cry to take him off the scent of the one composite iniquity which had been fastened upon the helpless masses. Whatever might be the economic phases, sufficient in themselves to justify his action, the moral phases of the whole issue were more than convincing to him. "From the depths of my soul," he said, "and in behalf of American citizenship, do I repudiate the doctrine of a distinguished politician who has said, 'The Decalogue and the Golden Rule have no place in a political campaign.'"

He above all others brought prohibition to Mississippi, and he was easily and conspiciously a leader of the cause throughout the South. His controversy on the subject with the Hon. Jefferson Davis, conducted for the most part on both sides with great ability and in high ethical tone, gave him the opportunity to say some things on the fundamental principles of prohibition which have hardly needed to be said since in the better circles of the South. "It is certain," said one who had labored with him in his contests for temperance, "that no man excelled him in planning against the invading hordes of liquor leeches in our State, or in meeting the liquor advocates in the arena of debate, or in the use of his facile pen to meet the vile misrepresentations of liquor dealers in the newspapers."

3. The oratorical style is not easily transferred to the pen. The temperament of the orator is not easily adjusted to the best literary standards. But Galloway possessed a style marked by perspicuity, elegance, and energy, whether in spoken or written matter. His editorial and other literary work gave congenial employment to his talents. He might sometimes say "these parallels" when simply to say the South would have been more impressive. He might say "far Cathay" when just to say China would have been more effective. But when it is considered how readily his mind ran to music, whether in utterance of the tongue or by the pen, the wonder is that he kept himself so free from literary blemish or excess.

The *New Orleans Christian Advocate* under his editorship prospered, and its influence increased in the affairs of both Church and State. It gave him the peculiar approach which the press has to great and commanding current issues, and on these issues he spoke in a commanding way. The paper made him more widely known to the Church, and greatly assisted in his election to the episcopacy.

He published a "Handbook of Prohibition" with special reference to the needs of Mississippi; wrote the life of Bishop Linus Parker; delivered a series of the Cole Lectures at Vanderbilt University on "Modern Missions: Their Evidential Value"; was the author of the first series of Quillian Lectures in Emory College, under the title, "Christianity and the American Commonwealth"; and there was published after his death fifteen of his more important addresses delivered on various occasions, in a volume called "Great Men and Great Movements."

4. The last-named volume is really an undesigned tribute to the breadth and scope of his citizenship. He was the

first citizen of Mississippi in the confidence and affection of her people, in his ability and readiness to champion her highest interests, and in the power of his influence upon her welfare. Jefferson Davis was still alive, to be sure, but he was living in retirement at Beauvoir; and no other Mississippian was more loyal to the great chieftain's fame and honor than Galloway himself. Concluding a memorable address delivered at the annual Commencement of the University of Mississippi, on June 3, 1908, the one hundredth anniversary of Mr. Davis's birth, he uttered this fine tribute: "Soldier, hero, statesman, gentleman, American, a prince of Christian chivalry, the uncrowned Chief of an invisible republic of loving and loyal hearts, when another hundred years have passed, no intelligent voice will fail to praise him and no patriotic hand will fail to place a laurel wreath upon his radiant brow." If he had not been capable of saying this about Davis, he could not have been justly accounted to be Mississippi's first citizen.

At the dedication of the new and beautiful capitol of the State, in 1903, Galloway was invited to make the address. The man and the occasion could not have been more happily blended. He was to speak of the Mississippi of which in a distant land he had said, *I prefer the Mississippi pines to the Singalese coconut-palms.*

In no other part of the address was he more felicitous than in his reference to the great men of Mississippi. "There was Jefferson Davis," he said, "our greatest chieftain and highest citizen and grandest hero, who led no army save at Mississippi's command and championed no principle or policy without her direction or cordial support. . . . There was Sargent S. Prentiss, the entrancing music of whose eloquence was equaled only by the majestic sweep of his invincible logic. . . . There was Lucius Q. C. Lamar, whose stainless character and broad statesmanship and

dauntless leadership Mississippi will ever be proud to remember and delight to honor." These were not all, but
they are sufficient for our purpose here.

But Mississippi alone did not afford adequate scope to
Galloway's citizenship. He was a first citizen of the South,
then a loyal citizen of the nation, and a no mean citizen
of the world.

5. In nothing else was he nobler, more manly, more Christian, more statesmanlike than in his friendship for the
Negroes. He delighted to preach to them, to dedicate their
churches, and to enter into fellowship with their Christian
aspirations. Referring to some full-blooded Africans whom
he observed serving as stokers on a ship in distant Orient
seas he wrote: "They really gave me a home feeling. For
their brethren in America I have a genuine affection and
the strongest spiritual concern."

With the palpably superficial and prejudiced cry that
efforts for the progress of the Negro would lower the prestige
of the white man he had less than the slightest sympathy.
"With every executive, judicial, and legislative office of the
State in the hands of the white people and with suffrage
qualifications that have practically eliminated the Negro
from political affairs, the old slogan is the emptiest cant,"
he affirmed. He insisted especially that there should be
guaranteed to the Negro as a man and as a citizen "the
equal protection of the law," and that his right to an
education should be regarded "as at once a duty and a
necessity."

But he was too wise to be a partisan friend of the race
even as against the unkindness and injustice they had
suffered. A partisan or prejudiced advocacy aids no good
cause. Wherever he went, whether as a fraternal messenger
to the General Conference of the Methodist Episcopal
Church, or in like capacity to the mother Church of the

Methodists in England, or as a speaker on the platform of the Conference for Education in the South, as sponsored by Mr. Robert C. Ogden, he expressed his convictions on the whole question very frankly, clearing up misunderstandings about the better attitude of the South toward the Negro, removing prejudices that needed not to exist, and opening a wider way for united and sympathetic action.

His speech at the Birmingham (Ala.) meeting of the Conference for Education in the South elicited a good deal of criticism, some of it unfavorable; but in the main the drift of the widely extended comment was to approve his position. Concerning the reception of this speech in circles so wide that opinion might well have greatly varied he said: "I am profoundly grateful for the cordial and general commendation of my address at Birmingham. . . . It was my earnest and sincere desire to render a substantial service to my country—to aid even in some moderate way both races and all interests. The address was designed to be a dispassionate and entirely impersonal discussion of a delicate and vital question in our national life, and that it has been almost unanimously so interpreted occasions the deepest gratification and inspires a larger hope."

When he died the Negro preachers of Jackson sent a floral offering, and requested that their people be allowed to follow his body to the cemetery.

Endowment and Endeavor

Shall a man be measured more by his endowment, or by his endeavor? The ideal course is that endeavor shall be commensurate with endowment, though there are very few who use all their powers. In Charles B. Galloway these two fundamental factors of achievement were admirably proportioned.

1. He possessed unusual native endowment. His very

presence was formed for the mastery of assemblies. His expansive head thrown back upon broad shoulders, the magnificent shock of his hair, the sweeping and penetrating glance of his eye, his easy command of his whole person—who that have seen these brought into action before a great audience can forget a certain majesty and militancy there was about him? Then his ringing and melodious voice as he parted his responsive lips completed the equipment and the action of the orator.

Yet he has been known to say that he had never learned to appear before an audience without a certain uneasiness and anxiety growing out of the responsibility he felt for the occasion. He made perpetual and continuous in his experience the saying which Christlieb in his "Homiletic" attributes to Cicero, "that if any one treads the rostrum for the first time and does not feel as if he were going to execution, he will never make a good orator." It was reported that after his magnificent address at the Missionary Conference of his Church in New Orleans, in 1901, at the end of which a then unprecedented offering for missions was made, he did not sleep at all through the entire night.

2. He had made so intense and intensive an employment of his powers that nature herself impeded the reaction to normal. This intensity was more characteristic of the man than was generally supposed. What he did seemed so easily done that others could not count the cost. He might have lived longer had he labored less strenuously. Yet who can say? Could he have laid any considerable constraint upon the exercise of his powers without its operating as a hindrance and not a help? It will be remembered that Phillips Brooks said to Canon Farrar, who ventured to advise him upon the point, that he could not restrain the impetuosity of his speech. Bishop Galloway's ardent

24

nature never slept; or at any rate, only as a mother sleeps who is always awake to the call of her child in the night.

3. There was in him an unfaltering fealty to truth. He had little time for the pursuit of truth as expressed in the abstract terms of philosophy. But to the truth of the Christian gospel, to truth as declared in terms of the Christian redemption, his very soul was bound. He had little confidence in the mind's finding its way to God unless God had first found his way to the mind, and to the conscience as well. For him the Christian revelation sufficed. In this time he could have been neither a *fundamentalist* nor a *modernist* in the more or less technical sense which these terms have come to bear. But he would most certainly have been a preacher of the Christian salvation.

Nowhere did he fail to care more for the substance than for the form. There is a peculiar temptation to the oratorical temperament to court approval and to stir popular applause. If the mere manner can please without the substance, why be careful about the substance? At the New Orleans Missionary Conference Bishop Galloway had occasion to make a presentation in honor of Rev. Sostenes Juarez, so highly esteemed for his ability and devotion in forwarding the interests of early Mexican missions. Both his bearing and speech in discharging the delicate function were full of grace and charm. The finest tastes of a cultured audience were captivated. But he had no more idea of neglecting the substance of his brief address than if there had been no charm in his manner.

4. He was characterized by a conspicuous and cultured catholicity of spirit. He was a Methodist, a Southern Methodist, an American Methodist; but most of all he was an ecumenical Methodist. Both Christ and John Wesley were to him broader than any sectional, national, racial, or denominational lines. Nothing less than this breadth could

make the sort of Methodist he was. He claimed all Methodism for his own, and all Methodism claimed him. He claimed all Christianity for his own, and all Christianity claimed him. There could hardly have been found among the Methodists of his time one more widely known, more highly honored, or more truly loved.

He was especially fraternal toward the Methodist Episcopal Church, and lost no occasion to cultivate closer relations between the two greater branches of American Methodism. Some of his warmest friendships were with ministers of the Northern Church. Bishop W. X. Ninde visited one of his Conferences in Japan, and Galloway wrote concerning him: "With the poise of a jurist, the breadth of a statesman, and the fervent piety of an apostle, he has eminent capability for leadership. Too broad to be a bigot and too great to be a narrow partisan, he finds Christly fellowship in every company of the Lord's anointed. He kindly assisted me in the ordinations, worshiped with us on the Sabbath, and addressed the Conference with eloquence and Methodistic heartiness. We wanted him to preach, but a temporary indisposition compelled him to decline."

He was naturally called to represent his Church before great ecclesiastical assemblies, and this congenial task he always discharged with distinction. His address before the third Ecumenical Methodist Conference meeting in the historic City Road Chapel in London, in 1901, on the topic, "A Timely Restatement of the Methodist Fundamentals," made a profound impression, and had the inevitable effect of making the representative body of Methodists to feel more deeply their oneness among themselves, and with all others who bore the Christian name throughout the world. Not only the Church of the present but also the Church of the future loses when such a man untimely dies. He goes

"Down like a kingly cedar green with boughs,
With a mighty shout upon the hills,
Leaving a vacant space against the sky."

5. The impression of his high appreciation of preaching must not be lost amid his other multiplied and multiform activities. Whatever else he might do, this he must do. Indeed, all else that he did lived upon his preaching. This was the fountain from which all the other streams of his influence were drawn. This was the trunk from which all his other activities branched out. There is this singular and significant thing about preaching, that whatever else the preacher does is best done when this is done first of all. If he seeks first the kingdom of preaching and its comprehensive implicates, all the other things are added unto it. When Charles B. Galloway preached, he was his truest self at his best. Neither the educator, nor the editor, nor the temperance advocate, nor the bishop, nor the champion of men and races ever submerged or swallowed up the preacher. Preaching in the First Methodist Church, Huntsville, Ala., early in 1906, he had for his theme "The Authority of Christ," from the text, "He taught them as one having authority, and not as their scribes." Having proceeded at some length in the exposition of his theme, he wished to enforce the idea that authority has its clearly defined sources and its avenues of access to life and character. Adverting to the case of Mr. Gladstone in his coming forth from the retirement of his old age to speak on the behalf of the then bitterly distressed Armenians, with all the accumulation of authority which the experience and the wisdom and the trial and the fidelity of his long life had brought to him, the bishop swept the audience, intent upon his every word, into a profound insight into the significant truth which he proclaimed in a manner which was in itself truly Gladstonian. The pastor of the Church who sat behind him in the pulpit recalls

hardly another such telling incident in all the preaching he has ever heard. Such a preacher might be solicited, as Galloway was, to become a candidate for the United States Senate; but he is doing a greater work, and cannot come down.

At the General Conference in Birmingham, in 1906, Bishop Galloway had an illness, but nothing serious was thought of it at the time. But he was never well again. He went on, however, until 1909, when in Nashville, Tenn., on the night of May 5 he suffered a severe prostration. At his home in Jackson on Monday, May 10, he was stricken with pneumonia. Early on the following Wednesday morning, May 12, he died. On the afternoon of the next day his funeral services, thronged by sorrowing friends and admirers, were held in the First Methodist Church, and in the loved city of his adoption his body was buried. His noble, lofty, loyal soul had gone to enrich the fellowship of the redeemed.

But all that he was he fain would not carry with him. He left treasures which moth and rust doth not corrupt, and which thieves shall not break through nor steal, even in this world. His career was nobly sustained, progressive, and brilliant; his achievement was benevolent, enduring, and conspicuous; his fame is just, deserved, and unstained by any complicity with selfishness, sordidness, or scheming. He conquered by merit, died wishing still to labor, and lives in unquenchable esteem.

XI

FRANCIS PAGET

(1851-1911)

Unacclaimed Misfortune

Francis Paget had the misfortune to be born and reared in London. Now, poverty is acclaimed a misfortune. So is ill health, or blindness, or a crooked nose, or a leaky roof. To be born in an isolated or ill-conditioned region of country, or among a narrow and intolerant people is openly acclaimed a misfortune. But to be born and reared in London need not be a misfortune. John Henry Newman was born there. And so was Robert William Dale. No peculiar misfortune in the case of either of them seems to have attached to this circumstance of his birth. And in the case of Francis Paget it certainly was not a disastrous circumstance. Nevertheless, it was a misfortune. He suffered no conspicuous disadvantage of any sort from the fact of his birth and upbringing there; but he sorely missed some of the things he might have had elsewhere. He needed more of the open spaces. He needed the country more than the city. He needed an outlet for those physical energies which were never developed because he never had the incentive nor the opportunity which he required. He was not without some vigor of physical constitution, but what he had was by nature and rather in default than by means of education. London did not afford him the scope which the development and building of the physical man required. He lived from March 20, 1851, to August 2, 1911. But a man born to some of the natural advantages which were his should have lived longer. The wear and tear of the epis-

copacy made inroads upon his strength and brought distress
upon him which he ought to have been able to escape. His
power of resistance did not always register in accordance
with the demands made upon him.

Neither did London furnish him certain other contacts
which his temperament required. The great city to certain
temperaments is too lavish of its outer contacts and too par-
simonious of those which arise from within. Some persons
are more isolated the more they are in the crowd. They are
more lonely in the city than they would be almost anywhere
else in the world. This is true economically, socially, and
even religiously. The city is not their true habitat. It does
not constitute the true earnest of their environment.

Francis Paget did not suffer in all these ways, but in some
of them he did. With him temperament counted for so
much that the effect of environment was augmented. There
was about him a certain frailty which could not beat its way
against the obsessions of a rough and clamant world. He
could not toss himself upon the waves of a tumultuous life.
The city about him was so near, and yet so far. The ocean
at its shore may lave the feet of a little child, but who without a ship can compass the great spaces beyond?

Sir James Paget, one of the most famous surgeons of his
time, and bearing still a justly distinguished name, was the
father of Francis Paget. He was connected with a London
hospital, and Francis was born in a house on the hospital
grounds and baptized in the hospital church. Leaving the
hospital and its grounds the family had still but a humble
home, and the ways of the children were much circumscribed. It was a time of great anxiety for the father, but
he was too considerate of his children to allow his cares to
distress their tender years. Francis naturally "was more
solemn than was good for him, and had moods of depression
which made him, sometimes, difficult; not aggressive, but

very hard to play with." "It is sixty years too late," continues his brother, Stephen Paget, one of the joint authors of "Francis Paget, Bishop of Oxford," "to be wishing that he had been brought up far from London, and had run wild in some more inspiriting playground than Cavendish Square, far from the professional atmosphere of the neighborhood. Even in play he tended to solemnity: there was a skull in the children's little museum of curiosities, and he gave a lecture on it to a nursery audience, the first of all his many lectures, standing on tiptoes to reach it on the nursery table: 'Gentlemen, the object before us is a specimen of the human skull.'" This may be conceived to be rather too austere a start in natural history.

Four or five years later Sir James Paget began to have a large consulting practice and the family fortunes were much improved. The education of the children went on apace. First their mother taught them, and then a tutor; and next they were off to the schools.

The Making of a Scholar

When Francis Paget was thirteen he was sent to Shrewsbury, a grammar school noted throughout England for the excellence of its teaching. "It found him," says his brother, "come from a bad preparatory school, a boy of no more than average learning, and of rather less than average vigor; backward at games, unable to stand up for himself, hindered by self-consciousness, and sick with longing for the love and comfort of home; hard to understand, but easy to bully. He was at first utterly wretched: one of his letters home was so wild that his people came tearing back from Innsbrück, traveling night and day, fearing they knew not what." But "Shrewsbury left him an accomplished scholar, a lover of Greek and Latin, with a keen sense of criticism and style. It put into him self-confidence, ambition, and the enjoyment of accurate work. It did not stop there; for it taught him how to make friends, how to exercise his singular power of drawing men to him."

He was at Shrewsbury from 1864 to 1869. These five years constituted one of the epochal and formative periods of his life. Shrewsbury not only made up for the foundations which should have been earlier laid, but laid also its own foundations for future achievement. It was in itself already an achievement that he should come out with scholarly tastes and habits, and in some parts already a scholar, particularly with respect to his attainments in Greek and Latin. His acquisition also of a sense of criticism and of style, and the striking of a note of accuracy in his work all meant well for his future labor and attainment. He had but to continue in the course already begun, and not to be laying over again the foundations.

Moreover, the man himself had been notably built up, both in mind and character. Established in a surer self-confidence, moved by deeper and worthier ambitions, and holding a stronger hand upon himself, his life, upon the whole, now became very happy and prosperous. Both in his home and school connections he had come to be more advantageously situated. His home had never wanted the finer elements, but it could now provide more liberally the cultural elements.

On all sides he had been both steadied and enlarged for all his ampler achievement. Such studies as Greek and Latin, so frequently pursued in school as a mere requirement of the curriculum and neglected and forgotten when school is over, Shrewsbury had built "into the very structure of his mind." They became to him the very sinews of his intellectual training. Studies once proved to be so serviceable and stimulating to the mind are not easily dissociated from an active mind's further pursuits. Paget's knowledge of Greek and Latin he kept and increased. Indeed, his very proficiency in them tended to a fault. These languages exercised a more marked influence upon his intellectual development than English itself, and that too, not only because of their intrinsic excellence for the purpose, but also in part because the English, since it was native, was neglected. In his private notes made in preparation for public prayer or sermons he would use the Latin. And this usage he would recommend to younger men preparing for ordination. "He would send his love, in Greek or Latin, with his presents on birthdays or at Christmas."

Shrewsbury left him much to learn much even in the field of his own language and its literature, and in the history of his own times, and everything to learn in natural science; but it did give him a mind trained and talented to fine themes and accustomed to doing its own work. And this put all learning within his reach. With this beginning life itself, if he took it seriously, as he was sure to do, would force him into wider interests and a broader culture.

CHRIST CHURCH COLLEGE, OXFORD

Among twenty-nine candidates Paget came out first in the Christ Church College examinations fixed for entrance in October, 1869. He writes home to his eldest sister during his first term that he is already forming distinguished connections in the University, Tait and Liddon in particular being names he mentions. He speaks, however, in no strain of foolish pride or undue adulation, but out of a feeling of natural and not unworthy gratification. The lives of few men about him moved in a more distinguished circle than that which thenceforward marked his career; but he was never puffed up about it. The distinction of association with the distinguished, along with many other of the amenities of life, comes to some men and not to others; but those to whom they do not come are not by any means necessarily less worthy. Paget was worthy; and he kept ever the love which "vaunteth not itself." And to no distracting influence of Oxford does he mean to sacrifice academic excellence. When he is fairly under way he writes to his sister that he has worked a little over seven hours a day ever since he matriculated.

One grave danger he did run at Oxford, and that was that his tendency to ultra-refinement should too strongly assert itself. This had been his tendency at Shrewsbury, where it was easier to resist than at Oxford. He was fastidious to a fault. About his personal appearance, the arrangement of his room, the direction of his tastes, the choice of his acquaintance, and similar matters he felt an unnecessary concern. Manners make the man; but over-made manners make the man as artificial as his manners. A made-up man should have a place in a shop window. Paget escaped these extremes. He had too much character and good sense really to care for the merely meticulous in manners. But he needed to be less attentive to personal ceremony and procedure.

His intellectual employment went steadily on. At the end of his first scholastic year he won the Chancellor's Prize for Latin Verse, and was also distinguishing himself as a student in other ways. On his longer vacations, whether spent at home or on family sojourns elsewhere, he occupied five or six hours daily in reading. With Scott Holland and other congenial minds he formed annual reading parties, when members of the group, taking up quiet quarters in a more or less secluded resort, gave themselves up to very earnest intellectual work. In the main each one pursued his own path. Nevertheless, their deeper interests were common; and Paget found in the arrangement a profit of a sort which he had not found in home or school, or in any other way.

One of the reading parties resulted in an attack of typhoid fever for five of the group. One of the five died, and Paget himself was very ill. This illness and the gaining of the friendship of Scott Holland have been indicated as the most influential events of this immediate period of his life. In a letter after this illness he wrote: "I felt when I was ill, and I think any one must feel in an illness so full of what we call risks as typhoid is, that every day I lived, and every hour, was God's direct, unaided, uncovenanted gift to me; and, if He should help me to live well, then to you and to all who prayed for me. . . . One could not help seeing what one forgets, or at least what I had forgotten, in the stupidity of health and strength; and I used to feel that nothing but prayer and meditation was between me and God's anger; and to prayer, yours and mine and the much-availing prayer which you won for me, God granted my life; I knew all along that there was nothing for it but to pray."

Eight years more were to be spent at Oxford, eight years "divided between Oxford in term-time and London in vacation." He was passing, even in his appearance, from youth to manhood. His health was good, partly because he had learned something of the secret of a wise indifference toward himself and certain of his intimate and yet not essential personal concerns. He was very fortunate in his closer Oxford relations, more especially as concerning Liddon and Holland; and he was happy in London too, and began to be sought after there as a preacher.

He was appointed an examining Chaplain to the Bishop of Ely, and of addresses delivered to candidates for ordination he made his first book. In 1881 he was appointed Select Preacher to one of the Royal Chapels. With this arrangement he was not especially pleased, first, because he thought it would "hinder one's preaching at places where one would be much happier and might do more good; and, secondly, because there seems an uncomfortable flavor of courtliness about it, which it is sickening to bring into contact with the thought of preaching."

All his affairs now converged to the conclusion that he had lived long enough in Oxford. He was too close to some, notably Pusey and Liddon, to be very close to others; and so there was a rift between him and some others, these latter in some cases being members of the Governing Body of the College.

These years had been for Paget calm, but very earnest. His was not the type of either mind or character to reveal seasons of crisis or cataclysmic change. But he was just as far from the other extreme of settling on his lees. In 1875 he had gone to Cuddesdon Theological College to prepare for his ordination. He had preached his first sermon a few weeks later, near Oxford, "in a little temporary church, built there for men working in some stone quarries." His ordination constrained him to resolve that he would bring himself into subjection to a stricter discipline of life and conduct. He gave up going to theaters, saying to a friend that he did not like the apologetic look he had to put on before people whom he did not like to have see him there. Withal he was not without some sense of humor. Having lost an umbrella he wrote about it: "If you find it, and if you remember, and if Dr. Pusey preaches again, and if you come to stay with me, and if you bring it with you, and if by chance we meet during your visit, will you give it me back? Meanwhile I think I had better get another."

He had not yet been a pastor; and when he had felt the strain and yet the exhilaration of preaching in St. Paul's he has this significant word: "What I felt almost as much as anything else was the need of a better background to one's sermon, the miserable discrepancy between one's daily life and what one had to say. I am sure that, if one has not the purifying action of parish work, one must live with more regularity and concentration if one is to preach without unreality." His realization of his need of experience in pastoral work when as yet he had had none of it was a manifest token for good.

It is characteristic of the combination of the introspective and retrospective habit of his life that there should appear so fine and so mature a statement as this out of the reflection of his earlier years: "I think, as I look back over my life, that there is hardly a single thwarting of my wishes, hardly a single instance where things seemed to go against me, in which I cannot even now see, that by God's profound mercy they really went for me all the while; so that if I could have looked forward only so far as the time now present I should have longed for and welcomed all those things which I have feared and grudgingly accepted. . . . There is nothing that God does not work up into His perfect plan of our lives: all lines converge, all movements tend to do His will, on earth, as in heaven."

A Brief Tenancy of the Pastorate

Paget was wise enough to realize that he had gone too long without a pastorate. He needed to get away from Oxford, to have experience of that wider pastorate of human life without which no Christian minister ever comes to his best. Then, too, he was engaged to be married; and he and his betrothed had agreed that Oxford should not be their first home. While they were wistful what their course should be the way was strangely opened, and Paget wrote to a friend: "The Dean and Chapter of Worcester have appointed me to the vicarage of Bromsgrove. It is a large parish, four thousand and nine hundred people. I should never have dared to seek, or even to desire, so great a charge; but it has come unsought, by the free act of those who have the responsibility of choosing."

Bromsgrove is fourteen miles from Birmingham, and was a busy town when the latter was only a village. The parish church, one of the finest in Worcestershire, was renowned for its architecture and monuments, and recalled by means of these the great traditions of the town. Later in life Paget said that he had "felt so nervous, as he walked up from the station, that he nearly turned back." Even after a year's work there he is conscious of the hindrance to his efficiency imposed by his inexperience. "I feel so empiric," he says, "so deficient in never having been a curate. But it is too late now: and one can only go on, and trust that good is being wrought out of it all, and pray that the blunders and the presumption may be forgiven: and that at all events one may be saved from the folly of being content with one's self; wondering all the while at the abundant happiness that continually refreshes one, day after day."

On March 28, 1883, Francis Paget and Miss Helen Church, a daughter of Dr. R. W. Church, then Dean of the Cathedral, were married at St. Paul's in London, Dr. Liddon officiating. It was in every way a distinguished wedding— distinguished in the place of its performance and the great traditions clustered there, distinguished in the high character of the high contracting parties themselves, and of their ancestry before them, and distinguished in the character of the officiating minister. Helen Church, worthy entirely in her own person and right, could but be the continual desire of Francis Paget's heart. She was "in her simplicity as if she had come out of a poem by Wordsworth." No station to which her distinguished husband was ever called found her inadequate to any of its demands, and her heart as well as her head was in all his work. Her untimely death was the severest and most irrecoverable blow he ever had.

Their life was very busy at Bromsgrove. They were made drudges to economic necessity, though not altogether by reason of the slenderness of the stipend. It was due in part to the indiscretion of the pastor in giving away. The work of the parish prospered exceedingly. In less than a year after his settlement as pastor Paget is preparing a class of a hundred and thirty candidates for confirmation.

But Bromsgrove was to be a brief as well as a busy span in his life. The Regius Professor of Pastoral Theology at Oxford was made a bishop, and Paget was appointed to succeed him in that office, and also as Canon of Christ Church. He would gladly have stayed longer where he was. "I don't know," he said, "how we shall dig up all our roots." A second child had been born at Bromsgrove, and he writes to Lawrence Hardy: "Your godson is dethroned: or at least has only a divided empire. For on Thursday, to our great joy, a daughter was safely and happily born to us: and Richard, *mon roi*, no longer reigns alone."

A PROFESSOR OF PASTORAL THEOLOGY

Paget's preparation of his work as a lecturer was very thoroughly done. If he had a fault of preparation, it was that it was too thorough. He was too minutely careful. Preparation is as wise in what it leaves out as in what it takes in. It may be so extensive and diverse as to make impossible the closer and more direct pursuit of a subject to its proper conclusion. Paget's preparation was not excessive to this extent. But had he left himself freer of preparation his lecturing itself would have been freer and more effective. Effective, however, as a matter of fact it really was; and that too above the effectiveness of most men who wrought at the same general task. To most of the theological lectures which formed a part of the general course to which he contributed students are said to have come because attendance counted toward credit. To his they came for profit as well. "As Professor of Pastoral Theology," says one who was able to speak with authority, "Paget was one of a very few theological lecturers at that time whose influence followed undergraduates any distance outside the lecture room."

A good part of his success lay in his obvious delight in his own subject. Only his own real and abiding interest and his conviction of the worth of the work to be done could awaken and sustain interest on the part of others. This is all too obvious to be said; but some lecturers and some preachers have not yet learned it. Paget immersed himself in Hooker, for instance, until the enthusiasm which became incarnate in him communicated itself to others. And he had also his own long profiting thereby. For much of his own great reverence for the authority of law as evinced in all the administrative affairs of his life was imbibed from the same fountain whose refreshing drafts he poured out for others.

He delivered his lectures well, and uttered them in unusually good English. He could never have regretted any of the assiduous attention and care which at last he learned to give to the knowledge and use of the English language. For no remissness in the cultivation of the art of public speech is more reprehensible than the neglect of the tongue in which the speech is conveyed. This above most others is the place where the teacher must make his precept grow by his own example.

Paget was wise in practical suggestion. "The parish priest in his visiting," he said, "more especially in his visiting of the sick, should never let it be felt that he was in a hurry, or that he had other things to attend to which were

25

more important." He acted in cordial and full acceptation
of the principle of his own precept in receiving his own
students when they came to him, never suffering one of them
to go away with the feeling that his coming had been an
interference, or that he had been in any way an intruder
upon the privacy and the valuable time of a more important person. This was not because he did not value his
time, nor yet because he did not live to a great extent by
rule; but rather because he recognized the doing of this
thing itself as a duty, as, in truth, a sort of high pastoral
duty. True, he suffered by the interruption less than many
others would: for he had unusual power in taking up his
work again where he had left it off. But whether he suffered
or not, this was a thing solemnly counted to be done.

Perhaps no part of his work in Pastoral Theology had
higher value than his own attitude toward the work and
calling of the Christian ministry. He knew as well as any
one that the ministry has its disappointments and its disillusions, if a man has a mind to take them so. If one will,
life itself may be taken so. But it is not meant to be taken
so. And it is not truly taken so. There is a much braver
and a much truer way. And so it is with the ministry. It
is not made up of disappointments. Disillusions are not
the staple of its experience. The strength of the ministry
lay, as Paget conceived it, on the side of its great and positive
truth, and its great and positive endeavor. Only to an
ignoramus or to a weakling could it seem in its great intrinsic aim and qualities to be other than very noble and very
great. "He had little sympathy with the teaching of some
whose preparation of candidates for Holy Orders is largely
made up of warnings as to the difficulties and disillusions
which will form the chief portion of the history of the man
of God." If the Christian ministry were not worth the best

that the best man can put into it, it were not worth while to ask any man to go into it.

In 1889 Paget contributed to *Lux Mundi* the essay on the Sacraments. About this time his friendship with Dr. Dale began. On receiving a gift of one of his books he wrote him: "I trust that I may with humility take the word 'Evangelical,' in a very real sense, to designate the conception and hope of my work: and you have suggested to me point after point of self-examination in regard to it; so that your words will often help me, I hope, to test my loyalty and to be ashamed of my falterings in the service of our Lord, and in the preaching of his truth." Again when Dr. Dale was ill he wrote: "I shall be, please God, thinking of you every day in the way which I know you would wish. It must be a refreshment, I think, in your illness to know how very many, in England and elsewhere, are so remembering you before Almighty God."

In August, 1890, Cardinal Newman died, and Dean Church and Mrs. Paget attended his funeral. In September Canon Liddon, and in December Dean Church, died. The passing of the last two was as if death had hovered in the chambers of his own soul.

Francis Paget and Hugh Price Hughes lived contemporaneously, Hughes having been born four years earlier than Paget, while he died nine years earlier. They seem never to have hailed each other on the voyage of life. Each of them was an eminent minister of Christ, and each of them, moreover, an earnest Christian man. But one looks in vain in the index of the biography of either for the name of the other. What can it be—is it mere circumstance, or is it something deeper, which keeps two such men apart in a narrow land like England? They were living for a while at the same time in Oxford, and it seems inconceivable that they should not have known each other. Surely there must come a time when the breaches of this world shall be healed.

DEAN OF CHRIST CHURCH COLLEGE

Paget was installed as Dean of Christ Church College early in 1892 as successor of Dr. Liddell, one of the most eminent men that ever held the post. Paget felt keenly the responsibility of coming into the position. He could only long and pray, he said, that God would give him grace to work diligently and unselfishly, in humility and patience, in the hope that somehow he might be found useful. He brought over to his new position the disposition and aptitudes which he had acquired in his office as Professor of Pastoral Theology. There is a diversity of positions, but the same man. A former student said of him that *he raised administration to the level of a pastoral office.* Soon he had a serious illness and it was doubtful whether he would live through it. Said one of his physicians to Mrs. Paget: "My dear, your poor husband is very ill, very ill indeed; now, you just run away and have a good cry." Happily her weeping was not to be final.

Out of all the more serious experiences of his life there was developing a deepening wish to be Christlike. To George Romanes he wrote: "To desire to be like Him: to love the lives and ways that take their character from him: to follow the example of His patience and humility: . . . surely these are acts of faith from which He will never withhold His blessing."

His administration as Dean of the College was not lacking in trouble about discipline. But in the long run, as he had already said, hindrances turned out to his advantage rather than otherwise. Anyway, whether he could see his way through to the end or not, he trusted God and went on.

During this period the most of his printed works were issued—"The Spirit of Discipline," "Studies in the Christian Character," "Faculties and Difficulties for Belief and Unbelief," some of his work on Hooker, and a little book on "The Redemption of War." One is constrained to ask whether war can be redeemed. It must seem to many on reading this last book that his committal of himself to the belief that the call of one's country is the call of God passed the bounds of a just judgment.

In 1900 Mrs. Paget died. Dr. Talbot spoke very tenderly of her in the service for her departure held in Christ Church Cathedral. Hers was "the memory of a life with the dignity and freedom of entire simplicity, with something in it still of the brightness of a girl, but enlarged by the tenderness of mother and wife to take in every gladness or sorrow of others' lives."

Preaching in the Cathedral his last sermon as Dean of the College Paget himself said in part: "I have not said how sorry I am for my mistakes and faults: partly because you have shown me that you have put them out of sight, partly because what they really need is God's forgiveness, and God's overruling. And I have not tried to say good-by. I have simply wished to gather up for you and for myself the lessons that seem to rise out of the years that I have spent here. First the duty of reverence and loyalty toward Christ Church. Then the duty of reverence and gentleness toward all, with that charity which suffereth long and is kind, and hopeth all things. And then the lesson of that plain, upholding trust that if a man will only try to do his best, and keep clear of worldliness and selfish plans, and to cast out the love of praise and power, seeking and relying on God's grace, then, in spite of all his weakness and blundering and failure, God will somehow find a use for him, and somehow bring things right after all. For He in very truth, without

Whom nothing is pure, nothing is holy, is and will be the strength of them that put their trust in Him; even though the trust with which they cast their care on Him may be but indeed a very poor answer to all that He has taught them of His love." To speak like this is for a man to reveal the strength of his own soul.

"The Christian Character"

Nothing that Paget ever published more fairly represents and preserves the man than his "Studies in the Christian Character." This character he defines as "the coherent group of traits evinced in lives surrendered to the rule of Christ with reliance on His grace." The subject he thinks has less than its due attention.

The power of the Christian character in its appeal to those who disbelieve or doubt the truth of Christianity is in many cases, he thinks, "at once haunting and uncontentious; it is associated with thoughts and memories which are rightly dear to men; it is apt to speak to them most clearly when they know themselves to be at their best." One signal service it is peculiarly apt to render to the cause of faith: "It is often the only power which can confront the steady, surreptitious, miserable pressure with which the sins of Christians fight against the work of Christ." It suffers "some harm at times, as everything must suffer that is projected boldly into the tumult and treachery of the world." Yet it recovers its health "as if by the power of an endless life; moving like a great river, now broader, and now deeper, through the ages since Christ came; referred and traced to Him, as its one Source and Principle and Guide and Strength, by the accordant voice of all in whom its might and beauty have been manifest."

Goodness as a quality of character is very simple. But behind the simplicity of the result there are qualities which

"are among the greatest attainments of a human nature.
. . . The unembarrassed insight which goes straight to
the real character of an action or suggestion; the just imagination which can enter into another's position, and trans-
pose without altering the parts of a transaction where one's
self is interested; the kindly shrewdness which is never
credulous and never cynical; the strength of mind that re-
sists the temptation to be clever; and, above all, that sense
of things unseen which makes palpable the folly of ever
fancying that there can be through evil a short cut to good—
these are some of the faculties which are required and exerted and developed in that simple goodness which is
enlightened and sustained by trust in God; that consistent
and unwearied doing good, that purity both of purpose and
of method, which is the distinction of the souls that humbly
and sincerely rest on Him."

Dependent upon others all of us are, and we should not
be reluctant to confess it: "It is a dreary wintriness that
settles down upon the life that would be wholly independent; the life of one who shuts out sympathy and service
and compassion; who uses reserve not for self-discipline, but
for self-exaltation—not as distrusting himself, but as trust-
ing no one else; who hides his sorrow not in patience, but
in pride."

Courtesy, he believes, "is nothing else than sympathy
with the self-respect of others. . . . It helps men to sustain their self-respect by the quiet, frank, unquestioning
respect it shows to them; and it helps them to recover self-
respect by presuming that they have not lost it." Courtesy
does indeed, in this view of it, become a quality of the
Christian character.

More notable than any sermon in this volume, in the
known influence it exerted, was that on "The Sorrow of the
World" in the volume the title of which was "The Spirit of

Discipline." This sermon, to Paget's surprise, "was talked of far and wide." The idea is an old one; but he was stirred to fresh attention to it through his reading of Dante. In his descent to the Fifth Circle of the Inferno Dante finds "a black and loathsome marsh, made by the swarthy waters of the Stygian stream pouring down into it, dreary and turbid, through the cleft which they have worn out for themselves." In the putrid fen "he sees the souls of those whom anger has ruined." But in a lower deep, he is told, there are others still "whom he cannot see, whose sobs make those bubbles that he may mark ever rising to the surface of the pool—others, plunged further into the filthy swamp." What is the sin which thrust them into this unutterable wretchedness? Fixed in the slime, and gurgling through their throats, for they cannot speak in words that are full, they themselves give the answer: "*Gloomy* were we in the sweet air, that is gladdened by the sun, carrying sullen, lazy smoke within our hearts; now lie we *gloomy* here in the black mire."

Thus does he derive the setting for the sermon. He has but to deal with the ancient sin—for after all it is not a *Christian sin*—of surliness and of sloth, the sin of gloom and despondency, a sin committed in all ages and by all people. The Greeks called it *acedia*. Following some later forms Paget in his introductory essay calls it *Accidie*. He had fought the dark-hued and treacherous beast himself, else he had never written this sermon. The sermon may be seen in a separate volume in which form he was led to publish it, together with the long introductory and scholarly essay which originally accompanied it.

Having opened up the nature of "this wistful gloom," he proposes several ways in which we may do battle against it. In the first place, it will help "to see more, to think more, to remember and to understand more, of the real, plain, stub-

born sufferings that others have to bear; to acquaint ourselves afresh with the hardships of life, the trials and anxieties, and privations, and patience of the poor—the unfanci-
ful facts of pain." Another way is in turning promptly and
strenuously to work, "to whatever work one can at the
moment do." But there is yet one way above all other
ways; and that is the way of "the serious and resolute consideration of that astounding work of our redemption which
the Love of God has wrought at so immense a cost." In a
word, it is the religious way, the way of love, and trust, and
of confidence in God, of faith in his will and his works. "It
is strange indeed," says Paget—"it would be inconceivable
if it were not so very common—that a man can look back to
Calvary and still be sullen."

Solemnly to his heart he had laid the balm of the brave
lines of Robert Louis Stevenson in "The Celestial Surgeon":

> "If I have faltered more or less
> In my great task of happiness;
> If I have moved among my race
> And shown no glorious morning face;
> If beams from happy human eyes
> Have moved me not; if morning skies,
> Books, and my food, and summer rain
> Knocked on my sullen heart in vain—
> Lord, thy most pointed pleasure take
> And stab my spirit broad awake;
> Or, Lord, if too obdurate I,
> Choose Thou, before that spirit die,
> A piercing pain, a killing sin,
> And to my dead heart run them in."

BISHOP OF OXFORD

In May, 1901, Francis Paget was appointed Bishop of
Oxford. He was consecrated in St. Paul's by Archbishop
Temple, of Canterbury. Canon Scott Holland preached the
sermon. He came to a diocese which extended over three
counties, embracing a territory of more than two thousand

square miles, with a population of more than 600,000. The number of parishes was six hundred and forty-eight. The episcopal palace was two miles from Oxford, at Cuddesdon, where there is also a theological college.

None of the functions of his office was more congenial to him than the ordinations. The candidates, under his guidance and direction, were prepared with the greatest care and about their fitness in character he exercised the gravest concern. He spent much time with the candidates themselves, taking in them a most conscientious interest; and also with his chaplains, directing them in their part of the work. At the ordination itself, "as he came out of his oratory to take his place at the end of the long procession, with the marks of a week of prayer and spiritual effort clear upon him, with the intense seriousness of his approach to the altar, with the simplicity and sympathy of one who, after all, was at heart a parish priest, men must have felt thankful to have been with him for their Embertide devotions, thankful to be beginning their ministry under such a shepherd of the sheep."

The Confirmations laid upon him an equally earnest claim. Indeed, Crum, writing the latter part of his biography, says that "if one work had to be chosen as that through which the Bishop found happiness in his office, the choice would, I do not doubt, fall upon the Confirmations."

His employment as a bishop tended, inevitably perhaps in a person of his temperament and training, to an increase of the stress he had always laid upon authority in church administration. He loved order, reverenced authority, and esteemed the stately and the ceremonial in the offices and services of the Church. "He was as restless in the absence of authority as some men are restless under its discipline." He was a born conservative, too. Change tends to weakness as well as to strength, and he was afraid of the former.

To him the weakening of discipline and of the authority of law was "a serious and ill-boding thing." He was, as the Archbishop of Canterbury said, "by deliberate conviction, an Anglican High Churchman of the older school, with strong and clear Sacramentarian opinions." Therefore, "it was in proportion to the earnestness of those opinions that he suffered so acutely in the unswerving exercise of his Episcopal authority on behalf of loyalty to the teaching of the Book of Common Prayer." This exercise of authority, however, when it had to be done in restraint of the opinions and conduct of others, gave him acute pain. Dr. Temple had seen him with tears standing in his eyes "as he debated with himself and with me in what way he could, with least counterbalancing detriment, take the disciplinary or penal steps from which he was determined not to shrink."

The affairs of the diocese kept him very busy. Besides those which were necessary, a man in his position would have to give attention to a thousand other things. "I am very, very tired," he says to his brother; "I must get time to *think*." "You needn't be afraid of a very long letter," he says to another; "for it's close on midnight."

His services were frequently requisitioned by royalty. Both his personal and his official presence was peculiarly acceptable in these circles. He preaches at Windsor Castle, and is "to christen the child of the Prince and Princess of Wales." He is there again to bear a part "in the Investiture of the King of Portugal as a Knight of the Garter." He is called to be one of the two Bishops to be "in attendance on the Queen at the Coronation." "I'm told that Her Majesty wished it," he says. Again he was at Windsor for "the Investiture of the Prince of Wales as a Knight of the Garter." He bore an official part at the funeral of King Edward VII.

At the end of June, 1910, he had a very severe illness.

After a bad night as the illness came on he went and read prayers in the House of Lords. Then he went to a physician, with half an apology for troubling him. He got out again after the attack. But thenceforward he lived in the shadows which presage the end of the day. But in his illness he had learned the kindness and love of his diocese. "I can only bow my head and thank the Giver of all Grace," he said.

The Archbishop of York visited him and after a sermon he had preached Paget approached him for a very intimate and revealing interview. "He said," reports Dr. Lang, "that my words had somehow described what was becoming his own experience before his illness. . . . The point of it was, I think, this—after his great sorrow, the death of his wife, he had determined, as the only means by which he could fortify his soul against it and prevent it clouding his whole life, to devote himself with unsparing absorption to his daily tasks of work. The result was that his work became almost, as it were, an idol which demanded an exacting and painstaking devotion. Gradually, instead of his possessing it, and retaining his own freedom, it came to possess him, and to enslave him. He came, almost unconsciously, to resent anything which might have lightened it—pushed aside, e.g., such conveniences as dictating his letters or using a motor car for his journeys. The fear of realizing the blank in his home-life created by the loss of his wife's companionship led him—almost without his perceiving the tendency— to detach himself from that home-life, from the interests and occupations of his children, and to hold on with a sort of grim determination to his work. . . . He had begun to lose buoyancy of spirit; to let toil tell upon his nerves; to see the problems of his own diocese and of the Church in dark colors. The oppression of work resulted in depression of spirit. He became inwardly tired—in a word, dispirited."

His illness and the weeks of convalescence gave him an

opportunity for thought and self-review, and he saw all this. He came to himself, was revealed by his illness to himself, and realized that he had made a mistake, and must recover his liberty. What a godsend was such an illness, however it may have come.

The last year of his life moved swiftly on as if unconsciously impatient of the end. He again greatly enjoyed his work. His spirit was buoyant once more. But in midsummer a second surgical operation was found to be necessary. He was attended by two eminent surgeons. The operation was on Tuesday. A serious condition was revealed. Many whose presence he craved could not reach his bedside. He particularly desired to see his wife's twin sister, Mary, who after Mrs. Paget's death had taken the home. Late on Wednesday he died. Last of all he followed with steady voice the Psalm, "The Lord is my Shepherd."

The Mirror of the Man

1. Crum in his part of the biography, himself for a time associated with Paget in the ministry, expresses the opinion that the truest image of the man is seen as he is reflected in the character of those whom he most loved and admired. A man's appreciation of others is all but a faultless mirror of his own insight and sympathy, and his estimate of values in character and conduct. The good he sees in others must first of all exist as a capacity in himself. The power to appreciate involves the potentiality of becoming. This is one of the deepest principles of character formation and transformation. "But we all, with unveiled face beholding as in a mirror the glory of the Lord, are transformed into the same image from glory to glory, even as from the Lord the Spirit." Men live and grow, and renew their courage, and enhance all higher human values, and invigorate their im-

mortality by the high faculty of admiring. The chief employment of the saints in glory is praise.

"The face of Marcus Aurelius," says Crum, "is seen reflected in the mirror of his friendships, his admirations, his love. Describing them, he has unconsciously let us know himself." And this principle he applies to his own subject. He names Hooker, Pascal, and Butler among "the first three" of Paget's mighty men. Launcelot Andrews was not far away; but he hardly "attained unto the first three." "Among all his teachers it was with Hooker that the Bishop most put his mind to school." And what a man is Hooker for just that purpose. While Pascal is just as good, and, for many, even better. And Butler could hardly be the least of any three. He also "read much of Pusey and Newman and Liddon and Lightfoot and Westcott; and everything that Church and Mozley wrote."

More ardently still his heart admired. His devotion to his father, his unmeasured affection for his noble wife, his admiration for Dean Church, his love for Liddon and Holland, his esteem for Charles Gore and Dr. Dale—all these constitute but a composite mirror in which is seen the reflection of his own soul. To be associated with the Archbishop of Canterbury he always found to be "a sort of moral seaside: . . . he bears his great load so gallantly, with so ready a heart for kindness and sympathy, and so clear and steady a head, and so single a will. I can't be thankful enough for his friendship."

Liddon, "possessing in extraordinary measure the gifts most perilous to simplicity and modesty, and so wielding those gifts that men of all sorts gathered round him in thousands and listened to him as to no other preacher," he could not sufficiently admire. He "yet remained unmarred by admiration, and kept quite out of his heart all the degrading thoughts of what is called success; remained apparently one of the least self-conscious of men, ready to enter with undivided interest into anything that was of real interest to others; as simply grateful as a child for the simplest kindness shown to him; never talking about himself, nor talking as men do who, when they are silent, think much about themselves; and making others somehow feel that it would not do to talk to him as though they thought him remarkable or great." Perhaps Liddon more than any other helped him to set his own standards.

And yet so justly apportioned and so widely distributed was his admiration that it is difficult to give the preëminence to any. Among the minds which had distinctly impressed him with "the sense of distinction, power, penetration, swiftness, fearlessness," he mentions in one connection his father, Dean Church, Holland, and Gore. "And I could easily add to this list," he continues. Lord Salisbury, in another sphere, he cordially esteemed as "a high example of unworldliness amidst all the world's clamor and competing; of utter freedom from ambition; of great strength loyally given to a great task; of perseverance in hard work through personal sorrow and through failing health; of a life simply, frankly, steadfastly Christian."

These were people for the most part to whom he was not bound in any official way. His appreciation of those who labored directly with him for the bringing in of the kingdom of God is abundantly attested in the records of his official administration.

He could be brotherly beyond the bounds of his immediate ecclesiastical connections. So it was conspicuously in the case of Dr. Dale. At a time when the Judicial Committee of the Privy Council made a decision which deprived the United Free Church of Scotland of large funds held and administered in trust he wrote to a minister of that Church in terms of unrestrained sympathy. Dr. Scott Lidgett he regarded very highly, speaking of him as the "ablest Non-conformist" he knew.

And yet he remained an unbending High Churchman. To the clergy of his own diocese he wrote a letter in regard to the attitude which they should hold toward certain undenominational movements for a religious revival. "I believe that by the Will of God and under the guidance of the Holy Spirit," he said, "the historic Church of Christ has received and maintained the threefold ministry of Bishops, Priests, and Deacons: that in this threefold ministry the Church has the right and regular provision for guarding the tradition of the faith, for upholding the discipline of Christ, for ministering the means of grace." He held back, and yet "with a feeling of great sadness." He would not, he said, he could not coöperate with the power of his great office: and yet he would pray. He would do what was perhaps "much more worth doing"; he would pray "that God, Who 'fulfils Himself in many ways,' may be with those with whom I cannot see my way to go." This would seem to make his inconsistency complete; and yet he did not see it so. As early as his Bromsgrove pastorate he had refused to attend Bible Society meetings because he "should have to bear part with Nonconformist Ministers in a joint Devotional Act." His very capitals seem to be High Church.

2. At the heart of the man was his religion. His fine conscientiousness was a Christian virtue. "It was not so much an offended conscience as a never-satisfied conscience, which led him across the frontiers which divide the land of the Classical Virtues from the land of the Christian Graces." He was a great believer in the power of Christ's grace to work in human character, to quicken the conscience, to arouse the latent capacities of the soul, and to reconstruct the moral and spiritual nature. To all the searching process he strenuously submitted himself. And he hoped for it and

he labored for it in others. In an intimate letter to one of his sons he writes of one in whom he was interested: "I should like him to watch some one like your mother, or my father, or the Bishop of Lincoln, and see the strength and purity and gentleness and brightness that Christ works in a life simply set towards Him. . . . It is Christ Himself, and the characters He forms and animates, that really reach the heart and win it." The very strength and effectiveness of all his work all his life as a minister was the religious motive. After the serious illness of the last year of his life he wrote of what he had learned of his devotion to his diocese: "I did not know, in my dullness and faithlessness, that one could have quite that sort of feeling toward so big and scattered a thing as a Diocese, but, of God's mercy, it has come, and it seems to light up the thought of whatever years of work may yet remain. Of course, I ought to have learned it long ago, and I'm ashamed I did not."

3. His humility never hardened into formality and a mere habit. He could find fault with himself and never be affected about it. He wished to exercise an influence upon others, not by finding fault with them himself, but by leading them to do it themselves in a sincere and edifying way. "The mere sense that he had the advantage over the other man tended to send him down on his knees to him; the greater the contrast between them the more he felt the need of self-abasement." The other man might not understand him, and think him "merely affected and elaborate." But all the while "Paget would be remembering him in his prayers, and full of anxiety for his spiritual life."

Hard as he worked, he accused himself of failure in industry, and said that he ought to have worked harder and more intensely than he had done. "With, perhaps, more of praise than most men win," says Crum, "and perhaps, more in his own nature that he might have tempted him to linger

26

where the Merits are reckoned, he found his home in Prayer, in Forgiveness, in Simplicity, in Love." This was his humility. "I am more cheered and confirmed," said he, "by the clear faith of the loving, the patient, the unselfish, the beneficent, the humble, the thankful, the unself-conscious, the pure in heart, than I am ever troubled by the skepticism or denials of those of whom I only *know* that they are clever."

His very melancholy tended to humility. "He took things to heart as though it were a duty to feel them as deeply as possible." He fought the specters of the mind, and found them not easy to conquer. His very tasks would assume shapes of gloom. "More than anything else," says Crum, "his ten years as Bishop seem to me to have been a struggle against melancholy." A feeling of both unworthiness and unfitness assails such a man. But he struggled on, and gained strength by the very weakness which he suffered. Only God, after all, knows the cost of our labor.

4. He had the heart of a pastor. Administration itself, whether in his capacity as tutor, professor, or bishop, he raised to a pastoral rank. At a time when there was distress among farmers from seasonal causes he wrote in his *Diocesan Magazine:* "I venture to ask all those who read this letter to remember in their prayers the special necessities of our farmers and laborers at this time."

He visited a boy in a hospital apparently dying of typhoid fever and deeply impressed the matron with the fineness and tact of his action. "The good Bishop came to see him," said she; "but the mother hesitated till I told her she could never say no to the Bishop's desire to see a patient, and so he came to see the poor boy; who just knew him, for the Bishop had confirmed him the autumn before; which the Bishop referred to, and with his usual quiet helpful way he said a few prayers, and bid the boy good-by: and a few moments after the Bishop left the room, the poor boy's first sleep came, and from that hour he began to recover."

The opportunities of usefulness and happiness as attaching to the pastoral work of the office of a bishop he fully realized, and he used them to good account. One of the great lessons of his life is the fineness and value of the pastoral qualities of the Christian minister, in whatever sphere his ministry may be exercised, or however diverse from the routine of the pastoral office his station may seem to be.

5. Of his unobtrusive ability in council the Archbishop of Canterbury has generously testified. He was wise in counsel; that was his first value in the councils of the Church. But he had the necessary knowledge, too. He loved his Church, honored her traditions, appreciated the genius of her institutions, delighted in her worship, and knew her history and liturgy. Says the Archbishop: "From the very first he brought to our councils in matters ecclesiastical a wealth of matured opinion upon the distinctive history, position, and opportunities of the Church of England, which compelled attention. . . . His historical and liturgical knowledge, his unfailing courtesy, his quiet resourcefulness, and his facility of speech and pen were assets invaluable to the discharge of our task." This is a kind of usefulness which wins no great appreciation among the populace, but it is not without value on that account.

6. The preacher in Francis Paget was not absorbed in the other offices of his ministry. He possessed that sense of spiritual reality which is the greatest of all the qualities of preaching. In one of his diocesan charges he dealt with this aspect of worship; but he could only have felt the same way about preaching. He has felt how hard it is "to keep the act of worship truly, purely spiritual; to be always lifting up our hearts to the Unseen, the Eternal, the Incomprehensible; always striving beyond the thoughts, the scenes of

sense and time; always remembering that the ultimate
reality of worship is in the light that no man can approach
unto, and that our highest acts are but as hands stretched
out, as avenues of access toward the everlasting adoration
and intercession that is on high, where 'Christ ever liveth to
make intercession for us': where St. John saw 'in the midst
of the throne and of the four living creatures, and in the
midst of the elders, a Lamb standing as though it had been
slain.'" He had a "somewhat homiletic tone of voice in
which his terse, lucid, well-finished sentences fell upon the
ear"; but not "well suited to a promiscuous public gathering, or specially acceptable in the House of Lords." But
there was recalled "one notable occasion, the great Albert
Hall meeting of protest against Congo misrule, when he rose
to the level of highest oratory and his words rang out with
incisive force as, after the manner of some prophets of old
days, he wielded without loss of dignity the scathing scourge
of indignant irony."

Preaching was to him a high and serious task, and he
could no more permit himself to do it without discipline than
he could plant a field and not tend it. The discipline to
which he subjected himself in his better school days he
never relaxed. He had no fancy that preaching could issue
from any but a disciplined mind. Could a sermon be produced by any other than a disciplined mind, it would be alien
to the very mind that produced it. Such a product cannot
be preached, for it is not a sermon: it is a mere fortuity, a
sort of homiletical stepchild. Discourse is always dead if
the man who delivers it is dead. Spurgeon said he had not
infrequently seen a dead man in the pulpit. Preaching
material may be as multitudinous as the heaps of men's
bones in the valley of the prophet's vision, and also as dead.
There must be the breath of a living soul as well as the

might of the Spirit of God to lift this material into life, and
to set it forward as an army in conquering action.

But Paget was more severe in moral than in mental discipline. He believed that the ascent to heroism was through
drudgery. The doctor, he has been saying, through seasons
of drudgery and the doing of common tasks may find an
opening toward great and heroic endeavor. And so it must
be with the priest, he continues. "There may be long spells
of quiet and safe and almost uneventful work; and then
comes the call to a real venture of self-sacrifice, . . . the
choice between worldly prospects and loyalty to divine
truth: and he, too, must show what he really means, of what
sort he really is, and how far the gospel he preaches and the
example of his Lord have indeed been taken into his own
heart."

Two things he thinks we may learn as we study men's
characters. First, that the difference between the man who
will not fail, and the man who may, "is deep down in them,
and it does not show in fair weather; it is the sudden demand, the need for something great, that brings it out."
And secondly, most men will likely be at a crisis what they
have been all along. "They will make their choice then—
save for a miracle of God's grace—as they have been choosing all along." As an illustration of his point he instances
the final setting of the tide toward Wellington's victory at
Waterloo. "On both sides of the contrast we may see in rare
magnificence the same commanding qualities of intellect,
the same unwearied energy, the same personal courage,
the same masterful intensity of will; but writes the historian, 'Napoleon was covetous of glory; Wellington was
impressed with duty.' Singleness of heart was the characteristic of Wellington, a sense of duty was his ruling
principle; ambition pervaded Napoleon, a thirst for glory
was his invariable incentive. . . . There is not a proc-

lamation of Napoleon to his soldiers in which glory is not mentioned, nor one in which duty is alluded to; there is not an order of Wellington to his troops in which duty is not inculcated, nor one in which glory is mentioned."

In another sermon he speaks but to the same effect: "On the drift and tone which our minds are now acquiring it may depend whether, when the time comes, we recognize our work or not; whether we press forward with the host of God, or dully fall away, it may be, into the misery of a listless, aimless life." Only in disciplines such as these, he reiterates, is controlling greatness of character to be acquired.

In a sermon on "Freedom of Thought" he insists that freedom in this sphere does not mean that a man may think willfully, or as he lists, but only according to truth. And such thinking requires conscientious self-discipline. It must be "free from prejudice and conventionality; free from willfulness and pride; free from despondency and sloth; free from self-interest and the desire of praise; free from our moods and tempers; free from the taint of our old sins, and the shame and misery of those that still beset us; free from all delight in saying clever things; . . . free from the yet wilder perversions of jealousy or party strife, or personal dislike; free from the secret influence of timidity or impatience." "Are these conditions of the intellect's true liberty easily to be secured?" he asks.

His preparation, whether for a confirmation address, a charge to his clergy, a letter to his diocese, or a sermon from the pulpit, was diligent, thorough, and conscientious. He could not bear to carry unbeaten oil to the sanctuary. And all the acts of his ministry, public and private, were dispensed as if in a sanctuary.

His method of sermon construction, or other preparation of material for public discourse, was very simple. There were notes prepared in a form rather full, and a distinguishing of the principal heads of the discourse. But construction there was, and it served him, and it served its purpose. Not once in a hundred would one have to go back over a sentence in one of his printed sermons to know what his meaning was. The principle of economy of attention as propounded in Herbert Spencer's essay on the "Philosophy of Style" he admirably observed.

The simplicity and modesty of the man, the courtesy of his nature, his humility, his melancholy, the melancholy which so loves music and is transported by it as he was, that seriousness of soul which is but an undertone of the finest music a life can make—all these were blended in him, and sweeping his soul as the fingers sweep the lyre the Spirit of God made the music of his devoted life.

XII

JAMES MONROE BUCKLEY

(1836-1920)

DEBTS THAT CAN NEVER BE DISCHARGED

THERE are debts which could never be contracted were they not of such a nature that they can never be paid. If there were ever any discharging the obligation imposed by a mother's love, it would cease to be an obligation that could be contracted at all. We could establish our ability to pay for the glories of a star-strewn night only on condition that the skies ceased from their glory.

So the debts that can never be paid constitute our richest inheritance. Even such a man as Lord Shaftesbury, or Arthur Christopher Benson, or Archbishop Tait could be in this manner indebted to his nurse, the power of the nurse in each case to create such an indebtedness being able to reach from the lower to the higher condition. There could hardly be any life so circumscribed and humble as to be entirely without the power either to impose or to be in bonds to such an obligation.

James M. Buckley possessed in an unusual degree the power to create such obligations. It was not that he sought to make himself a creditor in general. Seeking to do so, he would have failed. Through doing it without design he greatly succeeded. He became a veritable mentor to many, not because he assumed the rôle, though it might appear sometimes that he thought himself equal to it; but because of the very readiness and fullness of the man and his method. A young preacher of one of the Methodist Churches less multitudinous than Dr.

(408)

Buckley's own, into whose hands the *Christian Advocate* began to come in his early ministry and continued until the editor's death, has been known to say that to read the paper for twenty years as he edited it was like a university education. If therefore these lines, whether directly or indirectly, should seem to be seeking to discharge one of those debts which can never be paid, they may be running only according to fact.

THE SPRINGING OF THE STREAM

John Buckley, father of James Monroe Buckley, was born in Lancashire, England, in 1805. He came to America in 1827. He had earlier been affiliated with the Church of England, but became a Methodist in America. He became impressed that he should preach, and wishing to prepare himself he attended Wesleyan Academy, Wilbraham, Mass., where Wilbur Fisk was principal. Failing health forced him to leave. He was licensed to preach, and admitted on trial in the Philadelphia Conference. In 1883 he was appointed to Mount Holly, N. J. His record as a man was above reproach. He was passionately devoted to preaching. His talents as a preacher are reported to have been of a superior order.

He was ill adapted physically to the hardships of the itinerancy; but knew neither how to spare himself nor to regain his health. He fought a protracted but losing battle with tuberculosis, and retired to a farm, hoping to recuperate. But the dread disease carried him off at the early age of thirty-seven.

At the home of her father in Mount Holly John Buckley met Abby Lonsdale Monroe. She became his wife and the mother of James Monroe Buckley. She was eight years younger than her husband. Her only brother was a Methodist preacher of some prominence. In early life she had a very definite experience of religion, and joined the Methodist Church at thirteen. She was married to John Buckley at the age of twenty-two. She fulfilled with diligence and devotion all the obligations of her station. She was left a widow at the age of twenty-nine, with the responsibility of caring for two children, both of them boys, one of them being not yet six years old, and the younger scarcely three. "They knew not," said the more distinguished of these sons when life had taught him more of real values, "the meaning of their loss, . . . nor that God had given them a mother, who to her tenderness would join the authority, self-control, and wisdom of a father."

The younger brother lived to a good old age, and died in Mount Holly, the place of his birth.

To the rearing of her children Mrs. Buckley gave herself in "incessant and self-sacrificing devotion." At her husband's death she went to live with her father, but was not willing to throw on him the burden of their support. She established a private school and kept it with success until she was offered an important position in public school work and accepted it as being less taxing than the conduct of a school upon her own responsibility. "Through winter's cold and summer heat," subscribes a grateful hand, "for twenty years and more she wrought for her children. What they learned in the schools was less than what she taught them by correcting their language, directing their reading, and reading to them." Amid all her toil she was faithful to her Church and its interests, and disciplined her children in religion.

At the age of fourteen James Buckley entered Pennington Seminary and remained for three years. He was not distinguished as a student during these years. His precocious intellect exposed him more to danger than to profit. When about sixteen he fell in with some infidels of the Thomas Paine type. They talked with him frequently; and one of them induced him to write a paper against Christianity. He read the works of Paine and others, and "doubted the truth of Christianity for more than a year."

He was out of school for two years, and attempted several kinds of employment. "He was, by turns, an errand boy in a dry goods store, a clerk in another store, an errand boy for a large auction house, the same in a hardware establishment, and was also employed in a lumber yard, where he met with a serious accident." He became apprenticed also to a harness maker, and became very proficient in sewing traces by hand.

He entered Pennington again in the fall of 1854. Here he met Thomas H. Landon, and their lives were sealed in lasting friendship. But his behavior was exceedingly lax. His habits of study were very unequal. In other habits he was not a model. An older student reproved him for profanity. The rebuke entered his conscience, and was a turning point in his life. He faced about and began to seek the companionship of Christian students.

In the debating society at Pennington he took very great interest; and his work in composition showed maturity of thought and facility of expression.

Thomas H. Landon was to lead him into the new life. "It was at a meeting led by Mr. Landon," said he, "that the writer attended for prayers, and in his room in private conversation, that he was enabled to learn the alphabet of the new life." Landon dealt very faithfully with him. He was honest, but a poor believer. They parted after midnight. Buckley came to class meeting, as Landon had advised him to do. He recited the plain facts of his case from time to time, but seemed to make little progress. "Well, Buckley, how have you gotten along this week?"

Landon asked at one of the meetings With a serious shake of the head he answered: "Not at all well, for to-day I got into a fight with P. C." Subsequent inquiry justified the fight on his part; and in course of time Buckley came into the light. He continued in school for two years, teaching school himself in the intervals.

THE MINISTRY AND THE LAW CONTEND

Buckley was fitted at Pennington for Wesleyan University. He intended at the time to become a lawyer. If talent, and talent alone, constitutes the call, then surely he was called to the law. If there is to be no compulsion of the Christian conscience, and a man may dispose of himself precisely as he will, then the ministry need not contend with the law in the determination of Buckley's vocation. At this time the law might by the very compulsion of his own talents have said to him: This is the way; walk ye in it.

His passion for running down a fact and nailing it to its place for his own possession, the penchant he had for searching out the secret doings of a man whom he suspected of dishonesty or double-dealing, would admirably have served his purpose as a lawyer. "He knew to minute details the entire personal history of more individuals than any other man I ever knew," says Dr. William V. Kelley. "I once told him that he made me think of Javert, the officer of justice in Victor Hugo's 'Les Miserables,' and that if I had had the assignment of him to a profession by some of his most conspicuous talents, I would have made him a criminal lawyer, a prosecuting attorney, in which he would have had no equal anywhere."

He had given some actual attention to the study of law, and esteemed it to be quite according to his taste. As if to make the conquest complete temptation conspired with taste and talent to draw him in that direction. More than once he was offered attractive positions with practicing lawyers. It is of reliable record that a prominent law firm in New York city made him a most flattering offer even after he became a minister. Dr. George P. Mains in his life of Buckley quotes the head of the firm as saying: "When Dr. Buckley was a young minister I offered him three thousand dollars if he would begin the study of law in our office, and I told him that when he had completed his course we would take him into the firm, and that ever after he would have an income that would stagger the minds of most Methodist preachers." On being asked why he had offered so large a sum he replied: "In ten years it would be worth one hundred thousand dollars a year to my firm to have Dr. Buckley a pleader in the courts of the State and of the nation."

At his matriculation in the University he "was in a very indifferent state of mind, filled with skeptical questionings, to which he had lent a willing ear, and which were increased by very free and outspoken utterance."

He took an active part in the presidential election of the same year, speaking from the stump for Fremont, and obtaining as a by-product of his effort a valuable experience in the art of public speech. Requiring a supplement to his income he turned at the end of the campaign to teaching, and had charge of a district school in Connecticut. There was no church in the town; and though not yet a preacher, he was invited to speak on religious subjects. During the same season he was invited by pastors to fill their pulpits, but could not feel that he was able to create any religious impression upon the minds of his hearers. Still there was all the while a vague notion in his mind that he might some day become a preacher.

At the last he was brought in an unusual way into the

ministry. A year or two after the experiences just related he was teaching school in another town and was fixed upon as the champion of the affirmative in a debate with an Adventist on the immortality of the soul. The debate stirred the interest of the community and lingered long in the memory of the older inhabitants. The effect upon Buckley himself was very decided. He had gone as deeply as possible into the subject, and had begotten within his own mind an intense conviction of the truth he had sustained. There came to him out of this conviction "a vitally different view of life from that which he had previously entertained."

Then there came to the community an extraordinary religious awakening which powerfully influenced a very wide constituency. In this awakening young Buckley actively participated greatly to the advantage of his religious life. His health was gravely impaired; he was more seriously than ever impressed that he ought to enter the ministry; and under the impression that he had but a little time to live he decided not to return to college, but to take up at once the work of a full and regular ministry.

He became engaged to serve for a year as the pastor of a small Wesleyan Methodist Church in Exeter, N. H. There were forty-eight members, all but four of them women. He almost equaled Beecher's early versatility and served all the requirements of the church except that of a sexton. Though still only a layman, his preaching prospered. His congregations grew and gradually filled the church. Many of the students and principal citizens of the town regularly attended his services.

THE FINAL FIXING OF HIS COURSE

While still serving as an unlicensed preacher he received an invitation to become the pastor of a Congregational

Church. But when he had made a trial of that offer for several weeks, and had studied critically the doctrines and polity of the Congregational Churches, he concluded that Methodism "could furnish for him the more congenial and fitting field of labor."

The timely intervention of Dr. E. O. Haven, then the editor of *Zion's Herald*, assisted and strengthened his decision and "seriously persuaded him that he ought to be a minister in the Church of his father." Taking the certificate of Church membership which he held from the Church at Middletown, Conn., he presented it to the Church at New Market, N. H., where he was received as a member, licensed to preach, and recommended to the Annual Conference all in one evening.

At Portsmouth in the spring of 1859 he was admitted according to the rules and regulations of the Methodist Episcopal Church in the New Hampshire Conference. Though entirely contrary to his own expectation, he was appointed to Dover, one of the largest churches of the State. Having found unusual favor with the people, he remained for two years, which at the time was the limit of the pastoral term.

His pastorate in a large church in Manchester, following Dover, was marked by intricate difficulties of discipline, involving several church trials. He met the situation in a way to establish his own position in the church and community, and in the end to bring about the purification of the Church.

His physical condition now became graver than ever. It was supposed that tuberculosis had taken a fatal hold on him. His presiding elder advised him to relinquish his charge and go home to his mother to die. Buckley thought it not advisable to follow this course with respect to any of the ends which it proposed. On the contrary he determined not to die. In 1872 he met this presiding elder at the General Conference in Brooklyn.

At the end of his second year in Manchester, Buckley went to Europe on a journey which occupied him from the spring of the year until late autumn. On his return he seemed to be in much better health. He had an offer of a Church in California at a salary of twenty-five hundred dollars, gold tender, but declined in compliance with the wishes of his mother. She could not see why a widowed mother should be separated so far from her son unless there were considerations of duty which did not seem to appear in this case. Shortly afterwards Bishop Simpson appointed him to Central Church, Detroit, where there was erected during his pastorate a splendid church of "cathedral proportions," and adequate in all its design and structure long to meet the needs of one of the historic congregations of American Methodism.

At the Spring Conference season of 1866 he was transferred to the New York East Conference, and stationed at the Summerfield Church in Brooklyn. "For the ensuing fourteen years his pastorates alternated between Brooklyn and Stamford, Conn."

In the spring of 1878 he was appointed to the Hanson Place Church, Brooklyn. From its pastorate he was elected by the General Conference of 1880 to the editorship of the *Christian Advocate*, New York.

These details chronicle his entire regular pastoral and pulpit work. But they are only the details in a career already beginning to be notable. He had acquired a wide reputation for pulpit and platform ability; and was in frequent demand for sermons and addresses before university audiences, in theological schools, in the dedication of churches, and upon a still greater variety of occasions, literary, civic, ecclesiastical, and religious.

His qualities as a preacher were but the resultant of the man and his characteristic method. The genuineness of his religious devotion, the sincerity of his character as a Christian, his love for the Church, his concern for the total condition of man and his need first of all of the grace of God offered in the gospel, his sympathy for every good cause, and for truth in all its manifestations constituted in the combination and sum of them a no mean contribution to a pulpit which issuing from them could not itself be narrow, or mean, or sectarian, or sectional, or secular.

He read as nearly everything as a man could, and retained what he read to an unexampled degree. His knowledge of the Bible in particular was full and accurate to an amazing extent. He said that if the English Bible were destroyed "he could reliably restore two-thirds of it from memory." Scarcely less extensive was his knowledge of other departments of knowledge—literature, history, science, and so forth.

None surpassed him and hardly any equaled him in his knowledge of the genius, the progress, the facts, the forces, the personnel of Methodism. For its propagation and defense his pulpit was firmly set.

His method of acquiring, and of retaining what he had acquired, enabled him to focus upon an occasion or to concentrate upon a point at issue in the readiest and most effective manner his all but inexhaustible accumulation of material. He could hardly have had an equal in his day in marshaling the forces of attack and defense, and in calling into service what was required and in eliminating what was not pertinent. All this appeared to the best purpose in debate and before great popular assemblies. But it was not without service to his preaching.

27

He had neither the voice, nor the manner, nor the temperament of the popular orator. But his voice had reaching capacity, was capable of modulation to his mood, and was readily subservient to his purpose. "He acquired the art of easy enunciation, so that when speaking to the largest audiences he made himself distinctly heard without appearance of laborious effort or undue physical strain."

Whether as a pastor, or otherwise, he had no hesitation in throwing himself into any contest for important moral and social reforms. Once at the end of a temperance campaign in Stamford the liquor interests had him arrested on a charge of conspiracy, the specific allegation being that he had hired detectives to contrive the sale of liquor against the law that evidence might be obtained. During the agitation he answered the charges in the town hall and delivered what was by many considered to be the most eloquent speech of his life. The trial itself proved to be "one of the biggest temperance rallies ever held in the town." Able attorneys represented his cause. But he "summed up" for himself, occupying more than two hours in the act, and commanding the closest attention throughout. He was bound over, but the case was never called in the higher court.

Serious-mindedness was a distinctive quality of his pulpit. He could brook no trifling with sacred things. A laugh provoked from the pulpit for the laugh's sake he counted irreverent. A discriminating hearer said: "He had a way of saying things which was so original that he frequently had his audiences smiling. What he said in a humorous strain seemed to come incidentally, and although many years have gone since he was here, his preaching made a deep impression for that very reason. His manner was grave, and the lesson was always the important thing."

Though he could not be counted an evangelist in any

professional sense whatsoever, there were marked religious revivals attendant upon his ministry. Whatever
his appeal it went through the understanding. Through
the reason he reached heart and will and conscience; and
all lower methods he straitly discounted.

"He excelled as a pastor." In quiet and unobtrusive
ways, and through patient and methodical attention to
his pastoral duties, he won the poor and the unprivileged;
and through gifts of another sort he could easily win the
rich and the cultured. "His pastoral ministry," it was
said, "was continuously and exceptionally fruitful."

Could the Pale Conqueror Be Conquered?

In early life James Buckley had assigned him a task
like unto that of dethroning the rider of the white horse
in the Apocalypse, who went forth "conquering, and to
conquer." Such was the import of the tuberculosis of
which he found himself a victim. In his case the vitals of
his own body carried the grim rider.

At about the age of twenty he applied for life insurance.
Was his father living? Dead at the age of thirty-seven,
of consumption. Had this father brothers and sisters?
A brother who died at twenty-eight; cause, consumption.
"Of what disease did their mother die?" "Consumption,
aged about thirty-five." "And their father?" "Of acute
lung disease, aged forty-three."

Should he succumb to the pale conqueror too? He had
always been slight of stature, but as a boy had not been
without average strength. In his fourteenth year he had
an attack of bronchitis, was very ill, and made a slow recovery. He seemed at the same time rather carelessly
to accept the fate of a short life, his own and the general
expectation being that he would soon go the way of his
father. At Middletown he went into a severer climate;

and also undertook an unwise experiment of self-boarding. The political campaign into which he had entered made matters worse. In the ensuing winter he undertook teaching, and engaged in a form of popular debating which was current about the country. Irregular habits induced frequent colds. There was fever, and hemorrhages began. "The year passed away broken with attacks of illness, including hemorrhages while preaching, and many other things not necessary to detail, that, in the opinion of physicians, pointed unmistakably to death."

He was temporarily improved when he entered the New Hampshire Conference. But he had heavy work. He acquired a morbid dread of colds, and took an imprudent care of himself, bundling himself up in coats, caps, scarfs, and the like to an excessive degree. The hemorrhages grew worse, and the spring of 1860 failed to bring him the usual annual relief.

Physicians advised and prescribed in vain. He became his own physician, basing his treatment in the main upon his own reading. He began a measured and systematic course of out-of-door walking, and practiced deep breathing. He used an inhaling tube which he described as being so constructed as to admit the air without difficulty, but to obstruct its expiration. This notable statement forms the conclusion of the whole matter: "To the use of the tube, the amount of time spent in walking and riding in the open air, and the observance of certain additional hygienic methods, together with the determination not to die, I owe my recovery."

The first year of this regimen there was no marked improvement; the second there was visible progress. Climbing the Alps in Europe, he was so exhilarated that he thought the last vestige of disease had disappeared. But on the relaxation of his diligence the disease returned and

he had to resort to his cure again. In a short time all
portentous symptoms disappeared, and not one indication of a tendency to pulmonary disease was seen again.
His feet and legs, combined with the benefits of the breathing tube, had saved his lungs and his life. There was no
more relaxation of physical discipline. He became a renowned pedestrian, and wiser than most physicians as a
hygienic adviser.

Editorship of the Christian Advocate

James Monroe Buckley was elected to the editorship of
the *Christian Advocate* in 1880, following in the position
such men as Nathan Bangs, John P. Durbin, Thomas
Bond, Abel Stevens, Edward Thomson, Daniel Curry,
and Charles H. Fowler.

He announced his policy in his salutatory. He was
under bonds to neither men nor measures, and had only
to put forth every effort to make the paper what it ought
to be. It ought as a Christian advocate to explain and
vindicate Christian principles. As the organ of a Protestant communion it should declare and vindicate the truth
and soundness of Protestant principles and polity.

He thought a Christian newspaper should furnish intelligence of the progress of Christianity, and that his
paper should in particular do this for the Methodist Episcopal Church; that it should discuss everything that related to the moral welfare of mankind, including all that
was in any proper way connected with that welfare; that
it should denounce political corruption, but obey non-
partisan principles; that it should keep its readers informed
of philanthropic enterprises; that it should speak for the
oppressed in whatever section of the country, or the world;
that denominationally it should express the mind of the
body of which it was the organ; but that it should not be

debarred the privilege of seeking the improvement of the Church.   He was determined to be as diligent as if the paper were a private enterprise, and should "rely upon the sympathy, the prayers, and the loyalty of the Church" whose representative and servant he was.   There were certain clearly defined features of the paper which admirably reflected his gifts and qualities as an editor.

1. A file of the issues for the term of the thirty-two years of his editorship constitutes as nearly an encyclopedia of religious and general information as could anywhere be obtained from a similar source.   The variety of its contents from week to week was one of the most striking features of the paper.   He writes on the newly acclaimed wonders of wireless telegraphy; on what grace did for John Wesley; on the visit of the Bishop of London to the United States, pointing some fine lessons for other ministers as they might learn them from this himself notably successful minister.

He writes on the work of Christian colleges; on the favorite passages of Scripture of certain great men; on Mrs. Steunenberg's forgiveness of Harry Orchard, murderer of her husband when he was Governor of Idaho, calling it "An Almost Supernormal Act of Forgiveness"; on the supremacy of the Bible even in literary values as testimony to the fact was evoked in the discussions of a distinguished company where literature was the topic.

He writes on Goldwin Smith and his theory of evolution; on Dr. John P. Newman's fidelity as a pastor in Washington City; on W. T. Stead and the outbreak of the great revival in Wales which he traces to the trembling utterance in a prayer meeting of a poor girl in a Cardigan village; on Bishop Thoburn at the missionary conference in Edinburgh as by the might of his own simple faith he lifted the whole assembly out of the mists and fog of a dull and

profitless debate into an assurance of the Divine presence,
evoking on adjournment the tribute of a titled Englishmen who threw his arms around him and exclaimed: "O
Thoburn, Thoburn, you have lifted as from earth to
heaven!"

He writes on Lecky's statement in his "England in the
Eighteenth Century" concerning Roman Catholicism as a
political institution; on Ambassador Bryce's description
of Gladstone's oratory; on Peter Cartwright, who described
himself as "born in a canebrake, cradled in a gum tree,
and graduated in a thunderstorm"; on President Mc-
Kinley's "Last Words"; on the Mayor of New York's
gifts as a letter writer and his power to compress wisdom
into a nutshell; on the decision of the judges of a debate
on prohibition in the Boys' High School in Atlanta, Ga.

He writes on "What Shall We Read?" and ridicules the
illiterate man who, newly grown rich, wanted to buy some
books. Having been supplied with a pile of catalogues by
a bookseller, he was asked to make some selections. "He
looked at them blankly for a minute or two, and then, with
the air of one who could not be bothered with such unim-
portant details, he said, 'O, send some blue books, some
green books, some black books, and a few red ones!'"
Another phrased his order for books as follows: "I have
sixty feet of shelving. I want ten feet of poetry, ten feet
of history, ten feet of science, ten feet of religion, the same
of novels, and fill up the rest with any kind of books."
This was a fairer distribution of the chief departments of
literature, but neglected philosophy. But the editor remarks that "the man had that in himself."

2. Fitness followed fast upon the heels of the variety
which enlivened the columns of the *Advocate*. It may be
doubted whether there ever appeared as much as a single
paragraph in the paper which did not in Dr. Buckley's

mind bear some definite or implied purpose of edification. He had the most remarkable facility in taking an incident and weaving out of it a whole fabric of moral admonition. There was almost anything in his luminous pages; but it always had value, and, though only a quotation, was apposite to some implied or expressed design to instruct and to suggest improvement.

Here is a mere paragraph; but its purpose does not require to be argued:

Punta Arenas, in South America, is the most southern town on the globe, and Hammerfest in Norway is the northernmost, and there are Methodist Episcopal churches in both places—and pretty much everywhere between, to use a Yankeeism.

Looking in an entirely different direction is another; but still without moralizing there is an evident purpose of warning and edification:

Alphonse Karr knew "a man of eighty years who frequently said, 'Well, I really must set about thinking of my future.'" He did not "set about" nor did he "think" of his future. He merely chattered.

The centenary of the sailing of the first American missionaries affords his alert mind the opportunity for a broad and effective generalization:

Now in February, 1912, there is not a national movement in Turkey, Persia, China, Japan, or India whose history can be written without giving large place to the Christian factor. To read the foreign news of the day without a knowledge of Christian missions is to miss half its significance.

He could turn the minutest incident into a homily:

A famous and eccentric clergyman in Philadelphia one day was striding down one of the principal streets of that city, when he was accosted by a merchant from the West, who asked him, "Sir, can you tell me how to find the sheriff's office?" The minister instantly stopped and said, "Yes, sir! Every time you earn *five* dollars spend *ten!*" and strode on. . . . Extravagance is the besetting folly of the American people. The extravagant man squanders property which would have saved him from poverty, or contracts debts which he cannot pay. Either of these habits, much more both, may crush him to the dust and keep him there.

William E. Gladstone had to select bishops for the Church of England and wrote out for his private use a list of the qualifications that ought to be looked for in men who were called to the office. Dr. Buckley knew of this circumstance and had the list. Just before a session of the General Conference in his own Church, when bishops would be elected, he published Gladstone's qualifications as follows:

Piety.
Activity.
Courage.
Eloquence.
Corporal Vigor.
Circumspection.
Sacred learning.
An equitable spirit.
Administrative power.
Some legal habit of mind.
Maturity of age and character.
Accomplishments and literature.
Liberal sentiments on public affairs.
Faculty of working with his brother bishops.
Tact and courtesy in dealings with men: knowledge of the world.
Faithful allegiance to the Church (and to the Church of England).
A representative character with reference to shades of opinion fairly allowable in the Church.

Attention to these qualifications he said would not only aid in selecting bishops, but "would serve as tests by which to judge how the bishops in existence are filling their position." After the election he said no more.

3. The deliverances made in the *Advocate* upon practical affairs were as sound as a true philosophy of life, and as wise as a book of proverbs. In the course of the conduct of a questions and answers department this question came in:

Should ministers labor for the conversion of a stated number of persons? *A*. No. To do so is superstition or presumption. A man standing on the shore endeavoring to save the victims of a shipwreck does not fix a number. He struggles so long as his strength lasts, or until all within his reach are brought in.

A physician serving as a health officer published some findings on the Bible and health. Among other things he said:

"God never created a direct law of man's nature that would necessarily produce sickness, under any circumstance in life." . . . The editor commented as follows: This is an extravagant statement. As the earth and man are now and always have been, there are direct laws of man's nature that would necessarily produce sickness *under some circumstances in life*. He says that sickness and disease are the direct results of transgression and disobedience of the laws of God. Are they the direct result *in all cases* of transgression and disobedience of God *in the sufferers* of sickness and disease?

Writing of the destruction of the *Titanic* and referring to the fact that "some dark hints have been thrown out that the great majority of the passengers were wicked people, forgetting God, and that this was their punishment," he controverts the idea:

No human being has the right or the privilege to ejaculate such a theory. Any man may believe that divine Providence works in the natural world as well as in the spiritual world, and he who believes it has the right to assert it; but to attempt to fix definitely upon 2,000 people a wholesale condemnation is a presumption that implies a distorted mind or a proud heart, or both. If such profess to be Christians, let them turn to the gospel of Luke and read: . . . "And Jesus answering said unto them, Suppose ye that these Galileans were sinners above all the Galileans, because they suffered such things? I tell you, Nay: but except ye repent, ye shall all likewise perish. Or those eighteen upon whom the tower of Siloam fell, and slew them, think ye that they were sinners above all men that dwelt in Jerusalem? I tell you, Nay."

Buckley never ceased to be the preacher and could not forbear to counsel ministers if it were only upon the proper care of their voices:

Ministers are guilty of grievous errors resulting frequently in the total breakdown of their voices, but still more frequently in their having at all times a harsh, ineffective tone. Before delivering a speech of any length, or sermon, a person should be silent at least an hour, and should retire from society in order to do it. One who would pursue this course could speak in public four times in a day without any injury to the vocal organs, while to talk two hours during the Sabbath regularly is enough to lay the foundations of disease of the vocal organs.

A layman had approached him and provoked an editorial on "The Absolute Simplicities":

A few days ago a cultivated lawyer, an alumnus of one of the best colleges in the country, a traveler in many countries, liberal in religious views but holding to the fundamental principles of orthodox Christianity, approached the editor of this paper on the cars and said, "Here is a problem for you that I cannot solve. I do not see why clergymen, when they find men in their audiences supposed to be learned or eminent, do not understand that if they wish to gain their respect or admiration the surest way to do so is to stick to the absolute simplicities as they would if they were not present." The "absolute simplicities" are adhered to by minds of the highest grade in the ministry, and they are most frequently departed from by the half-educated, the persons who are addicted to phrase-making rather than thinking, who take their language from the books they read, or who are afraid to be simple in speech lest they should not be able to preach a sermon of the conventional length. . . . The days of pompous styles are past . . . . Beecher drew vast crowds, and he was a man of the absolute simplicities; so is Dr. Cuyler, so was John Hall; so was William M. Taylor; so, preëminently, was John Wesley, and, in language and ideas, also George Whitefield.

The manager of a theater wrote him a letter:

Dear Sir: The tendency to affiliation between the church and the stage, etc., leads me to believe that a play that I am now presenting will prove of great interest to clergymen. It is with great pleasure that I invite you, with one friend, to be present as my guests. Your presence is desired for its own sake, for the advantage which I think will accrue to the theater as an institution by countenance of pure and wholesome plays by the clergy in numbers, and especially "for the recognition it would imply of the ancient and acknowledged right of the drama, to treat, with proper reticence and respect, of those truths of life that are a force for good, interest the earnest mind, and convey a moral lesson to every auditor."

Publishing this letter as a part of a long editorial, headed "The Spider to the Fly," he said in reply:

All such letters as these to the clergy are practically illustrations of ministers of Satan appearing "as angels of light," and not a few clergymen have been caught by this kind of flattery and chaff. Only two or three weeks ago an old friend of ours, an Episcopal minister, took his family to one of these plays, and was so shocked by a portion of it that he had to write a letter to the manager condemning it, which letter was made public.

Referring to an evangelist some of whose methods he thought extravagant, he commends him as being thoroughly sound on an important point:

He does not believe in making the second or after meeting "a *sine qua non.*" He thinks that is not the true focus. The focus of preaching, according to him, "is the moment and the act of preaching." "While Peter yet spake these words the Holy Ghost fell." . . . Our eyes were opened to this fact long ago by reading Wesley's Journal. Many conversions took place while he was preaching, and the converts came up at the close and reported the fact to him, and were immediately classified.

4. Character sketching was an eminent editorial feature of the *Advocate* under Dr. Buckley's administration. His wide acquaintance with men, and keen observation of their character and conduct, with unusual ability to fathom their motives, his discriminating descriptive powers, and his judicial temper combined to produce notably valuable results in the delicate task of weighing the worth of the distinguished or the humbler dead and estimating their title to the esteem of their fellows. What he touched in delineating the lives of men he adorned; but it was his writing and not necessarily the subject of it that was adorned. He might not always seem to be perfectly fair; but he always had a reason for the judgment he expressed. He did not feel bound to applaud indiscriminately even the dead. There is a marked difference between the mere habit of eulogy and applause and a discreet appraisal of

merit. He expressed in the paper the meaninglessness of much applause:

Not long since a young man was arrested by the Paris police as a vagabond. He proved that he gained a living as a professional "applauder" at public meetings, for which he was paid about sixty-five cents a night. It would appear from the absurdity of much applause that there must be quite a number of people in this business. An English writer descants wittily and wisely on a trunkmaker who was employed as a professional applauder. So hearty, emphatic, and rhythmical were his "whacks" that he could make most people applaud the very opposite of their sentiments.

Indiscriminate eulogy he could not have thought less absurd than these schemes for raising spurious applause. The applause and the eulogy are alike dishonest, and tend directly to break down moral distinctions.

Nevertheless appreciation is one of the finest of all the organs of truth and knowledge, and the editor of the *Advocate* was too discerning not to know this. Praise where praise was due was just as high an obligation as truth where truth was due.

In an editorial written on one of the Lincoln anniversaries he furnishes a fine specimen of the breadth of his generalizations in character treatment:

The date of the birth of Abraham Lincoln is almost as important to history as that of George Washington. We say almost, for had there been no Washington there could have been no Lincoln. The date of the death of George Washington was not of the first importance. His work had culminated. His mental faculties were not enfeebled, nor was his physical strength by any means exhausted. For Washington to have lived as long as Thomas Jefferson or John Adams would have been a boon to the United States, but could not have added to his fame.

The date of the death of Lincoln is momentous. Washington died in his sixty-eighth year; Lincoln in his fifty-seventh year His work was done; and yet not done. The love for him already engendered in the hearts of the people of the United States was doubled and trebled in wideness and intensity because of the horror of his taking off. He was a true martyr. . . .

The savior of the country may not be equal to the creator of the country, but certainly the inequality is extremly small. When the first voting for those who should be admitted to the Hall of Fame took place, we feared that Abraham Lincoln would receive more votes than George Washington for that honor; others there were who feared that many of the Southern electors would not record their votes in favor of the admission of Lincoln, and thus cause him to take a minor place. Lo! George Washington received ninety-seven votes, the whole number of votes cast, and Lincoln received ninety-six. So should it be: Washington the father of his country; Lincoln its savior. There let them stand side by side, arm in arm, Washington on the right and Lincoln on the left, the admiration of the world!

His delineation of the bishops in the last chapter of the "Constitutional and Parliamentary History of the Methodist Episcopal Church" has been regarded as an extraordinary piece of portrait painting. "Every bishop from Thomas Coke to Henry Spellmeyer is delineated with respect to his ability as a presiding officer, while other phases of his personality are incidentally revealed. . . . No characteristic indispensable to a right understanding of a man is omitted, even when it subtracts from his dignity. . . . Contemporaries of some of the bishops can scarcely repress a smile as they look. . . . A few strokes and the picture is done, the likeness perfect."

When he had written on the death of Bishop McCabe, Dr. W. V. Kelley, who had at the same time *The Methodist Review*, wrote him:

When I had finished reading your editorial on Bishop McCabe, and tried to read its effect on my mind, I found such things as these running in my thoughts: . . . "Why does Dr. Buckley want to organize himself into an octopus and do everything better than the rest of us can do anything? The most extraordinary delineator, portrait painter Methodism has produced—one of the most magnanimous and generous of men in his tributes to his brethren, alive or dead."

5. Among their contemporaries in the Methodist Episcopal Church there was none to dispute with the *Christian Advocate* and its editor the title to first place in the ability to expound the principles and polity of Methodism. This Methodist Episcopalian was first of all a Protestant, and after that a Methodist. If Protestantism was not secure,

$200,000, and ultimately he more than doubled this. The editorial and Seney's action started a stream of beneficence which has not yet ceased to flow.

8. Any editorial chair in which James M. Buckley sat was a watchtower of men and events. He looked toward every horizon, and over all the space between. If anything happened he knew it, and could tell the significance of it. He did not wait for the news to come to him. He went out to get it. He is but reflecting his own method when he makes the following reference:

> When Horace Greeley had been called on six times by an important personage without being found at his desk, he replied to an ill-tempered reference thus: "A farmer might as well wait for a cow to back up to him to be milked as for an editor to depend for the material of his editorials or the determination of his policy only on what is brought to him in the office."

He has been looking through the editorials in the New York newspapers on the going down of the *Titanic*, and finds but one reference to God. Among their millions of readers who else noticed this? But just this is what he would notice.

He notes that a certain gentleman of the platform is advertised as "the most popular temperance orator living or dead," and produces some of the most eminent names from the "long list of the dead." It includes

> Lyman Beecher, who had brains enough and eloquence enough to justify the introduction of his son, Henry Ward Beecher, in England by a very eminent man as "the son of the great Dr. Beecher, of America"; Eliphalet Nott, a man second to none in a peculiar, most persuasive, ever-to-be-remembered style of oratory; Father Mathew, whose words shook nations, and reverberate to this day in tones that are softened, but not weakened, by the echoes; and John B. Gough, who captured the impassive and, on his first appearance, half-unfriendly critics of England, and the analytical, semi-cynical, anti-total abstinence listeners of Scotland, with the same ease with which he enslaved the eyes, ears, and hearts of the common people of both sexes of all ages and races. . . .Young Mr. Murphy is not

28

to blame for this advertisement. . . . He is deservedly popular, but by such eulogy he is "wounded in the house of his friends," and put into contrast with his own father, whose name is known round the world.

He discovers Mr. Gladstone in a new light through a story which had appeared in a British newspaper. A crossing sweeper had been sick, and the Chancellor of the Exchequer had been to see him:

The vicar asked the crossing sweeper if any one had lately visited him. "Yes, Mr. Gladstone," answered the invalid. "But how came he to see you?" asked the vicar. "Well," answered the crossing sweeper, "he had always a nice word for me when he passed my crossing, and when I was not there he missed me. He asked my mate, who had taken my place, where I was, and when he heard that I was ill he asked my address, and when he was told he put it down on paper. So he called to see me." "And what did he do?" asked the vicar. "Why, he read some Bible to me and prayed," was the answer.

A man who can find an edifying and instructive editorial alike in an incident of the street corner and in the swing of an empire to a new policy need not lack for material. "He was . . . the most extraordinary and tireless observer of people and things, great and small, that we have ever known," says Dr. Kelley.

Readers knew the *Christian Advocate* who had never seen its editor, and had hardly heard his name. Dr. Buckley himself relates this incident:

Traveling westward, about twenty years ago, I found the cars crowded, every seat being taken save one. Behind me was one of the most gigantic men I had ever seen; he was much larger than ex-President Taft, even before he reduced his weight by sixty pounds. As I was scanning him he took out of his coat pocket several papers, and lo! they were copies of the *Christian Advocate*. I asked him if he took that paper. A deep voice resounded through the car: "No! I don't, but my wife does; and I tell you they have an old cuss at the head of it who gives things their right names."

At the General Conference of 1912 Dr. Buckley declined another election, and said in his valedictory: "I highly estimate and gladly acknowledge the favor shown

to me by the eight General Conferences which have placed
and continued me in office." An editor of the Methodist
Episcopal Church, South, who was present said:

If ever a man could carry into the reflective twilights of age the comfort
and bracing tonics of appreciation, that man is Dr. Buckley. What could
this last General Conference do that was left undone? Did it not stand
and respectfully pay Dr. Buckley its homage, when he came forward and
read his memorable letter declining reëlection to the *Christian Advocate?*
Did not the lilies of a thousand handkerchiefs blossom as he moved down
the aisle when the document prepared by a specially equipped committee
was read, and the Conference awaited some word from him? His appearance was always certain of a salvo of applause. And observing him that
hour when speaker after speaker paid his eulogy, one could see a certain
detachment of soul as if he were listening to the praises of another. When
he spoke it was to caution against exaggeration.

A Proponent of Public Speech and Debate

Young Buckley began the study and the practice of
oratory and debate when a student in Pennington Seminary. In the virtues of the debating society for the young
man who aspired to efficiency in public speech he was a
firm believer to the end.

On coming into the New York East Conference he acquired two new and notable arenas of debate—the Conference itself and the New York Preachers' Meeting.
Into the intellectual contentions of both of them he entered
with all his might. He measured lances at once with Dr.
Daniel Curry and other experts in debate. His audacity
was quite astonishing. He was still quite a young man;
they had won their spurs by long exercise and steady pursuit. But there was no lack of either self-confidence or
perseverance in Buckley; and soon he not only had attention, but there began with him the sway of an influence which none excelled, and once acquired was never
lost. "The old knights, filled with a proprietary sense and
a pride of possession, were somewhat slow to give room

to this latest arrived candidate for forensic honors." They challenged him, but wished they hadn't.

Methodism has rarely produced his like as a debater. His greatest fame was achieved in the General Conference. It was a stage built for his powers; and the influence he exerted there through the long course of his membership in the body was nothing less than a marvel. He had not been there long before he "was without dissent, and by common assent, acclaimed the greatest debater in Methodism, if not in the nation."

The extent of his information was hardly less valuable to him there than in the editorship of the *Advocate*. Indeed, his marked ability to hold practically the total accumulation of his knowledge at his tongue's end stood him in better stead there than elsewhere. The writer may take occasion to verify, and to pursue his investigations further, and to judge of the fitness of his material for its intended use. But the speaker must speak as the moment flies or else forever thereafter hold his peace. To introduce an allusion, or an incident, or a fact, or an argument when the occasion has gone and the subject grown cold may be worse than to deprive the matter of its value; it may turn out to the positive disadvantage of the unready debater. Woe to the speaker who must arise the second time and untimely remark that he forgot to say so and so.

This was not Buckley's way. His battalions of debate were always unlimbered and standing at attention. He marshaled them instantly for action. It is related that once in a General Conference a speaker was anticipating his opposition and undertook to suggest the direction that opposition would take. Immediately after him Dr. Buckley obtained the floor, and quoting accurately a proverb said: "He that answereth a matter before he heareth it, it is folly and shame unto him." That kind of readiness, other things being equal, is about nine-tenths of debate. And he had not only this readiness in retort, but the other qualities too: extent and accuracy of information; readiness in the command of all his resources; luminosity, simplicity, and directness of utterance; self-confidence and courage in demeanor; complete knowledge of parliamentary law, and quick apprehension of parliamentary practice. His celebrity as a debater was as wide as the nation. At the close of the General Conference of 1908 the *Baltimore Sun* said that it "is unquestioned that the most potent factor in the deliberations of the Conference was Dr. J. M. Buckley." Dr. Charles Parkhurst, of *Zion's Herald*, whose differences from him were neither slight nor few, generously said:

American Methodism has produced only one Dr. Buckley, nor is there another man in the denomination with whom fitly to compare him. Many will have it that as "Master of Assemblies" . . . he has shown most striking superiority. Assuredly in this assembly [the General Conference] there has been no one to compare with him. His perfect self-mastery, his resourcefulness, always equal to any emergency, his strength in argument, his unanswerable logic, his sparkling wit, and, when needed, his stinging sarcasm—in all these and many other qualities, we have never seen his equal.

As a student of oratory, both in theory and practice, he produced one of the best treatises on the subject in the English language, or in any language since the ancients wrote. Many of the principles and much of the practice which the book suggests were wrought out in his own experience. He found public speaking a good exercise for his diseased lungs and the general state of his health, when done under proper safeguards, and so had an additional incentive to its practice. Dropping in one morning on the Philadelphia Preachers' Meeting he was asked to speak. "I have known this city many years," he said. "In my youth I served as barker on the sidewalk for a clothing store in Market Street, in which occupation I cultivated two things which have been of use to me ever since—my voice and my cheek."

The title of his book is "Extemporaneous Oratory for Professional and Amateur Speakers." He defines his theme, and insists that his method "is compatible with protracted and special preparation." He institutes a comparison of the several modes of delivery, and argues well for his own. The basic physiological factors in public speech; the immediate preliminary physical preparation; the training and culture of the voice; general preparation with respect to language; and the acquisition and use of a vocabulary—all these have ample treatment.

Lincoln's disciplined command of language is traced to its source in Lincoln's own statement of how it was acquired:

Well, if I have got any power that way, I will tell you how I suppose I came to get it. You see, when I was a boy over in Indiana all the local politicians used to come to our cabin to discuss politics with my father. I used to sit by and listen to them, but father would not let me ask many questions, and there were a good many things I did not understand. Well, I'd go up to my room in the attic and sit down or pace back and forth till I made out just what they meant. And then I'd lie awake for hours just a-putting their ideas into words that the boys around our way could understand.

He refers also to Dr. John P. Durbin, who acquired his "marvelously simple style" in an earlier period of his life, when an enfeebled voice compelled him to desist from public effort, by going from "cabin to cabin among the Negroes on the plantations of Kentucky, conversing with them on religion."

General preparation of thought and feeling; gesture both as to its philosophy and practice; the value of public oral debate; and character as an indispensable general preparation are given adequate emphasis.

. He assumes that in addressing the assembly the speaker will be conscious of agitation; but this solicitude he accounts to be creditable, a help and not a hindrance. "Woe to the extemporaneous orator who has reached such an impassive condition that he knows nothing of this experience!"

From this point onward the book is addressed more specifically still to the standpoint and work of the extemporizer, his advantages and disadvantages, temptations, defects, difficulties, protection against failure, the guidance and inspiration he has in celebrated extemporizers, suggestions to beginners, and the setting of the highest ideals. The "matchless Prentiss" closes for him with the impressive statement of the principle which he made the rule of his own life: "It is impossible to speak too well to any audience."

COUNSELS AT CHAUTAUQUA

For more than thirty years Dr. Buckley spoke annually at Chautauqua. The only exceptions were the years when he was out of the country. He became an institution of the institution. Among the many distinguished men brought to the platform there he was chief instructor and entertainer. This was due in part to the frequency of his attendance. But more than that it was due to the signal gifts which he applied to the service of the institution. His presence was hardly less appreciated than that of Bishop Vincent himself, and his influence in some directions was even greater.

His contribution to the Assembly consisted mostly in sermons and lectures, of which in the total he delivered about a hundred. There was the usual variety and range in his topics and his accustomed comprehensiveness and thoroughness of treatment. On the occasion of his twenty-seventh lecture the *Assembly Herald* said: "An audience limited only by the standing and seating capacity of the vast Amphitheater is a strong attestation to the popularity of Dr. Buckley at Chautauqua."

More unique in interest even than his lectures was his conduct of an annual question box. It was a study to see him in this capacity. Nowhere else did his combination of shrewd wit and practical wisdom, the fullness and accuracy of his store of knowledge, and his readiness in response and repartee appear to better advantage. No doubt some questions were asked just to see what he would say. But he always had his say.

He was asked the perennial question, "Who was Cain's wife?" and answered: "The woman he married." And so the course of questions and answers went on without any intimation of what would turn up next, and amid unflagging attention:

Q. Does the pope take the *Christian Advocate?* *A.* A copy of the *Christian Advocate* goes regularly to Rome to a high Roman ecclesiastic. Don't you think for a moment that the Catholics depend on omniscience or infallibility for information.

Q. What do you think of Elisha's making the iron swim? *A.* I think it was a very remarkable circumstance.

Q. Is it possible for an honest man to get a drink of liquor in Kansas? *A.* I don't know, I never tried.

Q. What is the seating capacity of the Chautauqua Amphitheater? *A.* When they exhibit something here that does not *tax the brain*, count the people, and you will have your answer.

Q. Is marriage a failure? *A.* You know what the Jew said, when they put that question to him. He said that if the girl is an orphan, and has $150,000 in her own right, it is *almost* as good as a failure.

Q. What do you consider Roosevelt's strongest trait of character? *A.* Push.

Q. Do you think it is possible for any of our dead friends to come back here and shake hands with us? *A.* I once called for one that had only four fingers and he came back and shook hands with me with five.

Chautauqua gave him a fine opportunity to thrust at
fads, fakirs, and fanatics, to all of whom he was a sworn
foe. He was opposed to woman suffrage and his attitude
evidently comes out in his answer to the question, "What
is the real object of the new woman?" Answer: "The
Lord knows; I do not. But I am a very careful observer."

"Travels in Three Continents"

Books already mentioned do not form a complete record
of Dr. Buckley's authorship. Nor need the list be made
complete. He delivered a series of the Quillian Lectures
at Emory College and published them with the title,
"The Fundamentals and Their Contrasts." There were
some other books besides.

His "Travels in Three Continents" gave an account of
journeys in parts of Europe, Asia, and Africa. He carried
with him a carefully acquired store of information about
the countries visited; and saw them all the better through
the eyes of this information when he came to them.

At Lourdes, famed for its healing fountain and the multitudes of pilgrims who throng it, he observed: "The town
contains the ordinary proportion of cripples, lunatics,
sick children, and more than the average number of per-
sistent beggars."

At Toledo in the cathedral he was ordered to remove a
cap which he wore in order to avoid taking cold in a chilly
building. Presently the command was revoked and he
found himself treated with unusual courtesy. On asking
the cause of this change his courier replied:

I told him that you were a bishop of the Holy Roman Church, whose
health had failed, and who on account of important services in mission
fields had received a dispensation to wear a cap and a beard.

In Malaga he saw an assistant appointed to guard the
treasures of the cathedral asleep at his post in the presence

of an entire assembly gathered for a performance then proceeding. "I record this merely as a fact," he says, "having seen a Protestant minister asleep in the pulpit when a bishop was preaching."

He went into the chapel of St. John the Baptist in the cathedral of San Lorenzo and was shown the body of John without his head. He said he was interested in this, "as there are eighteen heads of John exhibited in different parts of the world."

As he travels he seems to know everything of interest that everybody has said about everything. Over the bronze statue at the entrance of a church in Florence he saw the letters I. H. S. and explains the origin of their use.

These initials were originally placed in front of the church by St. Bernardino. He expostulated with one of his flock for manufacturing playing cards. The man told him he did not know how to make a living in any other way. The saint "told him to put these letters on his blank cards and sell them." It was successful, and the man soon grew rich. Now they are to be seen in every Roman Catholic church in the world.

In Rome he visits the catacombs and says:

Thousands of bones, supposed to have miraculous healing properties, have been peddled over Europe. As all sorts of people were buried in the catacombs, it has been truthfully said that it is probable that the bones of the greatest sinners have been exhumed and revered as saints.

Of the ass of Verona he writes:

At Verona is exhibited, for the edification of the pious and the gratification of the curious, the skin of an ass. It is affirmed that this is the skin of the animal on which our Lord rode, and that the ass, after having had such an illustrious rider, refused ever to bear another. He made his way to Venice, where he rang the bell of a convent. As the porter did not recognize him he kept on to Verona, and there rang a bell, was instantly recognized, admitted, lived a long and holy life, died in the odor of sanctity, and his skin is preserved and exhibited as incontrovertible evidence of the truth of the account.

He reports his reflections from the top of a pyramid in Egypt, tells of the influence of the Nile upon the intellectual and material development of the country, and, still in Egypt, thinks that the telegraph poles stretching toward Khartoom seem "like civilization on stilts stalking across the boundless expanse of sand."

He saw the Samaritans in their home in Nablus, and was attracted by the handsome appearance of their high priest. Paying him a compliment, he learned that the reverend gentleman had photographs of himself, and was not averse to selling them. *Apropos* thereto he remarks:

George Eliot, in "Middlemarch," declares that none are so proud of their photographs, or give artists more trouble, than doctors of divinity who have renounced the world. When it is considered that a stock in trade is done by photographers in Great Britain and the United States in pictures of ministers and bishops in their prelatical robes; that peddlers of photographs of the successful revivalist follow him in his spiritual labors, and that a snug sum is derived from their sale, I will say nothing against this man who, so far as personal beauty is concerned, had a better reason for putting his photographs upon the market than a majority of those who find so much pleasure in it.

And so on through the book he succeeds in quite an effective way in communicating to the reader the interest and something of the insight which he himself had in his travels.

THE AMPLITUDE AND IMPRESSIVENESS OF THE MAN

He was an ample and an impressive man. No other terms seem to suffice. A simple narrative of his life cannot be given that unusual qualities do not appear. He was not impressive in physical appearance. He had not that massive and commanding aspect which convinces the eye before the ear hears. There was nothing about him of adventitious importance. His contemporary of the *Brooklyn Eagle*, St. Clair McKelway, thus describes him:

As a matter of fact, Dr. Buckley is rather insignificant as to frame. It is his head and face that take and hold attention. Candor compels the statement that it is not the beauty and regularity of his features that is impressive, but, rather, the massiveness of the head, the intellectual strength and power stamped on the face, and those remarkable eyes—glowing, absorbing, penetrating, all-embracing.

1. The impressiveness of the man is reflected in the influence he exerted. Men waited to see what he would say in the *Advocate* before they formed their own opinions. They rectified their judgment by his; corrected their opinions by his; tested their convictions by his. He had information to which they did not find access. He had the habit and process of forming conclusions to which they were not accustomed. They trusted him, both in his judgment and his integrity, with an implicitness of which they themselves often were not aware. It was a sign of that silent and spontaneous approval which is seldom seen; and which is precious in proportion to its rarity. He was a mentor of the Methodist Episcopal Church if ever it had one.

In the General Conference he exercised an influence which was unmatched by any of his contemporaries, unmatched, indeed, by that of any man who has appeared in its counsels since the Church grew to be so large, and the General Conference itself so influential a body.

He was a master of parliamentary procedure, and had a natural advantage in that. He knew the history, polity, doctrine of the Church almost as if this were the alphabet of his education; and there was a conspicuous advantage in that. He was a master of debate; and crowned all his advantages with that.

As a legislator he left an indelible impress upon the laws and institutions of the Church. It was once reported that he had taken the floor as many as seven hundred times in a single General Conference. This could hardly have been true even of him, but the exaggeration grew out of the patent fact of the frequency of his appearance. In five successive General Conferences he was chairman of the influential Committee on Episcopacy. This position would mean that in a peculiar way he had opportunity to influence legislation affecting the episcopacy. Says Dr. Eckman:

He guided the movement which developed our system of general superintendency from a plan of genial accommodation to the preferences of the bishops to an order of strict surveillance of the episcopal office by the General Conference and a quadrennial accounting of the great stewardship not uniformly agreeable to those who occupy it.

Naturally there were ever recurrent proposals that he himself should be made a bishop. Some wanted him because they thought him admirably fitted for the office. Others wanted him because they wished to remove him from the floor of the General Conference. The final determination of the whole matter lay in his own attitude which he expressed as follows·

I cannot say that I believe I am called of God to the office of a bishop in the Church of God. On the contrary, I am sure I am not called. If I were, there would be some indication of it in my prayers. When I draw near to God in prayer, he does not give me the slightest intimation that he wants me in that office. There is not the slightest drawing of my mind and heart in that direction. Another reason is this: I know my limitations. While I am in the *Advocate* I can travel abroad without compulsion or direction. I can avoid rigorous climates which would soon break me down. If I should accept the office of a bishop, I cannot choose. I cannot shirk. I am certain that in that case I should not live two years. I should break down as E. O. Haven did, and as Edward Thomson did, and be swept away by the storms. I do not believe I am called to make this sacrifice while there are other men, vigorous in body, who can do this work as well as I could, and possibly better.

2. He was an uncompromising conservative. His temperament might seem to incline him otherwise: but he was a conservative in conviction, and a conservative in practice. He was a conservative in his theological position, rather rigidly so, some thought; and he was conservative in resisting innovation. His attitude of opposi-

tion toward woman suffrage and the introduction of women into the administrative and legislative assemblies of the Church was sharply criticized. He was accused of being an egotist, and a few counted him for years as being colossally so. But it was more difficult to criticize for this than for the other. One was a personal fault; the other mostly a matter of opinion and of intellectual attitude. "Organically," said one of his critics, "Dr. Buckley is the same yesterday, to-day, and forever. . . . He knows exactly what he thought on any given subject at any given time by what he thinks about the matter now." A reviewer said of his "Wrong and Peril of Woman Suffrage": "The book neither takes notice of the modern argument for woman suffrage nor successfully controverts the old ones."

3. He was a tremendous toiler. Concede to him the possession of all his native gifts, and the result demonstrates that they were unusual. Still it "remains inexorably true that he reached all his wonderful proficiency by dint of tremendous toil." He read omnivorously, and retained prodigiously. Once on an ocean voyage an elderly clergyman advised him "to read an average of fifty pages a day in books of permanent value." Later in life he declared that he had done this for twenty years to his satisfaction "both in the consciousness of knowledge gained and its ready utility."

There is perhaps no more conclusive way of indicating his sagacity and diligence as a student than by reverting to the fact that as a General Conference approached he would as a means of preparing himself for the discharge of his duties as a member study for weeks in advance the Journals and *Daily Advocate* reports of preceding sessions. "Every conceivable subject that promised but faintly to appear on the horizon was rehearsed in his mind."

He arranged his material as carefully as he gathered it. How many scrapbooks he had nobody knew; but it is reported that there was a "mountainous pile of them." Yet he said, "If I were beginning life over again, I would make more scrapbooks." This is the drudgery that makes a man a master of his material, and gives him facility in the command of it.

4. His practice of self-discipline was carried to the point of austerity. He was reckoned to have had "one of the most highly self-trained minds ever active in Methodism." And that mind was sustained by a highly self-trained body. When past eighty years of age he asked a friend to feel his muscles how hard they were.

His memory, phenomenal as it was, "was more the product of assiduous training than it was of congenital endowment." He trained it until it had almost the precision of a machine, though there was nothing mechanical in its action. In the main it was "as reliable as it was capacious." One hardly dared to question his statement of a matter of fact. Twenty years' reading of the *Christian Advocate* revealed to one reader one error of fact: in quoting another he repeated the error that Phillips Brooks when a young man was advised by the President of Harvard that he could never make a preacher on account of an impediment in his speech.

His accuracy and facility in the use of words was itself the result of long self-training. Early in life he established a habit of critical observation of his own speech and never allowed himself to construct an awkward sentence, even in ordinary conversation; or to be careless or inaccurate in the use of a word, or the expression of an idea. Accuracy became the soul of his speech, as genuineness was a note of his character.

Impressive in personality, ample in accomplishment,

unsurpassed in readiness of resource, encyclopedic in the range of his knowledge, a master of debate, unparalleled in influence, a prodigy of memory, a "Rupert of repartee," true in his friendships, loyal to his Church, steadfast in the faith, his like is not often seen among men.

The span of his life extended from December 16, 1836, when he was born at Rahway, N. J., to February 8, 1920, when he died at Morristown, in the same State. Eight years of retirement and increasing infirmity constituted the last stage of his notable career. A life of such large discourse must find employment in a sphere where neither life nor employment is interrupted, or the life of man loses its economic as well as its rational integrity.